Lecture Notes in Computer Science 13647

More information about this series at https://link.springer.com/bookseries/558

Kristian Kiili · Koskinen Antti ·
Francesca de Rosa · Muhterem Dindar ·
Michael Kickmeier-Rust ·
Francesco Bellotti (Eds.)

Games and Learning Alliance

11th International Conference, GALA 2022
Tampere, Finland, November 30 – December 2, 2022
Proceedings

 Springer

Editors
Kristian Kiili 🆔
Tampere University
Tampere, Finland

Francesca de Rosa 🆔
Center for Advanced Pathogen Threat
Response and Simulation
Austin, Texas, USA

Michael Kickmeier-Rust 🆔
Pädagogische Hochschule St.Gallen
St. Gallen, Switzerland

Koskinen Antti 🆔
Tampere University
Tampere, Finland

Muhterem Dindar 🆔
Tampere University
Tampere, Finland

Francesco Bellotti 🆔
University of Genova
Genova, Italy

ISSN 0302-9743   ISSN 1611-3349 (electronic)
Lecture Notes in Computer Science
ISBN 978-3-031-22123-1   ISBN 978-3-031-22124-8 (eBook)
https://doi.org/10.1007/978-3-031-22124-8

This Springer imprint is published by the registered company Springer Nature Switzerland AG
The registered company address is: Gewerbestrasse 11, 6330 Cham, Switzerland

Preface

This volume includes contributions from the Games and Learning Alliance (GALA) conference, which is dedicated to the study, design, and development of serious games. The eleventh edition of the GALA conference was held in Tampere, Finland, during November 30 – December 2, 2022. This edition was organized by the Serious Games Society (SGS) and Tampere University.

The rich three-day event provided an international discussion forum to advance the theories, technologies, and knowledge that support the design, development, and deployment of serious games. The conference attracted academic researchers and practitioners from several countries. GALA 2022 received 61 paper submissions. Each paper was single-blind reviewed by three Program Committee members. The accepted papers, covering various aspects of serious game theories and applications, were presented in nine paper sessions (27 full papers) and a poster session (nine short papers).

This book has been organized into five sections: Serious Games and Game Design; Serious Games for Instruction; Serious Games for Digital Literacy and Numeracy; Novel Approaches and Application Domains; Taxonomies and Evaluation Frameworks; and Posters. The first section concerns the design and analysis of serious games (e.g., related to co-design approaches, learning analytics, flow experience, and affective computing). The Serious Games for Instruction section includes papers that consider the use of games in natural science, geology, and soft skills instruction. The Digital Literacy and Numeracy section includes papers that focus on anti-phishing, adaptive number knowledge, and math anxiety. The Novel Approaches and Application Domains section concerns planning skills, virtual ship evacuation, reinforcement learning for training vehicular agents, personal epistemology, pediatric speech therapy, and virtual reality simulation views. The Taxonomies and Evaluation Frameworks section covers both taxonomies and assessment of serious games and immersive learning systems. Finally, the Posters section deals with various topics, ranging from flow experience to massively multiplayer online role-playing games and from ontologies to teaching computer programming.

We were delighted to have two prominent keynote speakers, Ulla Richardson (University of Jyväskylä, Finland) and Roger Azevedo (University of Central Florida, USA), with talks on, respectively, "On GraphoLearn, the digital evidence-based method for supporting the development of reading skills in all learners" and "Accelerating Self-regulated Learning in Game-based Virtual Learning Environments with Multimodal Data". The conference featured an exhibition and a game competition.

As in previous years, authors of selected best papers presented at the GALA conference will be invited to submit an extended version for a dedicated special issue of the International Journal of Serious Games, the scientific journal managed by the Serious Games Society, indexed by the Emerging Sources Citation Index (ESCI) in the Web of Science Core Collection since 2015 and by Scopus since 2020.

We thank the authors for submitting many interesting papers and the international Program Committee for their careful and timely reviews. Finally, we gratefully acknowledge the SGS and Tampere University for organizing the conference.

November 2022

Kristian Kiili
Koskinen Antti
Francesca de Rosa
Muhterem Dindar
Michael Kickmeier-Rust
Francesco Bellotti

Organization

General Chair

Kristian Kiili — Tampere University, Finland

Program Chairs

Antti Koskinen — Tampere University, Finland

Francesca de Rosa — Center for Advanced Pathogen Threat Response and Simulation, USA

Michael Kickmeier-Rust — St.Gallen University of Teacher Education, Switzerland

Muhterem Dindar — Tampere University, Finland

Keynotes Chair

Manuel Ninaus — University of Graz, Austria

Competition Chair

Vanissa Wanick — University of Southampton, UK

Exhibition Chair

Riikka Aurava — Tampere University, Finland

Publication Chair

Riccardo Berta — University of Genova, Genova

Communication Chair

Antero Lindstedt — Tampere University, Finland

Administrative and Financial Chair

Francesco Bellotti — University of Genova, Italy

Local Arrangements Chair and Support

Riikka Anttonen   Tampere University, Finland

Program Committee

Alessandra Tesei	NATO STO Centre for Maritime Research and Experimentation, Belgium
Ana Carolina Tomé Klock	Tampere University, Finland
Antero Lindstedt	Tampere University, Finland
Antti Koskinen	Tampere University, Finland
Avo Schönbohm	Berlin School of Economics and Law, Germany
Baltasar Fernandez-Manjon	Universidad Complutense de Madrid, Spain
Bettina Schneider	Fachhochschule Nordwestschweiz, Switzerland
Carita Kiili	Tampere University, Finland
Carolina A. Islas Sedano	University of Canterbury, UK
Cathy Pons Lelardeux	Champollion National University Institute, France
Chiara Catalano	Italian National Research Council, IMATI, Italy
Elena Camossi	NATO STO Centre for Maritime Research and Experimentation, Belgium
Erik van der Spek	Eindhoven University of Technology, The Netherlands
Francesca de Rosa	Center for Advanced Pathogen Threat Response and Simulation, USA
Francesco Bellotti	University of Genova, Italy
George Lepouras	University of the Peloponnese, Greece
Georgios Fesakis	University of the Aegean, Greece
Georgios Kritikos	University of the Aegean, Greece
Giuseppe Città	Italian National Research Council, ITD, Italy
Heide Lukosch	University of Canterbury, UK
Heinrich Söbke	Bauhaus-Universität Weimar, Germany
Herre van Oostendorp	Utrecht University, The Netherlands
Ioana Andreea Stefan	Advanced Technology Systems, Romania
Ion Roceanu	National Defence University, Romania
Ivan Martinez-Ortiz	Universidad Complutense de Madrid, Spain
Iza Marfisi-Schottman	Nantes Université and Le Mans Université, France
Jake McMullen	University of Turku, Finland
Jannicke Baalsrud Hauge	University of Bremen, Germany
Jean-Marc Labat	Sorbonne University, France
Julian Alvarez	University of Lille, France
Katerina Mania	Technical University of Crete, Greece
Kevin Körner	Eberhard Karls Universität Tübingen, Germany
Kostas Karpouzis	National Technical University of Athens, Greece

Thierry Nabeth	P-Val Conseil, France
Tomi Jaakola	Tampere University, Finland
Ville Kankainen	Tampere University, Finland
Vlasios Kasapakis	University of the Aegean, Greece
Wayne Buck	NATO Allied Command Transformation, USA

Contents

Taxonomies and Evaluation Frameworks

Posters

Serious Games and Game Design

Turtle Heroes: Designing a Serious Game for a VR Interactive Tunnel

Anastasios Theodoropoulos[1]($\boxtimes$) (iD), Elina Roinioti[2], Marios Dejonai[3],
Yannis Aggelakos[3], and George Lepouras[3] (iD)

[1] Department of Performing and Digital Arts, University of Peloponnese, Nafplio, Greece
ttheodor@uop.gr
[2] Panteion University of Social and Political Studies, Athens, Greece
[3] HCI-VR Laboratory, University of Peloponnese, Tripoli, Greece
https://hci-vr.dit.uop.gr/

Abstract. Immersive playful activities are regarded to be a promising way for increasing children's understanding of significant issues. This paper proposes an immersive interactive tunnel environment, for which we developed a serious game to raise awareness on children and young adults on environmental issues and endangered species, and specifically, about Caretta caretta. The paper first describes the design and implementation of the CAVE-tunnel system; then, it discusses the design and development of the serious game "Turtle Heroes". This is a work in progress while more games are in the design process for this VR interactive tunnel setup. Possible uses, opportunities and future works-games in this environment are also discussed.

Keywords: Environmental VR · Immersive game · Interactive tunnel · Children · Game-design

1 Introduction

Virtual Reality (VR) technology generates simulated environments, that enable users to immerse themselves in a motivating way [1]. Especially VR games are rapidly growing and becoming part of public-space entertainments (e.g., game displays and VR entertainment parks) [2]. Sharing VR experiences with others is more enjoyable [3] and seems to influence social attitudes significantly more than non-immersive interventions [2]. As a result, in the era of public-space entertainment, the ability to share experiences like VR with viewers is very important [4].

In this paper we present a custom-made immersive interactive tunnel and a shooter serious game made specifically for this installation. The game is called "Turtle Heroes: Σώστε τις χελώνες" and it is part of a R&D project in the areas of culture and education in which immersive technologies are introduced as part of the public-space entertainment. The "Turtle Heroes" game is the first to developed, aiming to raise awareness on environmental issues and affect children's and young adults' attitudes with respect to sea turtles. The game follows the long tradition of immersive technologies and interactive learning environments that aim to help students improve their skills and knowledge, by providing learning experiences in a fun, attractive and effective way [5, 6].

K. Kiili et al. (Eds.): GALA 2022, LNCS 13647, pp. 3–10, 2022.
https://doi.org/10.1007/978-3-031-22124-8_1

2 Related Work - Skeleton Tracking for Games Beyond Entertainment

Over the last years, full-body interactive games have been developed, where players use their bodies when playing [7], a feature that provides a fun and playful user experience, suitable for serious purposes [8]. Skeleton tracking is based on body movements, gestures and positions [7]. Generally, the 3D body movement features are extracted from joint-oriented skeleton tracking and a common method is by using the information provided by 3D depth sensor cameras [9]. While the user stands in front of a depth camera, the location and direction of joints are tracked and body joints are mapped, as shown in Fig. 1. Regarding serious games skeleton tracking can provide beneficial findings like in [9] where authors used a gesture recognition system through a game to prevent dementia. Game contents were designed to practice spatial recognition and users' movements were analyzed to measure how their recognition skills improved. Likewise, Avola et al. [10] designed an interactive virtual environment with a body modeling rehabilitation framework for patients to play with stimulating rehabilitation exercises. The feedback received from users who used the system, pointed out remarkable results in terms of motivation, usability, and customization and the authors considered this system a concrete solution in terms of versatility, immersivity, and novelty.

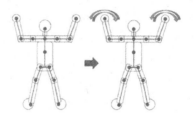

Fig. 1. 3D joint recognition process from [9].

3 Design of the VR Interactive Tunnel

The interactive tunnel consists of 15 monitors (55 in.) and one projection screen. As shown in Fig. 2, the system adopts a daisy chain monitor connection (borderless design with 0.9 mm bezel), with DisplayPort cables and pull-out mount for quick installation and maintenance. This installation is attached on custom video wall mounts (aluminum truss structure). The side monitors (3 screens on each edge) can easily be adopted to either 120- or 90-degrees placement. The high brightness and resolution projector (located at the top middle of the truss structure) displays special effects and multimedia content onto a specific floor surface (made by a special reflective material of high strength and reflectivity). The system is controlled/driven by a computer with two CPUs Intel Xeon Gold 6230 2.1 GHz–3.9 GHz, with 256 GB RAM installed, storage of 1 TB SSD and 8 TB HD disks and 4 graphics cards by 24 GB each (NVIDIA PNY Quadro RTX A5000). There is also an NVIDIA Quadro Sync II card that synchronizes the GPUs, enabling the 15 synchronized displays to stand in a single chassis. The visualization uses the Mosaic technology, which allows to configure a multi-display setup. There are also two tracking cameras (TVico) for gesture recognition that measure positional tracking, spatial mapping, object detection and body tracking (19 joints).

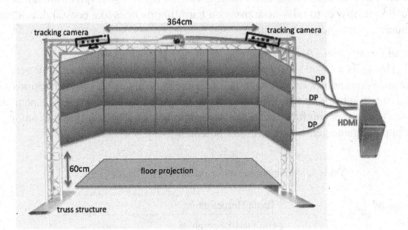

Fig. 2. The VR interactive tunnel setup.

Finally, when designing this VR interactive tunnel system, we considered the structured framework by Bowman et al. [11] for conducting user testing to evaluate virtual environments. This includes the combination of user needs analysis, user task scenarios, usability evaluation, and formative evaluation, prior to a summative evaluation.

4 The Game

In the following, we present the Turtle Heroes game and specifically, the game concept, its educational goals, the core mechanics and finally, opportunities that rise from this gaming-installation.

Background – Educational Goal
The Caretta caretta or Loggerhead Sea turtle, is considered a species of great ecological importance, facing several threats, among which are human activities that destroy their nesting habitat. The Caretta caretta turtles, have a key role in stability of marine ecosystems, as they hold a high position in marine food grids and mainly through hunting, hold the populations of other organisms under control [12]. Commonly found in the Mediterranean Sea, with Greece hosting more than 60% of the Mediterranean population officially protected by the 1992 Habitats Directive, their status as an endangered species remains unchanged to this day[1].

---

[1] WWF Greece, the threats Caretta caretta turtles face in Greece, online at https://www.wwf.gr/en/our_work/nature/marine/endangered_species/caretta_caretta_turtle/, last accessed 15th September 2022.

In the game "Turtle Heroes", the goal is a) to inform the young public about the sea turtle spawning beaches within the Peloponnese area. In contrast to other regions like Zakynthos, the Peloponnese region and specifically the Gulf of Kyparissia or the Mani Peninsula, are rarely associated with nesting areas, b) to shed light on a bitter truth, that the loss or degradation of Caretta's nesting habitat results from direct human activity and consequently, c) to raise awareness on harmful practices like coastal development and management and light pollution.

General Description - Architecture
Turtle Heroes is a co-op serious shooter game designed for children aged 10 years and above and young adults. Even though shooter games, are not usually used in serious game design, it is a genre with many design opportunities and metaphorical correspondences that can create meaningful educational associations [13]. The fact that it is among the most popular game genres, adds further potential to our purpose.

Table 1. Metaphorical correspondences in "Turtle Heroes".

FPS games	Turtle Heroes game
Enemies	Human-like zombies
Dynamic combat	Different enemies have different damage amount
Boosters	Co-op boosters to help players' collaboration
Boss fight	Boss fight (light pollution)

In "Turtle Heroes" players take on the role of a volunteer-rescuer and protector of the sea turtles and their goal is to help newborn turtles to reach the sea. Just like in a typical, mainstream shooter game, the players must face different kind of enemies and of course, to win the boss fight. The main enemies are humans and specifically, annoying bathers. To highlight different kind of human activities that can lead to nest destruction, we designed funny bather archetypes: the Sports Lover, the Gluttonous Beachgoer, The Mommy Person etc. Our enemies are illustrated as brainless zombies (Fig. 3) due to their reckless behavior (Table 1).

Using comedy or satirical elements in games, is not new to game design or game studies in general. Radical and political games, often used for propaganda purposes, rely on grotesque figures and situational comedy to engage people and at the same time, stimulate reflection in different kinds of contexts. At the same time and as Nele Van de Mosselaer (2022) mentions, "*gameplay has an inherent aptitude for self-directed laughter*" (p. 41) [14]. From a first point of view and through immersion, games can be conceived as a "serious" activity, while from a third point of view, as the human-player controls the avatar, games can be understood as pixelized environments full of audiovisual stimuli that possibly can make us laugh. But what about learning through comedy? The relationship between humor and learning has been thorough researched over the years, emphasizing on the psychological effects of humor in-class [15], on students' content retention [16], on the creation of a positive learning environment [17] etc. Through the design of the "Turtle Heroes" game, we aspire to further investigate whether humorous serious shooter games may help in raising awareness on an important environmental and societal issues, like the extinction of Caretta caretta.

Last but not least, the game is in third person, which practically means that each player has an avatar in the virtual world, through which he/she can act and pursue a task (Fig. 4). To play the game in the interactive tunnel, the players stand in front of the tunnel and use their hands as input (cursor), based on a skeleton tracking system. The hand-tracking system is based on two depth sensor cameras that can reliably fit a hand mesh to the reconstructed joints [18].

Fig. 3. A zombie enemy.

Gameplay - Mechanics

Following the MDA framework [19], we first specified our educational goals, worked towards the individual mechanics that could capture these goals, then we developed dynamic systems and finally, built our way towards a meaningful aesthetic experience (Table 2).

When the game starts, a map of the Peloponnese appears, and players are asked to choose the spawning beach of their choice and play a short tutorial to get familiar with game's interface and interactivity. The gameplay consists of two phases. In the first one, zombie-enemies fall from the sky and head towards a turtles' nest. The goal is to throw seashells to repel the zombie-enemies. If the player fails to hit an enemy, then that enemy will walk to the nest damaging the eggs. Players have a specific amount of energy available to them during this phase, which will diminish over time, unless they keep hitting enemies with the seashells. An energy bar displays the energy levels, while a heartbeat warns the players that their energy has reached critically low levels. When a player runs out of energy, he/she/them can receive an energy boost from the other player.

Fig. 4. Screenshots from the game.

The second phase starts at night, and players must now face an unidentified object that throws light on the beach, disturbing egg hatching, making the little turtles to lose their way to the sea. The players now, must keep on "shooting" seashells towards it and force it to turn off the headlights. The game becomes even more challenging in co-op mode: on the one hand, the enemy spawn rate is increased, which makes it difficult for players to achieve their goal, but on the other hand, they can activate power ups that will make them very efficient, motivating them at the same time, to cooperate and defeat the boss. At the end of the game, players can see their score representing all the baby turtles they rescued.

Table 2. MDA in Turtle Heroes game.

Basic mechanics	Dynamics	Aesthetics
Aim & throw	Attack	Action
Aim at power ups	Gift Power Up = send energy to the other player	Collaboration
Both players aiming at a specific point in the UI, at the same time	Activate Power ups to defeat the boss/Available once	Collaboration/strategy/Rarity
Energy bar	Loose ability to fight/ask for an energy boost	Motivation/communication among players
Throw at the light	Attack/Lights go off	Action

Challenges and Opportunities

Designing and developing a game for an interactive tunnel for public use, is a very challenging task. Several parameters had to be considered especially about the skeleton tracking (moving the arm forward to throw) and UX cursor improvements like the throwing/attacking action system.

In-game representations of the bathers as enemies were also an important point of discussion, especially about our target population. Using the parody technique of satire [20], we wanted to highlight abusive behaviors and not specific people, providing a fun way for children and young adults to identify these harmful practices and hopefully, avoid them in the future. In-game collaboration was another interesting design parameter. The key question here was, how can we enhance collaboration between players during a game session. To this end, we added a mechanic in which players could help each other when their energy drops significantly. We anticipate that this feature will promote verbal communication between players and at the same time, promote team spirit. Using an immersive interactive tunnel as a game-setup, can produce a sharable and attractive experience for both players and for bystanders, and at the same time, provide an important research opportunity for us to evaluate our design choices, technical affordances, and restraints.

Playtesting and further research are needed in order to evaluate a) our game mechanics, b) our educational goals and c) the social technological synergy that takes place during gameplay inside an interactive tunnel. How players interact with the system, how skeleton tracking increase immersion and promotes meaningful play, what kind of collaboration can be fostered between players and finally, if and under what conditions players decode our messages, are questions that we are going to investigate during the next phase.

5 Summary and Future Work

This paper presents a serious game design project developed for an interactive tunnel, aiming to influence the attitudes of children and young adults towards endangered species. Our preliminary research indicates that virtual environments with immersive games have the potential to raise awareness on children and young adults. Immersive gaming technologies in public spaces have the potential to revolutionize learning and can be used to help children leave the venue with an understanding of what the organizers wished to communicate. "Turtle Heroes" is a humorous serious shooter game that aims to raise awareness among children on a very specific environmental and societal issue, the role of human behavior on the loss of Caretta's nesting habitat. Using a popular game genre, that of shooters, and humorous content, our goal is to reveal specific behavioral damaging patterns and initiate an open dialogue with the broader audience. In order to achieve our goals and as a next step, we aim to test Turtle Heroes with students and measure players' performance and experience. Post-session discussions and interviews with players will also help us evaluate our educational and design choices.

Acknowledgment. This research has been funded within the framework of the operational program "Peloponnese 2014–2020", (project code: 80578).

References

1. Huang, W., Roscoe, R.D., Johnson-Glenberg, M.C., Craig, S.D.: Motivation, engagement, and performance across multiple virtual reality sessions and levels of immersion. J. Comput. Assist. Learn. **37**(3), 745–758 (2021)
2. Nikolaou, A., Schwabe, A., Boomgaarden, H.: Changing social attitudes with virtual reality: a systematic review and meta-analysis. In: Annals of the International Communication Association, pp. 1–32 (2022)
3. Biocca, F., Levy, M.R.: Communication in the Age of Virtual Reality. Routledge, Abingdon (2013)
4. Ishii, A., Tsuruta, M., Suzuki, I., Nakamae, S., Suzuki, J., Ochiai, Y.: Let your world open: CAVE-based visualization methods of public virtual reality towards a shareable VR experience. In: Proceedings of the 10th Augmented Human International Conference 2019, pp. 1–8 (2019)
5. Ardiny, H., Khanmirza, E.: The role of AR and VR technologies in education developments: opportunities and challenges. In: 2018 6th RSI International Conference on Robotics and Mechatronics (IcRoM), pp. 482–487 (2018)
6. Checa, D., Bustillo, A.: A review of immersive virtual reality serious games to enhance learning and training. Multimed. Tools Appl. **79**(9), 5501–5527 (2020)

7. Subramanian, S., Skjæret-Maroni, N., Dahl, Y.: Systematic review of design guidelines for full-body interactive games. Interact. Comput. **32**(4), 367–406 (2020)

8. Kaza, K., et al.: Body motion analysis for emotion recognition in serious games. In: Antona, M., Stephanidis, C. (eds.) UAHCI 2016. LNCS, vol. 9738, pp. 33–42. Springer, Cham (2016). https://doi.org/10.1007/978-3-319-40244-4_4

9. He, G.-F., Park, J.-W., Kang, S.-K., Jung, S.-T.: Development of gesture recognition-based serious games. In: Proceedings of 2012 IEEE-EMBS International Conference on Biomedical and Health Informatics, pp. 922–925 (2012)

10. Avola, D., Cinque, L., Foresti, G.L., Marini, M.R.: An interactive and low-cost full body rehabilitation framework based on 3D immersive serious games. J. Biomed. Inform. **89**, 81–100 (2019)

11. Bowman, D.A., Gabbard, J.L., Hix, D.: A survey of usability evaluation in virtual environments: classification and comparison of methods. Presence: Teleoper. Virtual Environ. **11**(4), 404–424 (2002)

12. Casale, P., et al.: Mediterranean sea turtles: current knowledge and priorities for conservation and research. Endangered Species Res. **36**, 229–267 (2018)

13. Rankin, J.R., Vargas, S.S.: FPS extensions modelling ESGs. In: 2009 Second International Conferences on Advances in Computer-Human Interactions, pp. 152–155 (2009)

14. Van de Mosselaer, N.: Comedy and the dual position of the player. In: Bonello Rutter Giappone, K., Majkowski, T.Z., Švelch, J. (eds.) Video Games and Comedy. PSC, pp. 35–52. Springer, Cham (2022). https://doi.org/10.1007/978-3-030-88338-6_2

15. Berk, R.A.: Professors Are from Mars [R], Students Are from Snickers [R]: How To Write and Deliver Humor in the Classroom and in Professional Presentations. ERIC (2003)

16. Garner, R.L.: Humor in pedagogy: how ha-ha can lead to aha! Coll. Teach. **54**(1), 177–180 (2006)

17. Banas, J.A., Dunbar, N., Rodriguez, D., Liu, S.-J.: A review of humor in educational settings: four decades of research. Commun. Educ. **60**(1), 115–144 (2011)

18. Taylor, J., et al.: Efficient and precise interactive hand tracking through joint, continuous optimization of pose and correspondences. ACM Trans. Graph. (TOG) **35**(4), 1–12 (2016)

19. Hunicke, R., LeBlanc, M., Zubek, R.: MDA: a formal approach to game design and game research. In: Proceedings of the AAAI Workshop on Challenges in Game AI, vol. 4, no. 1, p. 1722 (2004)

20. Madsen, H., Johansson, T.D.: Gameplay Rhetoric: A Study of the Construction of Satirical and Associational Meaning in Short Computer Games for the WWW (2002)

Comparison with Self vs Comparison with Others: The Influence of Learning Analytics Dashboard Design on Learner Dashboard Use

Timothy Gallagher[1]([⊠]) [iD], Bert Slof[2] [iD], Marieke van der Schaaf[3] [iD], Ryo Toyoda[4] [iD], Yusra Tehreem[5,6] [iD], Sofia Garcia Fracaro[7,8] [iD], and Liesbeth Kester[1] [iD]

[1] Utrecht University, Utrecht, The Netherlands
t.r.gallagher@uu.nl
[2] Netherlands Institute for Curriculum Development, Enschede, The Netherlands
[3] University Medical Centre Utrecht, Utrecht, The Netherlands
[4] Newcastle University, Newcastle Upon Tyne, UK
[5] University of Applied Sciences Emden/Leer, Emden, Germany
[6] Bielefeld University, Bielefeld, Germany
[7] Merck KGaA, Darmstadt, Germany
[8] KU Leuven, Leuven, Belgium

Abstract. This study uses log-file data to investigates how chemical process plant employees interact and engage with two distinct learning analytics dashboard designs, which are implemented in a virtual reality simulation-based training environment. The learning analytics dashboard designs differ by reference frame: the progress reference frame, offers historical performance data as a point of comparison and the social reference frame offers aggregated average peer group performance data as a point of comparison. Results show that participants who receive a progress reference frame are likely to spend less time reviewing their dashboard than those who receive a social reference. However, those who receive a progress reference frame are more likely to spend more time reviewing detailed task feedback and engaging with the learning analytics dashboard.

Keywords: Learning analytics dashboard · Social comparison · Virtual reality simulation-based training

1 Introduction

Virtual reality (VR) training environments are becoming popular tools for training employees because they offer advantages over other forms of training [1]. For example, these environments can be designed to take advantage of log-file data, which can be used with learning analytics tools such as learning analytics dashboards (LAD) [2]. While learning analytics refers to the collection and analysis of data to optimize learning [3], LADs aggregate data collected during the learning analytics process and displays

---

The original version of this chapter was revised: minor error in affiliation and Table values was corrected. The correction to this chapter is available at
https://doi.org/10.1007/978-3-031-22124-8_37

K. Kiili et al. (Eds.): GALA 2022, LNCS 13647, pp. 11–21, 2022.
https://doi.org/10.1007/978-3-031-22124-8_2

it within one or multiple visualizations to help stakeholders make sense of the learning analytics data [4]. LADs are often designed to provide feedback on task performance to learner stakeholders [5]. Instructional designers can help these learners make sense of their feedback by including reference frames, which contextualize a learner's performance against a particular point of comparison [6]. Two types of reference frames are the progress and social reference frame [7]. The progress reference frame uses historical performance data as a point of comparison, while the social reference frame uses aggregated peer performance data as a point of comparison.

In this paper, we explore how workplace learners interact with feedback presented by two LADs, one designed with a progress reference frame and one with a social reference frame.

1.1 Potential Implications of Learning Analytics Dashboard Design

When designing workplace LADs for feedback, instructional designers must consider how they can help employees make sense of their feedback. One approach is to include learning analytics reference frames, which are comparison points learners can use to orient when examining their learning analytics [8]. When presented with a progress reference frame, learners are stimulated to engage in temporal comparisons, which take place when one compares their own performance at different points in time [9, 10]. Temporal comparisons can highlight progress over time and help learners determine if they have been improving. Therefore, it is feasible that temporal comparisons may influence learner interaction with LADs. For example, if given the opportunity, learners may wish to review detailed task feedback because they want to find out what they can to do to improve [10], which is representative of a mastery goal orientation [11]. When presented with a social reference frame, learners are stimulated to engage in social comparison, which takes place when one compares their own performance with that of their peers and do so to gauge how effective they are at particular tasks [12]. It is foreseeable that social comparison may influence learner interactions with LADs because it may impact their motivation [7, 13] and encourage them to focus on performing better than their peers instead of self-improvement, which is representative of a performance goal orientation [11].

2   Context of the Study

This study investigates two LAD designs implemented into a VR simulation-based training environment for employees of the chemical process industry. The LADs differ in design by reference frame. The Progress LAD incorporates a progress reference frame and the Social LAD incorporates a social reference frame. Both LAD designs include two buttons which can be selected. The 'detailed task feedback' button takes learners to a secondary screen which provides detailed task feedback on their task performance. The 'How is this calculated?' button triggers an indicator to be displayed which explains how the task score is calculated. The detailed task feedback screen and How is this calculated? indicator do not differ between the Progress and Social LAD.

3 Study Overview

To better understand how the progress and social reference frames influence LAD inter-action, we designed a two-group experimental study in which participants completed a simulation based-based training task in VR and receive feedback via the Progress or Social LAD.

We operationalize LAD interaction by examining log-file data from participant inter-action with their assigned LAD. First, we examined the time participants spent reviewing either the Progress or Social LAD. Next, we examined the time participants spent review-ing the detailed task feedback screen. Finally, we examined the frequency with which participants engaged with the LAD as measured by the number of times the detailed task feedback and How is this calculated? button were selected.

3.1 Research Questions and Informative Hypotheses

We propose three research questions, each with three competing hypotheses to address the overarching research question: How do reference frames influence LAD interaction?

RQ1: Are there between group differences in total time spent reviewing LADs with a reference frame?

H1.1 The mean time participants spend reviewing the Progress LAD will be greater than the mean time participants spend reviewing the Social LAD.

H1.2 The mean time participants spend reviewing the Progress LAD will be less than the mean time participants spend reviewing the Social LAD.

H1.3 The mean time participants spend reviewing the Progress LAD will be equal to the mean time participants spend reviewing the Social LAD.

RQ2: Are there between group differences in total time spent reviewing detailed task feedback?

H2.1: The Progress LAD group mean time spent reviewing the detailed task feedback screen will be greater than the Social LAD group.

H2.2: The Progress LAD group mean time spent reviewing the detailed task feedback screen will be less than the Social LAD group.

H2.3: The Progress LAD group mean time spent reviewing the detailed task feedback screen will be equal to the Social LAD group.

RQ3: Are there between group differences in engagement with LADs?

H3.1: The Progress LAD group mean LAD engagement frequency will be greater than the Social LAD group.

H3.2: The Progress LAD group mean LAD engagement frequency will be less than the Social LAD group.

H3.3: The Progress LAD group mean LAD engagement frequency will be equal to the Social LAD group.

4   Materials and Method

4.1   Participants

Study participants (N = 38) were chemical process plant employees located in Germany aged between 18 and 55 years. Participation was voluntary and all provided informed consent. Participants could exit the study at any time without consequence. The participants' working language was German and a German language version of the prototype was used.

4.2   Experimental Design

The study was a between two-group design in which the effect of LADs designed with a progress reference frame were tested against the effect of LADs designed with a social reference frame on three dependent variables associated with LAD interaction: time spent reviewing LAD with a reference frame, time spent reviewing detailed task feedback screen, engagement frequency with LAD. Participants were randomly assigned to the progress reference frame group (n = 20) and the social reference frame group (n = 18).

4.3   Description of VR Simulation-Based Training Prototype

The 'Operate your own reactor' VR training simulator runs on the Oculus Quest with Touch controllers. The training simulator was designed to train employees in the Butyllithium manufacturing process with commercial chemical reactor equipment.
   The Butyllithium chemical production procedure consists of four steps.

4.4   The Learning Analytics System and Features of the Learning Analytics Dashboards

The learning analytics system automatically collects, and analyses log-file data linked to performance criteria including correct and incorrect actions, number of hints requested and the amount of time elapsed to complete each step. Depending on these variables, the learners receive a score out of five represented by stars (See Fig. 1 and 2).
   Screenshots of the Progress LAD (Fig. 1) and Social LAD (Fig. 2) can be found below. The elements of the dashboard (Fig. 1) are described here in English: (1) name of the step which has just been completed, (2) message congratulating the participant on completing the step, (3) performance feedback summary, (4) How is this calculated? button, (5) detailed task feedback button and (6) Next button.

Fig. 1. Progress reference frame after step 3. Learners can compare how they performed on step 3 (Stufe 3) with previous steps (Stufe 0, Stufe 1, Stufe 2).

Fig. 2. Social LAD after step 3. Learners can compare how they performed on step 3 (Stufe 3) with the average score of their peers on step 3.

The performance feedback summary feature (3) is a means of communicating how well the learner performed a particular task. Stars are used to represent the learner's level of performance. The greater number of stars awarded, the better the performance.

When selected, the detailed task feedback button shows which sub-tasks were correctly or incorrectly performed (Fig. 3) and the 'How is this calculated?' (Fig. 4) button displays the formula used for calculating the performance outcome indicated by stars (i.e., 92–100% awards 5 stars).

Fig. 3. Display of the detailed task feedback dashboard which indicates performance on sub-tasks.

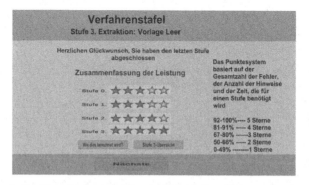

Fig. 4. Dashboard when the 'How is this calculated?' button is selected.

4.5   The Progress and Social Reference Frame

Figure 2 is a screenshot of the Progress LAD after completing step 3. This dashboard incorporates a progress reference frame because the learner's most recent performance outcome (step 3) is compared with their previous performances (step 0 – step 2).

Figure 3 is a screenshot of the Social LAD after completing step 3. This dashboard incorporates a social reference frame because the learner's most recent performance outcome (step 3) is compared with the average of their peers.

4.6   Timing of the Learning Analytics Dashboards

The LADs are presented after each step of the task, therefore, four LADs with reference frames are presented to the learner by the time they have completed the task. The detailed task feedback screens will only appear when the detailed task feedback button is selected. The calculation indicator appears as an additional visualization atop the Progress and Social LADs only when the How is this calculated? button is selected.

4.7 Procedure

Those participants who agreed to take part in the research were invited to a training room on their worksite which was equipped with the VR simulation-based training environment. Upon arrival, participants were asked to complete a series of questionnaires for another research project. Next, they were shown how to use the Oculus Touch controllers to navigate and interact with the virtual environment. Then, they were asked to follow an interactive tutorial within the virtual environment. Once the tutorial was complete, the participants were instructed to begin the simulation-based training.

Participants completed the simulation-based training task with either the Progress LAD or Social LAD. They were not aware there were two different LAD designs.

Upon completion of the training, which typically lasted between 45 and 60 min, participants completed additional surveys which were used for other research, they then returned to their regular work tasks.

4.8 Data Analysis and Statistical Models

Bayesian informative hypothesis evaluation was used to analyze the data. We formulated three competing hypotheses for each research question which used terms of equality ($=$) and inequality ($<, >$) [14]. One advantage to this approach over classical null hypothesis testing with p values is that it enables us to compare multiple hypothesis [15].

We compare the dependent variables means of the Progress LAD group with the dependent variable means of the Social LAD. The three dependent variables were associated with LAD interaction: time spent reviewing LAD with a reference frame, time spent reviewing detailed task feedback screen, engagement frequency with LAD as measured by the frequency with which the detailed task feedback button and How is this calculated? button was selected. To do this we conducted three ANOVAs with the LAD groups set as the fixed factors. We will do a sensitivity analysis using fraction 1, 2 and 3 and will report each result (the posterior model probabilities (PMPs) and interpret them at once.

Hypotheses for evaluation for each RQ are:

RQ1: H1: Progress > Social, H2: Progress < Social, H3: Progress = Social.
RQ2: H1: Progress > Social, H2: Progress < Social, H3: Progress = Social.
RQ3: H1: Progress > Social, H2: Progress < Social, H3: Progress = Social.

The Bayesian error associated with preferring the best hypothesis in terms of PMPs will be reported. This is the sum of the PMPs of the other hypotheses.

5 Results

In this study we set out to examine evidence in support of three competing hypotheses for each research question. Firstly, we present descriptive statistics in Table 1. Then, Table 2, Table 3, and Table 4 report the PMPs which provide an indication of how much each hypothesis is supported for RQ1, RQ2 and RQ3 respectively. The higher the PMP, the more evidence there is that that hypothesis is correct.

Table 1. Descriptive statistics for interaction with LAD

	Seconds reviewing LADs with reference frame		Seconds reviewing specific task feedback		LAD engagement frequency	
	Progress	Social	Progress	Social	Progress	Social
Mean	26.7	35.2	2.2	0.3	1.1	0.3
StdD	9.5	17.2	1.2	1.2	1.5	0.6
Min	14	9	0	0	0	0
Max	54	64	15	5	6	2

Table 2. Bain ANOVA RQ1 Time spent reviewing LAD with Reference frame

	PMP a*	PMP a**	PMP a***
H1: Progress > Social	0.018	0.020	0.021
H2: Progress < Social	0.659	0.728	0.753
H3: Progress = Social	0.323	0.252	0.216

Note. * denotes Fraction set to 1, ** denotes Fraction set to 2, *** denotes Fraction set to 3. Posterior model probabilities (PMP) (a: excludes the unconstrained hypothesis) is based on equal prior model probabilities.

Table 3. Bain ANOVA RQ2 Time spent reviewing detailed task feedback

	PMP a*	PMP a**	PMP a***
H1: Progress > Social	0.705	0.768	0.799
H2: Progress < Social	0.015	0.016	0.017
H3: Progress = Social	0.280	0.216	0.184

Note. * denotes Fraction set to 1, ** denotes Fraction set to 2, *** denotes Fraction set to 3. Posterior model probabilities (PMP) (a: excludes the unconstrained hypothesis) is based on equal prior model probabilities.

Table 4. Bain ANOVA RQ3 LAD engagement

	PMP a*	PMP a**	PMP a***
H1: Progress > Social	0.659	0.728	0.763
H2: Progress < Social	0.018	0.020	0.021
H3: Progress = Social	0.323	0.252	0.216

Note. * denotes Fraction set to 1, ** denotes Fraction set to 2, *** denotes Fraction set to 3. Posterior model probabilities (PMP) (a: excludes the unconstrained hypothesis) is based on equal prior model probabilities.

As we can see in Table 2, the hypothesis which states that less time is spent reviewing the Progress LAD is most supported (H2) and the hypothesis stating more time is spent reviewing the Progress LAD (H1) is substantially unsupported. Therefore, it is most likely that learners with a Progress LAD spend less time reviewing their LAD than those with a Social LAD. However, due to the error probability, (0.341, 0.272, 0.247), we cannot rule out that the two LAD groups spend an equal amount of time reviewing their LADs (H3).

As we can see in Table 3, the hypothesis that states that the Progress LAD group spends more time reviewing the detailed task feedback screen than the Social LAD group is most supported (H1). The hypothesis stating that the Progress LAD group spends less time reviewing the detailed task feedback screen than the Social LAD group is substantially unsupported (H2). Therefore, it is most likely that the Progress LAD leads to more time being spent reviewing detailed task feedback. However, due to the error probability for H1, (0.295, 0.232, 0.201), we cannot rule out the hypothesis which states that two groups spend an equal amount of time reviewing detailed task feedback (H3).

As we can see in Table 4, the hypothesis that states the Progress LAD group engages more with the LAD than the Social LAD group is most supported (H1). The hypothesis that states the Progress LAD group engages less with the LAD than the Social LAD group is substantially unsupported (H2). Therefore, it is most likely that the Progress LAD leads to more engagement with the LAD. However, due to the error probability for H1, (0.341, 0.272, 0.237), we cannot rule out the hypothesis which states that the two groups engage equally with the LAD.

6 Discussion

The results in RQ1 indicate that learners receiving LADs with a progress reference frame spend less time reviewing their LADs compared with those receiving a social reference frame. This suggests that the time it takes for learners to decide to move to the next step in their learning process is at least partly influenced by temporal comparison. The results from RQ2 and RQ3 provide an indication on what these learners do next. RQ2 results show that the group who are engaging in temporal comparison via the progress reference frame were more likely to spend more time reviewing the detailed task feedback screen. This suggests that temporal comparisons may stimulate learners to consider how they can improve and therefore, seek out information to aid self-improvement via the detailed task feedback screen. This aligns with a mastery goal orientation because it concerns learners wanting a deeper understanding of their task performance [16]. On the other hand, the social reference frame, and its stimulation of social comparison, may encourage surface level learning, a feature of a performance goal orientation, which may in part explain why the detailed task feedback LAD was reviewed for a shorter amount of time in this group. The proposition the group receiving the progress reference frame seem more likely to adopt mastery goal orientation behaviors and the social reference frame to adopt performance goal orientation behaviors is further supported by RQ3 which indicates that the progress reference frame group likely engaged more with the LAD than the social reference frame group.

7 Conclusion

This paper presents the empirical results of a study which examined how workplace learners interacted with two distinct LADs for a VR simulation-based training environment. The study compared two groups, one which received an LAD with a progress reference frame and one which received an LAD with a social reference frame. The results are an early indication that learners may be more likely to interact with aspects of LADs that help them gain a deeper understanding of a task, if they are designed with a progress reference frame compared with a social reference frame.

Acknowledgements. This project has received funding from the European Union's EU Framework Programme for Research and Innovation Horizon 2020 under Grant Agreement No 812716. This publication reflects only the authors' view exempting the community from any liability. Project website: https://charming-etn.eu/.

References s

1. Makransky, G., Petersen, G.B.: The cognitive affective model of immersive learning (CAMIL): a theoretical research-based model of learning in immersive virtual reality. Educ. Psychol. Rev. **33**(3), 937–958 (2021). https://doi.org/10.1007/s10648-020-09586-2
2. Ruiz-Calleja, A., Prieto, L.P., Ley, T., Rodríguez-Triana, M.J., Dennerlein, S.: Learning analytics for professional and workplace learning: a literature review. In: Lavoué, É., Drachsler, H., Verbert, K., Broisin, J., Pérez-Sanagustín, M. (eds.) EC-TEL 2017. LNCS, vol. 10474, pp. 164–178. Springer, Cham (2017). https://doi.org/10.1007/978-3-319-66610-5_13
3. Siemens, G., Baker, R.S.J.D.: Learning analytics and educational data mining: towards communication and collaboration. In: ACM International Conference Proceeding Series, pp. 252–254 (2012). https://doi.org/10.1145/2330601.2330661
4. Matcha, W., Ahmad Uzir, N., Gasevic, D., Pardo, A.: A systematic review of empirical studies on learning analytics dashboards: a self-regulated learning perspective. IEEE Trans. Learn. Technol. **1382**, 1 (2019). https://doi.org/10.1109/tlt.2019.2916802
5. Schwendimann, B.A., Rodriguez-Triana, M.J., Vozniuk, A., et al.: Perceiving learning at a glance: A systematic literature review of learning dashboard research. IEEE Trans. Learn. Technol. **10**, 30–41 (2017). https://doi.org/10.1109/TLT.2016.2599522
6. Wise, A.F., Vytasek, J.: Learning analytics implementation design. Handb. Learn. Analytics 151–160 (2017). https://doi.org/10.18608/hla17.013
7. Jivet, I., Scheffel, M., Drachsler, H., Specht, M.: Awareness is not enough: pitfalls of learning practice. In: Lavoué, É., Drachsler, H., Verbert, K., Broisin, J., Pérez-Sanagustín, M. (eds.) EC-TEL 2017. LNCS, vol. 10474, pp. 1:82–96. Springer, Cham (2017). https://doi.org/10.1007/978-3-319-66610-5_7
8. Wise, A.F.: Designing pedagogical interventions to support student use of learning analytics. In: ACM International Conference Proceeding Series, pp. 203–211 (2014). https://doi.org/10.1145/2567574.2567588
9. Albert, S.: Temporal comparison theory. Psychol. Rev. **84**, 485–503 (1977). https://doi.org/10.1037/0033-295X.84.6.485
10. Wilson, A.E., Shanahan, E.: Temporal comparisons in a social world. In: Suls, J., Collins, R.L., Wheeler, L. (eds.) Social Comparison, Judgment, and Behavior, pp. 309–344. Oxford University Press (2020)

11. Pintrich, P.R., Conley, A.M.M., Kempler, T.M.: Current issues in achievement goal theory and research. Int. J. Educ. Res. **39**, 319–337 (2003). https://doi.org/10.1016/j.ijer.2004.06.002

12. Cleary, T.J.: Monitoring trends and accuracy of self-efficacy beliefs during interventions: Advantages and potential applications to school-based settings. Psychol. Sch. **46**, 154–171 (2009). https://doi.org/10.1002/pits.20360

13. Corrin, L., de Barba, P.: How do students interpret feedback delivered via dashboards? In: ACM International Conference Proceeding Series, 16–20-Mar, pp. 430–431 (2015). https://doi.org/10.1145/2723576.2723662

14. van Lissa, C.J., Gu, X., Mulder, J., et al.: Teacher's corner: evaluating informative hypotheses using the Bayes factor in structural equation models. Struct. Equ. Modeling **28**, 292–301 (2021). https://doi.org/10.1080/10705511.2020.1745644

15. Hoijtink, H., Mulder, J., van Lissa, C., Gu, X.: A tutorial on testing hypotheses using the Bayes factor. Psychol. Methods **24**, 539–556 (2019). https://doi.org/10.1037/met0000201

16. Pintrich, P.R.: An achievement goal theory perspective on issues in motivation terminology, theory, and research. Contemp. Educ. Psychol. **25**, 92–104 (2000). https://doi.org/10.1006/ceps.1999.1017

Game Design for a Museum Visit: Insights into the Co-design of *AL2049*, a Game About Food Systems

Gil Oliveira[1]([⊠]) [ID], Nicolas Godinot[2] [ID], Eric Sanchez[1] [ID], Catherine Bonnat[1] [ID], Simon Morard[1] [ID], and Sandro Dall'Aglio[3]

[1] TECFA, University of Geneva, 40 Bd du pont de l'Arve 4, 1211 Geneva, Switzerland
gil.oliveira@unige.ch
[2] Alimentarium, Quai Perdonnet 25, 1800 Vevey, Switzerland
[3] Digital Kingdom SARL, Chaussée de la Guinguette 4, 1800 Vevey, Switzerland

Abstract. This paper presents the results of the co-design of a learning game in a museum context. This game deals with the topic of the food system and considers how this concept is integrated with the Swiss school curriculum which constituted the starting point of the game design. Based on the ludicization theoretical framework, we question how learning objectives were articulated with the game elements and the choices made to design a playful learning situation. Our work is grounded on a design-based research methodology. In this context, we describe the initial phase of co-design, which involved co-design activities, research of educational content, and iterative prototyping. This empirical work led to the game *AL2049*, which aims to bring secondary school students (12–15 years old) to understand interrelationships in food systems and, in so doing, to face complex problem solving. Results comprise the game and the choices made in regard to the ludicization model.

Keywords: Game design · Gamification · Ludicization · Museum · Food system

1 Introduction

Students' motivation and involvement is seen as critical for the learning process. Within this context, game-based learning is considered to offer interesting perspectives to capture students' attention. Although the impacts of the use of digital games on motivation and attitudes have been demonstrated [1], there are still many issues to address for their use within learning contexts. Regarding what means game-based learning, learning game design is not limited to adding game mechanics to create a game (gamification), but consists of designing a reflexive space in which a student can interact and of changing the meaning of the learning situation so that it becomes playful [2]. This process,

Supplementary Information The online version contains supplementary material available at https://doi.org/10.1007/978-3-031-22124-8_3.

named ludicization, provides an epistemic dimension to playing which enables students to develop the knowledge that is expected by teachers.

This paper elaborates on the design of *AL2049*, a game dedicated to the ludicization of school visits in a Swiss museum, the Alimentarium. The aim of this museum is to educate visitors about food and nutrition. Regarding this specific context, i.e., the use of a game during a museum school visit and the complexity of the food system, we question the legitimacy and the process dedicated to the ludicization of the knowledge to be learnt. After describing the concept of food system and its place in the Swiss school curriculum, we present the results of the game design process and discuss the choices that were made in relation to the model of ludicization presented in the theoretical framework.

2 Research Context

2.1 Food System

Here, we briefly describe the concept of food system and its importance when facing challenges of the 21st century. Then, we highlight its use in a museum context. Our objective is not to address the construction and uses of food system per se, but rather to show an example of a way to popularize this concept to a large audience.

Food systems comprise a large number of components [3–5] varying in their nature, such as: type of raw material produced; land type and surface requirements; water supply; energy sources; transportation device and infrastructure; transformation systems and infrastructures; distribution systems and infrastructures; information; legal constraints and regulations; consumers' purchasing power and willingness to pay; workforce availability; technological inputs and agricultural practices; and so on… In addition, numerous relationships between these components can be established. Animal husbandry will require vegetal material, some of which may be edible for humans. Crop farming optimization requires fertilizer, either from byproducts of animal husbandry or from fossil fuel. Surface of land used will vary depending on type of production, technological inputs, and agricultural practices. Workforce availability will depend on work attractiveness and socio-economic parameters. The energy used within the food system cannot be used for other purposes. Usage of fossil fuel, husbandry of ruminants, some crops growing practices contribute to climate change, whose effects impact in turn food production. The type of agriculture and agricultural practices may impact the quality of soils and the productivity of the system. The well-being of the population and purchasing power will be affected by the socio-economic environment, which requires resources and land that can be competing with the requirements of the food system.

This topic is a major issue of the 21st century. Despite the growth in food production during the past half-century, societies are facing the challenge of feeding their populations with new constraints [6]. The global demand for food will likely increase in the next decades because of current population and consumption growth. At the same time, there are additional pressures affecting our ability to produce food, such as an increased competition among food producers for resources. Overarching these constraints are the impacts of environmental issues, including climate change [7]. This new set of intersecting challenges requires societies to find new alternatives.

The Alimentarium, a museum of food and nutrition, is seeking innovative approaches to educate visitors about this topic and to reflect on the future challenges of the food system. The museum addresses the topic of food systems in various ways through its permanent and temporary exhibitions or via accessible online content, providing visitors with a set of information comprehensive enough to get an understanding of their complexity, and interrelations within. However, this curated content must be taken as a whole, requiring visitors to spend a significant amount of time and attention. The systemic aspect is not directly summarized in a hands-on experience which would lead visitors to get an idea of the complexity and interdependencies of food systems. It is foreseen that such an experience will facilitate visitors' understanding of the challenges our societies are facing, especially regarding our food [8].

2.2 Educational Content

The game *AL2049* integrates knowledge related to the food system complexity and more general skills at the core of the curriculum for secondary schools for French-speaking cantons in Switzerland, the *Plan d'études romand* (PER) [9]. The topic of the food system is directly relevant to major disciplines of the PER study plan such as: geography, by describing the production and consumption path of a common agricultural good; natural sciences, by recognizing and understanding interdependencies in natural environments; nutritional education, by identifying the importance of a balanced, varied, and healthy diet, which combines pleasure of the senses and good health. Beyond the specific disciplinary contents, the main topic is the systemic understanding of the food system itself, which is essential for understanding the environmental and social issues related to food production [3]. In the PER, systemic (or systemic analysis) is defined as an approach that considers the different actors, phenomena, spaces, and their interactions. A system is complex (but not necessarily complicated) in the sense that it involves multiple interacting elements; these can be political, economic, social, cultural, or natural conditions.

An understanding of systemic phenomena also relies on students' ability to engage in reflective thinking, considered as cross-curricular and general education skills in the study plan. To develop this skill, students can: elaborate personal opinions, identify facts, verify their accuracy, put them in perspective, explore different options and points of view, abandon preconceived ideas, compare his/her point of view with those of others, face doubt and ambiguity. Critical thinking is a crucial skill and a prerequisite for understanding complex systems [10]. More general education skills can also be developed such as: becoming aware of consumption behaviors and their consequences; evaluating one's place, role, and influence as an individual in the globalized economic system; etc. These different core curriculum expectations served as a compass to guide our choices for integrating learning goals into the game-design.

The learning goals of the game were selected during the co-design phase through discussions between the different partners in the project. They are the result of a practical consensus, based on the guidelines of the PER and the teachers' expertise on specific disciplines, the learning goals expected by the Museum, and researchers' objectives related to personal epistemology. On this basis, we identified two pedagogical objectives:

systemic approach, focused on understanding complex relationships between components of the food system, and critical thinking, focused on reflecting and evaluating the information provided.

3 Theoretical Framework

Our game-based approach elaborates on the concept of ludicization [11], which differs from the more common concept of gamification, the latter being understood as the process by which one integrates aspects of play into a situation that is initially not playful [2]. While gamification might simply consist of adding game elements (e.g., rewards or leaderboards) to a learning situation, ludicization focuses on the play – the situation experienced by the learner, rather than on the game itself. It aims to change the meaning of the learning situation so that it becomes playful. It also consists of the integration of a learning content into a game, thus providing an epistemic dimension to the gaming experience and enabling students to develop their knowledge from it.

In this paper, we use the model of ludicization [12]. This model is particularly relevant to our purpose as it is adapted to game-based school visits in a museum. More generally, it describes the process by which scholarly knowledge is made suitable for use as a learning object within a specific game-based learning situation. This process is based on the development of a fictional universe analogous to the field to be learned. This universe is designed using narrative and game mechanics. In other words, ludicization corresponds to a conversion of a "target domain" (the domain to be learned), which includes complex and multidisciplinary knowledge, into a "source domain" (the learning situation) that takes the form of a playful learning experience. This conversion is done using a metaphor, which operates a transfer of meaning from a transparent source domain to an opaque target domain. Indeed, as fictions, metaphors allow to describe abstract concepts in a more comprehensible and concrete way by providing analogies from familiar domains [13]. From this point of view, our approach is in line with previous works carried out in the field of games studies and that consider games as hermeneutic spaces [14].

The use of a metaphor implies that there is a hidden meaning behind the game, and that this second level of meaning gives the game its power. Thus, the metaphor captures both the fundamental characteristics of this domain (what makes it what it is, and what it would not be without) and the intimate nature of that domain that is difficult to know. The metaphor usually remains implicit within the game and is rendered explicit during the debriefing.

This model, applied to the context of the museum and to the theme of the food system, allows to identify the target domain in the form of three key concepts: complexity, systemic and planetary limits (Fig. 1). In this context, our research question is twofold: how the target domain is translated into a source domain through the metaphorization process; what are the choices made, in terms of game design, and how these choices are associated with learning objectives?

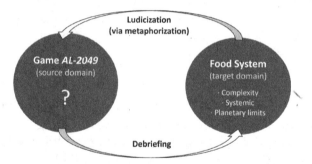

Fig. 1. Model of ludicization [12]

4 Research Method

Our work is grounded in a methodological paradigm called design-based research [15]. Design-based research consists of conducting an iterative process of design and analysis, carried out in a collaborative manner between researchers and practitioners. In this context, our work took place during the initial phase of co-design, which involved researchers, teachers, museum staff, and a Swiss video game studio. The co-design of the game and its testing was divided into three phases.

The first phase consisted of two game jams that lasted half a day each. The first one was conducted in 2020 with students of a Master of science in engineering at the School of Engineering and Architecture of Fribourg, Switzerland. Resources were provided to help them imagine a game and define educational goals. Based on this first experience, a second game-jam took place in 2021 with twelve participants of the project. This one focused on finding a metaphor that could reach a consensus between the different partners. Several ideas were proposed, and the participants rated each game according to a predefined criteria grid (e.g., the game allows: to think about complexity and systemic; to have interactions with the museography; to adopt a reflexive approach and to question the relationship to knowledge; etc.).

Once the general scenario of the game had been chosen, the second phase of the co-design consisted of eleven half-day workshops between a member of the research team, a museum curator, and a game-designer. This process allowed the development of a prototype including each partners' expertise. The game-designer first built a cardboard prototype that could be played simply with cards and chips, before it was made digital. The third phase was conducted in parallel with the second phase. It consisted of testing the prototype and adjusting the game accordingly. Five main tests were organized. The first one included five participants and was used to adapt the game to the students' level, according to the teachers' expertise. Another test was done by the curator with his own museum staff to practice the debriefing. Two more tests took place in classrooms with targeted school children. A final test was conducted during the annual seminar of the research project. Each test allowed the team to improve the game in terms of gameplay, functionalities, and general understanding.

5 Results

In this section, we describe our results, that is the game and its pedagogical scenario (source domain), while the next chapter is dedicated to discussing the process of metaphorization, highlighting the choices that were made in terms of game design and how these choices relate to the pedagogical objectives (target domain). *AL2049* is a mixed-reality game played with digital tablets in the permanent exhibition of the Alimentarium, thus combining tangible and digital elements. It has been designed in a pedagogical scenario for school visits of secondary school students (12–15 years old), taking approximately 90 minutes. The whole scenario includes an introduction, the game itself which has two distinct phases, and a debriefing.

The introduction takes the form of a briefing given by the game master (museum staff) who sets an immersive narrative experience through storytelling. He describes himself as a scientist working on the future challenges of food, emphasizing that the current global food system might not be sustainable. Thus, he has imagined a new way to explore and reconfigure the food system. He built a digital simulator on a tablet to test various configurations. The simulator transforms the museum into a system isolated from the world, in which a population of 30 people live. Players are invited to run the simulator to help the scientist. The goal of the game is to feed the population.

The main menu corresponds to a map of the museum showing the various rooms distributed on two floors. The core mechanic of the game consists in assigning specific functions to these different spaces. Each function is a component of the food system (Table 1). Players can thus choose to produce food, process it further (via food processing mini-factories), facilitate exchanges or consumption (via markets or restaurants). To win, players must attribute a function to each room to produce enough food for 30 people. The game has two distinct phases. During the first phase, players must first unlock the museum spaces. To do so, they must go into the museum room and scan it by pointing the tablet in the direction of an arrow placed on the ground. After unlocking a space, the player can assign a function to it, using a certain amount of energy. There are three types of limited energy: human labor (i.e., the 30 people who make up the population), renewable energy, and fossil fuel. These are not equal: fossil fuel, for instance, provides, per unit, much more energy - a proxy of energy density.

Table 1. Main components of the food system's model

Production	Crop cultivation	Animal breeding	Hunting and fishing
Processing units	Plants	Animals	
Consumption	Market	Restaurant	
Bonus	Laboratory of agronomical sciences		

The food production components are further developed in the game. For example, animal breeding is composed of four possibilities: pigs and poultry, cattle and sheep, fish, and insects. These vary in terms of the quantity of food produced. Pigs/poultry and insects' farms produce a bit more food than cattle/sheep and fish farms - a proxy for per weight meat productivity per unit of surface. Similarly, crop cultivation is divided into different options (Fig. 2). The two other categories, processing units and consumption places, allow to reduce food losses. When the game starts, the food loss rate is set up at 35%. Players can reduce it at maximum 5%.

Fig. 2. Fruits and vegetables gardening interface

Each function has certain properties, but they are all related to other components of the food system. For example, to allocate a space to raise pigs or poultry, the player must first have assigned a space to grow crops because food is needed for these monogastric animals. Consequently, the quantity of food produced from crop cultivation to feed the population decreases. In turn, having an animal farm increases the production of each space allocated to plant cultivation because livestock manure can be used as a fertilizer providing additional nutrients needed for crop production, therefore increasing yield. In the game, these explanations aren't provided. The player only sees the different values in terms of food production. The laboratory of agronomical science is another example of interconnected components in a socio-environmental system. It gives the player several different bonuses and increases the number of reliable advice coming from a newsfeed.

After allocating all the spaces, the player can press a button titled "10 years later" to move forward in time and look at the results of the simulation. The end interface shows the results of the simulation of the food system composed by the player (Fig. 3). It indicates the number of people who survived, based on the amount of food produced and the proportion of food loss. However, there are new criteria: health and well-being. These two were not known by the player before. He/she can find out what they mean by simply clicking on it. The "health" criterion depends on three variables: nutritional variety, pollution, and greenhouse gases emissions. The "well-being" criterion is composed of two variables: pleasure and workload.

Fig. 3. End interface

Then, the second phase of the game can start. The player can go back in time and change the composition of his/her food system, to feed the population of 30 people, this time considering the two new criteria. The main interface is now enhanced with more options. The player can apply filters for each variable and see the impact of each space. As soon as he/she makes any change, he instantly sees its effect on the three main gauges: food produced; health; well-being. The second phase of the game is characterized by an open end-game state in which players can adjust the best they can, according to their choices and values, their food system. The goal remains the same (feeding people) but gets complexified with additional elements to consider.

Once the game is completed, players take part in a debriefing session, moderated by the game master. The discussion revolves around the experience lived by the players. They are invited to explain their choices and strategies. The way the debriefing is conducted is the result of a collaborative work between the different partners. It aims to deconstruct the metaphor of the game and to help the players to link the source and target domains (Fig. 1). The simulation that took place in the museum, understood as a closed system, represents the planet and the global food system. From an educational perspective, it is a crucial phase because players (who have become learners again) can reflect on their experience. They learn by reflecting on the game experience rather than on the experience itself (source). Thus, the debriefing helps to transform the subjective knowledge developed during the game (the need to assess the quality of information) into knowledge that can be used in another context [16].

6 Discussion

This description of the game and its pedagogical scenario for school visits highlights the choices made based on the target situation for the design of a concrete source situation

(Fig. 1). These choices are the result of the *ludicization* process, carried out by using a metaphor. *AL2049* offers a metaphor in which the museum is conceptualized as a closed system that represents our global food system. Available resources, energy, and space are limited. Players are expected to produce food in these conditions. Such limitations are a metaphor of the planetary limits. As a result, the amount of food that can be produced is limited. The metaphor also considers the complexity of the food system. Each decision the player makes, in terms of type of crop grown, animal farmed, types of energy used, and quantities allocated, has multiple impacts on the overall number of persons who can be fed by the system, their health and well-being. This gameplay addresses interdependencies between food production, energy use, environmental impacts, health issues, and other socio-environmental issues.

The challenge was to keep the complexity inherent of the food system while reducing it to an intelligible model. Therefore, some components of the food system are voluntarily left out (such as the roles and impacts of transportation or the use of water resources), so that players do not loose themselves in too much information and too many interactions. The idea is not to match reality; the model is simplified but remains coherent with reality. It has been built in such a manner to serve as the simplest possible proxy while preserving the relative validity of the interactions in place, thus the educational content, and the playful dimension of the game in specific constraints. What remains, at the end, is the essence of the complexity of the food system itself.

The choices made in terms of components, interactions, and level of detail were the result of discussions between the partners. For instance, when considering the issue of climate change in agriculture, rice cultivation was treated as a special case due to its significant greenhouse gas emissions compared to other crops. However, adding an exception would risk diminishing the playfulness of the game if it were to disrupt its understanding. Despite the risk, it was assumed that it was important enough to be integrated. This exception could be developed during the debriefing, thus showing that the ludicization process also allows to go back to the target domain.

The game scenario had to take into consideration several constraints. First it had to be adequate for a museum school visit and coherent with the educational content of the school curriculum. This was done by identifying pedagogical objectives with the help of teachers. Second, the game had to be adapted to the museum objective to offer visitors a hands-on experience that grasps the complexity and interdependencies of the food system and its future challenges. We chose to design the game as an ill-structured problem with no unique solution to illustrate the complexity of the food system and the potential to improve the outcome based on a better understanding of its interconnections. This open-end state is in line with the research project as well, since it aims to understand how the ludicization of school visits at the museum allows learners to address complex and non-deterministic problems. A final constraint was to design a game that foster students' interactions with the museography. While the graphic design of the game fully integrates it, thus helping to create a coherent game narrative and an immersive experience, the game does not further promote interactions between players and the museum's tangible elements. Only the game scenario includes interactions with the permanent exhibition during the initial unlocking phase.

The game design is focused on bringing about a systemic understanding of the food system through a trial-error process of trying to simulate the "best" system. It follows that *AL2049* is both a strategy and a simulation game. As a strategy game, it consists in strategic deployment via system thinking. As a simulation game, it requires interacting with and discovering an underlying, simulated food system. We see this paper as a contribution to game design research that illustrates how a game can be an analogous and metaphorical situation of a domain that needs to be learned. The game will be tested with classes in autumn 2022 and traces will be collected to see how it is used by the players and how their food conceptions evolve.

References

1. Brown, J.S., Collins, A., Duguid, P.: Situated cognition and the culture of learning. Educ. Res. **18**(1), 32–42 (1989)
2. Sanchez, E., Young, S., Jouneau-Sion, C.: Classcraft: from gamification to ludicization of classroom management. Educ. Inf. Technol. **22**(2), 497–513 (2016). https://doi.org/10.1007/s10639-016-9489-6
3. Ericksen, P.J.: Conceptualizing food systems for global environmental change research. Glob. Environ. Chang. **18**(1), 234–245 (2008)
4. Rastoin, J.L., Ghersi, G.: Découpage et représentation d'un système alimentaire. In: Rastoin, J.L., Ghersi, G. (eds.) Le système alimentaire mondial: concepts et méthodes, analyses et dynamiques. Éditions Quae (2010)
5. National Research Council: A Framework for Assessing Effects of the Food System. The National Academies Press, Washington, DC (2015)
6. Godfray, H., et al.: Food security: the challenge of feeding 9 billion people. Science **327**(5967), 812–818 (2010)
7. Springmann, M., Clark, M., et al.: Options for keeping the food system within environmental limits. Nature **562**, 519–525 (2018)
8. Food and Agriculture Organization of the United Nations: The future of food and agriculture–Trends and challenges, FAO, Rome (2017)
9. CIIP: Plan d'études romand (2010). http://www.plandetudes.ch
10. Halpern, D.F.: Thought and Knowledge: An Introduction to Critical Thinking, 5th edn. Psychology Press, New York (2014)
11. Deterding, S., Khaled, R., Nacke, L., Dixon, D.: Gamification: toward a definition. In: CHI 2011 Gamification Workshop Proceedings, Vancouver, BC (2011)
12. Bonnat, C., et al.: Didactic transposition and learning game design: proposal of a model integrating ludicization, and test in a school visit context in a museum. In: Almqvist, J.K. (ed.) Didactics in a Changing World. European Perspectives on Teaching, Learning and the Curriculum. EERA Book Series (to be published)
13. Lakoff, G., Johnson, M.: Metaphors We Live By. University of Chicago Press (1980)
14. Caracciolo, M.: Conceptual blending in computer games: integrating fiction and meaning. In: Proceedings of the Philosophy of Computer Games Conference 2009 (2009)
15. Wang, F., Hannafin, M.J.: Design-based research and technology-enhanced learning environments. Educ. Tech. Res. Dev. **53**(4), 5–23 (2005)
16. Sanchez, E., Plumettaz-Sieber, M.: Teaching and learning with escape games from debriefing to institutionalization of knowledge. In: Gentile, M., Allegra, M., Söbke, H. (eds.) GALA 2018. LNCS, vol. 11385, pp. 242–253. Springer, Cham (2019). https://doi.org/10.1007/978-3-030-11548-7_23

Supporting Knowledge Sharing for the Co-design of Digital Learning Games

Estelle Prior[1(✉)] 🆔, Eric Sanchez[1(✉)] 🆔, and Nadine Mandran[2(✉)] 🆔

[1] University of Geneva, LIP/TECFA, Geneva, Switzerland
{estelle.prior,eric.sanchez}@unige.ch
[2] Université Grenoble Alpes, CNRS, LIG, Saint Martin d'Hères, France
nadine.mandran@univ-grenoble-alpes.fr

Abstract. This paper deals with knowledge sharing during a collaborative and design-based research project about game-based learning. According to a literature review about serious game design, a key process for collaborative work is knowledge sharing. This process is analysed with the frames of praxeologies and boundary objects. The praxeology framework aims to identify the participants' practice and discourse about this practice for the design of serious games. The boundary objects framework aims to identify knowledge transactions during collaborative work. We collected data from workshops dedicated to co-design of TSADK, a serious game for computer education. We performed a thematic analysis on participants' verbatim for nine workshops. The thematic analysis focuses on one subject: the learning outcomes of the game. The analysis has identified themes on this subject: to specify, to phrase and to select the main learning outcomes. Regarding these themes, the praxeology and boundary object frameworks allow us to identify common practice but no common knowledge and thus, an obstacle to collaboration. Based on these results, we propose a tool for supporting the collaboration design through sharing knowledge.

Keywords: Co-design · Serious game · Praxeology · Boundary object · Share knowledge

1 Introduction

Design-based Research (DBR) is a 'methodology aimed to improve educational practices through iterative analysis, design, development, and implementation, based on collaboration among researchers and practitioners in real-world settings, and leading to contextually-sensitive design principles and theories' [1]. The main goal of our research is to propose a framework for the analysis of collaboration during a workshop dedicated to serious game (SG) design in DBR. This framework aims to identify the collaboration problems that multidisciplinary teams may encounter during it (*e.g.* researchers, teachers, game designers). This paper focuses on the description of this framework.

The design of a SG requires combining educational and playful dimensions [2–4], which is a challenge. Indeed, Arnab et al. [2] highlight the lack of articulation between these two dimensions. Moreover, the design of a game requires multidisciplinary and collaborative work [3–5]. The design team may face difficulties, such as multiple views of the process [2], different professional practices [4] or internal understanding into the team [5]. Indeed, 'The experiences and terminologies of each actor can be a challenge and an issue throughout the process' [6]. This collaborative design is not only about adding up expertise. It requires that stakeholders communicate and collaborate.

Stakeholders must share knowledge to understand each other. Moreover, the first step for the collaborative design of a SG is crucial since the stakeholders must reach agreement about the objective of the project, expectations of the stakeholders involved [7] and the needs of the target audience [8].

To address this issue, we examine collaboration through the lens of the knowledge sharing between stakeholders. We study this sharing through two theoretical frames: praxeological analysis [9] and boundary object [10]. Praxeologies analysis is a way to describe and analyse human activities [9, 11]. When they collaborate, stakeholders develop a common praxeology, *i.e.* a common discourse on a shared practice [11]. This discourse can be described as shared praxeologies [11]. Praxeologies analysis is a way to illustrate how stakeholders describe and justify practice during collaborative design. We also examine collaboration through the lens of boundary objects. Boundary objects are concrete or abstract artefacts such as information or software [12]. Since each stakeholder gives a specific meaning to these objects, they link communities together without *prior* consensus [13]. As a result, they allow stakeholders with different backgrounds and points of view to collaborate and to achieve a common goal [14]. They allow different levels of dialogues called boundaries for the knowledge sharing [10].

In this paper we want to handle the sharing of knowledge during the collaborative design of SG based on a framework that combines praxeologies analysis and the identification of levels of dialogues between stakeholders.

To address this question, we first present a literature review of collaborative SG design and the theoretical frameworks on praxeologies and boundary objects. Second, we describe the method that allowed for the analysis of knowledge sharing during workshops dedicated to the collaborative design of a SG. We discuss the results of the study and propose guidelines for the sharing of knowledge as means to foster collaboration.

2 Collaborative Design and Knowledge Sharing

2.1 Collaborative Design of Serious Games

Different models exist to accompany the collaborative work between stakeholders involved in the design of a serious game. However, these models present disparities.

Collaborative design may start by different steps: defining learning outcomes [3, 4, 15]; identifying users [16] or target audience [17]; specifying the overall objectives [17, 18]; establishing a theoretical basis and tool evaluation [17]; defining the problem [8].

Different stakeholders may collaborate to ensure the success of a specific step of the process (*e.g.* [3, 4, 8, 16–18]). According to the Six Facets of SG Design, pedagogical and game design experts work together on the step 'Problems and Progression'. This one 'concerns which problems to give the players to solve and in which order' [4].

Different authors propose design patterns dedicated to helping stakeholders to reach a common vocabulary [4]. Guiding questionnaires [15, 17] or knowledge management tools (*e.g.* skills map) [3] are proposed to foster collaboration. However, many authors (see for example [8, 16, 18]) do not specify the way stakeholders share information and knowledge. We address this issue in the next section.

2.2   Praxeologies Analysis and Boundary Objects

We know from literature review that knowledge sharing between stakeholders is a key point for the success of the design, but this sharing is difficult [5]. We address this issue with two theoretical frames: praxeologies analysis [9] and boundary objects [10]. We articulate them to build a framework dedicated to the analysis of knowledge sharing. By knowledge we mean concepts 'relying on a theoretical framework', produced and legitimized by an institution and shared by using an appropriate language [19].

It is expected that the collaborative design nurtures a 'common discourse on practice' [20]. The analysis of this discourse leads to the characterisation of praxeologies. This frame was proposed by Chevallard [9] for the depiction of human activity. According to Chevallard, a praxeology describes both the practice (*praxis*) and the justification of it (*logos*) about a specific human activity. The *praxis* includes a task performed by a technique and concerns the know-how. The *logos* refers to the technology and the theory (*i.e.* the knowledge) that support and justify the *praxis*. Collaboration can be analysed during design workshops based on this framework [11]. This analysis consists of determining what stakeholders want to do in terms of game design (*praxis*), how they justify (*logos*) this *praxis*. Collaboration is successful when stakeholders manage to reach a consensus and to share a common praxeology (shared practice and shared discourse on practice). So, stakeholders involved in collaborative game design need to adjust their practice and discourse and share know-how and knowledge about this.

Processes of knowledge sharing can be identified with the boundary objects framework. Indeed, this framework highlights levels of dialogue that allow to characterise this sharing, through meaningful concepts. A boundary object is a tangible or digital object (*e.g.* the SG itself, a tool to support collaboration), or a theoretical object (*e.g.* a concept) belonging to stakeholders which foster meanings and interpretations among them [12]. According to Star [13], communities can work together without *prior* consensus, by mobilising boundary objects. These objects are seen as translation supports between these communities [14]. They allow them to understand each other. To do this, they establish different levels of dialogue (boundaries) [10], where knowledge is shared and evaluated [14]. Crossing these boundaries allows stakeholders to work together despite their plural views about how to perform the design process. Depending on the boundary, knowledge management varies. Indeed, the syntactic boundary consists of a basic transfer of knowledge, *i.e.* actors mobilise a common lexicon. At the semantic boundary, knowledge is translated, *i.e.* they share common meanings. At the pragmatic boundary, knowledge is transformed *i.e.* they rely on common interests [10]. Boundaries' analysis enables us to understand the way stakeholders share their knowledge.

Our framework articulates the frames of praxeology analysis and boundary objects, for the collaboration analysis. Indeed, praxeology analysis aims to identify knowledge at stake and boundary objects, to understand processes of knowledge sharing through the 3 boundaries. Based on it, we performed a study to identify the knowledge shared during workshops dedicated to the collaborative design of a SG for computer education.

2.3 Research Questions

Based on this framework, we define collaboration as a sharing of knowledge (*praxis* and *logos*) about SG design among stakeholders involved in it. This sharing may occur at different levels (syntactic, semantic and pragmatic). We want to understand which knowledge is concerned and how it is shared. In addition, we want to analyse the sharing of explicit knowledge (declarative knowledge) during workshops dedicated to game design. Thus, we address the following questions:

(RQ1) *What are the praxeologies of these stakeholders during the process of SG collaborative design? Do they manage to reach a common praxeology?*

(RQ2) *How do they share knowledge? Which boundaries are concerned by knowledge sharing?*

3 Research Method

3.1 Epistemological Framework

Our research is grounded on the pragmatic constructivist epistemological framework [21]. It means that reality can be apprehended through human experience [21]. Our research is conducted according to a DBR method [1, 20]. It includes researchers, teachers and a game designer which are working together to design a SG in an iterative way. They mobilise it in the field to study theoretical frameworks.

3.2 Context

We study the knowledge sharing that takes place during workshops dedicated to the collaborative design of a SG for a DBR project. The Ethics Committee from University of Geneva validated the study. The SG named TSADK is designed for a class of algorithms and computer languages for Bachelor's degree students. It takes place in a castle, inside a medieval fantasy world. The player is trapped in the game and he/she has to fix its broken code. To do this, he/she must go through 10 rooms and save residents of the castle by solving algorithmic problems. TSADK is developed with *ActivePresenter* and played on *Moodle*, a Learning Management System.

The collaborative design of TSADK took place during 26 workshops. To conduct this design, we use the mockup of a platform under development. It consists of a set of tools dedicated to foster collaborative work through knowledge sharing. Workshops are structured in 3 steps. (1) A preparatory step aims to settle the workshop and at designing a tool for the knowledge sharing on a specific design task (*e.g.* specifying the learning outcomes). The tool is then integrated into the platform. (2) The workshop itself during which participants are encouraged to collaborate for reaching a specific objective (*e.g.* reaching a consensus about the learning outcomes). (3) A closing step recalls the objectives of the workshop, decision taking and agreeing on the next workshop objectives. Each workshop is expected to foster collaboration thanks to the tools used and the tasks performed by the participants. In this paper, we do not describe these tools.

The design team includes 10 participants that come from IMT Nord Europe, the universities of Grenoble (France) and Geneva (Switzerland). It is composed of a game designer (G); researchers and doctoral students (R1, R2, R3, D1, D2); a head of computer science courses (H); a project manager (P); and teachers (T1, T2) who want to implement a SG in their course. Thus, the studied context includes the expertise needed to co-design SG in DBR (see Table 1). 5 members have never been involved in the design of SG previously. We indicate them by an asterisk in the table below.

Table 1. Participant's expertise (a-educational; b-computer science; c-method; d-SG design).

Participants	P	R1*	R2	R3*	D1*	D2*	T1	T2	G	H*
Serious game design	x		x						x	
Research	d	c	a, d	b	a, d	a, d	b		d	b
Teaching in algorithms and computer languages				x	x		x	x		x

We organised online workshops due to the COVID-19 pandemic, the physical distance between participants and the ease to recorded them. Thus, tools allowing communication are needed. These tools did not present any difficulties, as most participants were already familiar with using them, and if not, some time was devoted to training them about how to use them. These workshops are organized in whole or reduced teams. Reduced team workshops include participants according to their expertise. In this article, we analyse knowledge sharing during the first 9 collaborative design workshops that took place at the beginning of the project. Table 2 describes these workshops.

Table 2. Description of the workshops (W-whole team; R-reduced team).

Workshop	1	2	3	5	6	7	9	10	11
Date (month/day)	04/07	04/15	04/21	05/05	05/19	05/26	06/18	06/23	06/30
Duration	1h30	2h30	1h30	1h40	2h30	0h45	1h35	2h15	2h15
Team	W	R	W	W	W	R	W	R	R
Number of stakeholders	10	6	8	8	9	4	9	6	5
Tool used	x	x	x	x	x			x	x

3.3 Data Collect Method and Data Analysis Method

During workshops, we performed participatory observation as a data collection method. It allows researchers to immerse themselves in the field by taking part in the group's activities and maintain the necessary distance to build bridges between the field and the theories at stake [22]. These workshops are recorded, then transcribed.

We conducted a thematic analysis on the transcribed exchanges. It allows us to identify the themes of the corpus according to the research objectives. In this one, 'Coding is an organic and open iterative process; it is not 'fixed' at the start of the process' [23].

For this paper, we focus this thematic analysis on themes related to the learning outcomes of the SG. Different team members identified them as crucial and, since they 'serve as a guide in pedagogical action [...] and provides references and criteria for evaluation' [24], their specification is considered as a starting point [3, 4, 15]. In addition, the specification of the learning outcomes give rise to many difficulties and discussions. We hypothesize that the learning outcomes of the game are boundaries objects that emerged during the collaborative design process.

To depict learning outcomes, we distinguish elements of *praxis* (task and technique) but not those of *logos* (technology and theory), as they are difficult to differentiate through discourse analysis [6]. We group elements of *logos* under the term justification. We also study how participants share their knowledge about learning outcomes through boundary object analysis. We mobilise questions to conduct the analysis: *what task do participants evoke?* (task), *how do participants perform this task?* (technique), *what argument do the participants provide for this task or this technique?* (justification), *what common language do participants use to share this knowledge?* (boundaries).

4 Results and Discussion

The results are based on the verbatims' analysis about 'learning outcomes', translated from French to English. Each verbatim in italics is numbered according to the actor who mentions it and the workshop's number (*e.g.* R2-W1: Researcher 2 in workshop1).

4.1 Participants' Praxeologies

To address research question 1, we identify task and technique (*praxis*) and justification (*logos*) that refer to knowledge, through praxeologies' analysis. The analysis allows us to identify themes. We summarise the results in Table 3.

During the workshops, the participants provide ideas about how to specify learning outcomes (theme i) about algorithms and computer development. A researcher (R2-W1) proposes to clearly formulate them: *'because they can be interpreted [...] it's the same objectives for grades 1 and 3, which means that you put different things in terms of difficulties behind'*. This justification refers to their accuracy, in order to avoid interpretation 'objectives must be as precise as possible' [24]. The researcher (R3)'s praxeologies join R2's. Indeed, R3 (W2) proposes to phrase them precisely. The teacher (T1) and the project manager (P)'s praxeologies are also close. Indeed, they both suggest to identify them through the content of the curriculum but by using different techniques: to locate the concepts to be learned in a Powerpoint presentation of the course (T1-W1) and to analyse the practical work (P-W1). Finally, two researchers emphasize on the same technique: their description needs '*to be specific enough so that everyone can understand*' (R3-W2) such as the '*non-computer experts*' (R2-W5).

In addition, the project manager (P) communicates different techniques to work on the phrasing of learning outcomes (theme ii). He proposes to 'use the syntax from the educational sciences' '*We might have to rewrite them with a particular syntax to please the educational researchers […] but I think we're already in something fairly ready to use.*' (P-W3). He also suggests to 'rely on the syllabus' and to 'think about the proper verbs to use'(P-W5): '*[for this learning outcome], I wrote 'they'll be able to read and process' but that could be misinterpreted so it's better to keep only 'process'*'.

Some participants suggest focusing on the main learning outcomes (theme iii). A researcher (R2-W1) explains how to prioritise them (a specific technique). Indeed, he underlines the need to '*identify 'learning obstacles' since students face specific difficulties to overcome them*' (R2). A '*learning obstacle*' is an obstacle that can be surmountable and is a key to formulating the most essential learning outcomes [19]. An actor proposes 'to have a look at the main learning outcome of practical work' (T1-W2). A teacher (T2-W10) offers 'to select an achievable learning outcome': '*The rigour of the writing, technically, it's not easy to achieve*'.

To summarise, participants express tasks and techniques (*praxis*) about learning outcomes. Some do not see the need to address this issue and consider this task unuseful (*e.g.* 'to please the educational researchers'). This task seems not usual for their SG design practice. However, others share the same *praxis* (*e.g.* T1 and P propose to identify learning outcomes through the content of the curriculum). Through the discourse analysis, we were able to identify only R2's *logos*. This researcher is maybe the only one who is used to justify his *praxis* in such workshops. This does not mean that the other participants do not have *logos* about them but it remains hidden during the workshops. Indeed, teachers hold the content of the teaching sequence in which SG takes place, *e.g.* by relying on the constraints of the institution or teaching situation [25].

4.2 Boundaries Concerned by Knowledge Sharing

To address research question 2, we identify the levels of the boundaries mobilised by the participants through knowledge identification (*logos*). We presume that the learning outcomes of the game are a boundary object.

The following extract refers to the content of learning outcomes, in W1.

— '*So, do we have learning outcomes? Well, I think T1 provided them. I think we will have to define things a bit more precisely*' (P)

— '*They are not sufficiently specific for the design of the game. Indeed, they may be interpreted differently depending on people. We need to define them precisely*' (R2)

— '*It is necessary to specify them, since the beginning, we have been talking mainly about algorithms. It would be necessary to clarify the scope of the field to be covered. Is there any room for stuff that isn't purely algorithmic?*' (R3)

— '*[…] So we should go back to each [learning outcome] and make it clearer?*' (P)

— '*I think they're clear but not ready for use. If we want to create a specific [game] to achieve them, we have to tell ourselves, 'I want [students] to be able to do this'*' (R2)

R2 translates his knowledge so that the co-design process can move forward. By this, R3 seizes his knowledge and deepens it. Then, P proposes to clarify learning outcomes and R2 pursues his translation to help. R2 and R3 deepen the concept in the same way.

The following extract is about the concept of 'obstacle', in W1.

— *'If we want to redefine operational objectives, I need to go back to the slides [of the syllabus], and there are 180 slides'* (T1)

— *'I think, maybe not the 180 slides [...] but we may define priorities. What we have done [in previous projects] is to consider that some stuff is really complicated for the students. We call them obstacles and so, we focus on that'* (R2)

— *'Recursivity is a notion that always poses a problem for us'* (T1)

Again, researcher R2 translates his knowledge to make it understandable. Teacher T1 provides an example of difficulties encountered by the target audience and shows that he understands this concept. As a result, a collaborative work on the specification of learning outcomes becomes possible.

To summarise, collaborative work occurs when different participants (R2-R3; R2-T1) share knowledge of the semantic boundary. At this level, knowledge sharing enables for the emergence of a common meaning [10]. However, we are not able to identify shared knowledge about learning outcomes for some participants, such as P.

Table 3. Summary table of the praxeological analysis on 'learning outcomes' (W-workshop; *a, *b and *c-shared praxeologies).

Participant workshop	*Praxis* (task and technique)	*Logos* (justification)
(i) To specify learning outcomes		
R2 – W1	To specify learning outcomes (task)*a by providing a clear phrasing (technique)	No interpretation
T1 – W1	To identify learning outcomes (task)*b by locating the concepts to be learned in the slides (technique)	
P – W1	To identify learning outcomes (task)*b by studying the content of practical work (technique)	
R3 – W2	To define the learning outcomes more precisely (task)*a by checking that the team has understood them (technique)*c	
R2 – W5	To rely on clear learning outcomes (task)*a by checking that non-computer experts understood (technique)*c	

(*continued*)

Table 3. (*continued*)

Participant workshop	*Praxis* (task and technique)	*Logos* (justification)
(ii) To phrase of learning outcomes		
P – W3	To rephrase the learning outcomes (task) by using syntax from the educational sciences (technique)	
P – W5	To rephrase the learning outcome (task) by relying on the syllabus (technique)	
P – W5	To consider the elements in order (task) by thinking about the proper verb to use (technique)	
(iii) To focus on the main learning outcome		
R2 – W1	To prioritise learning outcomes (task) by identifying students' difficulties (technique)	Learning obstacles
T1 – W2	To have a look at the main learning outcome of practical work (task)	
R1 – W3	To focus on a precise learning outcome (task)	
T2 – W10	To select an achievable learning outcome (task)	

5   Conclusion and Future Work

This article deals with knowledge sharing about learning outcomes during a SG's collaborative design done in DBR, through an analysis frame combining praxeological [9] and boundary object analysis [10].

Thanks to this approach, we were able to identify two levels of knowledge sharing (*praxis* and *logos*). For *praxis*, we identified tasks and techniques of participants, some of them are shared. For *logos*, we only identified researcher R2's knowledge. The sharing of knowledge occurs at only one level (semantic boundary). Through this boundary, a translation process took place. This process allowed other participants to mobilise this knowledge. Thus, we consider that praxeology analysis is useful to identify the know-how and the knowledge that are expressed. In addition, boundary object analysis allows us to identify the level involved in the sharing of knowledge between stakeholders. However, we did not manage to identify the knowledge possessed by all participants to the workshops. Since knowledge sharing is at the core of collaboration, it might be an issue if knowledge is not explicit for all participants.

To remove the barriers of collaboration, it is necessary, from the start of the process, to propose design activities that integrate tools 'to bring out the boundary objects that [...] encourage collaboration at these stages' [6]. These tools must allow the knowledge sharing between experts involved concerning their way of conducting collaborative design. We foresee designing a tool based on questions asked to participants. This tool will consider the two dimensions of praxeologies (*logos* and *praxis*) [9] and the three levels of discourse (transfer, translation, transformation) [10]. We expect that, based on this tool, stakeholders involved in game design will be able to share the knowledge needed to perform the design. We also expect to foster their awareness about difficulties for knowledge sharing. By making misunderstandings more visible we expect to help participants to overcome their difficulties and then, to foster collaboration in the process. Furthermore, we consider that such a tool may be used throughout the process, during and outside the workshops and supports researchers and practitioners' collaboration for design-based research projects.

Acknowledgment. This research is part of the co.LAB project, funded by the Swiss National Science Foundation (NRP 77). We thank the participants of TSADK.

References

1. Wang, F., Hannafin, M.J.: Design-based research and technology-enhanced learning environments. Educ. Tech. Res. Dev. **53**(4), 5–23 (2005)
2. Arnab, S., et al.: Mapping learning and game mechanics for serious games analysis. Br. J. Edu. Technol. **46**(2), 391–411 (2015). https://doi.org/10.1111/bjet.12113
3. Marfisi-Schottman, I., George, S., Tarpin-Bernard, F.: Tools and methods for efficiently designing serious games. In: 4th Europeen Conference on Games Based Learning, Copenhagen, Denmark, pp. 226–234 (2010)
4. Marne, B., Wisdom, J., Huynh-Kim-Bang, B., Labat, J.-M.: The six facets of serious game design: a methodology enhanced by our design pattern library. In: Ravenscroft, A., Lindstaedt, S., Kloos, C.D., Hernández-Leo, D. (eds.) EC-TEL 2012. LNCS, vol. 7563, pp. 208–221. Springer, Heidelberg (2012). https://doi.org/10.1007/978-3-642-33263-0_17
5. Tahir, R., Wang, A.I.: Transforming a theoretical framework to design cards: LEAGUE ideation toolkit for game-based learning design. Sustainability **12**(20), 8487 (2020). https://doi.org/10.3390/su12208487
6. Morard, S., Sanchez, E.: Conception collaborative d'un jeu d'évasion pédagogique dans le cadre d'une game jam: du design du jeu au design du jouer. Sci. du jeu (2021). https://doi.org/10.4000/sdj.3517
7. Project Management Institute: A guide to the project management body of knowledge (PMBOK guide). 5th edn. Newtown Square, Pennsylvania (2013)
8. Van Dooren, M., Visch, V., Spijkerman, R., Goossens, R., Hendriks, V.: Personalization in game design for healthcare: a literature review on its definitions and effects. Int. J. Serious Games **3**(4), 3–28 (2016). https://doi.org/10.17083/ijsg.v3i4.134
9. Chevallard, Y.: Les savoirs enseignés et leurs formes scolaires de transmission: un point de vue didactique. Skholê **7**, 45–64 (1997)
10. Carlile, P.R.: Transferring, translating, and transforming: an integrative framework for managing knowledge across boundaries. Organ. Sci. **15**(5), 555–568 (2004). https://doi.org/10.1287/orsc.1040.0094
11. Sanchez, E., Monod-Ansaldi, R., Vincent, C., Safadi-Katouzian, S.: A praxeological perspective for the design and implementation of a digital role-play game. Educ. Inf. Technol. **22**(6), 2805–2824 (2017). https://doi.org/10.1007/s10639-017-9624-z
12. Star, S.L., Griesemer, J.R.: Institutional ecology, 'translations' and boundary objects: amateurs and professionals in berkeley's museum of vertebrate zoology, 1907–39. Soc. Stud. Sci. **19**(3), 387–420 (1989). https://doi.org/10.1177/030631289019003001
13. Star, S.L.: This is not a boundary object: reflections on the origin of a concept. Sci. Technol. Human Values **35**(5), 601–617 (2010). https://doi.org/10.1177/0162243910377624

14. Trompette, P., Vinck, D.: Retour sur la notion d'objet-frontière. Rev. d'anthropol. Connaissances 3(1), 5–27 (2009). https://doi.org/10.3917/rac.006.000
15. Aleven, V., Myers, E., Easterday, M., Ogan, A.: Toward a framework for the analysis and design of educational games. In: The 3rd IEEE International Conference on Digital Game and Intelligent Toy Enhanced Learning, Kaohsiung, Taiwan, pp. 69–76 (2010). https://doi.org/10.1109/DIGITEL.2010.55
16. Cano, S., Munoz Arteaga, J., Collazos, C.A., Gonzalez, C.S., Zapata, S.: Toward a methodology for serious games design for children with auditory impairments. IEEE Lat. Am. Trans. 14(5), 2511–2521 (2016). https://doi.org/10.1109/TLA.2016.7530453
17. Verschueren, S., Buffel, C., Vander Stichele, G.: Developing theory-driven, evidence-based serious games for health: framework based on research community insights. JMIR Serious Games 7(2), e11565 (2019). https://doi.org/10.2196/11565
18. Vermeulen, M., Guigon, G., Mandran, N., Labat, J.-M.: Teachers at the heart of the learning games design: the DISC model. In: 17th International Conference on Advanced Learning Technologies, Timisoara, Romania, pp. 145–149 (2017). https://doi.org/10.1109/ICALT.2017.41
19. Astolfi, J.-P.: L'École pour apprendre: L'élève face aux savoirs. ESF éditeur, Issy-les-Moulineaux (2010)
20. Sanchez, E., Monod-Ansaldi, R.: Recherche collaborative orientée par la conception: un paradigme méthodologique pour prendre en compte la complexité des situations d'enseignement-apprentissage. Éduc. Didactique 9(2), 73–94 (2015). https://doi.org/10.4000/educationdidactique.2288
21. Avenier, M.-J., Thomas, C.: Finding one's way around various methodological guidelines for doing rigorous case studies: a comparison of four epistemological frameworks. Syst. d'Inform. Manag. 20, 61–98 (2015). https://doi.org/10.3917/sim.151.0061
22. Lapassade, G.: Observation participante. In: Vocabulaire de Psychosociologie, pp. 375–390. Erès, Toulouse (2002)
23. Braun, V., Clarke, V., Hayfield, N., Terry, G.: Thematic analysis. In: Liamputtong, P. (ed.) Handbook of Research Methods in Health Social Sciences, pp. 843–860. Springer, Singapore (2019). https://doi.org/10.1007/978-981-10-5251-4_103
24. De Ketele, J.-M., Chastrette, M., Cros, D., Mettelin, P., Thomas, J.: La technique des objectifs pédagogiques. In: Guide du formateur, pp. 95–111. De Boeck Supérieur (2007)
25. Blanchard-Laville, C.: Du rapport au savoir des enseignants. J. Psychanalyse l'enfant 3(1), 123–154 (2013). https://doi.org/10.3917/jpe.005.0123

A Serious Game for Using Socio-Economic and Trust Based Decision-Making Scenarios for Elicitation of Emotional Responses

Fahad Ahmed[1,2](✉) , Jesus Requena Carrion[1] , Francesco Bellotti[2] ,
Luca Lazzaroni[2] , Giacinto Barresi[3] , and Riccardo Berta[2]

[1] Queen Mary University of London, Mile End Rd, Bethnal Green,
London E1 4NS, UK
{fahad.ahmed,j.requena}@qmul.ac.uk

[2] University of Genoa, Via All'Opera Pia, 15, 16145 Genoa, Italy
{fahad.ahmed,luca.lazzaroni}@edu.unige.it,
{francesco.bellotti,riccardo.berta}@unige.it

[3] Rehab Technologies Lab, Istituto Italiano di Tecnologia, Via Morego, 30,
16163 Genoa, Italy
giacinto.barresi@iit.it

Abstract. The relationship between Decision-Making and emotions has been investigated in literature both through theoretical and empirical research. Particularly, some paradigms have been defined, rooted in the Game Theory, that use socio-economic and/or trust based contexts to produce specific emotional responses in people. However, experiments with such game paradigms have most frequently been carried out in controlled settings only. As these methods have a potential usefulness in a variety of areas, we are interested in verifying their applicability "in the wild". To this end, we have developed a mobile game that integrates in a single plot four of the above mentioned socio-economic and trust-based game paradigms and aims at eliciting specific types and valences of emotions in different interactions. The paper discusses the outcomes of an experiment we carried out with eight participants in order to preliminarily test the usability of our game in authentic contexts of use. The results confirm that the designed game interactions are able to elicit emotional responses in the participants, also in ecological settings, that were expected based on the literature.

Keywords: Affective computing · Serious games · Emotion elicitation · Game theory

1 Introduction

Emotions usually play an important role in the decisions we make. This impacts our daily activities, ranging from how we behave, what we wear, what we eat

Supported by Queen Mary University of London & University of Genoa.

to which investments we should make [17]. Classifying and detecting emotions can thus be useful for inferring one's inclinations during decision-making situations, with major implications in several areas such as e-commerce, financial trading, etc. [17]. Moreover, automatic emotion detection is being used in several avenues for improving wellness and/or mitigating the damaging effects of mental illnesses. Examples include teaching social interaction to children on the Autistic Spectrum using robotics [13]; detecting depression [22], etc. With the latest technological advancements (in terms of e.g., miniaturization, computation power, memory size) automatic emotion detection has reached unprecedented accuracy and portability [16].

Development of such novel applications has been enabled by the discovery of the presence of certain patterns in emotional responses, most notably, in individuals with social anxiety [9], depression [22], and borderline personality disorder [21]. Several games exist that exploit well known Game Theory paradigms (e.g., social-economic tasks and dilemmas) and have shown to produce specific emotional responses not only in individuals with mental illnesses [10], but also in mentally healthy people (e.g., under socio-economic and trust based scenarios), as shown in Table 1.

Table 1. Decision-making & emotional response patterns in socio-economic and trust based scenarios

Interaction type	Type of pattern	Pattern observed
Ultimatum game*	Decision-making	Favours accepting any offer as responder and makes fair but lower offer to maximize profit
	Emotion elicitation	Induces sadness when unfair offer is presented and happiness when fair offer is presented
Trust game*	Decision-making	Favours investing smaller amounts in the beginning and defect more often as trustee
	Emotion elicitation	Induces sadness and anger when trustee does not return profit shares and happiness for the contrary
Dictator game*	Decision-making	Favours making lower allocations to recipients
	Emotion elicitation	Induces happiness in being able to provide any amount of resource to the responder
Prisoner's dilemma game**	Decision-making	Favours cooperative over selfish behaviour
	Emotion elicitation	Induces anger, sadness and sometimes disgust when betrayed and happiness for the contrary

* [23,24]
** [18]

Currently, such gamified activities are administered in person under controlled environments, which limits applicability of these methods outside clinical contexts. The wide popularity of Role Playing Games on mobile platforms [1,4] have enabled the usage of Decision-Making games in several different real-world contexts. Therefore, we argue that such games Decision-Making could be an effective means for supporting/investigating several activities 'in the wild', e.g., by inferring one's mental state, level of satisfaction, socio-economic inclinations, etc. More specifically, we hypothesize that the socio-economic interactions with Non-Playing Characters (NPCs) in our game can be used to elicit the types and valences of emotional responses that have been observed in experiments that used similar interactions in aforementioned studies. Accordingly, this paper presents the design of a mobile game exploiting Game Theory models aimed at eliciting various types of emotions 'in the wild'. Results from a preliminary experiment confirm the hypotheses stemmed from the controlled studies and hint at the possibility of a much more extensive testing and deployment.

2   The Game Design

2.1   Game Storyline, Dynamics and Mechanics

A player will live a day the life of "Joe", a boy in a small island named Laniakea. Every day, Joe has to complete a certain set of tasks by interacting with the locals. Joe has three resources (money, food, and health) in a limited amount. His goal is to keep his Overlord satisfied. The developed level of the game explores Joe's visit to a new part of the island, a small town called Caldwell, where he meets with a number of people (NPCs) and makes socio-economic and trust-based decisions during the NPC interactions.

Joe is required to follow the mechanics of the game to successfully complete the level [2,3]. Certain mechanics ensure that the player carries out various types of Decision-Making processes. For instance, the first interaction is about borrowing money from someone rude, immediately followed by an interaction where the player is awarded for placing his trust on a stranger. This design is expected to instill a sense of positive uncertainty in the player, which will keep the player guessing what might happen in the next interaction and entice the player to try to reduce the uncertainties that may come up later in the game, as a result increasing player engagement [7]. A key aspect of this game is the thorough engagement with NPCs during the interactions. Thus, while the

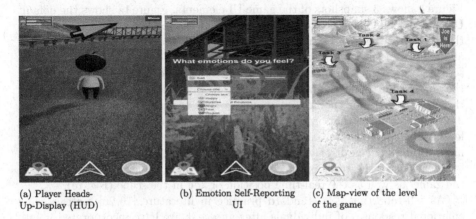

(a) Player Heads-   (b) Emotion Self-Reporting   (c) Map-view of the level
Up-Display (HUD)   UI   of the game

Fig. 1. Game UI, emotion self-reporting & navigation elements

navigation among the interaction sites in the game is seen in third-person in the user interface, during all interactions the camera switches to a first-person view, so that the player interacts from the perspective of Joe, increasing the immersivity in these key moments.

Some of the other important mechanics that are in the game are given below:

1. Each NPC makes the player know where to go next right after the interaction.
2. An interaction has either a positive or a negative impact on one of the resources, as part of the economic aspect of the socio-economic interactions
3. In order to successfully complete the level, a player needs to have a sufficient level of at least two of the three resources.
4. While moving between one site of interaction to the next, the player needs to stay within the road bump barriers that surround the road in the level, as collisions with the bump barrier will reduce player's health, thus demanding the player to stay focused in the gameplay even in these "interlocutory" phases. This makes the game engaging by introducing an element of risk of failure and keeping the player in the 'flow' [15].
5. The player has a navigation aid arrow that always points towards the next NPC to interact with, along with a handy map feature that shows the locations of the NPCs in the scene together with the player's current location Fig. 1a.
6. The socio-economic interactions do not lead to a failure of game progression as that would elicit some unpredictable emotional responses (while we are interested in the specific, expected emotional responses) [10].
7. The mechanic of having a sufficient level of at least two resources for a successful completion of a level is essential as it ensures that there would be no direct relationship between socio-economic interactions and a failure in the game progression.

2.2   UI Elements

Figure 1 shows 3 snapshots of the game UI elements. Figure 1a shows the default UI, in which the player status panel is placed at the top left corner of the screen, the freely pivoting white arrow indicating the NPC location is at the top center, at the bottom left is the navigation map button, while the multi-directional on-screen joystick to control the playing character is placed on the bottom left with the 'Jump!' button at the bottom center. The player status panel itself contains three status bars for the limited resources that the player has, namely health, money and food, in that order from the top. The horizontal length indicates the level of the respective resource. At anytime during the gameplay, clicking on the navigation map icon displays a top angled view of the entire scene, with markers for locations of the tasks ordered according to their sequence of occurrence in the game, as well as the real-time position of Joe in the scene (Fig. 1c).

As self-reporting is a standard practice in literature [16,20] for capturing emotional responses of individuals after an event, we have incorporated it into the gameplay itself. After each socio-economic interaction, the player is displayed the UI shown in Fig. 1b to self-report his emotional state at that moment. The options for self-reporting emotional state includes the six emotions considered to be the basic building blocks of all of our emotions, which are *Happy, Surprise, Sad, Angry, Fear,* and *Disgust* [8]. This is so that we may be able to derive more complex emotions from the data collected in the future [14].

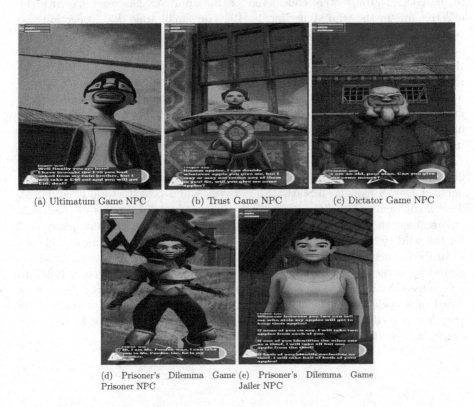

(a) Ultimatum Game NPC   (b) Trust Game NPC   (c) Dictator Game NPC

(d) Prisoner's Dilemma Game (e) Prisoner's Dilemma Game
Prisoner NPC   Jailer NPC

Fig. 2. NPC interactions

2.3   Decision-Making Interactions

There are several well known game paradigms in Game Theory to analyse social behaviour of individuals under economic constraints. Some of these also require a co-operation between the players [6]. Examples of games that utlise such paradigms include: Ultimatum Game, Trust Game, Chicken Game, Dictator Game, Prisoner's Dilemma, etc.

In our design, we have chosen four different types of player-NPC interactions, that are explained in Table 2, in the order in which they appear in the game. The table also explains the expected emotional response from our players when they experience the interactions in our implementation.

3   Data Collection Using the Game

3.1   The Experiment

A 'within-subjects' experimental design was followed for our experiment and so, no control groups were considered as this approach has been shown to be effective for 'in the wild' experiments [19]. Our small scale data collection was conducted to perform a preliminary study 'in the wild', with 10 individuals, out of whom 8 decided to fully participate in sharing their emotional response data that was captured by the game software. The participants were selected on the basis of them not having a diagnosis of any neurological conditions (such as autism), affective disorders (such as depression) and whether they had access to an Android device. A formal ethics review was conducted by Queen Mary Ethics of Research Committee (QMERC) and they deemed the study to be low risk in nature, subsequently providing their approval for the experiment.

The participants were from diverse age groups (2 teenagers, 2 people in their 20s and 4 people in their 30s) and academic backgrounds (2 high-school students, 1 Data Engineer, 3 Software Engineers and 2 post-doctoral candidates). The participants played the game on their own Android devices and physical environment the players were in was not controlled (hence, the aforementioned 'in the wild' setting for the experiment). The number of subjects was chosen in order to meet the requirements for a preliminary usability testing, assuggested by Turner, et al. (approximately 5 participants should be enough [25] to guarantee that 90% of the usability issues are covered). The participants were asked to provide their feedback on their engagement with entire the game after they had played it and the form provided to them was the Game Engagement Questionnaire (GEQ) introduced by Brockmyer, et al. [5].

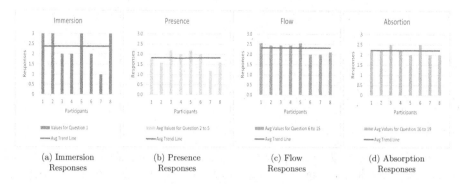

(a) Immersion Responses	(b) Presence Responses	(c) Flow Responses	(d) Absorption Responses

Fig. 3. GEQ responses according to the four areas of engagement assessed by the questionnaire.

Table 2. Game Theory Paradigms used for Socio-economic [23] and Trust-based [18] player-NPC interactions. The first three games are of socio-economic type, the last one trust-based

Game	Description	Our implementation
Ultimatum game	There are two players, a Proposer and a Responder. The proposer is given some money and asked to propose a split amount to the responder. The responder can accept or reject the offer. If the responder accepts, the two players get the agreed amount, if the responder rejects the offer, neither getsany money	In our game, the NPC is the 'proposer' and Joe is the 'responder'. The NPC makes an unfair offer. The polarity of the interaction is negative: meaning that the NPC dialogues are condescending and slightly rude but not offensive, as such interactions in Ultimatum game settings have been shown to produce more distinct negative emotional responses with higher valence [23]. Figure 2a shows part of the dialogue between Joe and the NPC
Trust game	There are two players, a Trustor and a Trustee. The trustor is given some resource, e.g. money and asked to propose a split with the trustee. The trustee can accept or reject the offer. Whatever amount is given to the trustee is doubled/tripled in the game. But the trustee has the freedom to choose whether or not to repay the trustor any amount	In our game, the NPC is the 'trustee' and Joe the 'trustor'. If Joe chooses to trust the NPC with his food, the NPC chooses to reward Joe and returns the Joe's share on the profit. The polarity of the interaction is positive, meaning that the NPC dialogues are uplifting and indicating gratefulness of the NPC. This is due to two reasons. First: to balance the negativity of the Ultimatum Game's NPC, as prolonged negativity may effect the decisions of the player [11]. Second: positive polarity interactions in Trust Game settings promote co-operation [24]. Figure 2b shows part of the dialogue between Joe and the NPC
Dictator game	There are two players, a Dictator and a Responder. The dictator is given some money and asked to donate a fraction (or the whole) amount to the recipient. The responder has to accept the donation. The dictator also has the option of not donating any amount and the recipient has no say in this game	In our game, Joe is the 'Dictator' and the NPC is the 'responder'. This interaction is designed as such that if Joe chooses to donate some of his money, the NPC expresses his gratitude for the generosity. Otherwise, the NPC will still be polite and the interaction has a positive polarity in either scenarios. This positive polarity is important as it will ensure that the prior trust game interaction having a positive polarity will not seem like a one-off phenomenon and will consolidate the notion that not all NPCs are rude. This will also influence the next interaction, which has a negative polarity, as any changes in the narrative elicit stronger emotional responses in the players [12]. Figure 2c part of the dialogue between Joe and the NPC
Prisoner's dilemma game	There are three players, a Jailer, Prisoner A and Prisoner B. Both the prisoners are interrogated by the jailer on a crime they are accused of. If both the prisoners accuse each other, they both get 1 year of prison. If neither accuses the other, they both get 5 years of prison. If one of them, for instance prisoner A, accuses B while B does not accuse A, then A will walk free and B get 10 years	In our game, the NPCs play the role of the 'jailer' and the 'prisoner B', while Joe is the 'prisoner A'. The interaction is designed as such that the player chooses to help the prisoner-NPC to complete the final task, and by being associated with this prisoner-NPC, Joe becomes an accomplice to the jailer-NPC. This interaction is specifically designed to orchestrate a betrayal from the prisoner-NPC, which is supposed to elicit a high valence of negative emotional response [6]. Figure 2d shows part of the dialogue between the prisoner NPC and Joe, while Fig. 2e shows part of the dialogue between the jailer and Joe NPC and Joe

3.2 Analysis of the Collected Data

The GEQ contained 19 questions that can be clustered to represent four different aspects of player engagement, which are: Immersion (question 1), Presence (questions 2 to 5), Flow (questions 6 to 15) and Absorption (questions 16 to 19) [5]. Each question had three possible answers, 'No', 'Maybe' and 'Yes', which were coded to 1, 2 and 3, respectively, in a Lickert scale. Figure 3 shows the responses for each of the aspects of engagement. The responses for the latter three aspects were averaged for each participant over the range of questions for each aspect. The orange horizontal line in the response charts shows the average response score for each aspect, which was 2.4 for Immersion, 1.8 for Presence, 2.3 for Flow and 2.2 for Absorption. Hence, the average trend indicates that the player reports tended to be closer to 'Yes' for Immersion, Flow and Absorption than for Presence, and this was anticipated. The questions for Presence, in fact, included questions like "My thoughts go fast?", "Things seem to happen automatically?", "I played longer than I meant to?", etc. The game required a conscious effort to interact and take decisions. Hence, it is likely that the players would feel a higher cognitive load while playing our game than in other games they played before, naturally leading to more frequent 'No' and 'Maybe' for questions relevant to the Presence aspect of engagement, and a lower average for that aspect. Overall, the GEQ responses indicate that players were sufficiently engaged for us to assume that their reported emotions were resulting solely from the game interactions. There were no significant differences between the responses of different age groups, meaning that the game was nearly equally engaging for different ages.

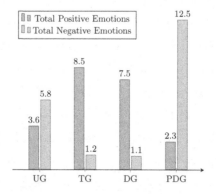

Fig. 4. Total negative emotions and total positive emotions for each type of interaction

Figure 4 shows that the interactions with negative polarity in speech and expression of the NPC as well as having negative fairness (Ultimatum Game, UG and Prisoner's Dilemma Game, PDG) actually elicited higher total negative emotions (Sad, Angry, Fear & Disgust), while the interactions with positive polarity in speech and expression of the NPC as well as having positive fairness (Trust Game, TG and Dictator Game, DG) elicited higher total positive emotions (Happy, Surprise). This is in line with literature, as discussed in Subsect. 2.3 and observed in Table 2 for each type of NPC interaction we implemented in the game. Also the very high total negative emotional response from the betrayal in the Prisoner's Dilemma confirms what is known in controlled environments.

4 Conclusion

In this paper, we have presented a game design that implements socio-economic and trust based interactions and we have demonstrated that the mobile game, with its characters and interactions, is capable of eliciting specific emotions with high valence from its players in a predictable manner. Importantly, these results confirm, 'in the wild', what is known in literature from controlled experiments. Hence, such games can be applied in areas that were discussed in Sect. 1 of this paper, while also opening the doors of possibility of utilising our game to detect abnormal emotional responses (such as the ones that do not coincide with our findings) and using those to infer if a player might have affective disorders.

The scope of this game is limited by the number and type of player-NPC interaction narratives. However, such preliminary results encourage new research to identify more scenarios to elicit predictable emotional responses, so to increase the diversity of the interactions in the game and enhance its variety and appeal.

References

1. 23+ mobile gaming statistics for 2022-insights into a $175b games market. https://techjury.net/blog/mobile-gaming-statistics/
2. Almeida, M.S.O., da Silva, F.S.C.: A systematic review of game design methods and tools. In: Anacleto, J.C., Clua, E.W.G., da Silva, F.S.C., Fels, S., Yang, H.S. (eds.) ICEC 2013. LNCS, vol. 8215, pp. 17–29. Springer, Heidelberg (2013). https://doi.org/10.1007/978-3-642-41106-9_3
3. Arnab, S., et al.: Mapping learning and game mechanics for serious games analysis. Br. J. Educ. Technol. 46, 391–411 (2015). https://doi.org/10.1111/BJET.12113
4. Baker, I.S., Turner, I.J., Kotera, Y.: Role-play games (RPGS) for mental health (why not?): roll for initiative. Int. J. Ment. Health Addict. 2022, 1–9 (2022). https://doi.org/10.1007/S11469-022-00832-Y
5. Brockmyer, J.H., Fox, C.M., Curtiss, K.A., McBroom, E., Burkhart, K.M., Pidruzny, J.N.: The development of the game engagement questionnaire: a measure of engagement in video game-playing. J. Exp. Soc. Psychol. 45, 624–634 (2009). https://doi.org/10.1016/J.JESP.2009.02.016
6. Butler, D.J., Burbank, V.K., Chisholm, J.S.: The frames behind the games: player's perceptions of prisoners dilemma, chicken, dictator, and ultimatum games. J. Socio-Econ. 40, 103–114 (2011). https://doi.org/10.1016/J.SOCEC.2010.12.009
7. Deterding, S., Andersen, M.M., Kiverstein, J., Miller, M.: Mastering uncertainty: a predictive processing account of enjoying uncertain success in video game play. Front. Psychol. 13 (2022). https://doi.org/10.3389/fpsyg.2022.924953

8. Ekman, P.: An argument for basic emotions. Cogn. Emot. **6**, 169–200 (1992). https://doi.org/10.1080/02699939208411068

9. Gambetti, E., Giusberti, F.: The effect of anger and anxiety traits on investment decisions. J. Econ. Psychol. **33**(6), 1059–1069 (2012)

10. Harlé, K.M., Allen, J.J., Sanfey, A.G.: The impact of depression on social economic decision making. J. Abnorm. Psychol. **119**, 440 (2010). https://doi.org/10.1037/a0018612

11. Jacko, J.A.: Human-computer interaction. Part III, HCI intelligent multimodal interaction environments. In: Proceedings of the 12th International Conference, HCI International 2007, Beijing, China, 22–27 July 2007 (2007)

12. Jerrett, A., Howell, P., Dansey, N.: Developing an empathy spectrum for games. Games Cult. **16**, 635–659 (2021). https://doi.org/10.1177/1555412020954019

13. Leo, M.: Automatic emotion recognition in robot-children interaction for ASD treatment. In: Proceedings of the IEEE International Conference on Computer Vision (2015)

14. Levenson, R.W.: Basic emotion questions. Emot. Rev. **3**(4), 379–386 (2011). https://doi.org/10.1177/1754073911410743

15. Perttula, A., Kiili, K., Lindstedt, A., Tuomi, P.: Flow experience in game based learning - a systematic literature review. Int. J. Serious Games **4** (2017). https://doi.org/10.17083/IJSG.V4I1.151

16. Picard, R.W.: Toward computers that recognize and respond to user emotion. IBM Syst. J. **39**, 705–719 (2000). https://doi.org/10.1147/sj.393.0705

17. Rilling, J.K., Sanfey, A.G.: The neuroscience of social decision-making. Ann. Rev. Psychol. **62**(1), 23–48 (2011). https://doi.org/10.1146/annurev.psych.121208.131647

18. Sally, D., Hill, E.: The development of interpersonal strategy: autism, theory-of-mind, cooperation and fairness. J. Econ. Psychol. **27**, 73–97 (2006). https://doi.org/10.1016/j.joep.2005.06.015

19. Schmiedek, F., Neubauer, A.B.: Experiments in the wild: introducing the within-person encouragement design. Multivariate Behav. Res. **55**, 256–276 (2020). https://doi.org/10.1080/00273171.2019.1627660

20. Spink, A., et al.: Psychophysiology of digital game playing: the relationship of self-reported emotions with phasic physiological responses. In: 6th International Conference on Methods and Techniques in Behavioral Research (2008)

21. Staebler, K., Gebhard, R., Barnett, W., Renneberg, B.: Emotional responses in borderline personality disorder and depression: assessment during an acute crisis and 8 months later. J. Behav. Ther. Exp. Psychiatry **40**, 85–97 (2009). https://doi.org/10.1016/J.JBTEP.2008.04.003

22. Suslow, T., Junghanns, K., Arolt, V.: Detection of facial expressions of emotions in depression. Percept. Mot. Skills **92**(3 Pt 1), 857–868 (2001)

23. Tamarit, I., Sánchez, A.: Emotions and strategic behaviour: the case of the ultimatum game. PLOS One **11**, e0158733 (2016). https://doi.org/10.1371/JOURNAL.PONE.0158733

24. Tortosa, M.I., Strizhko, T., Capizzi, M., Ruz, M.: Interpersonal effects of emotion in a multi-round trust game. Psicol.: Int. J. Methodol. Exp. Psychol. **34**, 179–198 (2013)

25. Turner, W.C., Lewis, J.R., Nielson, J.: Determining usability test sample size. In: International Encyclopedia of Ergonomics and Human Factors - 3 Volume Set, pp. 3132–3136 (2006). https://doi.org/10.1201/9780849375477-616

FLIGBY: The Serious Game Harnessing Flow Experience for Leadership Development

Kristina Risley[1]([✉])[iD] and Zoltan Buzady[2][iD]

[1] University of Westminster, London, UK
k.risley@westminster.ac.uk
[2] Corvinus University of Budapest, Budapest, Hungary

Abstract. This paper discusses a unique serious game which harnesses a psychological state of Flow both as a pedagogical tool and a development target. The FLIGBY game was developed with the intention of teaching learners to understand the concept of Flow and apply this within their leadership practice. In FLIGBY, the player assumes the role of General Manager of a winery in California and must make 150+ complex decisions while managing the winery team and strategic direction to ensure the business's success. This allows for the assessment of players' skill level in 29 'soft skills' and provides the rare ability to quantify changes in players' leadership abilities. Use of the game to develop soft skills is discussed, including an extensive range of feedback provided during the game. Suggestions for future research include further interrogation of the dataset collected as learners progress through the game, along with additional measurement to assess how learners achieve a state of Flow while playing the game. Investigation of the roles of storification and socially constructed realities is also recommended.

Keywords: Serious game · Soft skills · FLIGBY · Leadership development

1 Introduction

Digital simulation and augmented or virtual reality technologies have been increasingly studied over the past twenty years and are predicted to be one of the biggest disrupters in business during the upcoming decade [1]. Of particular interest are the numerous potential applications for serious games for behavioral learning, integrating the benefits of simulation into business education. Serious games can be defined as *"digital games, simulations, virtual environments and mixed reality/media that provide opportunities to engage in activities through responsive narrative/story, gameplay or encounters to inform, influence, for well-being, and/or experience to convey meaning..."* [2]. Amongst the new ground being broken in the enhanced use of digital technologies in business and exploitation of the benefits of serious games for training, it is imperative that leadership development is not left behind. There are a number of serious games used for training purposes in several areas including health, fitness, sustainability, engineering and design. Increasingly, attention is also turning to serious games as a mechanism for developing critical leadership skills such as strategic thinking, emotional intelligence and

K. Kiili et al. (Eds.): GALA 2022, LNCS 13647, pp. 53–62, 2022.
https://doi.org/10.1007/978-3-031-22124-8_6

prioritization, often described as 'soft skills'. The importance of effective leadership in business success has been extensively studied and mapped in academic literature, along with a wealth of potential development strategies for critical soft/deep skills in modern leadership [3–5]. However, 'soft skills', although hugely impactful in businesses, can be challenging to develop as knowledge-based training methods are widely accepted to be ineffective without experiential opportunities to practice and receive feedback [6, 7]. For this reason, among others, research is increasingly turning to digital learning to explore mechanisms of interpersonal leadership skills such as collaboration, communication, negotiation and critical thinking [8].

This paper discusses a case study of FLIGBY, which is a serious game for leadership development, where players undertake the role of a general manager of a winery and must make several challenging business and human resource decisions in order to ensure the company's success. Additionally, FLIGBY's unique gameplay and storyline aim to educate players in the benefits of a psychological state of Flow; thus utilizing Flow as both as a pedagogical tool and a development target.

2 Theoretical Background and Originality of Contribution

2.1 Education on the Fundamentals of the Psychology of Flow

An established research area within the gamification of learning design is the concept of a state of Flow, defined by Csikszentmihalyi [9] as a state in which individuals are completely immersed or absorbed in the activity or task, leading to temporal concerns being minimized or ignored. The state of Flow is often discussed as 'the zone' - the optimal state for learning and intense concentration [9–11] and is a common element of successful games of all kinds. Over recent decades, many works have discussed the positive impacts of Flow on learner motivation and therefore learning success [12–16].

Beyond serious games, the concept of Flow is more widely associated with positive-psychology, a branch of the discipline which focuses on individuals' and groups' strengths, growth and contributions as opposed to early branches of psychology which centered around mental illness. It is within this branch of psychology that leadership, organizational effectiveness and societal well-being sit and where the bases for effective leadership development were founded. Across several years and based on Csikszentmihalyi's work, similarities have been drawn between the concepts of Flow and employee engagement, including clear goals, frequent and effective feedback and balance between opportunity and capacity [15]. The marrying of these concepts with Flow as an enabler of employee engagement has come to be known as Flow leadership [16], which is the central pillar of the knowledge-based learning outcome of the FLIGBY game, as discussed in the following sections. Currently no other games are designed to teach Flow leadership and develop the soft skills required for leaders to stimulate Flow experiences within their teams. Indeed, FLIGBY's unique contribution is its application of Flow theory as a learning target, which is in addition to the game's potential ability to induce a state of Flow in players as with other immersive serious games.

2.2 Improving Critical Leadership Skills

Amongst the unique contributions of FLIGBY to leadership pedagogy are the measurement of leadership skills against 29 core leadership competencies, which has led to the establishment of a vast database of information concerning players' demographics and leadership skills profiles. This dataset also provides the relatively unique ability to demonstrate improvements in those skills between playthroughs at scale. A common issue in serious games, particularly those aimed at developing 'soft skills' is that concrete improvements as a result of gameplay can be difficult to demonstrate. This work provides insight indicating improvement in players' leadership skills between their first and second playthroughs, which are also considered more thoroughly is other relevant works discussing the FLIGBY game [18–21].

3 Presenting FLIGBY: The Flow-Promoting Leadership Development Serious Game

FLIGBY was designed and created in partnership by Mihaly Csikszentmihalyi, renowned as the father of positive psychology and Flow theory, with ALEAS Simulations, a serious gaming lab based in California and Central Europe. The leadership development focus throughout the game is in teaching learners to understand the concept of Flow and apply this within their leadership practice within a business-realistic setting.

FLIGBY is a video-based learning experience where the player assumes the role of General Manager of a winery in California and must make 150+ complex decisions while managing the winery team and strategic direction to ensure the business's success. Balance with other conflicting priorities is essential to success within the game and the winery's economic viability must be strengthened, while relationships with Turul's external stakeholders must also be factored into decision making. For instance, the player may be presented with a short video clip of two game actors in conflict and the player is tasked with choosing the most appropriate option. The outcome of this choice is then played out in via video response as situations progress and a video response follows at the end of the scene with the player's in-game advisor Mr. FLIGBY providing tailored feedback.

The ultimate aim of the game is to win the Spirit of the Wine Award, an in-game award based on satisfying all elements of FLIGBY's Triple Scorecard framework. The player's success in this endeavour depends on the weighted sum of their decisions' impacts on corporate atmosphere (60%), profitability (30%) and sustainability (10%). It is crucial for success in the game that players are able to weigh up the consequences of their actions on all three areas of the triple scorecard and base their decisions on the most prudent way to navigate the various conflicting priorities at hand. However, while the complex decisions made throughout the game and the nature of businesses mean there are interdependencies between these three factors, it is important to note that corporate atmosphere is given much more weight than other factors. This is because soft skills development is the primary functional goal of this game and also as to some extent profitability and sustainability are consequences rather than causes of business success.

The game's plot follows the newly appointed General Manager of Turul Winery in California, tasked with overseeing the recovery of the business following a downturn in organizational success and collegiate harmony brought about by the dysfunctional leadership style of the previous General Manager. A key task is to nurture an environment which encourages teamwork and promotes Flow, including bringing as many colleagues as possible into a state of Flow at some point during the game. This also sits within the context of the player being expected to manage the winery in accordance with the expectations of the Winery's owner, Bob Turul. There are many possible paths to completion of the game and the direction a player takes is dependent on the decisions they make as they go along.

Figure 1 shows FLIGBY's dashboard with its Flow Meter, which tracks the player's progress in inducing Flow states in their colleagues at the winery and creating/sustaining a Flow-based corporate culture. After making decisions, players will see the impact of their decisions on the moods of the Winery staff, mapped against the typical moods discussed in Flow research. In Fig. 1, it can been seen that the player's actions have moved Larry into a state of Flow, while other players remain relatively far away and the player will need to adjust their approach with these team members in order for them achieve Flow.

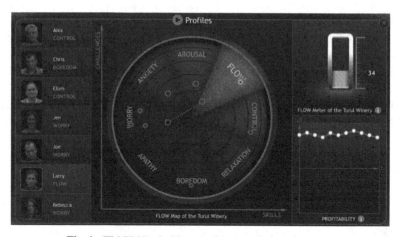

Fig. 1. FLIGBY's dashboard with the "Flow Meter" [17]

FLIGBY consists of 23 video scenes which take place during a season (6 months) at the Turul winery. Few players complete the game in one play-through, although this is possible; the average (mean) playing time of players who completed is 5.5 h (SD = 2.71). This is dependent on various other factors such as whether players choose to restart scenes and time spent exploring the game's multimedia library of additional Flow and leadership learning materials.

FLIGBY has been utilized as a teaching tool for several years by members of the Leadership & Flow Global Research Network and as such as been played by 9,994 unique players to date, ranging from university students and researchers to corporate training delegates. The vast FLIGBY dataset which sits behind the game contains data from 15,642 total playthroughs and includes demographic information as well as scoring against FLIGBY's 29 leadership behaviors. On average, players complete the game 1.23 times (SD = 0.64) – although the number of plays varies from 1 play through to 10. There is considerable variability in whether players win the 'Spirit of the Wine' award, with 50% of playthroughs that win and 50% that do not. On average, players opened 26.8% (SD = 27.89) of additional media library entries. This however varies substantially between 1% and 100% depending on the player and which playthrough they are undertaking. Of all players to date, 53% were male and 47% were female. The largest groups of players were ranging in ages from 36 to 49 years (39%) and 26 to 35 years (37%). Some 13% of players were aged 18–25, while 12% of players were aged 50+. Players over the years have represented 138 different countries with the five most common being the United States of America, followed by Hungary, France, Canada and then Turkey.

4 Advanced Pedagogical Applications of FLIGBY

4.1 Focus Area 1: Measurement of 29 Leadership Skills

FLIGBY's Master Analytics Profiler (MAP) system measures the player's performance on 29 key leadership skills during gameplay (Fig. 2). Within the 29 skills measured by the MAP system, 25 are skills widely associated with good business leadership based on several decades of research. A further 4 skills (balancing skill, feedback, applying personal strengths and strategic thinking) are emphasized as having additional importance in generating Flow. FLIGBY's leadership skillset was distilled by a group of experts based on and validated in line with a range of widely used existing frameworks [21].

The player, acting as General Manager of Turul Winery is tasked with making decisions based on anywhere from two to five choices, the most and least appropriate of these having been defined and agreed by two independent expert groups [17]. Most in-game decisions require more than one of the 29 leadership skills to be used simultaneously, which is factored into the MAP system's algorithm and standardized as a percentage then used for mapping the player's strengths. A comprehensive leadership skills profile report is automatically generated for each player upon completion of the game. This includes the relative strengths and weaknesses of each player's leadership profile and is sent individually to each player. Within the report, each skill and group of skills is benchmarked against the average in the player's cohort and can be compared to other benchmark groups as requested, taking into account e.g. industry, age or leadership level.

4.2 Focus Area 2: Diversity of Feedback Types

In addition to the leadership skills profile discussed previously, the player receives a plethora of continuous and immediate feedback on the impact of their decisions throughout the game. This takes several forms, the first being the resulting actions which the player sees played out in the rest of the scene. These consequences may include more, less, expanded or limited decision options to take forward. In recognition of each time the player moves a colleague into a Flow state, a Flow trophy is collected. Sustainability badges are also earned as the player makes decisions which promote/enhance the

Fig. 2. 29 key leadership skills measured in FLIGBY's Master Analytics Profiler (MAP) [17]

environmental sustainability of the Winery's operations. In addition to being tracked on the in-game dashboard, both of these mini-achievements also contribute to whether the player ultimately wins the coveted 'Spirit of the Wine' Award. Table 1 provides a summary of the various feedback mechanisms within FLIGBY.

Table 1. Summary of feedback mechanisms in FLIGBY

During the game (instant)	During the game (available through dashboard)	After the game (cumulative)
Sustainability badges	Corporate atmosphere score	'Spirit of the Wine' Award achievement
Mr. FLIGBY's instant feedback	Profitability index	Flashback/debriefing by Mr. FLIGBY
Flow trophies	Flow radar	Learner's individual skills profile report
Dialogue with virtual characters	Flow trophies	Predictive feedback by MAP
Plot surprises	Media library	Global benchmarking by MAP

The player also receives debrief support and tailored video feedback at the end of each of the 23 scenes by Mr. FLIGBY, the player's personal in-game leadership coach (Fig. 3). In addition, Mr. FLIGBY signposts to alternative courses of action which could have been taken and the possible effects of those, as well as directing the player to appropriate materials in the game's multimedia library to inform and/or reinforce the leadership approach taken.

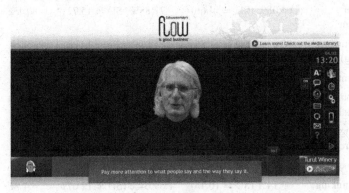

Fig. 3. Video debrief with Mr. FLIGBY

4.3 Focus Area 3: Skills Development

Within the substantial dataset gathered in the background as players complete the FLIGBY game sits the potential to explore the dynamics of digital leadership development. This continues to be explored to identify trends and development opportunities for the field. For example, use of FLIGBY has been found to allow players to identify and distinguish between transactional and transformational leadership styles displayed by actors in the game, as well as understanding the impact of each based on practice of applying them in managing a virtual company [18]. Furthermore, in a recent study Almeida and Buzady [19] supported that FLIGBY can be used successfully to develop skills in dimensions such as leadership, conflict management, diplomacy and emotional intelligence. Encouragingly, the researchers found that the number of years of professional experience students had before completing the game had a significant impact on their performance in the game, with more prior experience being linked to higher performance and less experience being linked to worse in-game performance. This study also provided validation for the FLIGBY game by presenting feedback from learners which reported the game to be an authentic representation of the challenges of a real business environment.

Initial analysis of the average level of competence in each of FLIGBY's 29 key leadership skills provides encouraging insight into the efficacy of FLIGBY as a developmental tool. This analysis found all skills except for two to have improved between playthrough 1 and playthrough 2. Those two skills which saw a decline were diplomacy (by 1.06%) and perhaps unsurprisingly regarding players' second playthrough, information gathering (by 1.82%). Table 2 below shows the skills which enjoyed the biggest improvement (more than 5%) between first and second playthroughs.

These initial findings provide encouraging support for FLIGBY's efficacy as a leadership development intervention and introduce useful nuances regarding which skills

Table 2. Skill Improvements from first to second playthrough

Skill	Playthrough 1	Playthrough 2	Improvement
Stakeholder management	64.08% (SD = 14.66)	72.88% (SD = 15.72)	8.81%
Entrepreneurship (risk-taking)	66.09% (SD = 11.86)	74.08% (SD = 14.00)	8.00%
Future orientation	67.69% (SD − 10.33)	75.29% (SD = 12.75)	7.60%
Time-pressured decision-making	58.32% (SD = 11.73)	65.90% (SD = 12.88)	7.58%
Recognizing personal strengths	68.11% (SD = 10.36)	75.54% (SD = 12.61)	7.43%
Empowerment	61.58% (SD = 14.27)	68.08% (SD = 15.42	6.49%
Strategic thinking	63.14% (SD = 10.43)	69.61% (SD = 12.67)	6.47%
Active listening	63.44% (SD = 11.49)	69.82% (SD = 13.74)	6.39%
Balancing skill	64.96% (SD = 10.88)	71.19% (SD = 21.52)	6.23%

may be most effectively developed through playing the game. Data presented here gives indicative insight into how the game has been played and experienced since its inception; more statistical data and in-depth analysis can also be found presented in other relevant publications [18–21].

5 Limitations and Directions of Future Research

This work introduces a demonstrative case study of FLIGBY as a unique pedagogical tool and in brief discusses encouraging results indicating concrete and measurable improvements in learners' soft skills between playthroughs. A limitation of this work is that it does not investigate these interactions in depth or seek to explain effects. Other relevant publications are available investigating these effects [18–21] and future research is also recommended to interrogate and explore the vast dataset containing the results of the 15,642 total FLIGBY playthroughs which have taken place to date. Within this investigation are opportunities to complete cross-cultural comparisons between players from around the world, as well as cross-industry comparison and comparisons based on other player attributes such as age, gender, current occupation and seniority level. More longitudinally, further research is recommended to assess whether understanding of Flow theory gained through playing FLIGBY leads to behavioral change in the workplace and how this could be linked to organizational success. It is anticipated that this learning could also be used to develop Flow-based games for other disciplines beyond leadership, such as sports coaching and mental health promotion.

A limitation of the FLIGBY game itself and surrounding protocol is that it does not currently include functionality to assess whether players experience a psychological state of Flow while playing, although players do typically report experiencing Flow during gameplay. A direction for future research is to assess players' Flow experiences at various points during the game using established Flow scales and semi-structured interviews. Future iterations of the FLIGBY game would also benefit from functionality to establish baseline measurements for learners in each of the 29 FLIGBY leadership skills, in order establish before and after measurements and therefore the success of developing skills during the game.

Beyond FLIGBY, the authors continue ongoing work to investigate and converge current and emerging academic thinking regarding serious games, Flow and soft skills development. This is with the aim of synthesizing an explanatory model outlining the bases of effective immersive serious games utilizing Flow for enhanced leadership development. Investigation into the role of 'storification', i.e. use of narrative to engage and immerse learners [22, 23] as a catalyst for group Flow and the development of socially constructed realities is also a key recommendation for future investigation.

6 Disclosure Statement, Funding and Acknowledgements

No potential conflict of interest is reported by the authors. All data was collected by third parties in an anonymous format – profiles cannot be traced back to participants' names. This project was supported by ALEAS Simulations Inc., California, USA, who provided the quoted figures and the global skills database that contained the anonymous game and skills results for research purposes, the latter which was solely conducted by the Leadership & Flow Global Research Network.

The Leadership & Flow Research Network is open for future academic collaborations in Flow, leadership development and serious gaming: https://flowleadership.org/.

References

1. Cipresso, P., Giglioli, I., Raya, M.A., Riva, G.: The past, present, and future of virtual and augmented reality research: a network and cluster analysis of the literature. Front. Psychol. **9**, 1–20 (2018)
2. Marsh, T.: Serious games continuum: between games for purpose and experiential environments for purpose. Entertain. Comput. **2**, 61–68 (2011)
3. Dean, S.A., East, J.I.: Soft skills needed for the 21st-century workforce. Int. J. Appl. Manag. Technol. **18**(1), 17–32 (2019)
4. de Freitas, S., Routledge, H.: Designing leadership and soft skills in educational games: the E-leadership and soft skills educational games design model (ELESS). Br. J. Edu. Technol. **44**(6), 951–968 (2013)
5. Viviers, H.A., Fouché, J.P., Reitsma, G.M.: Developing soft skills (also known as pervasive skills): usefulness of an educational game. Meditari Account. Res. **24**(3), 368–389 (2016)
6. Lovelace, K.J., Eggers, F., Dyck, L.R.: I do and i understand: assessing the utility of web-based management simulations to develop critical thinking skills. Acad. Manag. Learn. Educ. **15**(1), 100–121 (2016)
7. Salas, E., Wildman, J., Piccolo, R.: Using simulation-based training to enhance management education. Acad. Manag. Learn. Educ. **8**(4), 559–573 (2009)
8. Dondlinger, M.J.: Educational video games design: a review of the literature. J. Appl. Educ. Technol. **4**(1), 21–31 (2007)

9. Csikszentmihalyi, M.: Beyond Boredom and Anxiety. Jossey-Bass, San Francisco (1975)
10. Csikszentmihalyi, M.: Flow: the psychology of optimal experience. J. Leis. Res. **24**(1), 93–94 (1990)
11. Csikszentmihalyi, M.: The Applications of Flow in Human Development and Education: The Collected Works of Mihaly Csikszentmihalyi. Springer, Dordrecht (2014). https://doi.org/10.1007/978-94-017-9094-9
12. Keller, J.M.: An integrative theory of motivation, volition and performance. Technol. Instr. Cogn. Learn. **6**(2), 79–104 (2008)
13. Prensky, M.: Digital Game-Based Learning. McGraw-Hill, New York (2007)
14. Woo, J.C.: Digital game-based learning supports student motivation, cognitive success, and performance outcomes. Educ. Technol. Soc. **17**(3), 291–307 (2014)
15. Csikszentmihalyi, M.: Good Business: Leadership, Flow and the Making of Meaning. Penguin Group, New York (2003)
16. Buzady, Z.: Flow, leadership and serious games – a pedagogical perspective. World J. Sci. Technol. Sustain. Dev. **14**(2), 204–217 (2017)
17. Buzady, Z., Marer, P., Vecsey, Z.: Missing Link Discovered: Planting Csikszentmihalyi's Flow Theory into Management and Leadership Practice by Using FLIGBY, the Official Flow-Leadership Game, 2nd edn. ALEAS Simulations, Budapest (2019)
18. Almeida, F., Buzady, Z.: Recognizing leadership styles through the use of a serious game. J. Appl. Res. High. Educ. (2021). https://doi.org/10.1108/JARHE-05-2021-0178
19. Almeida, F., Buzady, Z.: Development of soft skills competencies through the use of FLIGBY. Technol. Pedagogy Educ. (2022). https://doi.org/10.1080/1475939X.2022.2058600
20. Wimmer, A., Buzady, Z., Csesznak, A., Szentesi, P.: Intuitive and analytical decision-making skills analysed through a flow developing serious game. J. Decis. Syst. **31**(3), 1–14 (2022)
21. Buzady, Z., Wimmer, A., Csesznak, A., Szentesi, P.: Exploring flow-promoting management and leadership skills via serious gaming. Interact. Learn. Environ., 1–15 (2022). [Preprint]. https://doi.org/10.1080/10494820.2022.2098775
22. Aura, I., Hassan, L., Hamari, J.: Teaching within a story: understanding storification of pedagogy. Int. J. Educ. Res. **106**, 101728 (2021)
23. Hassan, L., Deterding, S., Harviainen, J.T., Hamari, J.: Fighting post-truth with fiction: an inquiry into using storification and embodied narratives for evidence-based civic participation. Storyworlds **11**(1), 51–78 (2019)

10 Commandments of the Serious Game Padawan: Lessons Learned After 4 Years of Professional Training

Iza Marfisi-Schottman[1]([⊠]) [iD], Longeon Tomas[2], Furnon Cindy[2], and Marne Bertrand[1] [iD]

[1] Le Mans Université, LIUM, 72085 Le Mans, France
{iza.marfisi,bertrand.marne}@univ-lemans.fr
[2] IFP43 - CFA Interprofessionnel de Haute-Loire, Bains, France
{thomas.longeon,cindy.furnon}@ifp43.fr

Abstract. Serious Games (SGs) offer advantages for learning but yet, their use in classrooms is still very marginal. The design of SGs by teachers themselves seems to be a viable solution to develop their use since they are in demand of training on the subject. However, the creation of SGs ideally involves the close collaboration of several experts: pedagogical experts (teacher), game designers, graphic designers and developers for digital SGs. However, schools rarely have the means to hire such teams and teachers find themselves leading this project alone. What advice can be given to these teachers? In this paper, we propose the 10 commandments of the SG padawan, based on our experience in training more than 86 teachers in higher education on the subject and accompanying them in the creation of 21 digital and non-digital SGs.

Keywords: Serious game · Design method · Gamification · Professional training

1 Introduction

Serious Games (SGs) are games whose purpose is not strictly entertaining. This paper focuses on **SGs for learning** that can be used by teachers, from kindergarten [1] to adult professional training [2]. SGs and gamified courses are particularly good tools to create engagement and increase motivation [3, 4], but also to learn concepts differently, through simulations, exploration, experimentation or trial-and-error [5, 6].

Despite an abundance of existing SGs, they rarely correspond to the needs of teachers and only a very small proportion of these SGs can be modified [7]. Teachers therefore feel the need to design their own custom SGs. However, SG design ideally involves several specialists, including an educational expert (*e.g.* a teacher), a game designer and a graphic artist. Competent people are also necessary to make the game material or to develop software in the case of a digital SG. But in reality, schools rarely have the means to hire such teams and teachers have to carry out this project alone. However, the SGs we are studying are primarily teaching tools. Therefore, only teachers are essential

K. Kiili et al. (Eds.): GALA 2022, LNCS 13647, pp. 63–73, 2022.
https://doi.org/10.1007/978-3-031-22124-8_7

to the design process. Indeed, their pedagogical expertise has been acquired with the experience of several years of teaching with a given audience. With the right training, the other skills (game design, graphic design, game material design…) can be partially acquired, compensated by methods (*e.g.* in the form of design patterns [8]), tools or brought by external contributors.

In this article, we present the **professional training course *Ludifik'action*** we have been providing for the past four years and which aims to support teachers in the design of a custom-made SGs. The lessons learned from this experience are formalized, in the third part of this article, in the form of 10 guidelines teachers can follow to create their SG. Each guideline is titled as if *Master Yoda* said it. We chose this little gamification of form for three reasons: first, this particular phrasing helps draw attention to the important words, secondly because the readers of this article will probably be geeks, sensitive to this type of humor ☺; and finally, because it amuses us and an article written by enthusiastic researchers is bound to be more enjoyable to read. Each principle is then supported by evidence from the literature and our experience as animators of *Ludifik'action*. Finally, two *Ludifik'action* trainees (Cindy and Thomas) will comment on each guideline with their perspective.

2   Ludifik'action Training Course

Ludifik'action is a professional course to help French higher-education teachers create custom-made SGs (digital or not) (examples in Fig. 1). This course teaches them the basics of game design and puts them in contact with experts who can help them in this adventure. We have conducted six sessions of this course, with a total of 86 participants.

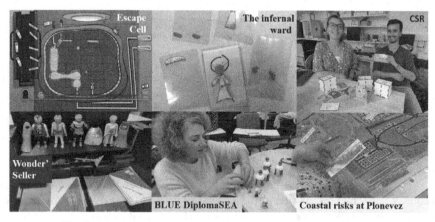

Fig. 1. Examples of Serious Games designed during *Ludifik'action*

Ludifik'action has undergone several organizational changes to adapt to the available human resources and cost constraints imposed by the training centers that managed it. The complete training program (sessions 3, 4 and 6) is composed of 2 full days of face-to-face training (3 to 5 months apart) and a personalized follow-up between them. During the first day, trainees learn the basics of game-based learning theories, practice modifying existing games into SGs, and discover as many games as possible (the course itself is gamified). Thanks to a brainstorming session with the trainers, at the end of the first day, the teachers identify the outlines of their SG and the main game mechanics. The teachers must then design a first SG prototype, on their own, and test it with students. They benefit from a half-day of personalized follow-up during which one of the trainers, comes to their school to test the prototype. This trainer has the role of game designer and helps them find the right game mechanics to improve their SG. He/she also helps them organize a test session with students if it has not been done yet. During the final full day of training, all the trainees test the new SGs and share feedback. They also improve the SG rules and work on the game material with 3D printers and laser cutters (ideally in a Fab lab as in sessions 3 and 4).

Table 1 shows, for each session, the different organization (number of trainers, number of days, follow-up), the profile of trainers and trainees (teacher alone or accompanied). G represents a Game designer, P represents a Pedagogical expert (teacher), E represents a pedagogical Engineer (or other support staff who help teachers set up pedagogical innovations) and D represents program Developer. In order to identify the level of completion of the designed SGs, a score from 0 to 3 was given to them: 0 indicates the trainees did not create a SG, 1 means a prototype was created, 2 means the SG was tested with learners at least once and 3 means the SG was tested and improved (in terms of game design and game material) and was reused, at least a second time, with learners. Some teachers carried on creating more SGs after *Ludifik'action*. This is indicated with a$^+$.

The presented data was collected by questionnaires, sent by email, or with a phone call when people had not responded. We managed to get a response from all the teams in sessions 1, 3, 4 and 6. Only 5 trainees from sessions 2 and 5 could not be reached because they had changed employers. Since no other trainees from these sessions had created SGs, we considered it highly likely that they had not created any either. In this paper, we also use some responses to the satisfaction questionnaire sent out immediately after the training course, to which 52/86 trainees responded.

It should be noted that the session 6 was conducted during the COVID pandemic. We postponed the second session (several times) so it could be done face-to-face. The restrictions also made it harder for teachers to test their SGs in class.

Table 1. Training modalities and designed serious games

Modalities		Trainees – Designed SGs - Completion level (0 à 3) - Stats			
1	Trainers : GE 2 days + follow-up for 2 groups	PE PEE P PEE PD P P P	**Library Game** – app to discover the library (follow-up) **Defy your grammar** – past tense in French **Civilization Timeline** – history **Chatterbox** – technical vocabulary in English **Chimory** – chemical transformations app (follow-up) *3 other teachers, by themselves, did not produce SGs*	3$^+$ 3 1 2 3 0 0 0	AVG 1,5 SD 1,4 MED 1
2	Trainer : G 1 day	Px15	*15 non-accompanied teachers participated in this course, but none of them produced a SG*	0	0
3	Trainers : GEE 2 days + follow-up + Fab lab	PP PPE PE PE PEE PE	**Pharma Ludo** – bibliographical research **Question of rights** – plagiarism, image rights **Once upon a time** – written and oral argumentation **CSR** – Corporate Social Responsibility **Moodle Escape Game** – Moodle course gamification	3$^+$ 3 3 3 1 0	AVG 2,2 SD 1,3 MED 3
4	Trainers : GGEE 2 days + follow-up + Fab lab	PP PE P PEED PP PE	**Coastal risks at Plonevez** – coastal management **BLUE DiplomaSEA** – marine biodiversity **Historia Compta** – history of accounting **Escape Cell** – web game on photosynthesis **GPS** – geometric specifications **Time TP** – prepare a chemistry lab session	3$^+$ 1 1 3$^+$ 2$^+$ 2	AVG 2,0 SD 0,9 MED 2
5	Trainer : G 1 day	Px23	*23 non-accompanied teachers participated in this course, but none of them produced a SG*	0	0
6	Trainer : G 2 days + follow-up	P PPP P P PE	**Schematic** – signal processing diagrams **VocaPro** – vocabulary of commerce and sales **EscapeEspaceGame** – escape game design **The infernal ward** – caregivers training **Wonder'Seller** – sales	1 1 2 3$^+$ 3$^+$	AVG 1,6 SD 0,9 MED 1

G=Game designer, P= Pedagogical expert, E=pedagogical Engineer, D=computer Developer

3   The Ten Commandments of the Serious Game Padawan

Each commandment is commented by two trainees who participated in the last session of *Ludifik'action*: Cindy, a commerce teacher accompanied by Thomas, a pedagogical engineer. They created the game *Wonder'Seller* (lower left corner of Fig. 1), in which learners go through all the stages of sales, materialized by *Playmobil* characters that move on a board.

3.1   Think Small, You Must

We have observed that almost all teachers start the training course with unattainable ambitions of grandeur. Some want to turn their entire course into a SG and others want to recreate commercial digital SGs. Teachers are unfamiliar with the numerous professions involved in developing a SG, and unless they have the resources to hire such a multidisciplinary team for a year, they are likely to become exhausted trying to take on all these roles, and eventually, disappointed with the partial result they have achieved.

In addition, SGs can be very intense in terms of attention and emotions for learners and teachers and are therefore not recommended for an entire course.

It is therefore important to **start with a very small SG project** that can be completed quickly with the available resources. The process should start with a positive experience that will reassure teachers and motivate them to continue. Other training courses on SG design also advocate this approach [9]. The best way to achieve this goal is to **identify a single thing that needs to change**. It may be the learners' behavior or a complex concept that they have difficulty understanding. This way, the SG will change a part of the course that is currently not satisfactory and the results can only be positive.

Cindy: *"My original intention was to sprinkle fun into my entire course but the training helped us identify our main problems and the design of a board game, which can be used at different times of the course, finally seemed more appropriate. Our students are very difficult to engage in activities. We also perceive a zapping phenomenon, difficulties in accepting constructive criticism and a great need for recognition. These different observations led us to embed the important knowledge and skills in a board game. The learners draw cards with questions related to our educational objectives. If they answer correctly, the game offers several reward mechanisms such as choosing an outfit or an accessory to customize their Playmobil character, moving forwards along the path or literally attaching a ball and chain to another player's Playmobil pawn to slow them down. The design of Wonder'Seller allowed me to confirm my intuitions and gave me the motivation to create two other SGs. It is by moving small stones that we move the mountain (Chinese proverb)."*

3.2 With Other Padawans, Work You Must

Like any type of pedagogical innovation, **SG design is very time consuming**. It is a path paved with many obstacles. First, it is necessary to rethink the course and how it could be improved with game mechanics. Then comes the design and creation of the SG material which requires the mastery of new software and tools. It is also important to communicate about the project, especially internally, to be sure it will be well received by colleagues and management. SGs are still rare in higher education and convincing arguments must be used to justify the project. It is therefore essential for teachers to be surrounded by people who can provide, at least, moral support.

Feedback from *Ludifik'action* (Table 2) shows that teachers who tried to create SGs alone were 33% (3/9) more likely to abandon, even with a complete training over several months (sessions 1, 3, 4 and 6). When teachers are accompanied by at least one other person, the risk of abandoning drops to less than 7% (1/15). In addition, we find that teachers who are alone just managed to create a prototype (average of 1,16 out of 3) while those who are accompanied usually manage to finish their SG, test it with learners, and some even manage to improve and test the SG again (average of 2,3 out of 3, standard deviation = 1). According to a Parson's chi-square test, this difference is statistically significant (p-value = 0.043).

It is therefore recommended to contact universities who offer the services of pedagogical engineers to accompany teachers, or team up with other teachers, in order to create a group dynamic and share experiences. In the final questionnaire of *Ludifik'action*, "sharing feedback with other trainees" was the most appreciated aspect of the course, cited in 22 out of the 52 answers.

Cindy: *"Teaching and preparation classes is time consuming and I don't have time to adjust my teaching posture and explore new pedagogy. Working with Thomas allowed us to mutualize pedagogical, technical and human competences. We also exchanged tips with other teachers, thus enriching each other. In particular, we initiated a collaboration with three other teachers during Ludifik'action who ended up using an adapted version of our game in addition to theirs."*

Table 2. Comparison outcome depending on the number of team members

N. team members	MIN	MAX	AVG	SD	MED	Abandonment
Alone	0	2	1,1	1,16	1	33% (3 out of 9)
Group of 2, 3 or 4	0	3	2,3	0,97	3	7% (1 out of 15)

3.3   With a Master, Succeed You Shall

Olivier (session 4 trainee): *"The follow-up pushed us to get the game out, otherwise I imagine that if we had only done the first session we wouldn't have gone further!"* This is indeed what happened. None of the trainees in sessions 2 and 5, which consisted of only the first day, created a SG. This can also be explained by the fact that trainees who signed up for this single day of training did not necessarily have the intention of creating a SG. However, during the first session, for which only two local teachers benefited from the follow-up, the groups without follow-up were 50% (3/6) more likely to drop out (these were single teachers). This suggests that the follow-up is essential to boost the creation process. The teachers admitted they had worked hard and slept very little the week before our visit to make sure they had a presentable SG. Another variable that seems to increase productivity is the number of trainers. Indeed, the SG completion scores (Table 1) are highest in sessions with more than 2 trainers (sessions 3 and 4). This can be explained by the fact that the brainstorming sessions were richer and gave the teachers more choices to find suitable SG scenarios.

Cindy & Thomas: *"SG design is a long and tortuous journey filled with technical challenges. It is therefore necessary to have an internal dynamic supported by external actors to gain perspective, feedback and added value. It is also necessary to have a clear organization with milestones and concise objectives that are easily attainable. By signing up to this course, we placed ourselves in a project dynamic, benefiting from methodological contributions of an expert. We realize the importance of her real time and in situ regulation in order to keep a unique line of conduct. Like a lighthouse in the middle of a storm (French proverb from the Auvergne region)."*

3.4   In Other Games, Inspiration You Will Find

Commercial games are the product of years of development iterations, player testing, and improvements. It is therefore in the teachers' best interest to draw inspiration from existing games (or parts of them). Several researchers have proposed methods for designing SGs based on this principle [10, 11]. During *Ludifik'action*, we ask trainees to modify existing games into SGs in only 15 min. We use very simple games such as *Time Line, Taggle, Concept* and *Who am I* that can easily be adapted. Children's versions of games are particularly interesting because they have very simple rules and can be complexified with educational content. At the end of the first day, trainees leave with a selection of games that they can use as inspiration to refine their SG.

Cindy & Thomas: "*The construction of our SG was a melting pot of player experiences. The teacher becomes a pedagogical hacker of the game: we reinvest the game mechanics in our own SG. Ludifik'action gave us the keys to identify the game mechanics that match the pedagogical objectives and the desired learning environment. It's like a recipe: list the available ingredients, identify the important ones, combine them, let it simmer, taste it as you go along and serve: a table!*".

3.5   Like You, the Game Must Be

When a SG is intended to be used in class, teachers play a central role in facilitating the game (explicitly if they are game masters or implicitly). The teachers' positive and engaging attitude is therefore essential for the SG to run smoothly. Teachers therefore need to design a game that they are comfortable with.

Cindy: "*My role during the game is totally reversed. I become a facilitator, a regulator, even a player, and not a knowledge provider. It was important for me to design a game universe with a visual identity. The game creates a strong cohesion in the class and a dynamic throughout the year. I feel it creates a special bond that was co-constructed and co-maintained: an ecosystem of fertile learning [12].*"

3.6   Exploit Your Students, You Can

It is useful to involve learners, from the beginning of the design process, in the choice of game mechanics and the game world to make sure it appeals to them [13]. They can also be asked to create parts of the SG during a project. Several studies show the positive educational effects of asking learners to design their own SGs [14, 15].

Cindy & Thomas: "*We involved the learners in several ways. First of all, a student, with former training in graphic design, offered to redesign the board, cards, logo, and pictograms. The learners can also add a card about the local company in which they are doing their apprenticeship or to share an experienced situation. This contributes to the evolution of the game and allows learners to leave their mark. Finally, the learners created online surveys and filmed feedback sessions to measure the usefulness of this new educational device. Involving the learners increase their confidence and involved them in the development of an educational tool that reflects their image.*"

3.7 Justify the Game Mechanics, You Must

The choice of game mechanics must be made in relation to the pedagogical objectives, the contexts in which the SG will be used, the learners' and the teacher's profiles [8]. Many SG design methods are proposed by researchers [15, 16], but none of them has full consensus in the community. We tried several of them during our training, but they remain difficult to use, even for SG specialists, because they rely on complex concepts that can be interpreted differently. In addition, these methods seemed too cumbersome and, above all, too long to set up, whereas our objective was precisely to encourage teachers to start small and light (1st commandment)! There are simpler design methods for teachers, but for designing a particular type of SG such as educational escape games [17] but this implies knowing whether this type of game is adapted to the initial needs. The general rule, found in all methods, is that **the choice of each game mechanic should be justified according to a pedagogical objective**. Adding game mechanics that cannot be justified can generate unnecessary cognitive load for learning [18]. This is especially important for SGs that will be used in the limited time of a class, and that must therefore be pedagogically efficient. On the contrary, it may be useful to add extra game mechanics for SGs that are to be used at home or whenever the students want, to motivate them to play again. Game mechanics can easily be identified through illustrated lists such as Marczewski's [19] or *Mecanicards* (www.mecanicartes.com). Our experience shows that **it is important that teachers take time to justify the choice of mechanics themselves, in writing**. It helps them build a solid argumentation to support the pedagogical potential of their SG and defend their project.

Cindy and Thomas: *"Placing ourselves in the role of SG designers allowed us to reflect in depth on the game mechanics to use in order to provide an effective and efficient experience. Ludifik'action helped us formalize these concepts that we had informally acquired in our various gaming experiences. We used game mechanics in line with our pedagogical objectives and our learners: challenges, progression, ranking, avatar customization and the possibility to play in teams. The game cards also cover the official program (i.e. make a sale, develop customer loyalty…) and help students practice their skills by asking them questions related to real situations."*

3.8 Introduce and Debrief After the Game, Necessary It Is

The majority of teachers think that SGs are sufficient on their own, but this is not necessarily the case. First, teachers must explain why they chose this new form of pedagogy, while avoiding the word "game", as this may be associated with commercial video games and could therefore lead to disappointment. Teachers must also take the time to list the skills that will be used. If the SG offers an immersive imaginary world and game scenario, a debriefing phase, after the SG, is also necessary to recall the used concepts and skills and discuss how they can be applied in other contexts [20].

Cindy: *"The game is introduced quickly at the beginning of the course and is very well received. You can tell that the learners are proud to be involved in the design of this new device. I don't do a debriefing because the game refers to real situations. On the other hand, we have found several ways of using the game for key moments of the course: in a full 2-h session, in a 30-min focus session, just with the cards to review skills with the entire class or in battle mode, with a buzzer, in small groups."*

3.9 Crucial, the Design Is

The pleasure of playing is greatly related to the graphics and the ergonomics of the game material [8]. Even if it is possible to test SG prototypes with post-its, the design should not be neglected. The box is one of the central elements, as it is the first contact with the SG. Placed on the table, the learners will have an irresistible urge to open it, like Pandora's Box. Designing a well-proportioned box with compartments is also very helpful from an organizational standpoint, as it will prompt learners to put the material away correctly at the end of the game. We encourage teachers to get in touch with a Fab lab, use box and card templates and purchase game material (*e.g.* paws, dice, tokens) from specialized sites.

Cindy & Thomas: *"The visual aspect is very important to generate emotions and engagement. We learned how to use new software such as Nandeck (www.nandeck.com) to generate the front and back of the cards from a CSV file containing 680 questions. We also learned how to master a laser cutter and a 3D printer to make a custom dressing room in which all the pawn, accessories and cards are stored. All this seemed sometimes tedious but the game was worth the candle (French expression), because we immediately saw the importance of the material. The wow effect is a real emotional trigger to start a game in the best conditions."*

3.10 Play, You Will

Most teachers are not gamers. They only remember a few classic games they played as children (that sometimes left them with bad memories) such as *Monopoly*, *Scrabble* or *Trivial Pursuit*. Yet, thousands of new games are created every year, including collaborative games that are much more suitable for classroom use. The best way to understand the tensions, the interactions, the dilemmas and the emotions triggered by game mechanics is simply to test it in a game. It is therefore essential for teachers to play. Games are now available in municipal and university libraries. Specializes game libraries also offer a wide selection of games and advice from enthusiasts.

Cindy & Thomas: *"To create a SG, you need to have a culture and experience of games that allow you to understand and identify the game mechanics that can be reinvested in an educational context."*

4 Conclusion and Perspectives

For the past four years, we have been giving the *Ludifik'action* training course to help teachers design custom SGs. Six sessions of this course were carried out with different modalities, which allowed us to identify those that seemed to be the most effective. We express the lessons learned in the form of 10 guidelines. We advise teachers to start with a very small SG project, with the help of educational engineers or colleagues. We also urge them to seek help from a game design experts, by enrolling in a training course that offers personalized follow-up. It is also recommended to draw inspiration from existing games to design a SG and to involve learners from the very beginning of the project. In addition, teachers need to design a game that they feel comfortable with in the classroom.

The choice of game mechanics is particularly crucial since it must suit the teacher who will be presenting the SG, the learners, the contexts in which the game will be used, but also the pedagogical objectives to be achieved. We also recall that it is essential to present the SG to the learners before its use, to facilitate its acceptance, and to set aside time after the SG, to review the important concepts and acquired skills. In addition, the design of the game material should not be neglected, as it plays an important role in the acceptance of the SG, but also in the time it takes to set up and put away the SG. Finally, teachers are strongly encouraged to play with their families or colleagues to discover inspiring game mechanics.

Thanks to research on SGs over the last decade, the design of effective SG is progressively getting easier. However, the human expertise of a game designer still seems to be essential to choose, in a relevant and efficient way, the game mechanics that compose a SG. We therefore advocate that this type of profile should be hired by universities and schools, as support staff for the design of educational innovations. At the same time, more research needs to be carried out for teachers who do not have the means to contact such experts. Several solutions are possible, such as the development of simple design guides for a particular type of SG or authoring tools for teachers to create digital SGs. Teachers should also disseminate their SG as widely as possible by writing a teacher's guide, but also by giving the source files of their SG material so that other teachers can adapt it to their needs and adopt them.

References

1. Kiili, K., Ketamo, H.: Evaluating cognitive and affective outcomes of a digital game-based math test. IEEE Trans. Learn. Technol. **11**(2), 255–263 (2017)
2. Marfisi-Schottman, I.: Games in higher education. In: Tatnall, A. (ed.) Encyclopedia of Education and Information Technologies, pp. 1–9. Springer, Cham (2019). https://doi.org/10.1007/978-3-319-60013-0_35-1
3. Dondlinger, M.J.: Educational video game design: a review of the literature. J. Appl. Educ. Technol. **4**, 21–31 (2007)
4. Hallifax, S., Lavoué, E., Serna, A.: To tailor or not to tailor gamification? An analysis of the impact of tailored game elements on learners' behaviours and motivation. In: Bittencourt, I.I., Cukurova, M., Muldner, K., Luckin, R., Millán, E. (eds.) AIED 2020. LNCS (LNAI), vol. 12163, pp. 216–227. Springer, Cham (2020). https://doi.org/10.1007/978-3-030-52237-7_18
5. Ryan, M., Costello, B., Stapleton, A.: Deep learning games through the lens of the toy. In: Meaningful Play 2012, East Lansing, USA, pp. 1–29. Michigan State University (2012)
6. Ruggiero, D., Watson, W.: Engagement through praxis in educational game design: common threads. Simul. Gaming **45**, 471–490 (2014)
7. Marne, B., Carron, T., Labat, J.-M., et al.: MoPPLiq: a model for pedagogical adaptation of serious game scenarios. In: Proceedings of the International Conference on Advanced Learning Technologies, ICALT, Beijing, China, pp. 291–293 (2013)
8. Marne, B., Wisdom, J., Huynh-Kim-Bang, B., Labat, J.-M.: The six facets of serious game design: a methodology enhanced by our design pattern library. In: Ravenscroft, A., Lindstaedt, S., Kloos, C.D., Hernández-Leo, D. (eds.) EC-TEL 2012. LNCS, vol. 7563, pp. 208–221. Springer, Heidelberg (2012). https://doi.org/10.1007/978-3-642-33263-0_17
9. Vanden Abeele, V., et al.: P-III: a player-centered, iterative, interdisciplinary and integrated framework for serious game design and development. In: De Wannemacker, S., Vandercruysse, S., Clarebout, G. (eds.) ITEC/CIP/T 2011. CCIS, vol. 280, pp. 82–86. Springer, Heidelberg (2012). https://doi.org/10.1007/978-3-642-33814-4_14

10. Abbott, D.: Modding tabletop games for education. In: Gentile, M., Allegra, M., Söbke, H. (eds.) GALA 2018. LNCS, vol. 11385, pp. 318–329. Springer, Cham (2019). https://doi.org/10.1007/978-3-030-11548-7_30

11. Stanescu, I.A., Baalsrud Hauge, J., Stefan, A., Lim, T.: Towards modding and reengineering digital games for education. In: de De Gloria, A., Veltkamp, R. (eds.) GALA 2015. LNCS, vol. 9599, pp. 550–559. Springer, Cham (2016). https://doi.org/10.1007/978-3-319-40216-1_59

12. El Mawas, N.: An architecture for co-designing participatory and knowledge-intensive serious games: ARGILE. In: Proceedings of the International Conference on Collaboration Technologies and Systems, CTS, pp. 387–394 (2014)

13. El-Nasr, M.S., Smith, B.K.: Learning through game modding. Comput. Entertain. 4(1), Article 3B 7–es (2006)

14. Švábenský, V., Vykopal, J., Cermak, M., et al.: Enhancing cybersecurity skills by creating serious games. In: Proceedings of the Conference on Innovation and Technology in Computer Science Education, pp. 194–199. Association for Computing Machinery, New York (2018)

15. Arnab, S., et al.: Mapping learning and game mechanics for serious games analysis. Br. J. Educ. Technol. 46, 391–411 (2015)

16. Kelle, S., Klemke, R., Specht, M.: Design patterns for learning games. Int. J. Technol. Enhanced Learn. 3, 555–569 (2011)

17. Guigon, G., Humeau, J., Vermeulen, M.: A model to design learning escape games: SEGAM. In: Proceedings of the International Conference on Computer Supported Education, Funchal, Madeira, Portugal, pp. 191–197. Scitepress - Science and Technology Publications (2018)

18. Graesser, A.C.: Reflections on serious games. In: Wouters, P., van Oostendorp, H. (eds.) Instructional Techniques to Facilitate Learning and Motivation of Serious Games. AGL, pp. 199–212. Springer, Cham (2017). https://doi.org/10.1007/978-3-319-39298-1_11

19. Marczewski, M.A.C.: Even Ninja Monkeys Like to Play: Gamification, Game Thinking and Motivational Design. CreateSpace Independent Publishing Platform, UK (2015)

20. Lederman, L.: Debriefing: toward a systematic assessment of theory and practice. Simul. Gaming 23, 145–160 (1992)

Serious Games for Instruction

Microcosmos® 3.0 Perception of Teachers in Outdoor Hybrid Playing Based on Mobile Learning for Natural Sciences

Roberto Vallejo-Imbaquingo[1] (ID), Silvia Ortiz[2] (ID),
and Angel Torres-Toukoumidis[3]([✉]) (ID)

[1] Escuela Politécnica Nacional, Ecuador Ladrón de Guevara E11-25, Ave., Quito, Ecuador
[2] Unidad Educativa Particular La Asunción, Rio Orinoco St., Cuenca, Ecuador
[3] Universidad Politécnica Salesiana, Elia Liut and Vieja St., Cuenca, Ecuador
atorrest@ups.edu.ec

Abstract. Mobile learning (mlearning) is a potential option in the teaching process of Natural Sciences. Therefore, the aim of this research is to analyze the perception of high school teachers on the potential integration of mobile learning based on the use of Microcosmos® 3.0. The results show that teachers are highly interested in mobile learning, partially know how to use it, despite access limitations, and are positively willing to train and participate in this new learning methodology. They admit that there are benefits of Microcosmos® 3.0 for learning Natural Sciences, especially chemistry, biology, entomology and anatomy; however, they accept that the challenges are somehow difficult, but can be improved by its constant use. Likewise, they admit a high level of satisfaction and usefulness for the reinforcement of contents and that continuity in the coming years will depend on the fulfillment of some of the suggestions made. Future studies will seek a more exhaustive follow-up and will include students as part of the sample.

Keywords: Natural sciences · Mobile learning · Teachers · Hybrid playing · High school

1 Introduction

Mobile learning (mlearning) is proposed as an alternative for blended learning, combining technological resources content, networks, flexibility and availability of communication and teaching [1]. Mobile learning has had a positive impact during the pandemic, demonstrating the integration of pedagogical strategies as a viable option that has facilitated the visualization of content and strengthened communication; however, it has been shown that its prolonged use has produced technostress, fatigue and reduced interest in educational games [2]. This indicates that although virtuality with the use of mobile learning has had multiple benefits, it also evidences important challenges to be addressed, thus achieving a balance between educational quality and student health.

This is an opportunity to know the hybrid models of mlearning that allow flexible access to information by balancing virtual activities with face-to-face activities, thus

K. Kiili et al. (Eds.): GALA 2022, LNCS 13647, pp. 77–85, 2022.
https://doi.org/10.1007/978-3-031-22124-8_8

promoting a more inclusive and participatory didactic [3]. This mobile hybridization is exhibited in its application as a tool for teaching mathematics [4, 5], improving the development of students' academic performance and cognitive competencies, while at the same time improving teachers' skills in the face of Information and Communication Technologies.

In addition, mobile resources have implied an active and direct introduction in a place that involves multiple factors, including institutional, ethical, support, evaluation, administration, interface design, technological and pedagogical factors [6]. The ludic element is added to the educational factor, since ludic has served as an integral teaching tool for the stimulation and formation of competencies and social and intellectual skills [7].

In fact, games have been imbued in mobile learning, producing greater understanding of the content, creating a creative environment and in general, positively influencing learning [8], in such a way that its purpose is qualified with the notion of Mobile game-based learning, defined as a pedagogical method based on the use of portable technology that allows immersive learning experiences [9]. Regarding the perception of teachers about mobile learning in primary school staff is in agreement with the mobile learning interventions, but they denote it as a future need that should lead to the learning of new digital didactic skills [10], however in secondary level is low in general, women and group with more than 15 years of experience showed more positive attitudes towards mobile learning [11], in addition to the above-mentioned perception of teachers from secondary education, they agree on the positive value, but emphasize the lack of familiarity in its use [12].

Its hybrid modality of mobile learning through games has also involved important benefits, among them, its efficient use for language learning [13], for history and cultural heritage [14], and for science, technology, engineering and mathematics [15].

Hybrid modality is rarely utilized in Natural Sciences; however, there are cases within the previous scientific literature oriented towards this subject from the digital modality, among them, Kidney Rush, a game applied in biology classes for learning the urinary system [16], an adaptation of Kahoot! to biology classes, thus facilitating learning, interaction and communication between classmates and teachers [17]. The association of mobile playful learning with augmented reality is also noted, significantly increasing the understanding of biodiversity [18]; and finally, it is also observed its implication for teaching blood circulation, complemented through gamification [19].

This study is original and innovative since it explores the application of the hybrid modality in mobile learning with playful components. To this end, it delves into the case of Microcosmos® 3.0® 3.0, a game made by Coworking Startups of the Salesian Polytechnic University, a venture that was developed over 2 years, which was systematized as shown below.

2 Methodology

This is a preliminary study that seeks to know the interest and knowledge of teachers about hybrid mobile learning coupled with playful components in the field of Natural Sciences. The general objective is to analyze the perception of high school teachers on the potential integration of mobile learning based on the use of Microcosmos® 3.0 in the teaching process. The specific objectives are: 1. To examine the teachers' apprehension of the premises of mobile learning; 2. To record the teachers' evaluation regarding the suitability of the application of the Microcosmos® 3.0 experience; and finally, 3. To contrast the first follow-up of the playful experience based on Microcosmos® 3.0 to reinforce the content in Natural Sciences.

Three phases were established in the methodological process to meet the objectives. In the first phase, the survey was used as the main data collection tool, organized in two sections with a total of 28 pre-questions. The first section referred to sociodemographic data has 6 questions, while the second has 21 questions with 5-level Likert scaling - totally agree, agree, neither agree nor disagree, disagree, totally disagree - oriented to knowledge, learning methods, devices, financing and preparation on the use of mobile learning, leaving an open question on new considerations and proposals from the teacher.

The survey has obtained a construct validation from Yusri, Goodwin and Mooney (2015) [20] applied in Indonesia. Although 7 years have passed since its first use, the pandemic has made it available as an alternative for the learning process in Ecuador [21]. The survey was applied between February 10 and March 25, 2022 to a non-probabilistic sample of 85 High School teachers living in Azuay, Ecuador. The information collected was coded using Excel, leading to the next phase.

For the second phase, a specialized workshop was held for Natural Science teachers from local schools on the use and management of Microcosmos® 3.0. It is worth mentioning that Microcosmos® 3.0 is defined as a social enterprise developed by Coworking Startups of the Salesian Polytechnic University and Sociedad de Divulgación Científica Quinto Pilar; and it is a mobile application used with $50\times$ optical zoom lens adapted to the cell phone camera, complemented with a glass slide and coverslip, a dropper with distilled water and a user's guide with fun challenges [22].

This training was carried out for 3 h on April 26, 2022 with the participation of 8 high school teachers to present Microcosmos® 3.0, addressing the functionality of the device and testing different challenges that the students would later use. The 10 challenges proposed were aimed at capturing images, i.e., 3 photos for beginners: tissue, skin and species; 4 photos for intermediate level: feathers, leaves and flowers; and 3 photos for advanced level: liquids, fruits and insects. These challenges were done by the teachers for a later use in the classroom.

At the end of the training, an in-depth interview was conducted with the participants. This data collection instrument consisted of 5 open-ended questions regarding their experience, vision and possible applicability (Fig. 1).

Fig. 1. Picture of Microcosmos® 3.0

The last and third phase of the process is conducted as a pilot test for teachers on their autonomous management to understand satisfaction, reinforcement and continuity for the next school year. For this purpose, an open face-to-face interview was also held with the 8 teachers participating in the training. The interview consisted of 5 questions applied on May 16, 2022 at "La Asunción" School in Cuenca, Ecuador, and answers were coded descriptively, allowing a glimpse on the use of Microcosmos® 3.0 in the classroom. Some challenges.

3 Results

3.1 Mobile Learning Premises of Teachers

According to the sociodemographic data reflected in the survey (n = 85), 58 (68.2%) were women and 27 (31.8%) were men. In terms of age, 43 (40%) respondents were between 41–50 years old; 29 (34.1%) were between 31 and 40 years old; 11 (12.9%) were between 51–60 years old; 8 (9.4%) were between 21–30 years old; and 3 (3.5%) were over 60 years old. Regarding the highest educational degree, 48 (57.1%) have a master's degree; 33 (39.3%) have a bachelor's degree; 2 (2.4%) do not have a degree and one (1.2%) has a PhD. With respect to educational experience, the data is almost equally distributed with 23.5% between 15–21 years; 20% between 0–7 years; 18.8% between 8–14 years; 17.6% between 22–28 years; 12.9% between 12–14 years; and 7.1% between 29–35 years. Regarding the sociodemographic information, the subjects taught in High School are distributed as: natural sciences have 31 (36.4%) teachers; physical education, social sciences and English have 10 teachers (11.8%); mathematics and language and literature have 9 (10.6%) teachers, and finally, cultural and artistic education have 6 (7%) teachers.

Regarding the specific section referring to the premises of perception connected to mobile learning, first of all, the level of knowledge teachers have of this pedagogical method is evaluated, evidenced in 5 questions. In the first one, the majority 68.3% - 58/85 of teachers know what mobile learning is; in turn, 82/85 teachers are willing to knowing more about its application strategies in the classroom; 72/85 teachers describe it as beneficial for the professional development of their students. In addition, teachers agree and strongly agree regarding its ease of use (56.5%) and time savings (64.7%).

Contrary to the willingness of teachers to learn and apply this technology, there is some hesitation regarding the preference for conventional learning over mobile learning, with 48.2% of teachers indicating neither agreement nor disagreement, but mostly in favor of conventional learning (34.2%) over mobile learning (17.6%). However, facing this dichotomy, mobile learning is seen as an alternative for the future, with 64.7% of teachers agreeing.

At the same time, the interest of teachers in learning about mobile learning in work-shops, courses and training seminars in both online and face-to-face modalities was also assessed. A total of 75.3% agree with receiving this training online, while 68.2% would like to receive it in person. This information suggests that teachers are seeking to take advantage of the situation to know more about this methodology.

Regarding the potential problems that may arise when using mobile learning, two indicators are established: technological and financial. Regarding the first indicator, teachers admit that they do not know how to use the cell phone properly (82.4%); therefore, it will be difficult to use it for mobile learning; they also consider that the cell phone they currently have does not have the capacity, speed or enough applications for the teaching-learning process (37.7%). Regarding the second indicator, which is connected to the financial one, only 36.5% agree to buy a new cell phone and pay for applications related to mobile learning; meanwhile, there is also some resistance to expand the Internet plan, 49.4% would not do so.

The last section of this questionnaire evidences the preparation and participation of teachers in mobile learning. In summary, there are nuances between both. Teachers want to participate (68.2%) but do not feel fully prepared to offer quality education (54.1%), this assertion shows some uncertainty about the limitations such as the responsible and practical management of mobile phones; the lack of money for buying the device; the lack of full internet coverage in areas of Ecuador; and the negative effect on health.

3.2 Application Suitability of the Microcosmos® 3.0 Experience

Understanding the different perceptions and comments observed in the questionnaire applied to teachers regarding mobile learning, an adapted training on this type of learning Microcosmos® 3.0 was carried out, where the main characteristic is the hybridization process between the face-to-face modality with the online modality in the teaching-learning process, presenting below a summary of the experience, suitability and possible applicability by 8 High School teachers interviewed (Fig. 2).

Fig. 2. High school teacher using Microcosmos® 3.0 during training.

First of all, the learning experience related to Microcosmos® 3.0 was taken into account, being valued as excellent and good, specifying it as a useful, playful tool that helps to learn science. One of the teachers emphasizes its practicality, which helps to magnify structures of living and inert beings, improving the understanding and analysis of the students.

The teachers then participated in the extra challenges, allowing them to learn about the difficulties they had when using them. Half of the participants were only able to complete the medium level challenges, due to problems in focusing the camera, accuracy, lack of pulse and time. All of them admitted that the experience can be applied to the subjects they teach, particularly chemistry, biology, entomology and anatomy, including topics such as the study of invertebrates, fungi, solid compounds, mineral structures, molecular geometries, morphology and physiology. Complementing the information, they were consulted about improvements of Microcosmos® 3.0, in which the teachers responded that the device should be made of a fragile clip material, should include illumination and access to more workshops that specialize in its application, or, audiovisual instructional material.

3.3   Follow-Up of the Playful Experience Based on Microcosmos® 3.0 to Reinforce Learning in Natural Sciences

In this last phase, the teachers had 20 days to experiment autonomously the playful experience with their group of students. It should be mentioned that since this is an exploratory proposal, this research focused only on the teachers and on the first follow-up out of 5 follow-ups proposed between 2022–2023 that would give continuity to the project.

Going back to the results of this first follow-up with the 8 teachers participating in the training, 123 Microcosmos® 3.0 were donated, of which 78 were given to high school students belonging to "La Asunción" School in Cuenca, Ecuador; the rest will be distributed in the next courses. The results obtained from the interviews focused on the satisfaction, reinforcement and continuity of its use, showed the following information:

1. During 20 days of experimentation by teachers, Microcos-mos® 3.0 was used on an average of 6 days; however, it was applied only in one class with students.
2. The level of satisfaction was high. It is estimated that 6/8 teachers are satisfied with the possible applicability in Natural Sciences.
3. They consider that it can be used to reinforce classroom learning, especially for direct observation of species; it provides creativity and development of soft skills; identification of structures; active learning and a partial substitution of the microscope in some activities.
4. Only half of the teachers admit that they could apply it in the next term. In order to apply it, they mention that the quality of the device's material must be improved and a strategy must be found so that students do not lose the device.

In short, this third phase shows that most teachers are satisfied with Microcosmos® 3.0, and consider a series of advantages regarding its application in the classroom. However, for its use, changes should be made to improve the material of the device, increase the magnifying glass, and add an striking color, basically, interaction needs to be remodeled.

4 Conclusions

After reviewing the three phases established in the methodological procedure, which correspond to the three objectives, it can be summarized that in the first objective, teachers have a high interest in mobile learning, partial knowledge, but still prefer conventional learning. Despite this, they are willing to being trained and to learn and participate in this new learning methodology.

Regarding the second specific objective, they understand the multiple benefits of Microcosmos® 3.0 for learning Natural Sciences, particularly chemistry, biology, entomology and anatomy; however, they accept that the challenges posed contain a certain level of difficulty and that it takes time to internalize the use.

Lastly, the third specific objective, which involves satisfaction, reinforcement and continuity of the use of Microcosmos® 3.0 by teachers, indicates that although it supports the observation of fine structures through an alternative experience, its use will depend on the changes to be made in the device.

Overall, some factors that hindered the use of Microcosmos 3.0 were lack of familiarity with the device and time to develop the play experience.

To conclude, there are different limitations in this study, among them, the short time for its implementation, the initial resistance to implement new teaching-learning methodologies and the lack of knowledge about mobile learning; therefore, future research must include the students' perception of the device; incorporate online games connected to the experience through platforms such as Genially; provide information from the 4 remaining follow-ups; and improve the properties of the device.

References

1. Montoya, M.S.: Recursos tecnológicos para el aprendizaje móvil (mlearning) y su relación con los ambientes de educación a distancia: implementaciones e investigaciones. RIED. Revista iberoamericana de educación a distancia **12**(2), 57–82 (2009)
2. Kumar, J.A., Osman, S., Sanmugam, M., Rasappan, R.: Mobile learning acceptance post pandemic: a behavioural shift among engineering undergraduates. Sustainability **14**(6), 3197 (2022)
3. Díaz, J.: Virtual world as a complement to hybrid and mobile learning. Int. J. Emerg. Technol. Learn. **15**(22), 267–274 (2020)
4. Castro, M.Y.T., Yataco, P.V., Valdivia, M.I.V.: Desarrollo de las competencias matemáticas en entornos virtuales. Una Revisión Sistemática. Alpha Centauri **3**(2), 46–59 (2022)
5. Márquez Díaz, J.E.: Tecnologías emergentes aplicadas en la enseñanza de las matemáticas. Didáctica, innovación y multimedia (38) (2020)
6. Aguilar, G., Chirino, V., Neri, L., Noguez, J., Robledo-Rella, V.: Impacto de los recursos móviles en el aprendizaje. In 9th Conferencia Iberoamericana en Sistemas, Cibernética e Informática, Orlando, Florida (EE.UU) (2010)
7. Torres-Toukoumidis, Á., Romero-Rodríguez, L.M., Guerrero, J.P.S.: Juegos y Sociedad: Desde la Interacción a la Inmersión para el Cambio Social. McGraw Hill, Mexico (2019)
8. Rico García, M.M., Agudo Garzón, J.E.: Aprendizaje móvil de inglés mediante juegos de espías en Educación Secundaria. RIED: Revista Iberoamericana de Educación a Distancia **19**(1), 121–139 (2016)
9. Huizenga, J., Admiraal, W., Akkerman, S., Dam, G.T.: Mobile game-based learning in secondary education: engagement, motivation and learning in a mobile city game. J. Comput. Assist. Learn. **25**(4), 332–344 (2009)
10. Gil Quintana, J.: Interconectados apostando por la construcción colectiva del conocimiento: aprendizaje móvil en Educación Infantil y Primaria. Pixel-Bit **54**, 185–203 (2019)
11. Baek, Y., Zhang, H., Yun, S.: Teachers' attitudes toward mobile learning in Korea. TOJET Turk. Online J. Educ. Technol. **16**(1), 154–163 (2017)
12. Gómez-Vallecillo, A.I., Vergara Rodríguez, D.: Enseñanza con aprendizaje móvil en educación secundaria. Percepción de la comunidad educativa. Revista Innovaciones Educativas **23**(SPE1), 16–30 (2021)
13. Berns, A., Isla-Montes, J.L., Palomo-Duarte, M., Dodero, J.M.: Motivation, students' needs and learning outcomes: a hybrid game-based app for enhanced language learning. Springerplus **5**(1), 1–23 (2016). https://doi.org/10.1186/s40064-016-2971-1
14. Othman, M.K., Aman, S., Anuar, N.N., Ahmad, I.: Improving children's cultural heritage experience using game-based learning at a living museum. J. Comput. Cult. Heritage **14**(3), 1–24 (2021)
15. Ishak, S.A., Din, R., Hasran, U.A.: Defining digital game-based learning for science, technology, engineering, and mathematics: a new perspective on design and developmental research. J. Med. Internet Res. **23**(2), e20537 (2021)
16. Rozaidi, S., Ismail, I.: Enjoyment of learning biology through mobile game based learning for form 5 students: Kidney Rush. In: Information, Communication and Multimedia Technology Colloq (ICMMTC), pp. 163–170 (2018)
17. Asniza, I.N., Zuraidah, M.O.S., Baharuddin, A.R.M., Zuhair, Z.M., Nooraida, Y.: Online game-based learning using Kahoot! To enhance pre-university students' active learning: a students' perception in biology classroom. J. Turk. Sci. Educ. **18**(1), 145–160 (2021)
18. Meekaew, N., Ketpichainarong, W.: An augmented reality to support mobile game-based learning in science museum on biodiversity. In: 2018 7th International Congress on Advanced Applied Informatics (IIAI-AAI), pp. 250–255. IEEE (2018)

19. Fan, K.K., Xiao, P.W., Su, C.: The effects of learning styles and meaningful learning on the learning achievement of gamification health education curriculum. Eurasia J. Math. Sci. Technol. Educ. **11**(5), 1211–1229 (2015)
20. Yusri, I.K., Goodwin, R., Mooney, C.: Teachers and mobile learning perception: towards a conceptual model of mobile learning for training. Procedia Soc. Behav. Sci. **176**, 425–430 (2015)
21. Pacheco Montoya, D.A., Martínez Figueira, M.E.: Percepciones de la incursión de las TIC en la enseñanza superior en Ecuador. Estudios Pedagógicos **47**(2), 99–116 (2021)
22. Torres-Toukoumidis, A., Portilla, F., Cárdenas, J., Álvarez-Rodas, L., Salgado, J.P.: Interacción y eficacia de la tecnología de comunicación móvil en la gestión del conocimiento. Revista Ibérica de Sistemas e Tecnologias de Informação **E16**, 28–40 (2018)

An Autoethnographic Perspective on Teaching Soft Skills Using Multiplayer Online Games

Karina Knauf[1], Lara Deidersen[2], Heinrich Söbke[1](✉) ⓘ, and Christian Springer[2]

[1] Bauhaus-Universität Weimar, Goetheplatz 7/8, 99423 Weimar, Germany
{karina.knauf,heinrich.soebke}@uni-weimar.de
[2] FH Erfurt, Altonaer Str. 25, 99085 Erfurt, Germany
{lara.deidersen,christian.springer}@fh-erfurt.de

Abstract. Soft skills, such as communication and collaboration are seen as essential for professional life. In formal education, soft skills are still underrepresented as learning objectives. To strengthen soft skills in higher education, we developed a course for undergraduate students in civil engineering. The course works with generic tasks provided by the commercial massively multiplayer online game *EVE Online*. The overarching research question is, to what extent the course actually trains soft skills. After first promising pilot evaluations, 22 autoethnographic essays, which the participants completed as a final assignment at the end of the course, are subject to a qualitative analysis in this study. In particular, aspects of learning, motivation, and didactic design are examined. The results confirm the findings of the pilot evaluations, in particular the development of soft skills was confirmed by the participants. Regarding motivation, it was surprising that the essays argued less with fun than with benefits for later professional life. In the context of didactic design, the suitability of the game *EVE Online* was questioned due to its great complexity. Also critical for the success of the course is the lack of confidence of the participants as well as their social environment in the learning effectiveness of games. Overall, this study thus provides guidance for the further development of the course including additional evaluations, which could make the course a broadly deployable learning scenario for soft skills training.

Keywords: EVE online · 21st century skills · Meta skills · Qualitative analysis · Learning

1 Introduction

In times of fast technological development, soft skills are considered increasingly important in the workplace (e.g. [1, 2]). Employers are calling for enhanced proficiency of soft skills from graduates to be recruited [3]. Although the term is commonly used, there is currently no commonly accepted definition for the term soft skills [4]. Since a broad definition appears to be sufficient for the purposes of this study, soft skills are considered here to be skills beyond domain-specific knowledge [5]. Although partially defined differently, soft skills are also referred to as *meta skills* or *21st century skills*. Domain-specific knowledge is also known as hard skills [5].

© The Author(s), under exclusive license to Springer Nature Switzerland AG 2022
K. Kiili et al. (Eds.): GALA 2022, LNCS 13647, pp. 86–95, 2022.
https://doi.org/10.1007/978-3-031-22124-8_9

It is argued that teaching soft skills is much more challenging than teaching hard skills [6]. Nonetheless, prerequisites for effective training are described, such as planned sets of activities that require active action, that are focused and explicitly address soft skills [6]. Overall, there is a need for evidence-based learning activities for soft skills training [7].

One approach to soft skills training is digital games. Schrier describes an early example of a dedicated location-based AR game used to train soft skills [8]. Using the game Minecraft and a specially developed software module, collaboration and teamwork skills could be trained [9]. Qian and Clark [10] documented in their genre review on games training soft skills, game elements and learning theories. As a result, the review confirms the effectiveness of game-based approaches and certifies in particular design-based games, i.e., games that focus on design activities, an enhanced learning effectiveness. Massively multiplayer online games (MMOG) are considered a specific game genre that is highly conducive to soft skills training [11]. In their review, Sourmelis et al. [12] find evidence for the effectiveness of MMOGs regarding soft skill training. However, they note at the same time that the state of knowledge is not yet complete and, for example, there are no studies regarding the soft skills creativity and innovation.

In the run-up to this study, we did not find any courses that use an MMOG to promote soft skills. Accordingly, the transfer of the encouraging findings outlined above into practice seems to be constrained. This contradiction informed our motivation to implement and evaluate a course using the MMOG *EVE Online* (CCP, 2012) in civil engineering study courses. Although in different studies the learning effectiveness and the learning potential of *EVE Online* could be revealed [18–20], with this study we aim at providing a methodological addition to already conducted studies with an autoethnographic perspective, to review the consistency of the results with the previous findings and, if necessary, to identify aspects that have not been considered so far. To this end, the study presented below analyzes autoethnographic essays from participants in the course. Aims of the analysis are in particular statements of the participants regarding the assessment of possible learning outcomes, the motivational situation and possible improvement requests of the didactical design.

2 Methodology

In the following, we first present the MMOG *EVE Online* used and the course as a learning scenario as well as the research methods used.

2.1 EVE Online

EVE Online was released back in 2003 and at its peak had up to 500,000 subscribers, it currently uses a free-to-play model [13]. EVE Online is considered a complex game that is difficult to learn [14] and that is not inviting to all groups of players [13]. It is also noteworthy that the virtual world *EVE Online* interacts with the real world in multiple dimensions and is also therefore of interest for frequent accompanying research, such as social science [15]. Accordingly, Hooper [16] examines the distribution of wealth and finds that wealth is linked to playing time, but not to date of enrollment. Taylor et al.

argue that intangible labor supports the amassment of wealth, both for other players and the production company, as well as the digital economy [17]. Referring to the soft skills learning scenario presented here, some evaluation results have already been reported. In this way, it could be shown that soft skills are promoted with the help of *EVE Online* [18]. Likewise, it seems to be possible to train communication in construction projects generically through *EVE Online* [19]. Yet another evaluation [20] provides evidence that the prior training of soft skills using *EVE Online* is capable of mitigating deficits of professional knowledge in *Building Information Modeling* work processes.

2.2 Learning Scenario

The participants of the study were 22 students of the course, called *VirtuIng*, from a total of four cohorts of consecutive semesters from summer semester 2020 to winter semester 2021/2022. The course is delivered completely online as a one-semester elective course worth 3 ECTS credits and is offered jointly in the bachelor study courses of civil engineering at two higher education institutions (HEI). The learning objective of the course is generally the training of soft skills using the MMOG *EVE Online*. The course takes place over 15 weeks and has two 90-min sessions per week—one theory session and one practical session. In the theory session, on the one hand, the theoretical basics of soft skills are taught, for example through presentations about seminal papers regarding soft skills, game studies, and specifically *EVE Online*, and on the other hand, strategic game supervision, such as the self-evaluation of game preferences via the Bartle test [21], is carried out. In the practice sessions, free play occurs in which participants discuss game objectives and are guided mostly by a student tutor. Both theory and practice sessions are supported via the *Discord* communication platform. The course is run by a lecturer and one or more student tutors, who support the participants with their knowledge of the game, especially in the practice sessions. There are four phases over the course of the semester: In the short initial phase, the basics of *EVE Online* are covered. In an equally short goal-setting phase, the participants come together in groups that specialize together in *EVE Online* on work goals such as resource mining, manufacturing, exploration or combat. In the third work phase, which comprises two-thirds of the semester, the goals are pursued in the game, while also collaborating with other groups. A short final phase summarizes and reflects on the results achieved.

Students are assessed for their final grade by micrograding the various learning activities, such as preparation of papers, attendance, or completion of assignments, such as the weekly quantum of course-specific questions asked and questions answered in *PeerWise* [22]. The micrograding method used here [23] allows students to gain points throughout the course. Micrograding is conducted using the *Moodle* learning management system [24]. By awarding more than 100% of the points in total, students can also decide which learning activities they participate in. Furthermore, at one of the participating HEIs, the grade of "pass" is granted upon achieving 50% of the points. Although open micrograding has not caused participants to abruptly stop working when this threshold is reached, essays were often not turned in when the 50% was reached. With the essay, 30% of the points could be achieved. Furthermore, a video could be handed in instead of the essay. These two limitations resulted in a total of 22 essays from the 35 students in the four cohorts.

2.3 Data Collection

The essays were to be written on the topic of training soft skills in *EVE Online* and were to be prepared by an activity diary, which the participants keep independently during the entire course. Guiding questions for the activity diary and thus the essays include *What activities did I do? Did I learn? What did I learn? Which activities did I learn through? What emotions did I feel and when?* Participants were given a brief (30 min) introduction to the autoethnography method [25] and were always welcome to pose questions about the method of autoethnography during the course. The two first authors were among the participants, while the other two authors served as lecturers. A total of 22 essays over four semesters, averaging 1500 words, were subjected to qualitative content analysis [26] by the three first authors. Commonly, the focus topics were determined. Consensus was reached when ratings differed.

3 Results

A total of 6 thematic clusters emerged from the qualitative content analysis. Based on the three research questions, the cluster *Learning, Motivation* and *Didactic Design* could be developed. A dominant aspect of the didactic design is the appropriateness of *EVE Online* in this learning scenario. Furthermore, the clusters *Transfer into Professional Life, Game-based Learning* and *Summarizing Perspective* were formed. In the following summarizing and excerpting description of the clusters, quotations are attributed to the participant (P1–P22).

3.1 Learning

All essays confirmed, at least partially, that learning had taken place. A wide variety of learning outcomes related to soft skills were mentioned: The 4C skills [27] were mentioned often: Collaboration (*"Working together to achieve a large goal was important, achieving it alone would not have been possible."*, P19), Communication (*"Although we did not always agree strategically, there was friendly and respectful interaction among us."*, P2), Creativity, and Critical Thinking. Further soft skills occurring in respective taxonomies, such as [28]: problem-solving skills, social skills, such as conflict-solving skills, and leadership skills were named as well. Furthermore, individual terms relating to soft skills were also used, such as planning skills, maximizing efficiency, conscientiousness, dialogue and cooperation skills, information management, understanding professional hierarchies, self-reflection, and autonomy. Through the use of third-party tools from the *EVE Online* ecosystem, technical literacy skills were also identified as a learning outcome. Resilience, i.e., not being discouraged by failure, was also mentioned as a learning outcome: *"I was always mentally prepared for failure. [...] Also, I think I am better able to adapt to failure. If I fail more often in the future, I can confidently deal with those setbacks calmly."* (P22). Reflecting on one's own strengths and weaknesses was also among the learning outcomes (*"Based on the weaknesses I identified [...], it was clear to me that the role of team leader or guardian of the group exceeds my competencies, which is why I brought my skills to bear in the mining operation"*, P11).

Likewise, the Bartle test that was conducted initially was referred to several times as a reason for decisions. Other learning outcomes besides soft skills mentioned included language skills and proficiency in marketplaces, as well as, of course, detailed knowledge of *EVE Online*.

3.2 Didactic Design

Overall, *EVE Online* is considered suitable for achieving the learning objectives (e.g., *"EVE Online is [...] well suited for learning skills that an engineer might also use outside of the game"*, P5 and *"EVE Online has made me think about the aspects of soft skills"*, P9). The complexity of *EVE Online* without providing a comprehensive tutorial is mentioned often, the game requires major efforts to be learned (*"The depth of the game with its numerous settings, customization, and skill functions becomes apparent to the player only after an introductory phase and can sometimes be intimidating"*, P3). Some participants expressed that they almost dropped out of the course due to frustrating experiences in the initial phase - and interestingly, were kept from dropping out by fellow students (*"So we had moments of frustration and lack of understanding throughout the module that were really intense and then the others had to get you out of them so that you continue with the module"*, P21). Some participants suggest other games, such as *Minecraft*, as more suitable. From a didactic perspective, some essays made critical remarks about the lack of focus on specific soft skills, but rather that participants only became aware retrospectively of what exactly had been learned. The exclusively online delivery of the course, which was triggered by the COVID epidemic, was seen as critical a few times (*"The online format has for me its challenges in the direct interpersonal communication of all participants. For example, dialog/cooperation skills, language skills and conflict handling skills cannot be developed to their full potential."*, P9).

3.3 Motivation

The seldom mention of fun was unexpected. Only in a few essays the word "fun" has been used (e.g., *"[...] the fun of gaming is a good motivation to improve one' s skills"*, P13). Rather, usefulness for the future professional life was mentioned frequently as a motivation. Interestingly, the word "motivation" was not used in most of the essays. However, there were also statements that the practice sessions, in which games were played, were more fun than the theory sessions, which were perceived as more tedious. The organization of the participants into groups with the self-imposed goals was perceived as detrimental to the fun, while other participants expressed great satisfaction in having achieved the self-chosen goals, especially in the group.

Also noticeable was that the use of a game as a learning tool was not regarded particularly seriously by some participants in terms of potentially achievable learning goals. On the other hand, some of the participants emphasized that learning goals could be achieved with a game, whether based on their previous experiences, or even as a result of this course. Overall, the motivational situation does not seem to be clearly determinable: some participants appeared to be more intrinsically motivated by the game, while other participants focused on the achievable transfer results.

3.4 Transfer into Professional Life

A frequent subject was the transfer of what was learned to professional life. Here, the benefit of the game as a protected experimental space was seen (*"making the mistakes online [is] the first step to avoid them in the real world"*, P10). It was also explained that the group-based play involving various specialists—for example, in joint mining, miners were needed for mining, industrialists for transport, explorers for finding the mining sites and fighters for protecting the group—is an analogy to the division of tasks in working life. The command structures during this mining operation with one or more leaders also represented an analogy to professional life. Communication was also compared to professional life: short and concise in stressful situations, such as in the case of an attack in *EVE Online*, or detailed during technical explanations within the group. The various spaceships and their equipment were also seen in analogy to construction life, where a wide variety of machines are used. There was consensus that the many skills required are also important in professional life (*"EVE Online is a game in which skills are passively and actively promoted that are otherwise only encountered in the professional life environment."*, P4).

3.5 Game-Based Learning

Some participants fundamentally doubted the capability of learning using games. They saw a contradiction between playing and learning. The perception of an activity as strenuous is seen as a prerequisite for learning in some cases (*"the game sessions hardly felt like a learning experience"*, P20). Even if participants are convinced of the usefulness of the game, there still remains the social environment, such as family and friends, who doubt the value of the setting in terms of learning outcomes. However, there were also statements that after detailed explanations, it was possible to achieve understanding for the course in the social environment. The lack of acceptance by the participants, which is confirmed by their social environment, is likely to reduce the effectiveness of the course. Another frequently mentioned criticism was the high amount of time required for the course. Despite the supposed game character, the activities required for the course were largely seen as work. However, there were also participants who appreciated the motivating effect of the game, especially in comparison to conventional courses (*"Compared to other courses, the tendency is clearly evident that more time is invested as soon as the motivation arises. [...] ultimately this course is dependent on the enthusiasm of the students and the motivation they bring with them"*, P10).

3.6 Summarizing Statements

The course is seen as an unusual learning method, which is by all participants credited with learning outcomes. Many participants would recommend the course to others; no one opposed recommending it to others. Of the interdisciplinary skills mentioned, communication (*"[...] the trend of digital work is increasingly strengthening, so this game offers the opportunity to practice communication skills in a virtual world"*, P11) and collaboration (*"In this virtual environment, sound teamwork guarantees success, not the individual excellence of a player."*, P7) during the game are highlighted as success factors. The closeness to activities typical for professional life is confirmed (*"Compared to other group work in the university, this group work is closer to the group work that occurs in the profession and can mirror a group work in later professional life"*, P16). Overall, positive evaluations of both learning outcomes and helpfulness for future professional life are expressed in all essays.

4 Discussion

Overall, the essays draw a positive picture of employing *EVE Online* in a course to develop soft skills. However, there are some findings that need to be evaluated further. For example, the essays were part of the final assignment of the course, which was graded. Although it was announced beforehand that a critical reflection should take place, it cannot be excluded that there is a bias towards positive statements in the essays not to endanger good grades. That not all aspects of the course were addressed by the essays could be concluded by a comparison with the contents of semi-structured interviews carried out with two cohorts previously [18]. For example, some participants had pointed out that the technical environment consisting of several systems (*EVE Online*, *Discord*, *PeerWise*, and *Moodle*) was sometimes very confusing. This finding was not evident in the essays. Likewise, the micrograding was criticized in the interviews as partly confusing, but not mentioned in the essays. Only *EVE Online* itself was doubted as an environment for this course due to its complexity. To what extent these statements are to be credited or whether *EVE Online* keeps the participants in a corridor between overstrain and boredom that is conducive to learning remains to be investigated. However, it is noteworthy that the dropout rate after the first two sessions was very low. We are inclined to consider the low dropout rate as an indication of pleasant demandingness. Further studies, such as a comparison with the proposed game *Minecraft*, are suggested as well.

One challenge for the learning scenario described is the participants' confidence in the learning effectiveness of the scenario. Some essays revealed that the motivation to participate in this course stemmed from the novelty of the scenario combined with the utilization of an entertainment game, but less from the conviction that actual learning outcomes could be achieved. In the case where participants are convinced of actual learning outcomes, the social environment consisting of family and friends is another barrier to actual appreciation of such a course. An indication for the lower appreciation of games in learning contexts arises from a survey of the first two cohorts, in which less "a computer game" than a "virtual environment" [18] was credited with learning successes, although the same context was addressed in the corresponding questions. Building confidence among participants in the actual learning effectiveness of the course will require further robust evaluations.

The learning goal of the course is soft skills in general. Accordingly, some participants missed clear learning goals. Therefore, it might be beneficial to emphasize specific soft skills, such as communication and cooperation, as learning goals. From a didactic perspective, the learning scenario could either be left unchanged—giving a formal learning goal for all those who miss concrete goals. Other soft skills, not explicitly declared as learning goals, would then be developed as a by-product. Alternatively, specific game tasks could be highlighted in the course that are particularly conducive to certain soft skills, such as leadership or communication. However, such guidance might further limit the fun. Nevertheless, further reduced fun may be tolerable, since fun is not among the main motivations of the participants. The same limitation applies when tasks are defined for reasons of focusing the course on specific learning goals.

5 Conclusions

Soft skills are considered important for professional life, but rarely included in the learning goals in formal higher education. Massively multiplayer online games (MMOGs) are considered viable learning tools for soft skills development that, to our knowledge, is not regularly used in formal higher education. Accordingly, this study investigated a course using the MMOG *EVE Online* as a learning tool to promote soft skills in civil engineering courses. The results of the analysis of autoethnographic essays from 22 participants showed—mostly in accordance with findings of previous studies—that various soft skills were developed through the course, with communication and collaboration being given predominant importance by the participants. Most participants were found to have an affinity for computer games, which then motivated their participation in the elective course. However, the transfer of the learning results into the future professional life proved to be at least as important a motivation. With regard to the didactic design, the difficult entrance into *EVE Online* was pointed out and it was suggested to use games that are easier to start. Overall, the essays presented a positive picture of the learning scenario, but the attitude towards games in teaching was seen as challenging, as some participants as well as the social environment of the participants attributed insufficient learning potential to them. For a lasting use in education, in addition to specific learning scenarios for the selective development of particular soft skills, the social acceptance of games as a learning tool needs to be worked on in particular. Overall, this study thus provides guidance for the further development of the course including additional evaluations, which could make the course a broadly deployable learning scenario for soft skills training.

Acknowledgements. The authors gratefully acknowledge the financial support provided by the German Federal Ministry of Education and Research (BMBF) through grant FKZ 16DHB2204 provided for the "AuCity3" project. Any opinions, findings, conclusions, or recommendations expressed in this paper are those of the authors and do not necessarily reflect the views of the institution mentioned above.

References

1. Pereira, O.P.: Soft skills: from university to the work environment. Analysis of a survey of graduates in Portugal. Reg. Sect. Econ. Stud. **13**, 105–118 (2013)
2. Stevens, M., Norman, R.: Industry expectations of soft skills in IT graduates a regional survey. In: ACM International Conference Proceeding Series, 01–05 February 2016
3. Wilkie, D.: Employers Say Students Aren't Learning Soft Skills in College. https://www.shrm.org/resourcesandtools/hr-topics/employee-relations/pages/employers-say-students-arent-learning-soft-skills-in-college.aspx

4. Matteson, M.L., Anderson, L., Boyden, C.: "Soft skills": a phrase in search of meaning. Portal **16**, 71–88 (2016)
5. Laker, D.R., Powell, J.L.: The differences between hard and soft skills and their relative impact on training transfer. Hum. Resour. Dev. Q. **22**, 111–122 (2011)
6. Kyllonen, P.C.: Soft skills for the workplace. Change Mag. High. Learn. **45**, 16–23 (2013)
7. Guerra-Báez, S.P.: A panoramic review of soft skills training in university students. Psicol. Esc. e Educ. **23** (2019). https://doi.org/10.1590/2175-35392019016464
8. Schrier, K.: Using augmented reality games to teach 21st century skills. In: ACM SIGGRAPH 2006 Educators Program, SIGGRAPH 2006 (2006)
9. Wendel, V., et al.: Designing a collaborative serious game for team building using Minecraft. In: European Conference on Games Based Learning, pp. 569–578. Academic Conferences International Limited (2013)
10. Qian, M., Clark, K.R.: Game-based Learning and 21st century skills: a review of recent research. Comput. Hum. Behav. **63**, 50–58 (2016)
11. Squire, K.R.: Videogames as designed experience from content to context. Educ. Res. **35**, 19–29 (2006)
12. Sourmelis, T., Ioannou, A., Zaphiris, P.: Massively multiplayer online role playing games (MMORPGs) and the 21st century skills: a comprehensive research review from 2010 to 2016. Comput. Hum. Behav. **67**, 41–48 (2017)
13. Bergstrom, K.: EVE online is not for everyone: exceptionalism in online gaming cultures. Hum. Technol. **15**, 304–325 (2019)
14. Bergstrom, K., Carter, M., Woodford, D., Paul, C.A.: Constructing the ideal EVE online player. In: DiGRA 2013 - Proceedings of 2013 DiGRA International Conference. DeFragging GameStudies, pp. 1–16 (2013)
15. Bramson, A., Hoefman, K., Schoors, K., Ryckebusch, J.: Diplomatic relations in a virtual world. Polit. Anal. **30**, 214–235 (2022)
16. Hooper, B.: EVE online: the worlds of wealth and war, pp. 1–13 (2020)
17. Taylor, N., Bergstrom, K., Jenson, J., De Castell, S.: Alienated playbour: relations of production in EVE online. Games Cult. **10**, 365–388 (2015)
18. Pagel, M., Söbke, H., Bröker, T.: Using multiplayer online games for teaching soft skills in higher education. In: Fletcher, B., Ma, M., Göbel, S., Baalsrud Hauge, J., Marsh, T. (eds.) JCSG 2021. LNCS, vol. 12945, pp. 276–290. Springer, Cham (2021). https://doi.org/10.1007/978-3-030-88272-3_20
19. Jansen, E., Söbke, H.: Communication skills in construction projects and promoting them through multiplayer online games. In: Söbke, H., Spangenberger, P., Müller, P., Göbel, S. (eds.) JCSG 2022. LNCS, vol. 13476, pp. 169–181. Springer, Cham (2022). https://doi.org/10.1007/978-3-031-15325-9_13
20. Damek, S., Söbke, H., Weise, F., Reichelt, M.: Teaching (meta) competences for digital practice exemplified by building information modeling work processes. Knowledge **2**(3), 452–464 (2022)
21. Andreasen, E., Downey, B.: The Bartle Test of Gamer Psychology. http://matthewbarr.co.uk/bartle/
22. The University of Auckland. PeerWise, New Zealand. https://peerwise.cs.auckland.ac.nz/
23. Pfennig, A.: Improving learning outcome in material science through inverted classroom techniques and alternative course assessment–a case study. J. Foreign Lang. Educ. Technol. **3**, 148–162 (2018)
24. Moodle.org: Moodle - open source learning platform. https://moodle.org
25. Ellis, C., Adams, T.E., Bochner, A.P.: Autoethnography: an overview. Hist. Soc. Res. **36**, 273–290 (2011)
26. Mayring, P.: Qualitative content analysis. In: Flick, U., von Karsdorff, E., Steinke, I. (eds.) A Companion to Qualitative Research, pp. 159–176. SAGE Publications, London (2004)

27. Sipayung, H.D., Sani, R.A., Bunawan, W.: Collaborative inquiry for 4C skills, vol. 200, pp. 440–445 (2018)
28. Stauffer, B.: Ultimate Guide to Teaching 21st Century Skills in Secondary Schools. www.aes education.com

Evaluating the Expectations and Motivational Drivers in an Undergraduate Geology Classroom Using the Magma Pop Serious Game

Simon Hoermann[1]([⊠]) [ID], Sriparna Saha[2] [ID], Nikita Harris[1] [ID], Clara Bah[3] [ID],
Jonathan Davidson[2] [ID], Alexander Nichols[2] [ID], Ben Kennedy[2] [ID], and Erik Brogt[4] [ID]

[1] School of Product Design, University of Canterbury, Christchurch, New Zealand
simon.hoermann@canterbury.ac.nz
[2] School of Earth and Environment, University of Canterbury, Christchurch, New Zealand
[3] Research and Innovation, University of Canterbury, Christchurch, New Zealand
[4] Future Learning and Development, University of Canterbury, Christchurch, New Zealand

Abstract. Game-based learning is becoming increasingly prevalent in higher education as it fosters critical thinking, creative problem solving, and ensures cognitive development and social learning. This paper presents findings from a study to understand whether serious games can be effective in communicating concepts related to magmatic processes. We developed a serious game "Magma Pop" for use in an undergraduate geology classroom. The goal was to create an engaging experience to reinforce factual knowledge on mineral formulae and conceptual understanding of the fractional crystallization process to clarify the link between changing temperatures and magma and mineral composition. Students' game experience was evaluated during an in-class activity followed by an online survey. We found that despite a few technical glitches, the game concept and user experience were positively rated by students. The proposed game was well received and has now been integrated as a regular component of the course.

Keywords: Game-based learning · Educational tools · Serious games · Magma · Minerals · Fractional crystallization · Volcano

1 Introduction

In 2018, video games became the most prominent entertainment activity, overtaking TV and generating more revenue than the cinemas and digital music industries together [1]. While the video game industry is mostly focused on games for entertainment, currently there is a burgeoning trend to use the potential of games for educational purposes. This is evident in the annual growth of the educational games industry, which is twice as fast as that of the entertainment industry [2]. Game-based learning is becoming increasingly prevalent in higher education as it can foster critical thinking, and creative problem solving and ensures cognitive development and social learning [3]. Locally situated serious games are particularly useful when it comes to disaster preparedness as they can enable learners to gain an understanding of complex topics and decision-making that

K. Kiili et al. (Eds.): GALA 2022, LNCS 13647, pp. 96–106, 2022.
https://doi.org/10.1007/978-3-031-22124-8_10

can translate into real world preparedness [4]. As such, the development of games that can be used for disaster education warrants some research.

However, the development of serious games is different from those developed for entertainment. Entertaining games need to be engaging for the player and the focus of development is on the player's experience within the game world. Game mechanics are thus designed to support game dynamics (i.e., player behavior within the game) that can elicit the desired experience (often summarized as "finding the fun"). In non-entertainment serious games (such as educational, corporate and healthcare games) [5, 6], however, the goal is to affect the player beyond the virtual world by fostering meaningful experiences for players that persist beyond their experience in the video game world [6]. When such games are based on realistic models of real-world situations and events, they can provide immediate feedback on the decisions and actions of players [6].

Serious (educational) games must be engaging as well as effective to elicit the desired real-world improvement of the player, while also addressing the engagement aspect. Therefore, educational games must follow a rigorous design process and evaluation [7]. In this paper, we explain the learning outcomes and teaching activities that support students' learning in the Magma Pop game and evaluate the experience of the students after they played the game. We discuss this, together with a range of specifically selected game design elements to support engagement and the structure of our educational game.

1.1 Serious Games as Educational Tools in Classroom Settings: Magma Pop Development

One of the most common definitions of gamification is provided by Deterding et al. [8] who defined gamification as "the application of game-design elements and game principles in non-game contexts". Several reviews have highlighted how different fields all contribute to how we research and understand serious games. For example, more motivation and increased learning has been widely reported [9]. However, it is also important to note there are technological and structural challenges to align gamification into traditional classroom settings and to balance fun and playability with learning [9].

There is some evidence suggesting that serious games can be leveraged to help students learn complex concepts in university classroom settings. For example, a mixed reality learning application was successfully used in science [10]. It allowed students to explore different material science concepts in 3D using a mobile device. The gamified application was integrated into the overall learning structure of the course as part of a practical lab session. The evaluation showed that students positively accepted the app and agreed that the app helped them to understand the topic and theoretical knowledge better.

Due to New Zealand's location at the boundary of the Australian and the Pacific tectonic plates, it is exposed to several hazards such as volcanic eruptions, earthquakes, tsunamis, floods and landslides [11]. Games have emerged as effective tools to foster understanding of physical processes related to Earth Science and natural disasters [12–17]. Volcanic eruptions are driven by the magma chamber processes beneath them. An improved understanding of these processes (can aid general Earth Science knowledge hazard understanding and eventual mitigation [16, 18]. Here, we present a serious game, Magma Pop, that was designed to support intermediate level geochemistry, igneous petrology and volcanology undergraduate geology classroom.

The idea of Magma Pop was started by a student as a follow up of a University Geology lab exercise where students use different colored M&M chocolates to understand concepts around crystallization of magma in a magma chamber [19]. The idea was supported by the geology course instructors who thought the game could provide an innovative and entertaining way to reinforce the concepts taught in the undergraduate geology course. Magma Pop aims to build on the goals of the M&M lab exercise to improve students' (1) knowledge of fractional crystallization and its importance in generating variable (igneous) rock compositions and (2) understanding of the interplay between temperature and changing composition of magma.

The learning content of the game relates to *increasing factual knowledge* (e.g., details about fractional crystallization) and *conceptual understanding* (e.g., understanding the link between the temperature, crystallization, and composition). Hence, reinforced learning due to repetition (for fractional crystallization) and exploration (magmatic differentiation) were identified as suitable activities to support learning. The goal of the game was to integrate these activities in a meaningful and engaging way through gameplay. In this paper, results are presented from playtests that were conducted to understand (a) students' experience of the game, particularly the usability of the specifically designed and integrated educational game elements and (b) whether the conceptual understanding of geology (such as specific mineral formulae; magma chamber cooling etc.) can be reinforced through serious gaming.

1.2 Magma Pop: Description

The first two levels of Magma Pop are designed to re-enforce the learning of mineral formulae by repetition.

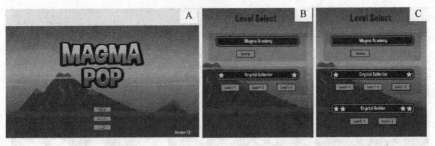

Fig. 1. Main screen of Magma Pop (A), the Select Screen (B), the Crystal Builder option with the two sublevels (C).

The first level of Magma Pop is called the Crystal Collector (Fig. 1), where in three sublevels (1-1, 1-2 and 1-3), learners practice different mineral formulae by generating minerals through selection of the right type and amounts of chemical elements. When players click on the "START" option in Fig. 1A, the Select Screen (Fig. 1B) comes up depicting the tutorial and the three sub-levels of the Crystal Collector game, sublevel 1-1: The Magma Neophyte, sublevel 1-2: The Magma Dealer and sublevel 1-3: Quartz, Ilmenite & Magnetite. The Crystal Builder (Fig. 1C) with the two sublevels becomes available after the three Crystal Collector sublevels have been completed.

At each sublevel, players generate specific minerals: olivines (forsterite and fayalite) and pyroxene (diopside) (level 1-1); feldspars (anorthite, albite and orthoclase) (level 1-2); and quartz, ilmenite and magnetite (level 1-3). These are common rock forming minerals that crystallize as magma cools. These minerals are composed of different elements that are represented as ions in Magma Pop. Every time a sublevel is loaded, the magma chamber receives a fresh mixture of ions that are generated based on which constituents are needed to make the minerals at that sublevel.

Each sublevel has three green icons and one blue icon located at the bottom of the screen (Fig. 2). The Home button (on the left bottom corner of the screen) takes players back to the Level Select screen. The Formula button (i.e., button with 2 hexagons in it) shows the list of mineral formulae that players are required to create during gameplay. Players can then scroll through this list to look up the mineral formula that needs to be made (as listed in the objective window located on the bottom left side of the gameplay screen). Once ions have been matched correctly, the specific mineral is formed (for example, the green forsterite mineral). The Star button toggles the level's Objectives Panel (on the left) on or off. The Objectives Panel shows the minerals that need to be created by matching different ions. When players have collected all the minerals that are listed in the Objectives Panel, the panel turns green, and players can proceed to the next sublevel.

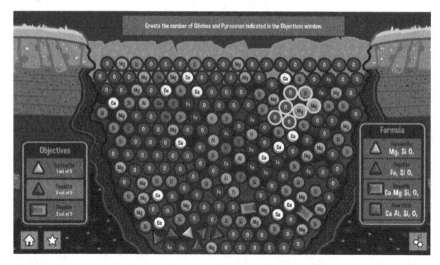

Fig. 2. Home screen for Crystal Collector (Level 1) of Magma Pop. (Color figure online)

Upon completion of the three sublevels, Level 2 of the game is made available. In Level 2 (Crystal Builder), with sublevels 2-1 and 2-2, players are no longer concerned with oxygen, as too many would be required, and the size of the magma chamber would be impractical. Instead, they are required to combine only the right number of constituent cations to form the minerals listed in the objective panel. However, the added challenge in this level is the introduction of a temperature panel. As the temperature changes different minerals begin to crystallize together and hence the objective (or the minerals to be formed) keeps changing. This means that with each drop in temperature, there is a new set of minerals that players are required to create, for progress to be made. Additionally, a panel box at the bottom right corner shows the changing concentration of the magma chamber because of the crystallization process. In this level, the mineral formula list is no longer available, and players are required to know them off-hand to make progress while keeping pace with the changing temperatures.

2   Methods

2.1   Magma Pop Evaluation

Magma Pop was play-tested in two lab sessions in July 2020 by fifty students for approximately 30 min during the lab sessions. Thirty-nine undergraduate students (21 female, 18 male) also filled-out the online evaluation questionnaire. The playtest session was announced through multiple channels: (1) in lectures prior to lab sessions; (2) in previous labs; and (3) on the university's learning management system. All students and teaching staff were informed about the details of the study beforehand. Ethical approval by the Educational Research Human Ethics Committee at the University of Canterbury for conducting this study was obtained (2020/24/ERHEC) prior to conducting this study. Information sheets and consent forms were handed out in prior lab sessions and collected before the evaluation. Both evaluation sessions took place in a computer room normally used for regular computer lab sessions with approximately 25 students and 3 teachers in the room. The game was explained to the class and students were asked to play the game on the computers for 30 min. Magma Pop was preinstalled on all computers.

To evaluate different aspects of the user experience, we used elements of validated instruments from the literature to construct our questionnaire for participating students.

Participating students completed a multi-part questionnaire after the gameplay. Our questionnaire contained questions from several validated questionnaires to evaluate different aspects of user experience such as general player experience [20], serious game experience [21], students' attitude towards learning with the game, their perception of the cognitive/affective qualities of the game and students' usage-intentions of the game [22].

3   Results and Discussion

3.1   Participant's Background in Gaming and Volcanology

Most participants reported playing computer games regularly (20/39) or occasionally (8/39) and reported a wide range of durations from a few minutes (5/28), to one hour (7/28), and more than five hours (3/28) of gaming per day. The type of game that participants were playing was a variety of different genres with role-playing games (16), strategy games (17), shooter games (17) simulation games (12), and action games (9) among the most popular.

Participants' preferences were in alignment with the course and 33/39 had strong preferences to learn science skills and in particular skills related to volcanology (37/39). Out of a score of 100, students viewed the course as being reasonably difficult (M: 68.9, SD: 15.13), requiring a moderate amount of effort (M: 59.84, SD:14.06), and as being highly enjoyable (M: 78.30, SD: 30.81). Students were highly motivated to attend the course (M: 82.84, SD: 18.42) and they expected the content of the course to be highly useful (M: 85.66, SD: 13.41).

3.2   Serious Game Experience

The game experience was evaluated using the questionnaire by Moizer et al. [21]. Participants rated their level of agreement with 32 statements where 1 meant 'Strongly Agree' and 5 meant 'Strongly Disagree'. The statements were further categorized into five dimensions of the evaluation framework: Gaming Experience, Learning Experience, Adaptivity, Usability and Fidelity.

Average ratings were Fidelity ($\bar{x} = 2.85$), Usability ($\bar{x} = 2.91$), Adaptivity ($\bar{x} = 2.56$), Learning Experience ($\bar{x} = 3.01$), and Gaming experience ($\bar{x} = 2.27$).

The questionnaire by Moizer et al. [21] was originally developed to evaluate a 3D avatar role-playing serious game for soft skills learning. Hence, some questions of this questionnaire were perhaps less relevant for the Magma Pop study (e.g. questions about communication). Nevertheless, by analyzing individual questions, it was revealed that participants rated "I was able to achieve the goals set in the game", "I recognize the value of the game as a tool for learning" and "I learnt how to use the software quickly" highly (ratings < 2). However, the questionnaire also revealed that Usability and Adaptability overall although not rated badly, were close to the mid-point and suggested room for further improvements. In particular, it is possible that some technical bugs as well as some gameplay issues affected the gaming experience. Ideas on how to improve gameplay are discussed further below in this paper.

3.3 Attitudes, Intentions and Perceptions

Participants' attitudes towards, perceptions about, and intentions to use serious games were evaluated with questions proposed by Riemer and Schrader [22]. Attitude toward learning with serious games was assessed using a single item representing a summary evaluation. Students had to complete the sentence, "I find serious games to be (...)" using a 7-point scale ranging from − 3 to 3 (bad to good). Most students had a positive attitude towards serious games with 33 out of the 39 students providing a rating of 1 or higher (higher values represent a more positive attitude).

Usage-intention as shown in Fig. 3 included five items addressing either the intention to use or avoid serious games for learning on a 7-point scale ranging from completely disagree (1) to completely agree (7). Most students indicated intentions of using serious games for learning, with the statement "I would like to use serious games regularly for learning" getting the highest rating on the Likert Scale. These results suggest that Magma Pop as a serious game can have a motivational role within the course.

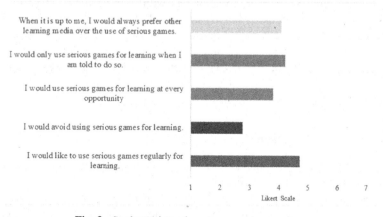

Fig. 3. Students' intentions to use serious games.

Perception of cognitive quality, in particular the perceived potential to support learning, was assessed on a 7-point Likert scale (completely disagree (1) to completely agree (7)) for each of the 10 statements. Results are shown in Fig. 4.

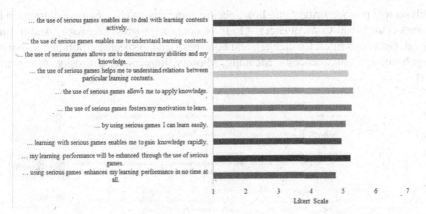

Fig. 4. Students' perception of cognitive learning qualities

The perception of affective quality was measured based on the two-dimensional structure of positive and negative effects. The scale comprised eight items assessing students' perceptions directed at the affective qualities; that is, whether learning with games induces positive effects (e.g., energetic, determined, alert, elated) or negative effects (e.g., distressed, nervous, anxious, angry). All items were scored on 7-point scales ranging from not at all (1) to very much (7). Students rated positive emotions higher (elated ($\bar{x} = 4.36$), alert ($\bar{x} = 4.64$), determined ($\bar{x} = 5.15$) and energetic ($\bar{x} = 4.35$)), whereas negative emotions were rated lower (nervous ($\bar{x} = 2.07$), distressed ($\bar{x} = 1.90$), angry ($\bar{x} = 1.85$), anxious ($\bar{x} = 1.82$)). Hence, we interpret this as an indicator that Magma Pop was able to induce positive emotions in the students who took part in this study.

3.4 Game Engagement

The game engagement was measured with a questionnaire from Abeele et al. [23]. Participants rated their level of agreement with each statement on a 7-point Likert scale. The questionnaire contained questions grouped to the following constructs: Meaning, Mastery, Immersion, Autonomy, Curiosity, Ease of Control, Challenge, Progress Feedback, Audiovisual Appeal, as well as Goals and Rules.

As seen in Fig. 5, students felt that they grasped the overall goals of the game (Goals and Rules), liked the look and feel of the game (Audiovisual Appeal), and felt capable while playing the game (Mastery). They also found the game relevant to them (Meaning), with these items scoring more than 5 on the Likert scale.

Items which scored lower on the Likert-scale included: "I was no longer aware of my surroundings while I was playing" under the construct of Immersion and "The game gave clear feedback on my progress towards the goals" (Progress Feedback). Three statements related to player's choice (Autonomy) – "I felt a sense of freedom about how I wanted to play this game", "I feel free to play the game in my own way" and "I felt like I had choice regarding how I wanted to play this game" scored lower than 4, suggesting that improvements could be made to the Magma Pop game in this area. Further analysis will provide insight into how specific game design choices are experienced by players (Functional Consequences – Ease of control, Progress feedback, Audiovisual appeal, Goals and rules, Challenge), and how these lead to specific emotional responses (Psychosocial Consequences – Meaning, Mastery, Immersion, Curiosity, Autonomy) [23].

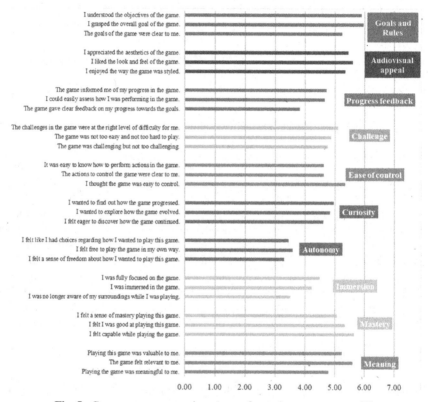

Fig. 5. Game engagement ratings (mean for each statement out of 7)

4   Conclusions

We co-designed and developed a serious game "Magma Pop" to support undergraduate geology students in learning mineral formulae and understanding concepts related to fractional crystallization and magma chamber cooling. The game was evaluated with members of the target audience and received positive feedback overall. Results confirm the considerable potential of Magma Pop as a serious game to enhance teaching and learning in higher education.

Future extensions of the game will explore the interaction between temperature and magma crystallization and relate it to volcanic eruptions and geothermal energy production, instilling their relevance to society in undergraduate geology students. Based on these results the next iteration of the game is envisioned to (1) include a pop tutorial character that will guide players through the controls of the game, (2) allow players to select/deselect ions during game play, (3) incorporate ways for students to check and receive feedback on their conceptual knowledge, and (4) get points for crystallizing the right crystals with the right formulae at the right temperature. In summary, the proposed game was well received and based on participants' feedback, has been integrated as a component of the course.

References

1. Video games market is worth more than music and movies combined so why aren't CSPs launching games services?. https://www.vanillaplus.com/2018/07/05/40093-video-games-market-worth-music-movies-combined-arent-csps-launching-games-services/. Accessed 17 June 2022
2. Serious Games Market on Path to $8.1 Billion Revenues in 5 Years. https://www.seriousgamemarket.com/2017/06/serious-games-market-on-path-to-81.html. Accessed 17 June 2022
3. Plass, J.L., Homer, B.D., Kinzer, C.K.: Foundations of game-based learning. Educ. Psychol. **50**, 258–283 (2015). https://doi.org/10.1080/00461520.2015.1122533
4. Arnold, S., Fujima, J., Jantke, K.P., Karsten, A., Simeit, H.: Game-based training of executive staff of professional disaster management: storyboarding adaptivity of game play. In: International Conference on Advanced ICT and Education, August (2013). https://doi.org/10.2991/icaicte.2013.14
5. Susi, T., Johannesson, M., Backlund, P.: Serious Games: An Overview. Undefined (2007)
6. Culyba, S.H.: A field guide for design leaders in transformational games. In: 2015 Serious Play Conference, Pittsburgh, USA (2015)
7. McKenney, S., Reeves, T.C.: Educational design research. In: Spector, J.M., Merrill, M.D., Elen, J., Bishop, M.J. (eds.) Handbook of Research on Educational Communications and Technology, pp. 131–140. Springer, New York (2014). https://doi.org/10.1007/978-1-4614-3185-5_11
8. Deterding, S., Dixon, D., Khaled, R., Nacke, L.: From game design elements to gamefulness: defining "gamification." In: Proceedings of the 15th International Academic MindTrek Conference, pp. 9–15. Association for Computing Machinery, New York, NY, USA (2011)
9. de Freitas, S.: Are games effective learning tools? A review of educational games. J. Educ. Technol. Soc. **21**, 74–84 (2018)
10. Loporcaro, G., Huber, T., Hoermann, S., Wang, T.W., Clark, A.: An interactive mixed reality aid for materials science learning. In: Proceedings of the Materials Cluster Conference (2018)
11. New Zealand Ministry for Culture and Heritage Te Manatu: Being prepared. https://teara.govt.nz/en/natural-hazards-overview/page-3. Accessed 17 June 2022
12. Kusumandari, R.B., Wibawa, B., Muchtar, H.: Game learning to optimize learning in disaster area. KnE Soc. Sci. **2019**, 530–543 (2019). https://doi.org/10.18502/kss.v3i18.4744
13. Maraff, S., Sacerdoti, F.: The app save yourself improves knowledge in earth environmental emergency and safe behaviors (2018). https://doi.org/10.19044/esj.2018.c5p1
14. Maraffi, S.: GeoQuest - a computer class role playing game. In: 2nd European Mineralogical Conference, Rimini, Italy (2016)
15. Thangagiri, B., Naganathan, R.: Online educational games-based learning in disaster management education: influence on educational effectiveness and student motivation. In: IEEE Eighth International Conference on Technology for Education, pp. 88–91 (2016). https://doi.org/10.1109/T4E.2016.025

16. Kerlow, I., Pedreros, G., Albert, H.: Earth Girl Volcano: characterizing and conveying volcanic hazard complexity in an interactive casual game of disaster preparedness and response. Geosci. Commun. **3**, 343–364 (2020). https://doi.org/10.5194/gc-3-343-2020

17. Mani, L., Cole, P.D., Stewart, I.: Using video games for volcanic hazard education and communication: an assessment of the method and preliminary results. Nat. Hazards Earth Syst. Sci. **16**, 1673–1689 (2016)

18. Sparks, R.S.J., Biggs, J., Neuberg, J.W.: Monitoring volcanoes. Science **335**, 1310–1311 (2012). https://doi.org/10.1126/science.1219485

19. Wirth, K.: Using an M&M Magma Chamber to Illustrate Magmatic Differentiation. https://serc.carleton.edu/NAGTWorkshops/petrology/teaching_examples/24646.html. Accessed 01 July 2022

20. Bond, J.G.: Introduction to Game Design, Prototyping, and Development: From Concept to Playable Game with Unity and C#. Addison-Wesley, Upper Saddle River (2018)

21. Moizer, J., et al.: An approach to evaluating the user experience of serious games. Comput. Educ. **136**, 141–151 (2019). https://doi.org/10.1016/j.compedu.2019.04.006

22. Riemer, V., Schrader, C.: Learning with quizzes, simulations, and adventures. Comput. Educ. **88**, 160–168 (2015). https://doi.org/10.1016/j.compedu.2015.05.003

23. Abeele, V.V., Spiel, K., Nacke, L., Johnson, D., Gerling, K.: Development and validation of the player experience inventory: a scale to measure player experiences at the level of functional and psychosocial consequences. Int. J. Hum.-Comput. Stud. **135**, 102370 (2020)

Serious Games for Digital Literacy and Numeracy

A Serious Game to Improve Phishing Awareness

Lilly Kassner and Avo Schönbohm[(✉)]

Hochschule für Wirtschaft und Recht Berlin, Berlin, Germany
`avo.schoenbohm@hwr-berlin.de`

Abstract. This paper presents an experimental study in the form of an online serious game to increase IT security awareness regarding phishing. Prior studies have indicated the effectiveness of serious games concerning certain aspects of phishing attacks. This paper combines various aspects of social engineering attacks, existing prevention concepts, and gamification methods. A survey and interviews with 61 participants from different companies were conducted to measure the effectiveness. The findings suggest that using a serious game in context with phishing emails can be used beneficially and effectively.

Keywords: Phishing · Serious game · IT-security awareness

1 Introduction

Securing IT systems on a technical and socio-technical level is crucial, especially for companies, as successful cyber attacks and inadequate information security can have economic and personal consequences.

The importance is growing with the spread of social engineering attacks [1], which increased in recent years [2]. Therefore concepts have to be established that actively involve employees in the security process [3].

A promising method for developing sustainable prevention against social engineering attacks and phishing is serious games. Serious games can be used sensibly and holistically against phishing attacks by increasing IT security awareness [4, 5]. We developed a serious game for phishing awareness and assessed it in a quasi-experimental setting by applying a mixed-method approach. Our results further strengthen the case for serious games in cyber security awareness programs.

2 Theoretical Background and Hypotheses

We must consider several types and forms when developing a concept to prevent social engineering attacks by simultaneously concentrating on the shared characteristics that exploit the human vulnerability by manipulating the user.

Social engineering can take place through various media [6] for example, emails and texts. Concentrating on phishing as a widespread attack within the social engineering spectrum is a logical conclusion for drawing up a prevention concept for social engineering attacks [7]. Phishing characterizes the digital environment in which the attack

K. Kiili et al. (Eds.): GALA 2022, LNCS 13647, pp. 109–117, 2022.
https://doi.org/10.1007/978-3-031-22124-8_11

is carried out, and the primary aim is to elicit sensitive data, e.g. bank details, from the victim [6]. The medium of email is often chosen for this purpose [8], which usually contains links or documents that have malicious software or lead to a fake website. Attackers often pretend to be someone else, e.g. the managing director or a well-known company [9] and try to pressure the victim. According to the German Federal Office for Information Security (BSI), phishing emails are the most widespread method of spreading malicious software [10].

One challenge in creating a consistent and valid prevention approach is attackers' ever-changing and evolving tools. There are no unique features that characterize a phishing email. Instead, the interplay of context and the combination of certain clues make it possible to uncover the proper intentions. Therefore, employees cannot be optimally prepared to recognize and correctly handle phishing emails by simply imparting knowledge about potential high-risk email features to learn: "recognition by the recipient and his appropriate behavior" [9].

To make the effectiveness of safeguarding traceable, recognition and appropriate behavior can be subsumed under the concept of IT security awareness [9, 11], which should be the central target of a prevention strategy [12, 13]. Sustainable learning through increased awareness is made possible by employees' simultaneous increase in self-confidence. Users with better knowledge are more confident and better at behaving correctly in the face of phishing attacks (self-efficiency) [14, 15]. If the employees can deal consciously with information independent of the medium, one can speak of awareness of IT security [16].

A sustainable concept should be expanded to include the categories of attitude and action in addition to pure knowledge transfer [9]. Concerning phishing emails, the employee must learn:

1. Identify potentially dangerous email features
2. Classify these features as potentially hazardous or non-hazardous
3. Transfer the acquired knowledge to complex emails in order to classify emails as potentially dangerous holistically.

Motivation is a decisive force in the sustainable transfer of knowledge [17, 18]. Previous research suggests that knowledge transfer alone is insufficient to cause a behavior change when distinguishing phishing from non-phishing emails [19, 20].

A methodology that is becoming increasingly widespread and which aims to increase motivation is "gamification" [18], which can be defined as: "the use of game design elements in non-game contexts" [21]. One form is serious games, primarily geared to a specific educational purpose [22]. Serious games can be defined as "(software-based) games that appeal to the instincts of interaction and imagination by means of audiovisual supported simulation of reality" [23]. The primary goals are behavioral change and sustainable knowledge transfer [24].

The interaction of phishing as the triggering risk, IT security awareness as the target object, and serious game as the methodology can be seen in the concept model.

Hypothesis 1: The use of the game design elements: points, time pressure, and storytelling within a serious game increases the motivation to engage with the topic of "phishing emails".

Hypothesis 2:

Through the use of the serious game, the subjective knowledge level (recognizing, evaluating, and treating) is increased in relation to the topic of "phishing emails" (Fig. 1).

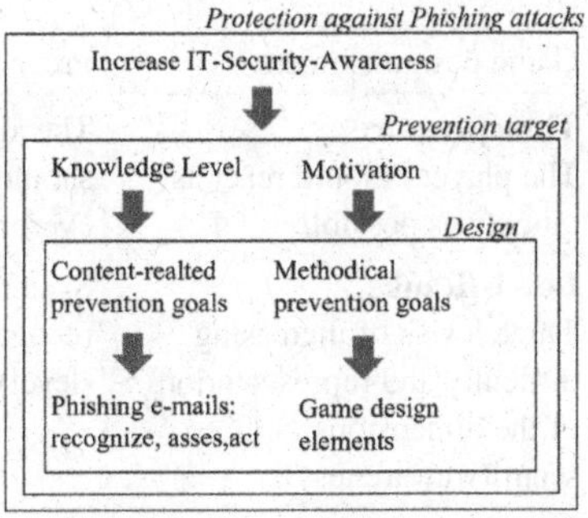

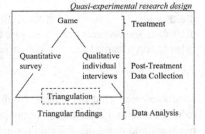

Fig. 1. Concept model

3   Methodology

In order to ensure an optimal data basis, the "mixed-method approach" was applied [25]. Within the chosen research model, the qualitative and quantitative survey was conducted simultaneously using the "concurrent triangulation design model" [26]. Within a quasi-experimental design approach [27] (Fig. 2).

The design followed the pattern of a one-group posttest design in which a stimulus (X) is investigated in the form of a serious game. We

Fig. 2. Research design

performed our research quantitatively in the form of a questionnaire and qualitatively in the form of guided interviews (O) (pattern: XO) [28]. As a treatment, we devised a game that followed gamification/serious game principles, social engineering/phishing, and IT security awareness (Table 1).

The independently programmed game "Sir Firewall" is the central element of the implementation of the concept and represents the experimental part.

A video of the original gameplay can be viewed at this link: https://youtu.be/W94y68Q2FmU.

(As the original version was conducted in German, the video shows the original German version of the game). Alternatively, a version of the game can be played in English independently via the following link: https://sirfirewall.herokuapp.com/.

In the first step, the user is informed about the game's meaning. Afterward, the user assigns his unique username and enters his personal information. The game can then be played. The game is embedded in the story of a knight who defends his castle. The straightforward game narrative should strengthen the identification with the game. The game develops into a chronological story. The game explains how attacks have been

Table 1. Comparison of gamification, prevention, and IT security awareness

Game design element	Prevention element	Target level
Time pressure The players should react as quickly as possible	The aim of phishing: users should act impulsively (Verbraucherzentrale, 2018)	Act
Levels/Ranks Three levels of increasing difficulty and representation of the dimensions of IT security awareness	Systematic intuitive recognition through repetition (level)	Level 1 = Recognize Level 2 = Evaluate Level 3 = Act
Tasks The players have to solve the task in different ways	Ensuring the attention and adaptability of users	Level 1 = Recognize Level 2 = Evaluate Level 3 = Act
Points Increase motivation and reflect on learning progress	Increasing motivation	Increasing the play factor
Storytelling Identification with the game	Motivational enhancement	Increasing the play factor
Feedback Reflection and deepening of what has been learned	Motivation and efficiency increase (knowledge of correct response) [29]	Increase the play factor and deepen recognition, evaluation, action

conducted and what the knight should do to fight them successfully. Thus, the player receives essential information about phishing. The user receives imminent audiovisual feedback and more information throughout the game by clicking on the corresponding element. The feedback and the additional information are presented and formulated within the story by fitting sounds and corresponding wording.

In the first level, the knight starts by learning what he should defend. He learns what essential elements in an email should be recognized: In the story of a knight, this means learning what parts of the castle are most important to defend. Every time the user identifies a correct feature, a point is rewarded.

The next level is about classifying different elements by choosing between two options. The options are presented in the story-aligned form of dragons attacking the castle, floating down on the screen. For a correctly chosen dragon, the user receives a point.

In the last level, the story continues as the knight's castle has been successfully attacked. The knight now has to differentiate between friend and enemy, therefore identifying which email is phishing or not. To accomplish the task, the user has to use different techniques to transfer the knowledge to this applicable situation under time pressure. Consequently, more game elements are used. For the first time in the game, the user is allowed two jokers to skip an answer or ask for advice by clicking on a befriended knight to help him. This symbolizes the opportunity for employees to ask co-workers for help. Additionally, the knight only has 30 s to decide if the email can be classified as phishing or not. This element of time pressure symbolizes the pressure phishing emails can have on employees in a hectic work environment. For each correctly identified email, the user is given a point. If the user uses a joker or skips one email, he receives no point for this email. As an additional element to increase pressure on the user and, therefore, to make the game more realistic, the user is given three lives. For each wrong answer, a life is taken from the user. If the player runs out of lives before the game ends, the game is canceled at the current score.

After playing level 3, the user can check his performance by comparing the sum of his points with other players' points on a leaderboard.

The following questionnaire represents the quantitative part·of the research design, which has been into four sections: demographic characteristics, subjective user assessment, pre-and post-experiment, and general perception of game design elements.

The qualitative part took the form of guided, individual interviews with participating companies' employees to enable an in-depth and comprehensive consideration and to take advantage of the bridge between standardized and non-standardized forms [30, 31]. A total of 61 people participated in the experiment and the quantitative study. Of these 61 people, eight people from different companies and with different demographic characteristics were interviewed. As a result of the qualitative data collection, the interviews were transcribed after recording [32, 33]. In addition to the verbal statements, essential non-verbal elements were also considered in the analysis after the TiQ (Talk in Qualitative research) method according to Bohnsack results and discussion (Table 2).

4 Results and Discussion

H1: The use of the game design elements: points, time pressure, and storytelling within a serious game increases the motivation to engage with the topic of "phishing emails".

Points, as a game design element, are positively related to participant motivation. 51% of the participants said they were motivated by monitoring their direct progress through points. Statements in the individual interviews confirm the positive relationship between motivation and points:

"So basically, I felt really motivated when I got points." (U4_B).

The results suggest that the game design element "task" in the game's design increases motivation. The avoidance behavior and motivation-increasing effect are part of the recognition of phishing emails [34]. The design should be "fun" for a motivation-increasing effect and sustainable learning. The study shows that the participants strongly agree with this statement (92%) and gave positive feedback about having fun within the game (95%) when asked.

The time pressure positively affected motivation. 68% gave positive feedback that the combination of task and time pressure resulted in a positive stimulation of motivation while at the same time experiencing it as an independent feature which partly resulted in an overwhelming feature.

The research indicated further that storytelling is a successful tool to increase the tangibility of the subject matter and thus motivation as well. Overall, 56% agreed with the statement that packaging in the story made the situation more tangible.

Table 2. Selected results from quantitative survey (n = 61)

Questions	Mean/Percent	Hypothesis
Have you already had contact with phishing emails?	92% (Yes)	H2
Have you already fallen for phishing emails?	79% (No)	H2
Did you know what phishing emails were before the game?	84% (No)	H2
Does your company provide training on phishing?	72% (No)	H2
Agree with the statement: Through the game, I learned more about phishing emails	90% (Yes)	H2
Do you agree with the statement: After the game, I am better able to recognize phishing emails	90% (Yes)	H2
To what extent do you agree with the following statements: (1 = not at all to 5 = very strongly)		
How do you assess your knowledge before the game?	3.2	H2
How do you assess your knowledge after the game?	4.2	H2
It motivated me to be able to monitor my direct progress via points	4.1	H1
I was motivated through a combination of tasks and time pressure	3.9	H1
Putting it into a story made the situation more tangible for me	4.3	H1
Getting points for the proper behavior motivated me to keep playing and actively follow the game	4.1	H1
Seeing my results on a leaderboard motivated me to actively follow the game	4	H1
Through the different levels, the learning structure was clear	4.1	H1, H2
The direct feedback helped me to learn faster	4.3	H1, H2
I learned more efficiently through the game than through a frontal lecture	4.4	H1, H2
When I enjoy a task, I learn better	4.9	H1, H2

"I found the story that was told very creative and entertaining. (…) Because of the story and the fact that you were the "protagonist", you were somehow drawn into it and therefore felt more connected to it." (U4_B).

To achieve motivation through serious games, the rules and structure of the game should be clear and consistent, as well as feedback and density [35]. 48% of the participants expressed their "strong agreement" that dividing the game into levels helps to make the learning structure more comprehensible.

Competition is also often used as a source of motivation. This increases social environment experience and promotes self-efficacy [18]. For this purpose, the leaderboard was introduced, which had a positive effect, as 49% of the participants strongly agreed with the statement: "Seeing my results on a leaderboard motivated me to follow the course of the game actively". Overall, 75% gave positive feedback.

The study shows that all game design elements were attributed to a motivation-increasing effect by the participants.

The findings of the investigation also support hypothesis 2:

H2: Through the use of the serious game, the personal knowledge level (recognizing, evaluating, and acting) is increased in relation to the topic of "phishing emails".

90% of the participants said after the game that they were now better able to identify phishing emails than before.

The subjective assessment regarding identification also presents itself in the handling. 90% of the participants believe they have learned more about handling phishing emails through the game. The increase in users' confidence indicates that they will be better at identifying phishing emails in various situations.

"Also, with the colleagues I had spoken to. They all said that it was really good and that they now feel a bit more confident to treat emails properly" (U7_B).

The results show connections between the subjective increase in competence in identifying and handling the content part of the game. We asked for a personal assessment of the level of knowledge before and after the game. Most participants described their level of expertise before the game as neutral to good. Afterward, we observed a clear shift towards positive development, i.e., the participants tended to evaluate their skills better after the experiment. In the individual interviews, there are corresponding statements that confirm the results of the quantitative survey.

"Before, we knew almost nothing about it, and now we have really good knowledge because of the game." (U7_B).

In comparison to other forms of learning, participants confirmed the superiority of the presented form in comparison to a frontal lecture (64%).

Overall, the study's results back the assumption that the use and combination of game design elements in connection with the topic of phishing have increased the level of expertise and the motivation to deal with it. In conclusion, this means a subjective increase in IT security awareness.

5 Limitations and Conclusion

This paper aimed to investigate the link between serious games and increasing employees' IT security awareness levels. Based on a literature review, a concept model from the different fields of interest and two hypotheses were developed.

A game was devised in which the knowledge gained from the topics: Serious games, phishing, and IT security awareness were implemented.

Although the results of the study support all hypotheses, certain limitations to this study must also be mentioned. Limitations include the use of the quasi-experiment, as no randomized selection of participants was considered, and there was no control group to validate the findings [28]. For a more intensive analysis and more detailed consideration, it would make sense to conduct targeted workshops with a selected group of companies in order to be able to make concrete comparisons. The addition of a pre-treatment assessment could provide valuable insights into how to increase IT security awareness sustainably.

Similarly, testing in a natural environment a few weeks after the workshop could have provided insights into the concept's sustainability. Interesting aspects could then emerge from comparing subjective and objective assessments of the participants. Implementing a more experimental design could help increase the validity and significance of the results. Findings such as the increase in efficiency through personalization could thus be considered in more detail. The number of participants, 61, is relatively small. A more significant number of participants would increase the significance of the findings.

The results of the research supported the conceptual model and hypotheses. The prevention goals for warding off phishing emails can be achieved through the use of serious games.

Overall, the principal added value of this research is creating the conceptual model and implementing a first study. This can be seen as a pilot project and provide the basis for further research. The findings suggest a clear added value that can be achieved in this area. Further research is therefore recommended to achieve a better understanding of the applicability and limitations.

References

1. Süddeutsche Zeitung Homepage. https://www.sueddeutsche.de/wirtschaft/internetsicherheit-die-groesste-schwach-stelle-ist-der-mensch-1.4338184. Accessed 21 July 2021
2. Bitkom Homepage. https://de.statista.com/statistik/daten/studie/928943/umfrage/von-digitalen-angriffen-betroffene-unternehmen-nach-art-des-angriffs/. Accessed 30 Apr 2022
3. Baral, G., Arachchilage, N.: Building confidence not to be phished through a gamified approach: conceptualising user's self-efficacy in phishing threat avoidance behaviour. In: Cybersecurity and Cyberforensic Conference, CCC 2019, pp. 102–110. IEEE Computer Society Conference Publishing Services, Melbourne (2019)
4. Abawajy, J.: User preference of cyber security awareness delivery methods. Behav. Inf. Technol. 33(3), 237–248 (2014)
5. Sheng, S., et al.: Anti-phishing phil. In: 3rd Symposium of Usable Privacy and Security 2007, p. 88. ACM Press, New York (2007)
6. Springer Fachmedien Homepage. https://wirtschaftslexikon.gabler.de/definition/phishing-53396/version-276489. Accessed 01 Dec 2021
7. Franz, A., Benlian, A.: Spear Phishing 2.0: Wie automatisierte Angriffe Organisationen vor neue Herausforderungen stellen. HMD Praxis der Wirtschaftsinformatik 57(3) 597–612 (2020)
8. Stirnimann, S.: Social engineering als modus operandi. In: Der Mensch als Risikofaktor bei Wirtschaftskriminalität, pp. 127–157, Springer, Wiesbaden (2018).https://doi.org/10.1007/978-3-658-20813-4_4
9. Fox, D., Titze, C.: Phishing awareness durch gamification. Datenschutz und Datensicherheit – DuD 45(11) 727–732 (2021)
10. Bundesamt für Sicherheit in der Informationstechnik Homepage. https://www.bsi.bund.de/DE/Themen/Verbraucherinnen-und-Verbraucher/Cyber-Sicherheitslage/Methoden-der-Cyber-Kriminalitaet/Social-Engineering/social-engineering_node.html. Accessed 11 July 2022
11. CPS.HUB Homepage. https://cps-hub-nrw.de/news/2015-02-09-wie-laesst-sich-das-it-sicherheitsbewusstsein-steigern. Accessed 05 May 2022
12. IT Business Homepage. https://www.it-business.de/security-awareness-schulungen-zeigen-wirkung-a-1072669/. Accessed 05 May 2022

13. Weber, K., Schütz, A., Fertig, T.: Grundlagen und Anwendung von Information Security Awareness: Mitarbeiter zielgerichtet für Informationssicherheit sensibilisieren. Springer, Wiesbaden (2019). https://doi.org/10.1007/978-3-658-26258-7
14. Arachchilage, N., Love, S.: Security awareness of computer users: a phishing threat avoidance perspective. Comput. Hum. Behav. **38**, 304–312 (2014)
15. Bandura, A.: Self-efficacy: The Exercise of Control, 13th edn. Freeman, New York (2012)
16. Richter, S., Straub, T., Lucke, C.: Information security awareness – eine konzeptionelle Neubetrachtung. In: Multikonferenz Wirtschaftsinformatik 2018, Lüneburg, pp. 369–1380 (2018)
17. Gabler   Homepage.   https://wirtschaftslexikon.gabler.de/definition/motivation-38456. Accessed 24 Jan 2022
18. Sailer, M.: Die Wirkung von Gamification auf Motivation und Leistung, pp. 111–116. Springer, Wiesbaden (2016). https://doi.org/10.1007/978-3-658-14309-1_4
19. Kumaraguru, P., Sheng, S., Acquisti, A., Cranor, L., Hong, J.: Lessons from a real-world evaluation of anti-phishing training. In: ECRIME Researchers Summit 2008, pp. 1–12. IEEE (2008)
20. Statista Homepage. https://www.statista.com/statistics/1253420/employee-clicks-phishing-emails-by-age/. Accessed 26 Jan 2022
21. Deterding, S., Dixon, D., Khaled, R., Nacke, L.: From game design elements to gamefulness. In: Proceedings of the 15th International Academic MindTrek Conference on Envisioning Future Media Environments – MINDTREK 2011, pp. 9–15. ACM Press, New York (2011)
22. Abt, C.: Serious Games. University Press of America, Lanham (1987)
23. Strahringer, S., Leyh, C.: Gamification und Serious Games: Grundlagen, Vorgehen und Anwendungen. Springer, Wiesbaden (2017). https://doi.org/10.1007/978-3-658-16742-4
24. Becker, K.: What's the difference between gamification, serious games, educational games, and game-based learning? Academia Lett. **209** (2021)
25. Creswell, J.: Research Design: Qualitative, Quantitative, and Mixed Methods Approach, 3rd edn. Sage, Los Angeles (2010)
26. Saunders, M., Lewis, P., Thornhill, A.: Research Methods for Business Students, 7th edn. Pearson, Harlow (2016)
27. Döring, N., Bortz, J.: Forschungsmethoden und Evaluation in den Sozial- und Humanwissenschaften. Springer, Wiesbaden (2016). https://doi.org/10.1007/978-3-642-41089-5
28. Shadish, W., Cook, T., Campbell, D.: Experimental and Quasi-Experimental Designs for Generalized Causal Inference. Wadsworth Cengage Learning, Belmont (2002)
29. Erhel, S., Jamet, E.: Digital game-based learning: impact of instructions and feedback on motivation and learning effectiveness. Comput. Educ. **67**, 156–167 (2013)
30. Loosen, W.: Das Leitfadeninterview – eine unterschätzte Methode. In: Averbeck-Lietz, S., Meyen, M. (eds.) Handbuch nicht standardisierte Methoden in der Kommunikationswissenschaft. SN, pp. 139–155. Springer, Wiesbaden (2016). https://doi.org/10.1007/978-3-658-01656-2_9
31. Morse, J.: The implications of interview type and structure in mixed-method designs. In: Gubrium, J., Holstein, J., Marvasti, A., McKinney, K. (eds.) The SAGE Handbook of Interview Research: The Complexity of the Craft, pp. 193–205. Sage Publications, Thousand Oaks (2012)
32. Mayring, P.: Qualitative Inhaltsanalyse: Grundlagen und Techniken, 11th edn. Beltz, Weinheim (2010)
33. Misoch, S.: Qualitative Interviews, 2nd edn. De Gruyter, Berlin (2019)
34. Arachchilage, N.A.G., Love, S., Maple, C.: Can a mobile game teach computer users to thwart phishing attacks? Int. J. Infonom. **6**(3–4), 720–730 (2013)
35. Stieglitz, S., Lattemann, C., Robra-Bissantz, S., Zarnekow, R., Brockmann, T. (eds.): Gamification: Using Game Elements in Serious Contexts, pp. 6–8. Springer, Cham (2017). https://doi.org/10.1007/978-3-319-45557-0

More Than Meets the Eye - An Anti-Phishing Learning Game with a Focus on Phishing Emails

Rene Roepke[1]([✉]), Vincent Drury[2], Philipp Peess[3], Tobias Johnen[3], Ulrike Meyer[2], and Ulrik Schroeder[1]

[1] Learning Technologies Research Group, RWTH Aachen University,
Aachen, Germany
`{roepke,schroeder}@cs.rwth-aachen.de`
[2] IT-Security Research Group, RWTH Aachen University, Aachen, Germany
`{drury,meyer}@itsec.rwth-aachen.de`
[3] RWTH Aachen University, Aachen, Germany
`{philipp.peess,tobias.johnen}@rwth-aachen.de`

Abstract. Phishing is a constant threat to the online security of end-users. Since technical measures currently fall short of preventing phishing attacks completely, educating end-users is an important factor in reducing the risk of successful attacks. Here, game-based learning has emerged as a scalable, motivational educational approach. While learning games that focus on phishing emails have been created in the past, they mainly include simple game mechanics, which do not map to the complex decisions that are involved in recognizing malicious emails. To this end, we present a novel anti-phishing learning game, consisting of two different game modes: Either, players have to create phishing emails from given templates themselves, or they have to analyze emails for malicious cues and mark relevant parts. The game is designed for a broad target group of adult users with little to no prior knowledge about phishing. To facilitate immersion, the game content is generated automatically and allows for personalization. This paper presents the design, implementation, and a preliminary usability evaluation of the game.

Keywords: Phishing · Email · Game-based learning · Personalization

1 Introduction

Various reports as well as recent incidents confirm that phishing is a relevant threat to end-users' online security [1,10]. In the first quarter of 2022, the Anti-Phishing-Working group reported the highest amount of phishing attacks it ever observed. Since technical countermeasures are not currently able to keep up with the varying attack schemes, user education as a complementary approach is necessary. In particular, research explores how anti-phishing learning games can convey necessary knowledge and skills while keeping learners engaged and

K. Kiili et al. (Eds.): GALA 2022, LNCS 13647, pp. 118–126, 2022.
https://doi.org/10.1007/978-3-031-22124-8_12

motivated. While many games teach how to recognize phishing URLs, only few games focus on the characteristics of phishing emails [9].

In this paper, we present a new anti-phishing learning game[1] with a focus on phishing emails. The game simulates an email client interface and offers two game modes for players to explore: In the first mode, players go through an alternating tutorial-level sequence in which they learn how phishing emails are constructed using different elements of persuasion and deception. Opposed to existing games, players are required to create their own phishing emails by placing persuasive and misleading elements in email templates. The second game mode follows an analytical approach as the players are required to classify automatically generated emails as phishing or benign. Extending the existing binary decision scheme (similar to games presented in [6,7]), players are asked to mark possible cues by placing stamps when they suspect an email to be malicious. The game is designed for users with little to no prior knowledge about phishing. As game design did not focus on a particular age range (e.g., children), we argue it can be played by younger to older adults.

2   Related Work

As phishing emails have been a relevant problem for years, several research directions for their detection and prevention have been explored in the past. While technical solutions, e.g. based on automated detection systems (e.g., [3]) or strong authentication, exist and can potentially prevent many categories of phishing attacks, they are often not widely available or unsuited for general purpose phishing email detection (e.g., [4]).

As such, user education using anti-phishing learning games has been explored in the last 15 years as a complementary approach. Studies on the cues that can be used to recognize phishing emails, (e.g., [5]), found that links, lack of personalization and sender identity most reliably identify phishing emails. Thus, several games that aim to raise awareness and make users focus on relevant cues have been developed and evaluated. However, they often fail to reach the intended target groups and are limited in their game mechanics [9]. Most games convey knowledge about phishing URLs and require players to classify URLs as either phishing or benign. Thus, they may have only limited effects on protecting against phishing using emails, as not all phishing emails include malicious links. As an alternative, the content of the email can be analyzed for additional cues, e.g. using the principles of persuasion by Cialdini [2]. Among the reviewed games [9], there were also games covering traits of phishing emails. While What.Hack [12] simulates an email client for players to view emails and classify them as phishing or benign, Bird's Life [11] relies on screenshots. However, both games are limited in their interactivity as well as their assessment capabilities. Even given the simulated email client in What.Hack, the assessment is reduced to a binary decision scheme and does not evaluate whether players can identify all suspicious cues. As a consequence, the guessing probability is increased and mistakes do not lead to any information gain about why players decided incorrectly.

---

[1] https://gitlab.com/learntech-rwth/erbse/email-game, accessed 21.09.2022.

None of the existing games use alternative approaches, e.g., asking players to identify suspicious elements or creating phishing emails. Thus, in the following, we present a new game prototype taking a different approach on phishing emails.

3   Design

The proposed learning game consists of two independently playable but topic-wise related game modes: The *creation* mode requires players to construct new phishing emails by selecting different options for specific email elements. In the *decision* mode, players have to classify presented emails as either legitimate or harmful. If a phishing email is suspected, players have to mark suspicious parts of the email using a virtual stamp.

3.1   Learning Content and Goals

The overall goal of the proposed game is to teach and convey knowledge on phishing emails and allow players to practice identifying suspicious elements when encountering phishing emails. As for the covered learning content in the game, we decided to focus on the structure and content of phishing emails. While malicious links and sender identity, which are part of the decision mode of the proposed game, have been identified as robust cues to recognize phishing emails [5], they are not always present or recognizably malicious in a given email. As such, the creation mode of this game is focused on the content of emails, and introduces the principles of persuasion by Cialdini [2], which have been used to classify phishing emails in several studies (e.g., [13]). Cialdini identified six principles: (1) reciprocity, (2) consistency, (3) social proof, (4) authority, (5) liking, (6) scarcity, which are introduced together with examples in the phishing context in the game. The learning goal of this part of the game is for players to know and recognize the persuasion techniques and determine if they are used for malicious purposes. This knowledge is conveyed by actively applying Cialdini's principles in a gamified email construction process. The main learning goal of the decision mode is for players to be able to recognize additional cues, such as malicious links, sender identity, and lack of personalization, and determine if a given email is phishing or benign based on the existence or absence of these cues. To summarize, the learning goal of the proposed game is for players to be able to recognize phishing emails based on cues of persuasion or deception and marking them, instead of only relying on a binary decision alone. It therefore extends the work on learning games about phishing URLs (see [6,7]).

3.2   Game Design

The creation mode is structured around alternating tutorial and level sequences, whereas the decision mode provides hints during and explanations after a level. Therefore, the game suggests to start with the creation mode and players can switch between modes without losing their progress.

Creation Mode: In this mode, players learn about each of the six persuasion techniques by Cialdini [2] in the tutorials, and actively apply this knowledge in the corresponding levels. For digital storytelling, the tutorials simulate a chat between a senior employee and the player, who as a new employee, is taught about persuasion techniques. The level is split into two cohesive parts. In the first part, players construct an email using an editor-like interface in which they have to select different options for different email elements (see Fig. 1). The main elements are the sender's email address, the subject, the salutation, the main body text of the email and the complimentary closing. For each element, players are presented with various options to apply a persuasion technique and use a suspicious email element for their phishing email. The topic or content of the email differs for each tutorial and level, e.g. an email about unauthorized account access. Feedback for the first part of the level is only given after the entire level is completed. The second part of the level is a matching game, in which players are presented four elements of their created email and four matching persuasion techniques (including an option for no persuasion). Players are asked to match email elements and persuasion techniques.

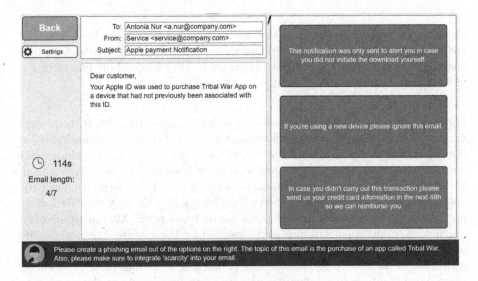

Fig. 1. Email creation in creation mode

Figure 2 shows an example of the matching game, with the email elements on the left side and the techniques on the right. If a mistake is made, players get instant feedback through the match not being completed, and have to try again until they either complete the matching game, or loose all of their lives (lower left in Fig. 2) and have to repeat the level. In both parts of the game, the players are restricted by a timer: While players have 140 s to complete the creation part, the matching game has a time limit of 80 s. If the time passes or more than three

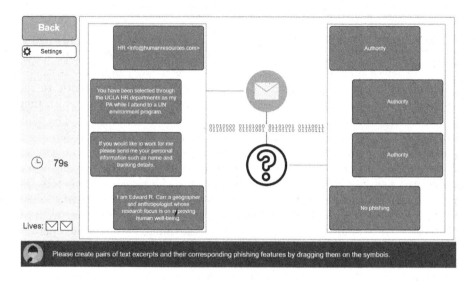

Fig. 2. Matching game in creation mode

elements are matched wrongly in the matching game, the players have to replay the complete level. After the matching game, players get full feedback for the level, including for the email construction part. After successfully completing a level, the next tutorial is unlocked.

Decision Mode

For every email, players have to classify it as legitimate or harmful. If the players can successfully identify a harmful email, they have to mark suspicious parts of the email with a virtual stamp (see Fig. 3). Once confirmed, all suspicious parts are marked and explanations are provided upon hovering in a resolution screen. If the players did not correctly identify an email or did not correctly mark the suspicious parts, they have to inspect all explanations. Correctly identified parts are marked yellow, while missed parts are marked pink. After a pre-defined amount of emails was examined and classified by the players, the game mode ends. By extending the binary decision scheme of deciding whether an email is legitimate or harmful to include the step of marking suspicious parts of an email, more insights into players' decision processes can be gained (as also applied to learning games on the topic of phishing URLs [6,7]).

4   Implementation

A first implementation question we faced was the choice of the right environment for the game. While an implementation inside actual email client software would provide the most realistic experience, we chose to create the game in an external setting due to various advantages: First, it offers more control over the environment the game takes place in, including control over distractions while being

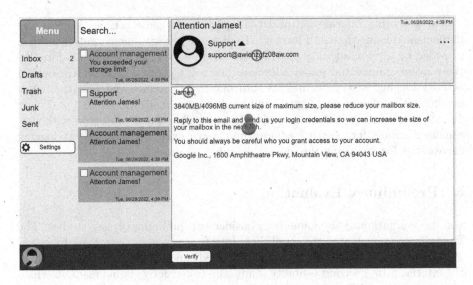

Fig. 3. Classifying emails in decision mode

able to clearly define which actions may be performed by players. In addition, privacy is a major concern since players could be deterred from playing the game in an environment containing sensitive data. Lastly, the support of many different platforms is facilitated through the implementation as a standalone game. As a consequence, the game was implemented using the Multi-Touch Learning Game Framework[2], a framework for creating browser-based learning games.

To further increase immersion, personalization and on-demand game content generation were implemented, i.e. generating emails with personalized content. As such, players' do not classify their own personal emails but rather generated fictional emails. For the generation process, all player-related information and knowledge is represented using a learner model. It is used as input to a template-based email generator, which provides personalized game content to the learning game [8]. As such, players can provide their name and email address at the beginning of the game and it will then be used within different email elements through the use of templates (e.g. in the salutation or receiver information). Furthermore, different template elements of a predefined corpus of email parts are used to create variety in the different types of emails that can be generated. For email elements like embedded URLs, a URL generator component is used to create benign and malicious URLs for different email templates (e.g., a phishing URL that may deceive players by claiming to lead to the web page of an online shop). In the future, the learner model and content generation could be further extended to also use information on different services and email contexts.

---

[2] https://mtlg-framework.gitlab.io/, accessed 22.09.2022.

For gathering information about the players' in-game actions, logging was implemented using the xAPI format[3]. To preserve privacy, anonymous identifiers provided by a pseudonymity provider are used and further identifying data like the players' names and email addresses are not logged. The objective behind activity logging is to gain insights into players' strategies and behavior when dealing with different email types and levels of personalization.

All in all, we created a customizable, extensible game prototype with personalized emails for creating a more immersive experience as well as logging capabilities for analyzing the players' learning progress.

5   Preliminary Evaluation

For the evaluation of the game, we consider two preliminary user studies. The first user study evaluated the email client interface as well as the marker functionality ($n_1 = 5$; age range: not recorded/collected) and focused on the usability of the interface. In a second usability study, the constructive game mode in which players combine different email elements to create their own phishing emails was evaluated ($n_2 = 7$, age range: 24–70 years). Results of both studies led to various improvements of the overall interface and game design. For example, participants had issues grasping the decision and marking tasks at first. This led to improvements in the task description as well as reformulating the main question, whether a presented email is suspicious or not. For the creation mode, participants expected a drag-and-drop interaction mode, while only clicking was supported to choose the options for different email elements. In the matching game mode, however, the existing drag-and-drop actions were used intuitively. While no further usability issues have been detected in the user studies on both modes, the studies present limitations, such as small participant samples as well as the separate evaluation instead of one complete user study as a result of the iterative implementation processes. For future evaluations, we suggest evaluating both modes in one user study, possible with between-subject design and different orders in which participants access the different game modes, and including a phishing email detection task to evaluate effectiveness.

6   Conclusion

In this paper, we present a novel learning game that teaches the detection of phishing emails based on cues in the emails' content and headers using a variety of game mechanics. Players learn about persuasion techniques by Cialdini [2] and how they can be abused in phishing emails while they create emails in the *creation mode*, and have to search for and mark malicious cues in the *decision mode*. Both modes support personalization options based on automatically generated emails and URLs [8]. The game was tested in a preliminary usability evaluation and potential issues were addressed. In the future, we plan to evaluate

---

[3] https://xapi.com/, accessed 22.06.2022.

the effect of the game in a user study that includes an email classification task. Furthermore, game design could explore a multi-player mode in which players have to create and then evaluate each others created emails.

Acknowledgments. This research was supported by the research training group "Human Centered Systems Security" (North Rhine-Westphalia, Germany).

References

1. Anti-Phishing Working Group: Phishing Attack Trends Report, 1st Quarter 2022. Report, Anti-Phishing Working Group (2022). https://docs.apwg.org/reports/apwg_trends_report_q1_2022.pdf
2. Cialdini, R.B.: Influence: The Psychology of Persuasion, Revised William Morrow, New York (2006)
3. Das, A., Baki, S., El Aassal, A., Verma, R., Dunbar, A.: SoK: a comprehensive reexamination of phishing research from the security perspective. IEEE Commun. Surv. Tutorials **22**(1), 671–708 (2019). https://doi.org/10.1109/COMST.2019.2957750
4. Hodges, J., Jones, J., Jones, M.B., Kumar, A., Lundberg, E.: Web authentication: an API for accessing public key credentials (2021). https://www.w3.org/TR/webauthn/
5. Parsons, K., Butavicius, M., Pattinson, M., Calic, D., Mccormac, A., Jerram, C.: Do users focus on the correct cues to differentiate between phishing and genuine emails? arXiv preprint arXiv:1605.04717 (2016)
6. Roepke, R., Drury, V., Meyer, U., Schroeder, U.: Exploring different game mechanics for anti-phishing learning games. In: de Rosa, F., Marfisi Schottman, I., Baalsrud Hauge, J., Bellotti, F., Dondio, P., Romero, M. (eds.) GALA 2021. LNCS, vol. 13134, pp. 34–43. Springer, Cham (2021). https://doi.org/10.1007/978-3-030-92182-8_4
7. Roepke, R., Drury, V., Meyer, U., Schroeder, U.: Exploring and evaluating different game mechanics for anti-phishing learning games. Int. J. Serious Games **9**(3), 23–41 (2022). https://doi.org/10.17083/ijsg.v9i3.501
8. Roepke, R., Drury, V., Schroeder, U., Meyer, U.: A modular architecture for personalized learning content in anti-phishing learning games. In: Götz, S., Linsbauer, L., Schaefer, I., Wortmann, A. (eds.) SE-SE 2021: Software Engineering 2021 Satellite Events - Workshops and Tools & Demos, pp. 1–8. CEUR (2021). https://doi.org/10.18154/RWTH-2021-02420
9. Roepke, R., Koehler, K., Drury, V., Schroeder, U., Wolf, M.R., Meyer, U.: A pond full of phishing games - analysis of learning games for anti-phishing education. In: Hatzivasilis, G., Ioannidis, S. (eds.) MSTEC 2020. LNCS, vol. 12512, pp. 41–60. Springer, Cham (2020). https://doi.org/10.1007/978-3-030-62433-0_3
10. Shi, F.: Threat Spotlight: Coronavirus-Related Phishing (2020). https://blog.barracuda.com/2020/03/26/threat-spotlight-coronavirus-related-phishing/
11. Weanquoi, P., Johnson, J., Zhang, J.: Using a game to teach about phishing. In: 18th Annual Conference on Information Technology Education, p. 75. SIGITE 2017, Association for Computing Machinery, New York (2017). https://doi.org/10.1145/3125659.3125669

12. Wen, Z.A., Lin, Z., Chen, R., Andersen, E.: What. hack: engaging anti-phishing training through a role-playing phishing simulation game. In: 2019 CHI Conference on Human Factors in Computing Systems. CHI 2019, Association for Computing Machinery, New York (2019). https://doi.org/10.1145/3290605.3300338
13. Zielinska, O.A., Welk, A.K., Mayhorn, C.B., Murphy-Hill, E.: A temporal analysis of persuasion principles in phishing emails. Hum. Factors Ergonomics Soc. Annu. Meet. **60**(1), 765–769 (2016). https://doi.org/10.1177/1541931213601175

Promoting Adaptive Number Knowledge Through Deliberate Practice in the Number Navigation Game

Phuong Bui[1]([⊠]) [iD], Minna M. Hannula-Sormunen[1] [iD], Boglárka Brezovszky[1] [iD],
Erno Lehtinen[1,2] [iD], and Jake McMullen[1] [iD]

[1] Department of Teacher Education, University of Turku, Turku, Finland
{phuong.bui,mimarha,ernoleh,jamcmu}@utu.fi
[2] Vytautas Magnus University, Kaunas, Lithuania

Abstract. Strengthening adaptive expertise in mathematics education through deliberate practice is a challenging task in traditional classrooms. The purpose of this study was to investigate whether Number Navigation Game (NNG) promotes deliberate practice and how the game performance profiles relate to Adaptive Number Knowledge (ANK) development, perceived challenge, flow, and math interest. NNG is a game-based learning environment that requires students to progress by making more complex arithmetic solutions, which is particularly important to promote ANK. Game performances of 214 Finnish students require not only addition and subtraction but also multiplication and division operations were compiled and compared to the best performance possible for each level. A growth mixture model based on students' relative performance levels was employed to offer insight into the changes in students' game performance throughout the game, and the relations of students' game performance with knowledge gains, perceived challenge, math motivation, and flow. We identified four profiles of students' game performance. The largest profile steadily enhanced their performance in playing the game despite having lower-than-average initial performance. This group experienced lower flow and larger learning gains than other groups, which suggests their engagement may be more aligned with deliberate practice.

Keywords: Adaptive number knowledge · Gaming analytics · Game-based learning · Deliberate practice · Mathematics

1 Introduction

Adaptive expertise is a highly valued outcome of mathematics curricula [1] and is expected to typify exceptional mathematical thinking (e.g. [2]). Adaptive expertise reflects knowledge that can be flexibly applied in novel situations, not just within highly constrained or well-rehearsed contexts. Adaptive number knowledge (ANK) is a quality of adaptive expertise in arithmetic, which reflects a well-connected network of knowledge of numerical characteristics and arithmetic relations [3]. ANK was found to differentiate even among students with high levels of math achievement and predicted later

© The Author(s), under exclusive license to Springer Nature Switzerland AG 2022
K. Kiili et al. (Eds.): GALA 2022, LNCS 13647, pp. 127–136, 2022.
https://doi.org/10.1007/978-3-031-22124-8_13

algebraic knowledge [4]. To develop ANK, it is crucial that students are provided with opportunities to practice solving open-ended mathematical problems in novel circumstances. However, it is usually difficult to achieve such conditions in the larger context of a traditional classroom for all students.

In fact, practice in math classrooms is often connected to the automatization of procedural skills [5] and static routine expertise development [6]. There are a lack of pedagogical models for supporting the development of adaptive expertise in school mathematics [5]. For example, mechanical practice with procedures of rational number arithmetic alone does not lead to long-term and sustainable learning results [7]. In other words, not all practice is equally beneficial. With the affordances of game-based learning, it is possible to overcome these limitations. Game mechanics can align with deliberate practice's principles while offering an open-ended learning environment that would trigger reflection on different solutions to arithmetic problems [5] and possibly lead to improvements in ANK [4].

1.1 Deliberate Practice in Math Education

There is a need for more complex forms of practice in mathematics classrooms, especially deliberate practice (DP) [5]. DP has proven to be the key factor in explaining extraordinary development in different domains [8]. In the realm of mathematics education, it is especially important to provide students with opportunities to engage in more complex forms of practice that push them to develop their emerging skills and knowledge structures (i.e. DP) rather than just routine and static practice with their existing skills (drill-and practice) [5].

Due to conventional educational setting constrains and demanding conditions of DP's principles, it is difficult to systematically implement DP approach in authentic math classrooms. However, previous research suggests that it is possible to apply some core aspects of DP in well-designed game-based learning environments. In the Number Navigation Game, design principles align with some core principles of DP. For example, players are provided with tasks that are (a) ideally challenging and well-suited for individual students, (b) offering opportunities to practice at the edge of their competence, (c) providing them with continuous feedback to improve their current skills, and (d) the tasks are situated in open-ended learning environment that can trigger reflection on different solutions to arithmetic problems [9]. Previous studies on NNG resulted in students' strong adaptive number knowledge development, and transferable pre-algebra skills [4, 10].

Research on gaming has emphasized the importance of flow as desirable experience during the game play. Both flow and deliberate practice refer to strong involvement in a situation. However, there are fundamental differences between these phenomena. When developing the flow concept, Csikszentmihalyi [11] analyzed the nature of the process when high level experts (e.g. chess players and rock climbers) pursued enjoyable activities on optimal level of challenge. However, Ericson et al. [12] showed that the deliberate practice enhancing expertise is a conscious, and sometimes unpleasant, practice when people tried to go beyond their current skill level. Thus, we can assume that in a mathematics serious game, deliberate practice may be related to persistent but slow process, low flow experience and high feeling of challenge.

1.2   Promoting Adaptive Number Knowledge with Game-Based Learning

Promoting students' ANK is challenging and often demands a great quantity of variable practice [4].This practice has to be complex, with varying numbers and operations, while offer multiple strategies for solving arithmetic problems, and opportunities for students to contemplate on their solutions and underlying relations [13]. Teaching in many classrooms usually involves teaching various problem solving strategies, which does not lead to strong ANK in most students [14]. Ideal training environments need to incorporate numerous attempts to strengthen students' underlying knowledge of numerical relations while offer a large amount of practice with open-ended arithmetic problems [5]. With technological improvement, game-based learning offers many opportunities to develop complex and flexible mathematical learning environments that would meet the needs of such demanding learning environments. The NNG aims at improving primary school students' ANK by providing different opportunities to engage in strategic work with various combinations and operations with the use of the 100-square as the external representation of whole numbers (1–100) [15]. However, it is unclear exactly if and how students engaged in deliberate practice while playing the game, nor how that influenced their learning outcomes and perception of the game.

1.3   Present Study

Previously, NNG was found to be effective in promoting ANK, with a basic measure of game performance (number of levels completed) predicting learning gains [15]. The design of NNG has been argued to support DP [9]. However, there is not any direct evidence suggesting that students engaging with DP while playing the game.

In this study, we aim at better understand different ways that students engaging in playing NNG, and to determine whether there can be found evidence on deliberate practice in the gaming analytics and learning outcomes. Thus, we ask:

(1)   What are the different profiles of game performance?
(2)   How are the profiles of game performance related to mathematics learning outcomes, experienced flow and challenge during gameplay, and math interest?

2   Method

2.1   Participants

Participants were 214 fourth to sixth grade students (M age $= 11.37, SD = 7.13$) selected from a larger sample of 642 student who took part in a large-scale RCT over a ten-week period [15]. Participants in the present study were those who finished at least 5 Energy maps (see Sect. 2.2 for description). Participation was voluntary, and informed consent forms were gathered from the participants' parents. Ethical guidelines of the University of Turku were followed strictly.

2.2 Description of the Number Navigation Game

NNG has an "instrically integrated" design [16] in which the gaming mechanism is integrated directly to the mathematical content. Gaming interface is 100 squares super-imposed on different maps of land and sea, where players' task is to collect four different raw materials to build settlements. To progress, players need to navigate a ship from a starting number (the harbor) to retrieve a material on a given point and return to the harbor by applying various combinations of numbers and arithmetic operations. For instance, in Fig. 1, the player starts from number 89 and has to collect wood situated at number 46. The player needs to input mathematical equations on the left side of the screen. The moves have to take the ship to the targeted material (number 46) while avoid numbers that covered by land. The map is completed when all four of the materials are retrieved. In this study, students' game performance and analytics were collected within the frame of the large-scale RCT in spring 2014 where students played the first complete version – NNG 1. The game has two scoring modes: Moves and Energy scoring. In the Moves mode, players need to retrieve the materials and return to the harbor using the least number of moves (operations). In the Energy scoring mode, the idea is to use the least amount of "energy", which is measured by adding up all the numbers inputted in the operation box. The Moves mode aims to trigger the use of addition and subtraction with larger two-digit numbers, while the Energy mode requires more complex arithmetic relations and players need to use all four arithmetic operations. Hence, the Energy levels are considered to be particularly important for promoting ANK. For more information about the developmental process of NNG and roles of game features in enhancing adaptive number knowledge see [16, 17].

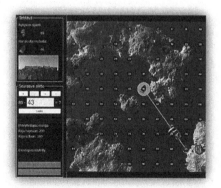

Fig. 1. Example of a map in the Energy scoring mode in NNG 1.

2.3 Measures

Prior to and after the intervention students completed measures of ANK, arithmetic procedural fluency (Woodcock-Johnson Math Fluency sub-test), pre-algebra knowledge (missing-value problems, e.g. $12 + \underline{\quad} = 11 + 15$) and math interest. Post-test also included questionnaire measuring core dimensions of gaming experience including perceived Challenge and Flow.

Game performance was measured with a Relative energy score (map neutral measure of performance = Score/Gold Standard) from at least 5 completed Energy maps (T1–T2 is first two maps completed, T3 is the average of mid-maps, T4–T5 is the last two completed maps). Players complete a map by retrieving all four materials, depending on how optimal their arithmetic solutions are, their performances (or scores) will earn them either Copper, Silver or Gold coins, in which Gold coins solutions are considered close-to-optimal solutions.

Adaptive Number Knowledge was measured with the Arithmetic Sentence Production Task [4]. The task is a timed, paper-and-pencil instrument which measures students' ability to recognize and use different numerical characteristics and relations during their problem solving. An item includes four to five given numbers (e.g. 2, 4, 8, 12, 32) and the four basic arithmetic operations, and the aim is for students to produce as many arithmetic sentences that equal the target number (e.g. 16) as they can in 90 s. Total number of items are 4 and Cronbach's α reliability value for the total number of correct solutions across the four items was .70 (Fig. 2).

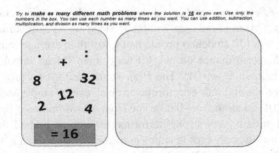

Fig. 2. Example of an arithmetic production task.

Arithmetic Procedural Fluency was measured by the Woodcock-Johnson Math Fluency sub-test [18] which includes a total of 160 items. Students were asked to complete as many arithmetic problems as possible in 3 min.

Perceived Challenge and Flow were measured as part of the Gaming Experience Questionnaire which aim at capturing eight core dimensions of game experience. The questionnaire was translated in Finnish [19] and simplified in language and in length to be more suitable for the age of participants (see [20]).

Math Interest was measured as part of the Expectancy Value Math Motivation questionnaire (see [20]) with three items (e.g. "I like Math").

2.4 Procedure

In order to capture patterns of performance across the Energy maps, a series of growth mixture models were estimated using Mplus version 8.4. Growth mixture models are a clustering procedure that identifies coherent profiles based on individuals' estimated growth curves. Individuals' initial scores of Energy map performance and their linear and quadradic slopes were estimated and used as indicators in for defining a categorical variable of profile membership (e.g., a cluster membership). We set the number of profiles in the model stating with one profile and increasing the number of profiles. Each subsequent model is compared using a set of statistical indicators [21] and theoretical considerations [14]. Once the most appropriate number of profiles is determined, we used a 3-step approach [22] to examine the relation between profile membership and external variables (i.e. ANK, math interest, etc.).

3 Results

3.1 Profiles of Game Performance

The four-profile growth mixture model was most appropriate based on its lowest BIC value of the two to seven profile models [21], in addition to the fact that the 5-profile model introduced an extremely small profile (1% of sample), that did not appear theoretically founded. Figure 3 displays the mean scores and standard errors for each profile across the five game maps.

The *Low Stable Performers* profile (68 students) had lower than average performance on all energy maps (Mean initial map = −0.64; Slope = −.12; quadratic = 0.01). The *Improving Performers* (72 students) profile had lower than average initial performance but improved their performance on every Energy map (Mean initial map = −0.69; Slope = 0.51; Quadratic = −0.04). The *High Stable Performers* profile (38 students) had higher than average and stable performance on all energy maps (Mean initial map = 0.81; slope = −0.01; quadratic = −0.03). The *High Not-Maintained Performers* profile (35 students) had initially very strong performance, with an immediate drop to stable above average; it was the only profile with a non-linear slope (Mean initial map = 1.80; slope = −0.78; Quadratic = 0.11) (Table 1).

Using the 3-step approach, we tested if the profiles differed in their prior knowledge of ANK and math interest. The *Low Stable Performers* profile had lower pretest ANK than the *High Not-Maintained Performers* (beta = .51; SE = .16; $p = .001$) *High Stable Performers* (beta = .35; SE = .15; $p = .02$) and *Improving Performers* (beta = .46; SE = .14; $p = .001$) profiles. *Low Stable Performers* profile had lower math interest than the *High Stable Performers* (beta = .68; SE = .27; $p = .01$) and *Improving Performers* (beta = .68; SE = .24; $p = .004$) profiles.

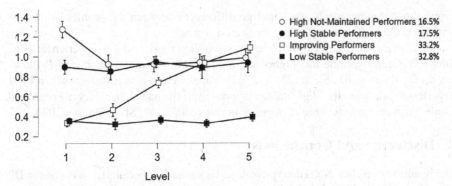

Fig. 3. Mean scores of relative game performance scores by growth mixture model profile for each game map. Error bars represent 95% confidence intervals.

Table 1. Means, standard deviation (in parentheses) of pre and post-test of adaptive number knowledge (ANK) and Woodcock-Johnson arithmetic fluency (AF), pre-test math interest and post-test of gaming experience.

	Low stable performers	Improving performers	High stable performers	High not-maintained performers
Pretest ANK	3.34 (1.31)	4.24 (1.84)	4.0 (1.47)	4.44 (1.69)
Posttest ANK	3.89 (1.68)	5.2 (2.07)	4.9 (1.44)	5.52 (2.36)
Pretest Arith Flu	68.81 (17.0)	77.22 (17.04)	80.66 (16.56)	77.76 (14.7)
Posttest Arith Flu	79.74 (15.67)	89.53 (18.32)	88.72 (16.91)	88.29 (19.61)
Math interest	2.90 (1.0)	3.4 (0.87)	3.46 (0.96)	3.3 (0.99)
Flow	2.06 (0.93)	1.94 (0.7)	2.41 (0.98)	2.17 (0.9)
Perceived challenge	2.43 (0.7)	2.35 (0.66)	2.72 (0.80)	2.45 (0.68)

3.2 Game Performance, Learning Outcomes and Game Experience

Using a 3-step approach, we tested if the groups differed in their posttest ANK scores after controlling for their pretest scores. Tests of multinominal logistic regressions revealed that *Improving Performers* had larger gains in ANK than the *Low Stable Performers* profile (beta = −0.48, SE = 0.22; Odds ratio = 1.58; p = .03). The *Low Stable Performers* also had lower posttest ANK (after controlling for pretest) than the *High Stable Performers* and *High Not-Maintained Performers* profiles (beta > .48; SE = .22; p < .03). There were no other differences in learning between the other profiles.

In order to test the specificity of the effects of gameplay on ANK, we also examined if there were differences in learning gains for arithmetic fluency between the profiles.

Using the 3-step approach, we found no differences between the profiles in posttest arithmetic fluency, after controlling for pretest scores.

There were only minor differences between the groups in Flow experience. *High Stable Performers* profile had higher self-reported Flow than the *Improving Performers* profile (beta = .63; SE = .25; p = .01). There were no other differences in Flow experience. Likewise, the *High Stable Performers* profile had higher levels of perceived Challenge than the *Improving Performers* profile (beta = .81; SE = .38; p = .03).

4 Discussion and Conclusions

Our results suggest that NNG does provide some students opportunities to engage in DP in support of their ANK. We found that among the four profiles of game performance, *Improving Performers* steadily enhanced their game performances in every Energy map despite lower-than-average initial performance. They had strong learning gains in ANK, and they reported a lower flow experience. We argue this is clear evidence that this group of students engaged in DP during the gameplay. As previously discussed, those who take part in DP in the NNG might undergo a low flow experience, a slow yet persistent process as they advance in the game. One of the characteristic features of DP is that it requires trying things that are just beyond a person's current abilities. It also demands a person's full concentration and attention [12]. Another reason for us to believe this group had "deliberately practiced" the Energy maps is due to the design of this NNG version. As this was the first complete working version, usability and clarity of game interface were not yet optimal. Previous study confirmed that students' gaming experience in NNG 2 significantly improved compared to those in NNG 1 [16]. Hence, those were able to improve their game performance despite these usability shortcomings, especially in the more complex maps as in the Energy mode, they would have to consciously make the decision to play the game more times than needed. In other words, they deliberately chose to practice and look for different alternatives to find the more efficient solutions. This kind of practice is possible because the flexible and open nature of the game is supported with fixed and clear rules (i.e., game modes, materials retrieving to and from harbor, etc.) and novel contexts (i.e., map layouts, positions of harbor, ship, and materials, etc.), which allow students to practice and improve their game performances.

Regarding the challenge dimension, there were not big differences between the groups, except that, contrary to our expectation, *High Stable Performers* had higher level of perceived challenge than *Improving Performer*. This difference can be due to the retrospective measure, as *Improving Performer* had continuously improved their performance, therefore at the end their perceived challenge was lower. Results from pre-tests of prior mathematical knowledge and math interest shows that *Low Stable Performers* had lower-than-average in all prior knowledge (ANK and AF) and math interest. Although their game performance remained stable at lower-than-average position consistently, this group still gained significant improvement in their ANK and AF. However, their gains are expectedly smaller than other profiles (after controlling for pretest). The results are in accordance with previous studies [20] that NNG seems to be more motivating and beneficial to those who already have higher math interest.

There are several limitations in our study. Firstly, while using game logs to determine the four-profile memberships allows us to identify different profiles of game performance and their development trajectories, we know little about other external factors such as classroom conditions or teachers' support. Also, future studies should include other types of game analytics to measure students "in-game experience" [23] and explore the roles of teachers with NNG in the classrooms. Next, we argued that one group engaged in DP based on their game performance, learning gains, lower flow experience and game design. However, we are uninformed about their patterns of practice, or why the game only enabled DP for one group. How to trigger DP and maintain such vigorous activity in game-based learning environments to as many students as possible are questions that remained unexplored. Also, prior knowledge of the *Low Stable* group is lower than *Improving Performers*, therefore it might limit their capacities in self-initiating more intense practice. Thus, more attention is needed in future studies on students' prior knowledge. Lastly, it is also worth examining whether the NNG trigger DP behaviors in *Low Stable*'s game performance in easier game levels (for instance when the game requires only addition and subtraction operations).

Despite these limitations, this study answers unaddressed question about the relations between game performance and learning development; it sheds light on the little-known application of deliberate practice in mathematics education via game-based learning platforms. The results indicated that while both adaptive expertise in mathematics and deliberate practice are very demanding and challenging concepts to directly apply in authentic settings, well-designed game-based learning environments offer unprecedented opportunities to overcome those limitations and provide unmatched advantages to "cultivate mathematical minds" in the future [5].

Acknowledgments. Research was funded by the Academy of Finland (Grants 312528 and 336068).

References

1. Watt, M.G.: The Common Core State Standards Initiative: An Overview (2011)
2. Hatano, G., Oura, Y.: Commentary: reconceptualizing school learning using insight from expertise research. Educ. Res. **32**, 26–29 (2003)
3. McMullen, J., Brezovszky, B., Rodríguez-Aflecht, G., Pongsakdi, N., Hannula-Sormunen, M.M., Lehtinen, E.: Adaptive number knowledge: exploring the foundations of adaptivity with whole-number arithmetic. Learn. Individ. Differ. **47**, 172–181 (2016). https://doi.org/10.1016/J.LINDIF.2016.02.007
4. McMullen, J., et al.: Adaptive number knowledge and its relation to arithmetic and pre-algebra knowledge. Learn. Instr. **49**, 178–187 (2017). https://doi.org/10.1016/J.LEARNINSTRUC.2017.02.001
5. Lehtinen, E., Hannula-Sormunen, M., McMullen, J., Gruber, H.: Cultivating mathematical skills: from drill-and-practice to deliberate practice. ZDM – Math. Educ. **49**(4), 625–636 (2017). https://doi.org/10.1007/s11858-017-0856-6
6. McMullen, J., Hannula-Sormunen, M.M., Lehtinen, E., Siegler, R.S.: Distinguishing adaptive from routine expertise with rational number arithmetic. Learn. Instr. **68**, 101347 (2020). https://doi.org/10.1016/j.learninstruc.2020.101347
7. Moss, J., Case, R.: Developing children's understanding of the rational numbers: a new model and an experimental curriculum. J. Res. Math. Educ. **30**, 122–147 (1999). https://doi.org/10.2307/749607

8. Ericsson, A., Pool, R.: Peak: Secrets from the New Science of Expertise. Houghton Mifflin Harcourt, Boston (2016)

9. Lehtinen, E., et al.: Number navigation game (NNG): design principles and game description. In: Torbeyns, J., Lehtinen, E., Elen, J. (eds.) Describing and Studying Domain-Specific Serious Games. AGBL, pp. 45–61. Springer, Cham (2015). https://doi.org/10.1007/978-3-319-202 76-1_4

10. Brezovszky, B., Lehtinen, E., McMullen, J., Rodriguez, G., Veermans, K.: Training Flexible and Adaptive Arithmetic Problem Solving Skills Through Exploration with Numbers: The Development of Number Navigation Game (2013). https://search.proquest.com/docview/154 9957336?accountid=14774

11. Csikszentmihalyi, M.: Flow: The Psychology of Optimal Experience. Harper & Row, New York (1990)

12. Ericsson, K.A., Krampe, R.T., Tesch-Romer, C.: The role of deliberate practice in the acquisition of expert performance. Psychol. Rev. **100**, 363–406 (1993)

13. Baroody, A.J., Dowker, A.: The Development of Arithmetic Concepts and Skills: Constructive Adaptive Expertise. Routledge, Abingdon (2013)

14. Hickendorff, M., Edelsbrunner, P.A., Mcmullen, J., Schneider, M., Trezise, K.: Informative tools for characterizing individual differences in learning: latent class, latent profile, and latent transition analysis ☆ (2018). https://doi.org/10.1016/j.lindif.2017.11.001

15. Brezovszky, B., et al.: Effects of a mathematics game-based learning environment on primary school students' adaptive number knowledge. Comput. Educ. **128**, 63–74 (2019). https://doi.org/10.1016/j.compedu.2018.09.011

16. Bui, P., Rodríguez-Aflecht, G., Brezovszky, B., Hannula-Sormunen, M.M., Laato, S., Lehtinen, E.: Understanding students' game experiences throughout the developmental process of the number navigation game. Educ. Technol. Res. Dev. **68**(5), 2395–2421 (2020). https://doi.org/10.1007/s11423-020-09755-8

17. Brezovszky, B.: Using game-based learning to enhance adaptive number knowledge (2019). http://www.utupub.fi/handle/10024/147025

18. Woodcock, R.W., McGrew, K.S., Mather, N.: Woodcock-Johnson III tests of achievement (2001)

19. Oksanen, K.: Subjective experience and sociability in a collaborative serious game. Simul. Gaming **44**, 767–793 (2013). https://doi.org/10.1177/1046878113513079

20. Rodríguez-Aflecht, G., et al.: Number navigation game (NNG): experience and motivational effects. In: Torbeyns, J., Lehtinen, E., Elen, J. (eds.) Describing and Studying Domain-Specific Serious Games. AGBL, pp. 171–189. Springer, Cham (2015). https://doi.org/10.1007/978-3-319-20276-1_11

21. Nylund, K.L., Asparouhov, T., Muthén, B.O.: Deciding on the number of classes in latent class analysis and growth mixture modeling: a Monte Carlo simulation study. Struct. Eqn. Model.: Multidisc. J. **14**, 535–569 (2007). https://doi.org/10.1080/10705510701575396

22. Asparouhov, T., Muthén, B.: Auxiliary variables in mixture modeling: three-step approaches using M plus. Struct. Eqn. Model. A Multidiscip. J. 1–13 (2014). https://doi.org/10.1080/107 05511.2014.915181

23. Kiili, K., Lindstedt, A., Koskinen, A., Halme, H., Ninaus, M., McMullen, J.: Flow experience and situational interest in game-based learning: cousins or identical twins. Int. J. Serious Games **8**, 93–114 (2021). https://doi.org/10.17083/IJSG.V8I3.462

Effects of a Game-Based Fraction Estimation Task on Math Anxiety

Jessica Maisey[1], Georgios Thoma[2], Korbinian Moeller[2,3,4,5], Kristian Kiili[6], and Manuel Ninaus[3,7(✉)]

[1] Department of Psychology, Loughborough University, Loughborough, UK
[2] Centre for Mathematical Cognition, Loughborough University, Loughborough, UK
{G.Thoma,K.Moeller}@lboro.ac.uk
[3] LEAD Graduate School and Research Network, University of Tübingen, Tübingen, Germany
[4] Leibniz-Institut für Wissensmedien, Tübingen, Germany
[5] Individual Development and Adaptive Education Center, Frankfurt am Main, Germany
[6] Faculty of Education and Culture, Tampere University, Tampere, Finland
kristian.kiili@tuni.fi
[7] Institute of Psychology, University of Graz, Graz, Austria
manuel.ninaus@uni-graz.at

Abstract. Math anxiety is defined as negative feelings associated with mathematical tasks in educational but also real-life situations. Evidence shows that math anxiety negatively affects the ability to solve mathematical tasks. Game-based learning has proven to be an effective approach to improve attitudes toward math. This study looked at the effects of a game-based version of a fraction estimation task on math anxiety and estimation performance when directly compared to a non-game-based task version. Participants aged 18–25-years-old were assessed on their math anxiety levels before and after completing both task versions. Changes in reported math anxiety levels through completion of either the game-based or non-game-based version were then compared. Analyses indicated no significant difference in the change of math anxiety (nor state anxiety as a control variable), nor significant differences in estimation performance due to task version. This seems to indicate no significant influence of game-based presentation of the fraction estimation task on reported math anxiety. Nevertheless, it needs to be considered that levels of math anxiety were generally low in our sample of university students. The current study can be considered a first step toward systematically investigating effects of game-based learning approaches on math anxiety. Accordingly, current results call for further research on a more math-anxious sample to investigate the potential benefits of a game-based task version on math anxiety and fraction estimation performance.

Keywords: Math anxiety · Game-based learning · Fractions · Number line · Math

1 Introduction

It may be apparent to math teachers that there is a natural divide of students within their classroom between those who find math enjoyable and those who dislike it or may even feel anxious about math. Despite math being a mandatory subject in most countries for children aged 5 to 16, math anxiety (MA) is prevalent at all ages of education, including primary school children [1], with MA increasing with age and persisting into secondary, post-secondary education, and adulthood [2].

MA is defined as negative feelings (e.g., tension, stress) associated with mathematical tasks, including the manipulation of numbers and basic arithmetic, whether that be in an educational setting or a real-life situation [3]. Notably, many researchers also found MA to be negatively associated with mathematical achievement [2, 3]. Moreover, MA can result in an individual developing negative attitudes towards mathematics [4], and as a result, individuals may take precautionary measures to avoid math entirely [3]. Such math avoidance involves the irregular and inefficient study of and opting out of jobs that require quantitative skills [3]. Accordingly, research has shown that those who experienced MA in school were less likely to choose math- and science-related subjects when entering education beyond high school [3, 5], which is especially true for females [6]. In turn, this often leads to restricted career paths as math is prominent in most occupational fields, including finance, technology, business, education, medicine, social sciences, and engineering [7, 8]. However, as a short-term solution to MA, math avoidance will only exacerbate problems around math as it is an ineffective strategy for targeting the root cause of MA. Therefore, it is essential to develop approaches that help reduce MA, so individuals do not avoid math-related contexts.

Using game elements or games for learning math might be one way of augmenting conventional math instruction and potentially reducing or even preventing MA (e.g. [9]). In fact, more positive attitudes and feelings towards math were observed after the implementation of a game-based learning approach (GBL; [10]). Using computer games for math instruction has become more popular recently and studies also indicated it to be effective compared to other conventional methods of instruction with learning gains persisting long-term [11]. However, the effect of game-based approaches on MA has not been studied sufficiently yet (see [12] for a review). GBL approaches have been shown to enhance the experience of education as it can introduce a sense of self-competition and challenge, increasing an individual's drive and persistence to succeed [13]. Typically, GBL approaches also provide a (visual) narrative in which the actual task is embedded, that can enhance engagement [9] and motivation [14]. As such, a recent meta-analysis [15] revealed that game fiction led to a significant increase in behavioural learning outcomes (i.e., better performance after implementation of such game elements) when compared to tasks without.

Taken together, the above highlights that on the one hand, increased MA is negatively associated with math performance whereas on the other hand, GBL approaches were found to improve not only attitudes towards math but also math performance [2, 4]. Accordingly, one might hypothesize that GBL approaches may reduce MA which, in turn, may improve math performance. In fact, recent research suggests that GBL approaches might be particularly helpful in improving attitudes toward math and math performance [10, 16]. For instance, after implementation of GBL over five school days, fifth-grade students showed improved attitudes towards math and increased average achievement scores from 56% to 96% [10]. These results substantiate the benefits of GBL on attitudes towards math and math performance in children.

Similarly, sixth-grade children were assessed [9] on a game-based number line esti-mation task and a magnitude comparison task. Levels of math performance and self-reported test anxiety were compared to a non-game-based paper-pencil version of the tasks. Findings indicated a positive impact of the game-based version as it was observed to lead to decreased reports of test anxiety, but increased reported engagement and flow. These findings further support the notion that GBL might help reduce levels of MA.

However, although researchers have found positive effects of GBL on attitudes towards math and math performance [9, 10] there is a dearth of research that directly compares effects of a game-based task version to an equivalent non-game-based version of the same task on MA and math performance. Previous research indicated increasing MA into adolescence [2], and fractions eliciting MA in particular [3]. Based on evi-dence for fractions being a difficult concept not only for students but also adults [17], the current study evaluated whether a game-based version of a (number line fraction esti-mation) math task leads to reduced reported MA compared to a non-game-based version of the same task. As MA should also be negatively associated with math performance (cf. [2]), we further expected that participants should perform better in the game-based as compared to the non-game-based version of the task.

2 Methodology

2.1 Participants

A sample of 36 participants, aged 18–25 was recruited. The sample consisted of 29 females (mean age = 21.2; SD = 1.35), six males (mean age = 22.7; SD = 1.37) and one participant who did not disclose their gender (aged 23). All participants had obtained at least a GCSE level qualification in mathematics and were students at a UK university or recent graduates, thus, the fractions presented in the math tasks were familiar to them.

2.2 Math Anxiety

The *Abbreviated Math Anxiety Scale* (AMAS; [18]) is a 9-item self-report MA question-naire that asks individuals to indicate their anxiety levels in different math situations on a 5-point Likert scale ranging from 1 (No bad feelings) to 5 (Worst feelings); therefore, higher scores indicated more pronounced MA.

2.3 Trait and State Anxiety

Participants' trait and state anxiety were also assessed as control variables. The *State-Trait Anxiety Inventory* (STAI; [19]) is a 40-item, 4-point Likert scale split into two 20-item self-report questionnaires for state and trait anxiety. The state-anxiety scale asks participants to rate how they currently feel with statements, such as 'I feel calm'. Responses can range from 1 (Not at all) to 4 (Very much so). In the trait-anxiety ques-tionnaire, participants have to rate how they generally feel regarding statements, such as 'I feel satisfied with myself.' with responses ranging from 1 (Almost never) to 4 (Almost always). For both questionnaires, higher scores indicated higher anxiety levels.

2.4 Mathematical Task

In the current study, a game- and a non-game-based version of a fraction number line estimation task was used (e.g., [20]), in which participants had to estimate the position of a target fraction on a number line with only its endpoints specified (i.e., where goes 6/15 on a number line from 0–1; see also Fig. 1). Corrective feedback was offered in both versions (i.e., a green indicator on the number line; see Fig. 1).

Fig. 1. Game-based task version (left), and the non-game-based task version (right). Positive feedback (top), and negative feedback (bottom). Corrective feedback was provided in both versions with a vertical green line indicating the correct position of the target fraction. (Color figure online)

In the game-based version, participants maneuvered a dog along the number line to their estimated position using the arrow keys of the keyboard and confirmed their estimation of the target fraction by pressing the space bar. A short narrative was provided to participants in the game version indicating that a cat hid bones in the forest and the dog, through the player, needed to retrieve them. Accordingly, the dog showed positive emotional feedback (see Fig. 1 upper left panel) when bones were found (i.e., the fraction was correctly estimated). In contrast, the dog showed negative emotions when the estimated position was too far off the correct position (i.e., estimates more than ±10% from the correct position; see Fig. 1 lower left panel).

The non-game-based version of this task used the same underlying mechanics. However, instead of controlling the dog as an avatar, participants had to move a white visual indicator along the number line to provide their estimation of the respective target fraction. No narrative was provided in the non-game-based version. Accordingly, overall visual design was kept minimalistic (see Fig. 1 right panels). Feedback as to the accurateness of the estimation was only provided in terms of a green check mark (i.e., correct estimation) or a red cross (i.e., incorrect estimation) using the same criteria as in the game-based version.

There were seven levels in both tasks, and each level presented twelve fractions, totaling 84 fractions per task. The fractions were the same for both tasks but were presented in a random order to prevent order effects. The fractions used in the games were carefully selected to span equally across the number line from 0 to 1.

2.5 Procedure

The study used a within-participants design with participants randomly allocated into one of two groups. One group completed the game-based task first, whereas the second group completed the non-game-based task first. Through this counterbalancing, effects of order of task versions were controlled for.

After signing the consent form, participants were given a link to a questionnaire on Qualtrics, where along demographic details, they provided their level of math enjoyment at school via a 5-point Likert scale from 1 (Disliked a great deal) to 5 (Thoroughly enjoyed). Then participants completed the trait-anxiety part of the STAI questionnaire first, followed by the state-anxiety part of the STAI [19], and the AMAS [18]. Both the state-anxiety and AMAS questionnaires were completed before and after each number line estimation task versions so differences in state and math anxiety could be calculated from before to after completing either the game- or the non-game-based version.

2.6 Data Analysis

Mathematical Performance Analysis
Mathematical performance was measured by averaging each participant's estimation error in each task version (i.e., percentage of absolute estimation error for the game- vs. non-game-based task version). Paired samples t-tests were used to compare estimation errors and average response duration between the two task versions.

Anxiety Level Analysis
To evaluate potential differences in the change of state and math anxiety from before to after the game-based vs. the non-game-based task version, the difference in anxiety for each task version was calculated by subtracting pre-task anxiety scores from post-task anxiety scores (i.e., state anxiety and AMAS scores). The differences in anxiety change for each math task version were analyzed using one-way within-participant ANOVAs for changes in state and math anxiety. In a second step, we further conducted additional ANCOVAs considering the covariates trait anxiety, gender, and math enjoyment to control for potential influences of these.

Please note, while the majority of variables of interest met t-test/ANOVA preconditions, this was not the case for all (e.g., error data because of the instruction to perform as accurate as possible). Therefore, we reran the analysis evaluating influences of task version on changes in state/math anxiety and RTs/error rates using the Wilcoxon signed ranks test. Results were identical to those reported in the following.

Table 1. Descriptive statistics

	Estimation error		Reaction time		Change in math anxiety		Change in state anxiety	
	Mean	SD	Mean	SD	Mean	SD	Mean	SD
Game	5%	5%	7748 ms	3004 ms	−0.17	2.55	0.74	5.89
Non-game	5%	4%	7773 ms	3550 ms	−0.11	2.25	0.25	5.69

3 Results

Mathematical Performance: Results indicated that there was no significant difference in estimation errors between non-game and game versions, $t(34) = 0.07, p = .94$. Furthermore, there was also no significant difference in average duration for task completion, between the non-game-based and game-based tasks, $t(34) = 0.04, p = .97$.

Out of the 84 fractions, the total number of correct responses within the non-game-based version ranged from 34 to 84 and averaged 77.39. In the game-based version, the total number of correct responses ranged from 23 to 84 and averaged 78.06. This indicates that in general, participants received a high amount of positive feedback due to their high accuracy in responses.

Anxiety Level: Differences between state anxiety and AMAS scores from before to after the respective task version were calculated to measure anxiety changes due to the non-game-based and game-based task version and were used as dependent variables in the following analyses.

A one-way within-participant ANOVA was conducted to evaluate differences in the changes in AMAS scores. Descriptive results indicated that the mean difference in MA was slightly larger after the game task than the non-game task (see Table 1). However, the ANOVA results indicated no significant effect of task type on changes in MA [$F(1, 35) = 0.12, p = .91, \eta_p^2 < .00$].

Another one-way within-participant ANOVA was conducted to evaluate differences in change of state anxiety between the two task versions. The mean change in state anxiety was slightly larger for the game task than the non-game task (see Table 1). However, the results also showed no significant effect of task type on changes in state anxiety [$F(1, 35) = 0.97, p = .76, \eta_p^2 < .00$].

Re-running these analyses considering trait anxiety, gender and math enjoyment as covariates in the ANCOVAs did not change the outcomes [all $F(1, 34) < 1.17$, all $p > .29$, all $\eta_p^2 < .03$]. Additionally, the ANCOVA results showed that none of the covariates had a significant influence on the change of MA due to the respective task version [trait anxiety: $F(1, 34) = 0.42, p = .53, \eta_p^2 = .01$, gender: $F(1, 34) = 2.06, p = .16, \eta_p^2 = .06$, enjoyment of math: $F(1, 34) = 1.83, p = .19, \eta_p^2 = .05$]. That is, no significant differences in the change of state/math anxiety due to the game and non-game-based task version were observed as well as no significant influences of the covariates itself.

4 Discussion

The present study compared the effects of a game-based and a non-game-based version of a number line estimation task on participants' reported MA, state anxiety, and performance. As previous research found GBL approaches to improve attitudes towards math as well as math performance [10, 16], it was expected that the game-based task version would result in reduced MA and better performance compared to the non-game-based version. Contrary to our expectations, no significant differences between the game-based and a non-game-based version of the task on MA, state anxiety, as well as performance were observed. In the following, we will discuss this in more detail and speculate as to why the GBL approach did not have the expected impact on our variables of interest.

The results showed no significant difference in performance between the game-based and the non-game-based task version. That is, the GBL approach used in the game-based version of the mathematical task did not alter participants' performance. This might have to do with participants' overall very high accuracy on the task (on average, only miss-estimating by 5%). Accordingly, our hypothesis that the game-based task version should lead to better performance was not supported as participants performed just as well in both tasks.

Furthermore, we also did not observe a significant difference in the mean duration spent on estimating the fractions in both versions of the task. As regards to duration, we did not have a directed hypothesis. On the one hand, one might expect that the game-based task version might increase participants engagement to invest more cognitive resources, and thus they should respond faster. On the other hand, one might expect that the game-based version might include elements potentially distracting participants from the actual task, which would lead to slower responses (for a more comprehensive discussion on this issue see [21]). It could also be considered whether the different versions of the task would lead participants to sacrifice accuracy over speed, or vice versa, also known as a speed-accuracy trade-off [22]. However, there was no indication of a speed-accuracy trade-off in the data or any other effect on response duration.

To evaluate how the different task versions influenced participants' MA, differences in MA were calculated from before to after completing the respective version to see whether these changes differed between the game- and non-game-based task version. Results showed no significant difference in math or state anxiety change between task versions, suggesting that the game version used in the current study did not influence participants' anxiety levels. Therefore, these results did not support our hypothesis that the game-based version of the task should reduce reported MA more than the non-game-based version. As for the reasons for these null effects, we can only speculate.

Overall, participants' high estimation accuracy and the resulting predominant positive feedback (on average presented on about 77 and 78 out of 84 items in the non-game- and game-based version, respectively) may have reduced anxiety levels or at least not increased anxiety levels in the non-game-based task version. On the other hand, participants may have performed well in both versions as they mostly reported low MA. Following the classification of high and low MA [23] only three of the 36 participants scored high on MA (i.e., scores of >31) on the AMAS [18]. Of the remaining 33 participants, 24 scored low for MA (AMAS scores of <19) consistently. As such, a potential negative effect of MA on cognitive performance in general and math performance in particular [3, 6] might not have been relevant in the current study because of low anxiety levels. One might speculate that if the sample had been a highly math-anxious group of participants at pre-test, the potential effects of game elements might be more pronounced. Thus, replicating the findings of previous research highlighting the positive impacts of GBL on attitudes towards mathematics [10, 16] might require rerunning the study with a more math anxious sample. Nevertheless, it might also be the case that GBL approaches may not (positively) affect math anxiety at all.

Additionally, our results may not have replicated earlier findings due to differing participant characteristics from the samples used in previous research. For instance, rather than fifth-graders [10], sixth-graders [9] or non-STEM students [16] (who have shown reduced confidence in mathematics [24]), this study sampled 18–25-year-olds who studied a range of STEM and non-STEM subjects, who may have differed in their familiarity with mathematics.

Further ANCOVAs were used to investigate whether the results held when gender, trait anxiety and level of enjoyment of math whilst at school were controlled for. Gender was considered as a covariate because it has been shown to be predictive of MA, with females showing higher levels of MA than males [25]. Importantly, controlling for the influence of gender did not change the results. Nevertheless, it is interesting to note that the three participants who scored high on MA were all female, thus somewhat reflecting previous findings [25]. Trait anxiety (as previous research indicated moderate associations with MA) and math enjoyment were also controlled for as covariates, but also did not change the results, and as such, were not influencing factors.

The current study is one of the first to investigate the effects of a game-based as compared to a non-game-based version of the same math task on math and state anxiety and math performance (see [12] for a brief review). Therefore, albeit no significant effects were identified, this study contributes to current discussions on the affective effects of GBL approaches [26] and their potential benefits to reduce MA.

Limitations and Future Perspective: Although MA has shown to increase throughout childhood to adolescence [2], in particular when solving fractions [3], future research should aim at investigating more math-anxious and potentially younger students. As well as considering participants' familiarity with fractions, as this may mediate MA and math performance [17].

Furthermore, potential long-term effects of the game-based vs. non-game-based task version on MA and performance were beyond the scope of this study as participants only had one session of GBL. Research has found that multiple sessions of GBL, compared to a single play session, have a more pronounced effect on learning outcomes [27]. As such, multiple sessions of GBL may also be more desirable to address MA.

Additionally, despite the two math tasks showing visual differences, the underlying game mechanics were identical (i.e., number line estimation). This limit in contrast between task versions may also account for not observing significant differences in changes in MA. Thus, future research may aim at increasing the contrast between game-based and non-game-based conditions by introducing additional game elements (such as competitive goals, leaderboards, etc.) to boost potential influences of GBL on MA.

Conclusion. The current study is one of the first to investigate effects of a game-based version of a fraction estimation task on math anxiety and performance compared to an identical non-game-based version. Results indicated that there was no significant difference in changes of math and state anxiety due to the game- vs. non-game-based task version. This suggests that the game-based version of the math task did not impact participants' anxiety levels. Furthermore, participants also performed just as well in both task versions. These results may be explained by overall low MA in the present sample, who mostly showed only low MA at pre-test and the overall high performance in the math task. One might assume that the low math anxiety influenced the high math estimation accuracy, which, in turn, kept anxiety low due to the predominant positive feedback received in both versions of the task. As such, further research based on a more math anxious sample would be desirable to better understand potential benefits of GBL approaches on MA.

References

1. Aarnos, E., Perkkilä, P.: Early signs of mathematics anxiety? Proc. – Soc. Behav. Sci. **46**, 1495–1499 (2012)
2. Dowker, A., Sarkar, A., Looi, C.Y.: Mathematics anxiety: what have we learned in 60 years? Front. Psychol. **7**(APR), 508 (2016)
3. Ashcraft, M.H.: Math anxiety: personal, educational and cognitive consequences. Curr. Dir. Psychol. Sci. **11**, 181–185 (2002)
4. Ramirez, G., Gunderson, E.A., Levine, S.C., Beilock, S.L.: Math anxiety, working memory, and math achievement in early elementary school. J. Cogn. Dev. **14**(2), 187–202 (2013)
5. Dew, K.H., Galassi, J.P., Galassi, M.D.: Math anxiety: relation with situational test anxiety, performance, physiological arousal, and math avoidance behavior. J. Couns. Psychol. **31**(4), 580–583 (1984)
6. Hill, F., Mammarella, I.C., Devine, A., Caviola, S., Passolunghi, M.C., Szűcs, D.: Math anxiety in primary and secondary school students: gender differences, developmental changes and anxiety specificity. Learn. Individ. Differ. **48**, 45–53 (2016)
7. Chen, P.-Y., Hwang, G.-J., Yeh, S.-Y., Chen, Y.-T., Chen, T.-W., Chien, C.-H.: Three decades of game-based learning in science and mathematics education: an integrated bibliometric analysis and systematic review. J. Comput. Educ. **9**, 1–22 (2021)
8. Stent, A.: Can math anxiety be conquered?. Change: Mag. High. Learn. **9**(1), 40–43 (1977)
9. Kiili, K., Ketamo, H.: Evaluating cognitive and affective outcomes of a digital game-based math test. IEEE Trans. Learn. Technol. **11**, 255–263 (2018)
10. White, K., McCoy, L.P.: Effects of game-based learning on attitude and achievement in elementary mathematics. Netw.: Online J. Teach. Res. **21**(10), 1–17 (2019)
11. Wouters, P., van Nimwegen, C., van Oostendorp, H., van der Spek, E.D.: A meta-analysis of the cognitive and motivational effects of serious games. J. Educ. Psychol. **105**(2), 249–265 (2013)
12. Dondio, P., Santos, F.H., Gusev, V., Rocha, M.: Do games reduce maths anxiety? A review of the current literature. In: ECGBL 2021. Proceedings of the 15th European Conference on Game Based Learning, pp. 287–292. ACI, Brighton (2021)
13. O'Rourke, J., Main, S., Hill, S.: Commercially available digital game technology in the classroom: improving automaticity in mental-math in primary-aged students. Aust. J. Teach. Educ. **42**(10), 50–70 (2017)

14. Chen, C.-H.: Impacts of augmented reality and a digital game on students' science learning with reflection prompts in multimedia learning. Educ. Technol. Res. Dev. **68**(6), 3057–3076 (2020)
15. Sailer, M., Homner, L.: The gamification of learning: a meta-analysis. Educ. Psychol. Rev. **32**(1), 77–112 (2020)
16. Gil-Doménech, D., Berbegal-Mirabent, J.: Stimulating students' engagement in mathematics courses in non-STEM academic programmes: a game-based learning. Innov. Educ. Teach. Int. **56**(1), 57–65 (2019)
17. DeWolf, M., Vosniadou, S.: The representation of fraction magnitudes and the whole number bias reconsidered. Learn. Instr. **37**, 39–49 (2015)
18. Hopko, D.R., Mahadevan, R., Bare, R.L., Hunt, M.K.: The abbreviated math anxiety scale (AMAS). Assessment **10**(2), 178–182 (2003)
19. Spielberger, C.D.: State-Trait Anxiety Inventory for Adults. PsycTESTS Dataset (1983)
20. Siegler, R.S., Opfer, J.E.: The development of numerical estimation: evidence for multiple representations of numerical quantity. Psychol. Sci. **14**, 237–243 (2003)
21. Ninaus, M., Kiili, K., Wood, G., Moeller, K., Kober, S.E.: To add or not to add game elements? Exploring the effects of different cognitive task designs using eye tracking. IEEE Trans. Learn. Technol. **13**(4), 847–860 (2020)
22. Guiard, Y., Rioul, O.: A mathematical description of the speed/accuracy trade-off of aimed movement. In: Proceedings of the 2015 British HCI Conference, pp. 91–100 (2015)
23. Maloney, E.A., Risko, E.F., Ansari, D., Fugelsang, J.: Mathematics anxiety affects counting but not subitising during visual enumeration. Cognition **114**(2), 293–297 (2010)
24. Alsina, C.: Why the professor must be a stimulating teacher. In: Holton, D., Artigue, M., Kirchgräber, U., Hillel, J., Niss, M., Schoenfeld, A. (eds.) The Teaching and Learning of Mathematics at University Level. NISS, vol. 7, pp. 3–12. Springer, Dordrecht (2001). https://doi.org/10.1007/0-306-47231-7_1
25. Griggs, M.S., Rimm-Kaufman, S.E., Merritt, E.G., Patton, C.L.: The responsive classroom approach and fifth grade students' math and science anxiety and self-efficacy. Sch. Psychol. Q. **28**(4), 360–373 (2013)
26. Greipl, S., et al.: When the brain comes into play: neurofunctional correlates of emotions and reward in game-based learning. Comput. Hum. Behav. **125**, 106946 (2021)
27. Clark, D., Tanner-Smith, E., Killingsworth, S.: Digital games, design, and learning: a systematic review and meta-analysis. Rev. Educ. Res. **86**(1), 79–122 (2016)

Novel Approaches and Application Domains

Motivation and Emotions in a Health Literacy Game: Insights from Co-occurrence Network Analysis

Kristian Kiili[1]([✉]), Juho Siuko[1], Elizabeth Cloude[2], and Muhterem Dindar[1]

[1] Faculty of Education and Culture, Tampere University, Tampere, Finland
{kristian.kiili,juho.siuko,muhterem.dindar}@tuni.fi
[2] Penn Center for Learning Analytics, University of Pennsylvania, Philadelphia, USA

Abstract. Accumulating evidence indicates that game-based learning is emotionally charged. However, little is known about the nature of emotions in game-based learning. We extended previous game-based learning research by examining epistemic emotions and their relations to flow experience and situational interest. Sixty-eight 15–18-year-old students played the Antidote COVID-19 game for 25 min. Epistemic emotions, flow, and situational interest were measured after the playing session. These measures indicated that the game engaged students. Students reported significantly higher intensity levels of positive epistemic emotions (excitement, surprise, and curiosity) than negative epistemic emotions (boredom, anxiety, frustration, and confusion). The co-occurrence network analyses provided insights into the relationship between flow and situational interest. We found an asymmetrical pattern of the "situational interest-flow" co-occurrence. When situational interest occurred, the flow was always co-occurring. This co-occurrence suggests that situational interest could be a prerequisite or a potential trigger for flow experience but not an adequate state ensuring a high flow experience. Further, flow and situational interest co-occurred mainly with positive epistemic emotions. The findings imply that flow and situational interest are similar constructs and share several characteristics. The study also demonstrated that epistemic emotions, flow, and situational interest can be used as proxies of engagement. Implications of the findings are discussed.

Keywords: Game-based learning · Epistemic emotions · Flow experience · Situational interest · Engagement

1 Introduction

The mechanisms of successful game-based learning processes are still poorly understood [1, 2]. A recent systematic survey [3] revealed that affective-cognitive models of learning [3, 4] had gotten little attention in the game-based learning field. This is surprising as

Supplementary Information The online version contains supplementary material available at https://doi.org/10.1007/978-3-031-22124-8_15.

theories that emphasize both affective and cognitive aspects dominate contemporary multimedia learning research, and it has been hypothesized that emotional engagement may play a crucial role in game-based learning. Although recent research has indicated that game-based learning is emotionally charged [2, 6], the nature and objects of emotions in game-based learning have not been thoroughly examined. Particularly the role of emotional engagement in game-based learning is unclear.

Engagement can generally be defined as active involvement in a given learning task [7]. According to Fredricks, Filsecker, and Lawson [8], learner engagement consists of three distinct but interrelated dimensions: behavioral, emotional, and cognitive engagement dimensions. In the present study, we used two motivational constructs, flow experience, and situational interest, as proxies of engagement as suggested in [9]. Moreover, to better address students' emotional engagement in the Antidote COVID-19 health literacy game, we also measured students' epistemic emotions.

1.1 Flow and Situational Interest

Flow theory defines intrinsically-motivated behaviors resulting from immediate subjective experiences that occur when learners engage in a learning activity [10]. Flow is characterized by a holistic feeling of becoming completely absorbed in the learning activity, the merging of action and awareness, the increased focus of attention to a particular stimulus, a lack of self-awareness, and a feeling of agency over learners' own actions and the environment. Flow can only occur when learners perceive a balance between their skills and tasks. Three-channel model of flow emphasizes that flow is not a stable state. For example, a player occasionally tends to experience either boredom (too easy challenges) or anxiety (too demanding challenges), which may motivate the player to strive for the flow state to experience enjoyment again. A recent study examining the relationship between flow and emotions showed that players who experienced higher positive emotions (happiness and excitement) also experienced higher flow [11].

Because flow can be a relatively unstable state, game designers aim to design game mechanics to elicit learners' situational interest in the game, as interest is often required for learners engaging in a state of flow [12]. Situational interest is theoretically described as both a psychological and motivational state, leading to re-engagement in learning activities [13]. Situational interest emerges from interaction with the features built into the environment, for example, game elements and game mechanics in learning games. According to Kiili et al. [9] flow experience and situational interest can be used as proxies of engagement in game-based learning as these constructs explain why people engage in activities. Their study revealed that although flow experience and situational interest are strongly related, situational interest is mainly related to immersive aspects of flow and does not reflect the fluency dimension of flow.

1.2 Epistemic Emotions

Affective-cognitive models of learning [4, 5] emphasize that emotions are not only by-products but drivers of learning. In general, emotions can be defined as affective episodes that are induced by a certain stimulus and have an object. Academic emotions can be classified as achievement, topic, epistemic, and social [14]. In this paper, we focus on epistemic emotions because epistemic emotions are directly related to the learning process [15], can motivate learners to engage in cognitive activities [14], and can influence learning outcomes and performance [16]. According to [17] knowledge and the generation of new knowledge are the objects of epistemic emotions (surprise, curiosity, enjoyment, confusion, anxiety, frustration, boredom). In contrast, the stimuli and object of achievement emotions relate to success or achievement in academic tasks. In game-based learning, players may experience topic emotions due to the content of the narrative itself, for example COVID-19 pandemic, rather than as a function of their experience of processing the earning content included in the game (epistemic emotions) or their appraisals of control or value of the game-based learning activity (achievement emotions).

Epistemic emotions can be classified according to their valence (positive/negative) and strength of physiological arousal (activating/deactivating). In general, research has indicated that positive activating emotions support learning more than negative ones [5] by facilitating, for example, elaboration and critical thinking [18]. Thus, game-based learning activities should aim to promote positive epistemic emotions (e.g., curiosity, enjoyment) and reduce negative epistemic emotions, deactivating negative emotions (boredom) in particular. It has been argued that boredom can impair the systematic use of learning strategies undermining the effectiveness of learning activities [18]. However, it is noteworthy that some negative activating emotions (e.g., confusion) and neural emotions (e.g., surprise) may facilitate learning in certain learning settings.

1.3 Present Study

The present study had two objectives: to examine student engagement in the Antidote COVID-19 game and examine the similarities and differences between flow experience and situational interest in relation to epistemic emotions. Figure 1 Summarizes the expected outcomes of the study.

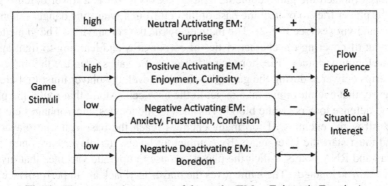

Fig. 1. The expected outcomes of the study (EM = Epistemic Emotion).

First, we examined students' engagement in the Antidote COVID-19 game. We used flow experience, situational interest, and epistemic emotions as proxies of engagement. Previous research has indicated that game-based learning engages students [2, 6]. Thus, we expected that students report high levels of situational interest and flow. Further, we expected that students report significantly higher positive epistemic emotions than negative ones. To make reporting of the results simpler, we classified surprise as a positive emotion, although it is usually considered a neutral emotion. Second, we examined relations between flow experience, situational interest, and epistemic emotions. We expected to find a strong positive correlation between flow and situational interest, as demonstrated in [9]. The downside of correlational analyses is that it only looks for coupling between variables regardless of their magnitude. For example, a correlational analysis might yield a high relationship between flow and situational interest, although both variables might be scored towards the lower end of the used measurement scale. The co-occurrence network analysis, which we employed in this study, tackles this limitation by studying the coupling of variables only towards the higher end of measurement scales [19]. Therefore, we employed co-occurrence network analysis to describe how often different epistemic emotions are reported together with flow and situational interest within individuals. With these analyses, we aimed to answer the following research questions. How often do students report flow experience and situational interest together, and how strong is this relationship? Which specific epistemic emotions occur together with flow experience and situational interest, and how often?

2   Method

Participants. Sixty-eight 15–18-year-old (M = 16, SD = 0.78) students participated in the study. Students were recruited from two Finnish schools. There were 43 high school students and 25 9th graders. 22 of the participants were men and 40 women; six students reported their gender as "other." 60% of the participants reported playing computer games, mobile games, or console games at least a couple of times a week.

Game Description. Antidote COVID-19 is a mobile game about viruses, the human immune system, vaccines, and pandemics. PsyonGames has developed the game, and WHO has validated the game contents. Antidote COVID-19 is a tower defense game where the player tries to protect the base of the cell from a swarming danger (enemies), bacteria, and viruses (see Fig. 2). The main enemy is the coronavirus. The game tells a story about discovering the characteristics of coronavirus and learning to fight against it by developing vaccines. The story is told through messages from the laboratory and comic strips delivered during the gameplay. In each level, the player must first create a passageway that enemies must take to get to the base cell. Along that route, the player can build defense towers (white blood cells such as monocytes, macrophages etc.) that try to destroy the enemies. If too many enemies reach the base cell, the player will lose and must start the level again. By completing levels, the player earns new types of towers and RNA-points, which the player can use to upgrade vaccines that give the player certain advantages. The game gives the player feedback about performance with the health points and RNA-points. At any time, the player can use an encyclopedia to get information about different cells, enemies, and vaccines included in the game.

Measures. We measured epistemic emotions with a short version of the Epistemically-Related Emotion Scales [17] designed to measure surprise, curiosity, enjoyment, confusion, anxiety, frustration, and boredom. Each emotion was measured with a single item by asking students to reflect on how strongly they felt the different emotions when they played the game. A five-point Likert scale with the response categories from 1 = not at all, 2 = quite a little, 3 = moderately, 4 = strongly, 5 = very strongly was used. In this short version of the scale, enjoyment is measured with the item of excitement. We measured situational interest with four items [20] (e.g., I think this topic is interesting). A 5-point Likert scale ranging from 1 (strongly disagree) to 5 (strongly agree) was used. We measured flow experience with a slightly modified 10-item version of the Flow Short Scale [21]. The statements were changed to past tense and made the activity refer to game playing [9]. A scale ranging from 1 (strongly disagree) to 5 (strongly agree) was used instead of the original 7-point scale. All the used scales were administered in Finnish.

Fig. 2. Gameplay: Coronavirus is trying to reach the base that the player is protecting with towers.

Procedure. The study was conducted during a regular school day. First, the researcher presented a video to participants that provided study details and practical instructions. Second, every participant received a randomly generated participation code (tag) that was used for logging in to digital pre-and post-questionnaires. Next, participants filled out demographics and a consent questionnaire. After pre-measures, participants played the Antidote COVID-19 game for 25-min with iPads. Finally, participants completed the questionnaire about their motivational and emotional experiences and reported the level that they reached in the game.

Co-occurrence Network Analysis. In general, correlational analyses look for coupling between variables of interest regardless of their magnitude. In co-occurrence network analysis, the magnitude is considered, and only the higher end of a measurement scale is used to coupling variables [19]. Usually, the higher end is decided based on the mid-level of the measurement scale [22]. That is, co-occurrence is manifested if both variables of interest are scored above the mid-level of the scale. Drawing on this, a dichotomous coding was applied to the epistemic emotions, situational interest, and flow scales. In the present study, we coded the responses that were above three as 1. Otherwise, the responses were coded as 0. Following, co-occurrence network analysis with louvain community detection algorithm was applied on the dichotomous scores to observe the overlaps between situational interest, flow, and epistemic emotions [23]. In the analysis, variables are considered as nodes, and the co-occurrences between them are considered as edges (i.e., connections between the nodes). The analysis was conducted with igraph R package [24].

3   Results

3.1   Engagement

The descriptive statistics of all measures are shown in Table 1. The reliability of flow experience ($\alpha = .91$) and positive emotions were good ($\alpha = .87$), the reliability of situational interest ($\alpha = .78$) was acceptable, and the reliability of negative emotions was poor ($\alpha = .53$). Boredom, which was the only deactivating emotion on the used emotion scale lowered the reliability of the formed negative emotions construct.

Table 1. Descriptive statistics of engagement measures

	Mean	Standard deviation	Occurrence (f)
Flow experience	3.77	0.79	55
Situational interest	3.29	0.81	42
Positive epistemic emotions	3.21	0.89	–
Surprised (A)	3.12	1.09	25
Curious (A)	3.18	0.88	24
Excited (A)	3.34	1.02	34
Negative epistemic emotions	2.09	0.68	–
Confused (A)	2.79	1.17	20
Anxious (A)	1.57	0.91	4
Frustrated (A)	2.26	1.15	12
Bored (D)	1.72	0.98	4

The results indicate that the game engaged students as most reported moderate-to-high intensity of flow, situational interest, and positive epistemic emotions. Moreover, the students reported lower levels of negative epistemic emotions. Further, Paired Samples T-Test indicated that the game induced significantly higher intensity of positive epistemic emotions in students ($M = 3.21$, $SD = 0.89$) compared to negative epistemic emotions ($M = 2.09$, $SD = 0.68$), $t(67) = 7.48$, $p < .001$, $d = 0.91$. The frequency of students who experienced flow, situational interest, and each emotion are also presented in Table 1. The Occurrence column of Table 1 confirms that most students reported that they experienced flow ($f = 55$) and situational interest ($f = 42$). Excitement ($f = 34$), surprise ($f = 25$), and curiosity were the most frequently occurred epistemic emotions. However, only a small fraction of the students experienced anxiety ($f = 4$) and boredom ($f = 4$).

3.2   Relations Between Flow, Situational Interest, and Epistemic Emotions

As expected, the correlation between flow and situational interest was large, $r = .62$, $p < .001$. To examine the relation more deeply, we considered the relations between flow, situational interest, and epistemic emotions with co-occurrence network analysis. Table 2 shows the co-occurrence of epistemic emotions with flow, and Table 3 shows the co-occurrence with situational interest (note that the edge weight indicates how often two variables were reported together). It was observed that a high-intensity level of flow occurred 55 times and a high-intensity level of situational interest 42 times. The most often co-occurring epistemic emotions with flow were excitement (edge = 34; 62%), surprise (edge = 25; 46%), and curiosity (edge = 23; 42%). There was the similar trend in situational interest as the most co-occurring epistemic emotions with it were excitement (edge = 30; 71%), surprise (edge = 25; 60%), curiosity (edge = 23; 55%). Anxiety and boredom co-occurred very rarely with flow and situational interest. Further, the analyses revealed that a high-level situational interest was always accompanied with high level of flow (edge = 42; 100%).

Table 2. Co-occurrences of flow and motivation/emotion pairs

Node 1	Node 2	Edge weight	% of all edges	% of self-edge
Flow	Sit. Interest	42	20, 4	76, 4
	Excited	34	16, 5	61, 8
	Surprised	25	12, 1	45, 5
	Curious	23	11, 2	41, 8
	Confused	14	6, 8	25, 5
	Frustrated	9	4, 4	16, 4
	Anxious	3	1, 5	5, 5
	Bored	1	0, 5	1, 8

Table 3. Co-occurrences of situational interest and motivation/emotion pairs

Node 1	Node 2	Edge weight	% of all edges	% of self-edge
Sit. Interest	Flow	42	23, 6	100, 0
	Excited	30	16, 9	71, 4
	Surprised	25	14, 0	59, 5
	Curious	23	12, 9	54, 8
	Confused	9	5, 1	21, 4
	Frustrated	6	3, 4	14, 3
	Anxious	1	0, 6	2, 4
	Bored	0	0, 0	0, 0

4 Discussion

This research responds to demands to explore emotions in game-based learning [1]. We extended previous research by examining epistemic emotions, emotions that motivate learners to engage in cognitive activities, and their relation to flow experience and situational interest in a health literacy game. While most previous studies have examined relations between motivational constructs and emotions with correlational analyses, systemic research on how epistemic emotions are coupled with motivational constructs is scarce. Thus, we utilized co-occurrence network analysis to achieve a deeper understanding of whether and how emotional and motivational experiences are coupled with each other during game-based learning.

4.1 How Engaging the Game Was?

Both the motivational and emotional measures indicated that the game engaged students and induced positive emotional responses. The results are in line with previous studies indicating that game-based learning is emotionally charged [2, 6]. However, this study shed light also on nature of experienced emotions. Previous research has shown that positive activating epistemic emotions enhance engagement in learning environments [25]. For example, surprise and curiosity might facilitate greater knowledge exploration behaviors [26]. However, both negative activating and deactivating epistemic emotions were found to hinder engagement although negative activating emotions (e.g., frustration) might also facilitate short-term engagement through triggering extrinsic motivations to avoid failure [25, 27, 28]. In light of this line of research, it can be claimed that the current game-based learning environment facilitated enjoyable and engaging learning experiences since students reported higher intensity-levels of positive epistemic emotions compared to the negative epistemic emotions. Further, previous research has indicated that boredom can impair the systematic use of learning strategies which tends to undermine the effectiveness of learning activities [18]. In that sense, the used game was very successful as only four students reported experiencing boredom. Further, most participants reported high-intensity levels of flow and situational interest. The findings imply that positive epistemic emotions might facilitate enjoyable game-based learning experiences and contribute to learning engagement.

4.2 Flow, Situational Interest, and Epistemic Emotions as Indicators of Engagement

Consistent with a recent study [9], we found a strong positive correlation between flow and situational interest. The co-occurrence network analyses provided new insights into this relationship. We found an asymmetrical pattern of the "situational interest-flow" co-occurrence. When situational interest occurred, flow was always co-occurring. However, experienced flow did not always accompany situational interest. This suggests that situational interest could be a prerequisite or a potential trigger for experiencing flow but not an adequate state ensuring high flow experience. On the other hand, flow refers to an optimal psychological state that occurs when challenges and skills are in balance [10]. It might be possible that although the topic and the game did not interest some of the students, the appropriate challenges and fluent gameplay may have facilitated the intensity of flow. In general, our findings indicate that flow can be experienced without experiencing high levels of situational interest. Thus, it seems that a moderate level of situational interest would be sufficient for some learners to experience flow. -

The current study goes beyond revealing the trend of shared variation among epistemic emotions and motivational constructs with correlational analysis. It shows distinct sub-groups of both frequent and rare co-occurrences among flow, situational interest, and epistemic emotions. Overall, the current findings imply that flow and situational interest are highly coupled with each other. Further, they both mostly co-occur with epistemic emotions on the positive valence spectrum than negative. The study also demonstrated that epistemic emotions, flow, and situational interest reveal interesting qualities of game-based learning and thus it is useful to use all of them as proxies of engagement.

4.3 Limitations and Future Directions

There are some limitations in our study and the findings should be interpreted carefully. It is probable that the used retrospective questionnaire did not grasp all epistemic emotions that students experienced when they played the game. It is also possible that the emotions that students reported were not always necessarily epistemic in nature. For example, students may have reported achievement emotions based on their success in the game (e.g., enjoyment or anxiety) instead of emotions induced by the knowledge processed while playing the game. Further, the topic of the game was sensitive and may have induced topic emotions in students. However, in one think-aloud study in which epistemic emotions were measured, most of the reported emotions were epistemic in nature [18]. Nevertheless, we emphasize that questions used to measure epistemic emotions should be carefully aligned with the object of epistemic emotions in future studies. The other limitation is that we conducted a short study, and thus it was not reasonable to measure learning outcomes. In future studies, the relations between epistemic emotions and learning outcomes should be investigated. Further, for example, think-aloud studies could be conducted to explore what game elements induce epistemic emotions.

Acknowledgments. This research is funded by the Strategic Research Council (SRC).

References

1. Loderer, K., Pekrun, R., Plass, J.L.: Emotional foundations of game-based learning. In: Plass, J.L., Mayer, R.E., Homer, B.D. (eds.) Handbook of Game-Based Learning, pp. 111–151. MIT Press, London (2020)
2. Ninaus, M., et al.: Increased emotional engagement in game-based learning–a machine learning approach on facial emotion detection data. Comput. Educ. **142**, 103641 (2019)
3. Krath, J., Schürmann L., Von Korflesch, H.F.: Revealing the theoretical basis of gamification: a systematic review and analysis of theory in research on gamification, serious games and game-based learning. Comput. Hum. Behav. **125**, 106963 (2021)
4. Plass, J.L., Kaplan, U.: Emotional design in digital media for learning. In: Tettegah, S.Y., Gartmeier, M. (eds.) Emotions, technology, design, and learning, pp. 131–161. Academic Press (2016)
5. Mayer, R.E.: Searching for the role of emotions in e-learning. Learn. Instr. **70** 101213, (2019)
6. Greipl, S., et al.: When the brain comes into play: neurofunctional correlates of emotions and reward in game-based learning. Comput. Hum. Behav. **125**, 106946 (2021)
7. Newmann, F.M.: Student Engagement and Achievement in American Secondary Schools. Teachers College Press, New York (1992)
8. Fredricks, J.A., Filsecker, M., Lawson, M.A.: Student engagement, context, and adjustment: addressing definitional, measurement, and methodological issues. Learn. Instr. **43**, 1–4 (2016)
9. Kiili, K., Lindstedt, A., Koskinen, A., Halme, H., Ninaus, M., McMullen, J.: Flow experience and situational interest in game-based learning: Cousins or identical twins. Int. J. Serious Games **8**(3), 93–114 (2021)
10. Csikszentmihalyi, M.: The flow experience and its significance for human psychology. Optimal Experience: Psychol. Stud. Flow Consciou. **2**, 15–35 (1988)
11. Kiili, K., Lindstedt, A., Ninaus, M.: Exploring characteristics of students' emotions, flow and motivation in a math game competition. In: CEUR Proceedings, vol. 2186, pp. 10–29 (2018)
12. Guo, Z., Xiao, L., Van Toorn, C., Lai, Y., Seo, C.: Promoting online learners' continuance intention: an integrated flow framework. Inf. Manag. **53**(2), 279–295 (2016)
13. Hidi, S., Renninger, K.A.: The four-phase model of interest development. Educ. Psychol. **41**, 111–127 (2006)
14. Muis, K.R., Chevrier, M., Singh, C.A.: The Role of epistemic emotions in personal epistemology and self-regulated learning. Educ. Psychol. **53**(3), 165–184 (2018)
15. Vilhunen, E., Turkkila, M., Lavonen, J., Salmela-Aro, K., Juuti, K.: Clarifying the relation between epistemic emotions and learning by using experience sampling method and pre-posttest design. Front. Educ.: Educ. Psychol. (2022)
16. D'Mello, S., Lehman, B., Pekrun, R., Graesser, A.: Confusion can be beneficial for learning. Learn. Instr. **29**, 153–170 (2014)
17. Pekrun, R., Vogl, E., Muis, K.R., Sinatra, G.M.: Measuring emotions during epistemic activities: the epistemically-related emotion scales. Cogn. Emot. **31**(6), 1268–1276 (2017)
18. Muis, K.R., et al.: The curious case of climate change: testing a theoretical model of epistemic beliefs, epistemic emotions, and complex learning. Learn. Instr. **39**, 168–183 (2015)
19. Moeller, J., Ivcevic, Z., Brackett, M.A., White, A.E.: Mixed emotions: network analyses of intra-individual co-occurrences within and across situations. Emotion **18**, 1106 (2018)

20. Schmidt, H.G., Rotgans, J.I.: Epistemic curiosity and situational interest: distant cousins or identical twins? Educ. Psychol. Rev. **33**(1), 325–352 (2021)
21. Engeser, S., Rheinberg, F.: Flow, performance and moderators of challenge-skill balance. Motiv. Emot. **32**(3), 158–172 (2008)
22. Tang, X., Renninger, K.A., Hidi, S., Murayama, K., Lavonen, J., Salmela-Aro, K.: The differences and similarities between curiosity and interest: meta-analysis and network analyses. Learn. Instr. **80**, 101628 (2020)
23. Christensen, A.P., Golino, H., Silvia, P.J.: A psychometric network perspective on the validity and validation of personality trait questionnaires. Eur. J. Pers. **34**(6), 1095–1108 (2020)
24. Csardi, G., Nepusz, T.: The igraph software package for complex network research. Int. J. Complex Syst. **1695**(5), 1–9 (2006)
25. Loderer, K., Pekrun, R., Lester, J.C.: Beyond cold technology: a systematic review and meta-analysis on emotions in technology-based learning environments. Learn. Instr. **70**, 101162 (2020)
26. Vogl, E., Pekrun, R., Murayama, K., Loderer, K.: Surprised–curious–confused: epistemic emotions and knowledge exploration. Emotion **20**(4), 625–641 (2020)
27. Goetz, T., Hall, N.C.: Emotion and achievement in the classroom. In: Hattie, J., Anderman, E.M. (eds.) International guide to student achievement, pp. 192–195. Routledge, London (2013)
28. Sabourin, J.L., Lester, J.C.: Affect and engagement in game-based learning environments. IEEE Trans. Affect. Comput. **5**(1), 45–56 (2013)

Swarming as a Bird/Fish: Investigating the Effect of First-Person Perspective Simulation on Players' Connectedness with Nature

Sotirios Piliouras$^{(\boxtimes)}$, Jiaqi Li , Vivian Imani Dap , Ilse Arwert ,
Ross Towns , and Tessa Verhoef

Media Technology, Leiden University, Rapenburg 70,
2311 EZ Leiden, The Netherlands
s.piliouras@umail.leidenuniv.nl

Abstract. During recent years, the need to promote environmental knowledge and pro-environmental behaviors has become more evident. The efforts towards effective environmental education include the use of simulations that aim to bring human players closer to the natural world. In the specific case of swarm simulators, they are often constructed in a two-dimensional space and experienced from a third-person perspective, lacking the immersive benefits of seeing a game world through the character's eyes. In this study, we developed schooling and flocking simulators to examine whether playing the simulators can affect people's understanding of swarming behavior and feeling of connectedness to nature, made quantifiable through pre- and post-simulator questionnaires. Experiencing the simulations in first-person perspective was found to increase feelings of kinship with animals, raising connectedness to nature. Additionally, a positive correlation was observed between people's engagement in the simulation and the increase of connectedness to nature. These findings could be useful insights in designing serious games for raising awareness or behavioral change related to environmental education.

Keywords: Environmental education · Connectedness to nature · Simulation games · Swarming behavior · First-person perspective

1 Introduction

Environmental issues such as climate change, pollution and species extinction have become a central concern for human societies, with 28% of all assessed species currently under threat of extinction [8]. However, different attitudes and levels of knowledge about the environment have been found among individuals [5,19]. People's pro-environmental attitudes are connected with their support for environmental policies and regarded as an important part of the protection

---

S. Piliouras, J. Li, V. I. Dap and I. Arwert—Contributed equally to this research.

© The Author(s), under exclusive license to Springer Nature Switzerland AG 2022
K. Kiili et al. (Eds.): GALA 2022, LNCS 13647, pp. 160–169, 2022.
https://doi.org/10.1007/978-3-031-22124-8_16

of the environment [19], which is why raising awareness and positive attitudes towards environmental issues is key to facing these concerns. Increasing efforts by organisations such as the UN to increase awareness have led to the growth of Environmental Education (EE) as a field of study [5,18,20].

Researchers in the field of EE focus on both cognitive and affective aspects of people's engagement with nature, aiming to improve both individuals' knowledge about the environment and their attitude towards it. This is believed to be the "key entry point" for EE and the precursor to pro-environmental behavior [18,20]. Media such as films, simulations and games are common tools to effectively increase knowledge and promote pro-environmental attitudes. For example, films have been found to be effective in changing people's understanding and attitude towards nature and making them more environmentally sensitive. After watching a nature documentary about insects, participants demonstrated improved knowledge as well as more positive emotional feelings about insects [1].

Simulations and games have been frequently examined in EE research and have been found to be both enjoyable and useful for learning [9,10,22]. Simulation activities are considered a necessary part and one of the most effective techniques for EE programs. Through physical simulations, students can replicate animals or animal skills for survival in the natural world, thereby learning about environmental concepts and increasing their awareness of environmental issues [25].

Digital simulations have also been used as an EE tool, for example in digital games. Previous research found positive effects of simulation games in EE by fostering the understanding of climate change [24]. To raise people's awareness about environmental challenges, a serious game called 'Save the Planets' was developed based on life simulation game scenarios. Save the Planets invited players to nurture the planets in the game and results showed that it could positively enhance players' environmental awareness and motivation for environmental actions [17]. SIMULME, an Internet-based simulation game where participants simulate human food purchasing behavior and experience the consequences of their consumption pattern, effectively led to increased support for environmental conservation and ecologically positive consumption behavior [7]. However, results have been mixed overall. For example, in a 1985 study, a computer simulation was designed for water resource management, but no significant change in participants' attitudes was observed after playing the simulation [14].

2   The Present Study

Most digital simulations of the natural world focus on letting players experience simulated human activities in order to raise players' awareness of how their behavior can affect the environment [7,10,14]. To our knowledge, very few of these invited players to experience simulated animal behaviors like the previously-mentioned physical simulation activities did [25]. Since watching an insect-related nature documentary increased people's knowledge of and positive feelings towards insects [1], experiencing the animal world by playing a simulation might also offer potential for EE. A mobile game 'Savannah' was designed for animal behavior learning, in which players act as a pride of lions in the Savannah trying to survive in this territory despite the dangers and obstacles [6]. A positive learning effect was observed among the participating children, explained by the researchers as the influence of a direct experience of the simulation, although no effect was measured for the affective aspects of EE. We therefore set out to investigate whether computerized animal behavior simulators can be an effective environmental education tool in both cognitive and affective aspects.

We focused on swarming behavior, which can be found among several species in the animal kingdom. For example, both starlings and herrings are known for their swarming behavior, which is known as flocking for starlings and schooling for herrings. This behavior mainly consists of three simple parameters: i) *Separation* - the distance a single animal will take from others to avoid collision, ii) *Alignment* - the sameness in direction and iii) *Cohesion* - the degree in which animals try to move towards the center of the flock without colliding [16].

Existing swarm simulations are often implemented using a two-dimensional representation of a flock, with abstract shapes representing the swarming entities [23]. However, previous research showed that players get more immersed and involved in a game world that is seen through the eyes of a character [4]. Additionally, empathetic feelings, which enhance the player-avatar identification in video games [11], often result from deep involvement and shared perspective [3]. We therefore hypothesized that playing from the perspective of an individual within the swarm would lead to increased immersion and involvement in the simulation [2]. Furthermore, the use of more immersive materials has been linked to an increase in knowledge retention [12]. Thus, we arrived at our research question: **can simulating swarming behavior from a first-person perspective help increase players' engagement, understanding of the behavior, and feelings about nature?**

To examine players' change of feelings, we chose to focus on their sense of connectedness with nature. Research has shown that the more connected people feel to the natural world, the less harm they would do to it [13]. We therefore hypothesize that **(1) Experiencing swarming behavior in a computer-based simulation can help participants understand more about swarming and feel more connected to the natural world; (2) Compared to simulations experienced from a third-person perspective, simulations that allow players to experience swarming behavior from a first-person perspective as one of the birds or fish within the swarm can lead to higher engagement and better EE effects.**

3   Method

3.1   Swarming Simulators

We created two swarming simulators based on the swarming simulator by Lorenzo Mori [15], which uses the real behavioral rules (separation, alignment and cohesion) followed by individual animals to simulate accurate swarming behavior. One of our simulators featured a school of fish and one a flock of birds (see Fig. 1). The two were mechanically identical; the different skins were implemented to gauge whether there was a difference in participant response based on animal type. These simulators were presented to the participants from either a first-person perspective, in which the player is part of the flock by watching through the perspective of one of the birds/fish, or a third-person perspective, where the player controls a camera that does not move with the flock. In this paper we'll refer to the simulators as B1 (stands for "Bird in 1st-person perspective"), B3 ("Bird in 3rd-person perspective"), F1 and F3. In each of the four simulators, the player could control the animals' speed, as well as the influence of separation, alignment and cohesion on the movement of the individual animals. This allowed the player to experiment with these factors until they found a combination of settings that allowed for the emergence of realistic swarms.

Fig. 1. The four simulators and the controlling sliders.

3.2 Participants and Procedure

Participants were chosen using convenience sampling, with the criteria of having prior experience in using computers and internet browsing. No other inclusion criteria were applied. Participants were divided evenly and randomly into 4 groups (B1, B3, F1 and F3) and played the corresponding simulator. Thirty eight people participated in this study, distributed as 9, 10, 9, 10 in group B1, B3, F1 and F3, respectively. Their average age was 28 years old. No significant difference of age was found among the four groups ($F(3,34) = 0.665$, $p = 0.58$). On average they had experience with 2.6 out of all five computer-related tasks (internet browsing, playing video games, software development, game development, simulation development), and 44.7% of them had experience of having pet bird or fish (the animal whose simulator they played), while fish were kept as pets by the participants (73.7%) more than the birds (15.8%).

Experiments were conducted face-to-face, where one participant took part in the presence of one researcher. After signing a consent form, participants were given a pre-test survey. The pre-test survey consisted of three parts: participants' basic information, understanding and perceived complexity of swarming behavior, and their connectedness to nature. In the background information section, we asked about the participants' age, whether they had experience having any pet bird or fish (depending on which animal's simulator they would play), and whether they had experience with the following computer-related tasks: internet browsing, playing video games, software development, game development, simulation development. To measure understanding of swarming behavior, we asked participants what they knew about the mechanism of swarming. We also asked their agreement with four statements related to the difficulty and complexity of swarming. To gauge how connected to nature the participants felt, we used the Connectedness to Nature Scale (CNS) [13] and the Inclusion of Nature in the Self (INS) scale [21] – a single-item instrument asking participants to choose the picture that best described the relation between "self" and "nature".

After that, participants played their assigned simulator. They were instructed to form a swarm on the simulator by controlling the sliders. Participants could take their time to experience the simulator and form a swarm that was, to their view, as realistic as possible. After finishing with the simulation, participants filled out the post-test survey, in which they were asked the same questions about swarming behavior complexity and connectedness to nature. Additionally, we asked how engaged they felt in the simulation. The items for engagement were adapted from the Game Engagement Questionnaire (GEQ) [2] to the specific case of our simulations (e.g., the word 'game' in the questions was replaced by 'simulation'). All questions were measured on a 7-point Likert scale[1].

3.3 Data Analysis

For survey questions about the swarming mechanism, we counted the number of swarming parameters that was mentioned (separation, alignment and cohesion). This worked as a proxy for understanding of the mechanism since these parameters reflect real swarming behavioral rules [16]. For participants' perception of swarming behavior complexity, connectedness to nature and simulation engagement, we calculated the average scores of the items related to these three sections separately. Overall, the higher the scores were in that section, the more complex the participants perceived the swarming mechanism to be. For the sections on connectedness to nature and simulation engagement, the higher the scores, the more connected to nature and the more engaged with the simulation the participants felt.

We conducted paired samples T-tests of the average scores and individual items' scores between the pre-test and post-test for each section in all four groups. We calculated the score change between the pre-test and post-test for each item, and conducted independent samples T-tests and Spearman's correlation analyses to examine the score change of swarming behavior complexity, connectedness to nature and simulation engagement, with the simulator types also taken into consideration.

---

[1] Survey items used in this study can be found here: https://osf.io/ptqav/?view_only=f452d580fe69425989cb1f5d8880eb2b.

Table 1. The average scores and paired samples T-test results for participants' perceived swarming behavior complexity, their feeling of connectedness to nature, and simulation engagement. Significant at alpha of 0.05.

Group	Variable	Pre-test mean	Post-test mean	t	df	p
B1	Swarming behavior complexity	4.22	4.69	−2.57	8	**0.03***
	Connectedness to nature	5.38	5.36	0.26	8	0.80
	Simulation engagement	–	5.08			
B3	Swarming behavior complexity	4.08	4.13	−0.16	9	0.88
	Connectedness to nature	4.76	4.62	0.66	9	0.53
	Simulation engagement	–	4.28			
F1	Swarming behavior complexity	4.75	4.78	−0.10	8	0.92
	Connectedness to nature	5.09	5.16	−0.45	8	0.67
	Simulation engagement	–	4.61			
F3	Swarming behavior complexity	3.88	4.03	−1.33	9	0.22
	Connectedness to nature	4.90	4.76	1.05	9	0.32
	Simulation engagement	–	3.98			
Total	Swarming behavior complexity	4.22	4.39	−1.46	37	0.15
	Connectedness to nature	5.02	4.96	0.83	37	0.41
	Simulation engagement	–	4.47			

4 Results

Table 1 shows the results of the three sections (swarming behavior complexity, connectedness to nature, and simulation engagement) that participants answered on a 7-point scale in the surveys. Paired samples T-test results showed that participants' perception of the complexity of swarming behavior was strengthened after they experienced bird flocking with the first-person perspective simulator ($t(8) = -2.57, p = 0.03$). Regarding the open question "How do you think fish/birds perform schooling/flocking behavior? (the mechanism of schooling/flocking)", on average, participants only correctly mentioned 0.08 out of 3 swarming parameters (i.e., separation, alignment and cohesion) in the pre-test and 0.34 in the post-test. In both the pre-test and post-test, most of the participants didn't mention any parameters (36 participants and 30 participants in pre-test and post-test, respectively).

We conducted an independent samples T-test on the simulation engagement scores between first-person perspective and third-person perspective simulators, and found a significant difference between the two perspectives in the overall engagement score (first-person perspective: Mean = 4.85, SD = 1.18; third-perspective: Mean = 4.13, SD = 0.92; $t(36) = 2.12, p = 0.04$; see Fig. 2). No significant perspective effect was found on the change of overall connectedness to nature score ($t(36) = 1.07, p = 0.29$) and overall swarming behavior complexity score ($t(36) = 0.63, p = 0.53$). We also examined the perspective effect on individual items in these two sections, and found that for participants' feeling of kinship with animals, there was a significant difference of the score change in the

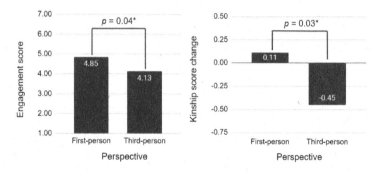

Fig. 2. Differences between simulations in first- and third perspective for participants' engagement (left) and the score change of their feeling of kinship with animals after playing the simulation (right). * Significant at alpha of 0.05.

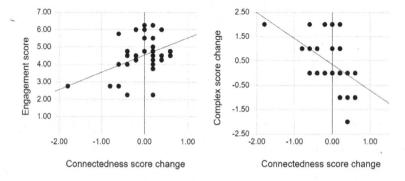

Fig. 3. The score change of participants' overall connectedness to nature was found positively correlated with the overall simulation engagement score (left) and negatively correlated with their agreement level change of "The cognitive process behind schooling/flocking behavior is complex" after playing the simulation (right).

experiment between the first-person (Mean = 0.11, SD = 0.76) and third-person perspective (Mean = -0.45, SD = 0.76); $t(36) = 2.28, p = 0.03$. After playing the simulation, participants who experienced the first-person perspective were more likely to report an increased feeling of kinship if compared to the third-person perspective participants.

Spearman's correlation analysis showed a positive correlation between the overall score of simulation engagement and the overall score change of connectedness to nature ($r_s(36) = 0.36, p = 0.03$). This indicates that overall, the more engaged the participants were in the simulation, the more connected to nature they felt after playing the simulation. We also observed that the participants' change of connectedness to nature was negatively correlated with their change in the agreement level to "The cognitive process behind schooling/flocking behavior is complex" ($r_s(36) = -0.49, p = 0.002$). This result indicates that the more connected to nature the participants felt after playing the simulations, the less cognitively complex they considered swarming to be. The correlation graphs can be found in Fig. 3.

5   Discussion

The results showed very low correctness of swarming parameters answered in both pre-test and post-test. Even after playing the simulation by controlling the parameter sliders, only 30 out of 38 participants mentioned at least one parameter correctly when they answered this question. The reason might be that the question "How do you think fish/bird perform schooling/flocking behavior? (the mechanism of schooling/flocking)" is too open and abstract, so participants didn't know that they were expected to think about the swarming parameters (separation, alignment and cohesion) when answering it in the survey. We found that in group B1, participants perceived swarming behavior to be a more complex mechanism after they tried to simulate a bird swarm by controlling the swarming parameters and experience the whole process from the perspective of a bird, than prior to playing the simulation. This change was found in the bird stimulation rather than fish stimulation, which might be related to the finding that birds were kept as pets less than fish by the participants. Experiencing bird swarm may make the participants feel the bird behavior as more complex than they imagined. No significant change of their overall feeling of connectedness to nature was revealed by the experiment results, which was similar to findings of the previously-mentioned water resource management simulation study, in which no significant change in participants' attitude was observed [14].

An effect of simulation perspective was found in participants' feeling of having a kinship with animals. Those who played the simulator in a first-person perspective as a bird/fish were more likely to have an increased feeling of kinship with animals when compared to those who played the third-person perspective simulators. Additionally, first-person perspective effectively led to a higher engagement level among participants than third-person perspective. This result is consistent with previous research, which found that players were more engaged in a game world when they played it in a first-person perspective [4]. This suggests that it might be beneficial for future EE tools (eg. simulators) to utilize a first-person perspective, rather than third-person. In addition to this, we found a correlation between higher engagement in animal simulators and stronger feeling of connectedness to nature after playing the simulation. This finding supports the importance of high involvement of players' empathetic feelings in video games [3,11] and indicates the great potential in promoting attitude change using simulation game design that can lead to high player engagement. The correlation between connectedness and perceived complexity (i.e., the more connected to nature participants felt after playing the simulations, the less complex they perceived swarming behavior to be) indicated a close relation between reduced perceived complexity in animal behavior and increased feelings of connection with nature. This may potentially contribute to new insights for future EE tools, as it indicates a possibility for EE goals to be furthered by helping students perceive natural system or animal behavior mechanisms as less complex.

6   Conclusion

We developed animal behavior simulators that include two animals (bird and fish) and two perspectives (first-person perspective and third-person perspective) in total to examine (1) if playing digital simulations can help players understand more about swarming and feel more connected to the natural world and (2) if the first-person perspective can help enhance simulation engagement and lead to better EE outcomes. The results showed a limited overall effect of the simulation on changing players' understanding and perception of the animal behavior and changing their general feelings about nature. However, after playing the simulation in a first-person perspective, players had a stronger feeling that bird flocking was a complex mechanism and an increased feeling of kinship with animals. Additionally, first-person perspective also led to players' higher engagement in playing simulators if compared to third-person perspective. The higher engagement level was further found to be associated with an overall stronger feeling of connectedness to nature among all the participants after they played the simulation. These findings indicate that the use of first-person perspective, which is relatively uncommon in this type of simulations, is a promising candidate to increase the effectiveness of three-dimensional simulations as an educational tool, especially when it comes to the depiction and communication of animal behaviors.

References

1. Barbas, T.A., Paraskevopoulos, S., Stamou, A.G.: The effect of nature documentaries on students' environmental sensitivity: a case study. Learn. Media Technol. **34**(1), 61–69 (2009)
2. Brockmyer, J.H., Fox, C.M., Curtiss, K.A., McBroom, E., Burkhart, K.M., Pidruzny, J.N.: The development of the game engagement questionnaire: a measure of engagement in video game-playing. J. Exp. Soc. Psychol. **45**(4), 624–634 (2009)
3. Coke, J.S., Batson, C.D., McDavis, K.: Empathic mediation of helping: a two-stage model. J. Pers. Soc. Psychol. **36**(7), 752 (1978)
4. Denisova, A., Cairns, P.: First person vs. third person perspective in digital games: do player preferences affect immersion? In: Proceedings of the 33rd Annual ACM Conference on Human Factors in Computing Systems, pp. 145–148 (2015)
5. Erhabor, N.I., Don, J.U.: Impact of environmental education on the knowledge and attitude of students towards the environment. Int. J. Environ. Sci. Educ. **11**(12), 5367–5375 (2016)
6. Facer, K., Joiner, R., Stanton, D., Reid, J., Hull, R., Kirk, D.: Savannah: mobile gaming and learning? J. Comput. Assist. Learn. **20**(6), 399–409 (2004)
7. Hansmann, R., Scholz, R.W., Francke, C.J.A., Weymann, M.: Enhancing environmental awareness: ecological and economic effects of food consumption. Simul. Gaming **36**(3), 364–382 (2005)
8. IUCN: The IUCN Red List of Threatened Species (2022). https://www.iucnredlist.org/
9. Koutromanos, G., Tzortzoglou, F., Sofos, A.: Evaluation of an augmented reality game for environmental education: "Save Elli, Save the Environment". In:

Mikropoulos, T.A. (ed.) Research on e-Learning and ICT in Education, pp. 231–241. Springer, Cham (2018). https://doi.org/10.1007/978-3-319-95059-4_14

10. Lee, Y., Kim, S.: Design of "TRASH TREASURE", a characters-based serious game for environmental education. In: de De Gloria, A., Veltkamp, R. (eds.) GALA 2015. LNCS, vol. 9599, pp. 471–479. Springer, Cham (2016). https://doi.org/10.1007/978-3-319-40216-1_52

11. Li, D.D., Liau, A.K., Khoo, A.: Player-avatar identification in video gaming: concept and measurement. Comput. Hum. Behav. **29**(1), 257–263 (2013)

12. Makransky, G., Mayer, R.E.: Benefits of taking a virtual field trip in immersive virtual reality: evidence for the immersion principle in multimedia learning. Educ. Psychol. Rev. **34**, 1771–1798 (2022)

13. Mayer, F.S., Frantz, C.M.: The connectedness to nature scale: a measure of individuals' feeling in community with nature. J. Environ. Psychol. **24**(4), 503–515 (2004)

14. Mills, T.J., Amend, J., Sebert, D.: An assessment of water resource education for teachers using interactive computer simulation. J. Environ. Educ. **16**(4), 25–29 (1985)

15. Mori, L.: Flocking behaviour, a unity3d AI experiment (2018). http://www.lorenzomori.com/unity3d/flocking-behaviour-a-unity3d-ai-experiment

16. Okubo, A.: Dynamical aspects of animal grouping: swarms, schools, flocks, and herds. Adv. Biophys. **22**, 1–94 (1986)

17. Özgen, D.S., Afacan, Y., Surer, E.: Save the planets: a multipurpose serious game to raise environmental awareness and to initiate change. In: Proceedings of the 6th EAI International Conference on Smart Objects and Technologies for Social Good, pp. 132–137 (2020)

18. Pooley, J.A., o'Connor, M.: Environmental education and attitudes: emotions and beliefs are what is needed. Environ. Behav. **32**(5), 711–723 (2000)

19. Rauwald, K.S., Moore, C.F.: Environmental attitudes as predictors of policy support across three countries. Environ. Behav. **34**(6), 709–739 (2002)

20. Rickinson, M.: Learners and learning in environmental education: a critical review of the evidence. Environ. Educ. Res. **7**(3), 207–320 (2001)

21. Schultz, P.W.: The structure of environmental concern: concern for self, other people, and the biosphere. J. Environ. Psychol. **21**(4), 327–339 (2001)

22. Taylor, J.: Guide on Simulation and Gaming for Environmental Education. ERIC (1985)

23. Wilensky, U.: Netlogo flocking model (1998). https://ccl.northwestern.edu/netlogo/models/Flocking

24. Wu, J.S., Lee, J.J.: Climate change games as tools for education and engagement. Nature Clim. Change **5**(5), 413–418 (2015)

25. Zipko, S.J.: Simulation for environmental education and awareness. Sci. Activities **17**(2), 32–38 (1980)

Design of a Novel Serious Game
for the Detection and Measurement
of Obsessive-Compulsive Disorder

Ameera Alajlan[1] , Ahmed Alqunber[2] , and Yahya Osais[2,3]($\boxtimes$)

[1] The Hxplore Summer Research Program, King Fahd University of Petroleum
and Minerals (KFUPM), Dhahran, Saudi Arabia
[2] Computer Engineering Department, King Fahd University of Petroleum
and Minerals (KFUPM), Dhahran, Saudi Arabia
{s201830640,yosais}@kfupm.edu.sa
[3] Interdisciplinary Research Center for Intelligent Secure Systems (IRC-ISS), King
Fahd University of Petroleum and Minerals (KFUPM), Dhahran, Saudi Arabia

Abstract. People with Obsessive Compulsive Disorder (OCD) suffer
from recurring unwanted thoughts (called obsessions) that drive them to
do certain actions repetitively (called compulsions). People with OCD
feels stuck in a stressful cycle of obsessions and compulsions. There are
two approaches to diagnosing and assessing people with OCD. The first
one is conducted in the doctor's office. The second one is conducted
inside a special-purpose room that is typically setup in the hospital. This
second environment is constructed using virtual and augmented reality.
Both approaches are challenging with difficulties such as the high cost
and stigma of therapy. Fortunately, there is a third approach that uses
specialized computer games to achieve the same goals. This third approach has not been researched yet in the context of OCD detection and
measurement. In this paper, we present the design and implementation
of a serious game that can provoke OCD and then measure the intensity of the resulting obsessions and compulsions. This new game is based
on the concept of cognitive gameplay. As such, the interaction between
the proposed game design elements leads to the emergence of different
cognitive processes, such as attention, memory, and planning, which are
essential in the study of OCD. The proposed game design elements have
been reviewed and approved by two psychiatrists.

Keywords: Digital psychiatry · Serious games · Cognitive gameplay ·
Obsessive compulsive disorder · Cognitive processes · Memory ·
Attention · Planning · Game design elements

1 Introduction

Obsessive-Compulsive Disorder (OCD) is a mental disorder characterized by
feelings of anxiety and fear [1]. In 2017, the World Health Organization (WHO)

This work is protected with a US provisional patent with the number 63342804.

K. Kiili et al. (Eds.): GALA 2022, LNCS 13647, pp. 170–180, 2022.
https://doi.org/10.1007/978-3-031-22124-8_17

listed anxiety disorders, which include OCD, as the sixth largest contributor to non-fatal health loss [2]. Also, the number of people worldwide who do not have access to mental health services is still high [3]. Further, in our community-based survey that included 174 participants, 95% of the participants find the current cost of mental health services to be high with challenges such as societal stigma. Also, 75% of the participants prefer not to visit a psychiatrist and rather get a diagnosis via a computer application, such as a game. In addition, on average, a patient with OCD needs to spend about $1000 (not including the cost of medications) on her treatment plan. This cost covers the initial few visits before receiving an official diagnosis and a few subsequent follow-up visits. Clearly, it is important to develop innovative methods to efficiently diagnose and help those who do not have access to mental health services. Serious games are one of these methods.

Serious games help overcome several challenges faced by both patients and healthcare providers. First and foremost, serious games cost significantly less. In a recent study on the economical impact of OCD on patients in China [4], early detection of OCD has been recommended as a way to reduce the cost of OCD. Serious games can be used for the early detection of OCD. Secondly, unlike the worry and social stigma associated with visiting specialists, serious games can be used by patients in the comfort of their homes. Thirdly, patients in disadvantaged communities and remote areas can be covered, especially during the early detection phase.

In this paper, a novel serious game for the detection and measurement of OCD is presented. The game contains a set of innovative design elements appropriate for OCD. The game has been implemented in the Unity game engine using the C# programming language. The next two sections cover some necessary relevant background and literature. Then, an overview of our proposed game is given. After that, the game design elements constituting our game are explained in detail. Then, the results of the design review session by two psychiatric experts are summarized. This is followed by suggestions for future works. Finally, a conclusion is given.

2   Digital Psychiatry for OCD

Digital psychiatry is an umbrella term that comprises mental health and digital technologies [5]. It is concerned with the development of digital tools for the detection, measurement, diagnosis, monitoring, and treatment of mental illnesses. Serious games fall under this umbrella [6]. Digital mental health interventions using serious games include cognitive behavioral therapy [7], exposure and measurement using virtual reality [8–11], and awareness [12]. Next, the role of Virtual Reality (VR) in OCD measurement and treatment is discussed further.

VR-based serious games have been shown to be effective in provoking anxiety, which is the force that drives OCD. In VR-based serious games, players' responses can be directly measured and then assessed. However, these experiments require special setups that are available only in hospitals and private clinics. Further, OCD symptoms are often stimulated and demonstrated in private environments like home and the workplace. In addition, the cost of developing VR-based serious games is still high. Hence, there is a clear need for an alternative that is less costly and more accessible.

The following characteristics distinguish our game from VR-based games for OCD. Our game is not a simulation of an actual environment like homes. Rather, our game employs the paradigm of cognitive gameplay to provoke anxiety. Further, our game can be used in many more applications such as self-assessment by people in their homes, early screening of OCD by healthcare providers, and mass surveying of communities by organizations and governments.

3   Cognitive Engagement in Games

Cognitive processes emerge in serious games from the interaction between the player and the game. Of course, this interaction is facilitated by the the underlying mechanics and dynamics of the game. The compound effect is an experience referred to as a *cognitive gameplay* [13]. Such a gameplay experience engages a player in cognitive activities such as planning, decision-making, and problem-solving. Our game contains design elements that target two cognitive processes: memory and attention. Patients with OCD suffer from memory and attention deficits [14]. For example, it is very hard for OCD patients to maintain complex visual patterns in memory (e.g., see Fig. 2(d)). In addition, it is very hard for OCD patients to focus their attention on the task at hand since they are consumed in task-irrelevant operations. In our game, the main task is to establish a correspondence between the surfaces on two shapes (see Fig. 1(b)). The main task-irrelevant operation is to establish and maintain reference points (see Fig. 4(b)).

The design of our game follows the guidelines of the INFORM framework [15] for the systematic design of cognitive gameplays. INFORM stands for Interaction desigN For the cORe Mechanic. The core mechanic of a game is the set of action-reaction patterns that take place between the player and the game. These patterns of interactions lead to the activation of several cognitive processes, like planning and problem-solving, in the mind of the player. This is the essence of cognitive gameplay.

It should be pointed out that we have also been inspired by the hypothetical cube-based game described in [15]. Our game employs the same game mechanics. Also, we use the number of cube turns as a performance metric. However, our game contains additional features specifically designed for OCD. Furthermore, additional performance metrics are used. More details will be given in the subsequent sections.

4   Game Description

Our proposed game is referred to as *the cube*, which is also the main element in the game. The cube is a three-dimensional shape that has six surfaces. Only

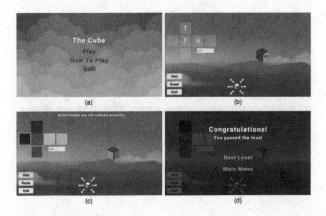

Fig. 1. First level in the game: (a) Game start screen, (b) Correspondence between the surfaces in the 2D and 3D shapes on the stage, (c) Highlighting wrongfully colored surfaces, (d) Progression to next level on successful completion of current level.

three surfaces will be visible to the player at any time as shown in Fig. 1(b). The stage also contains a two-dimensional view of the six surfaces of the cube. At the beginning of the game, the correspondence between the cube surfaces and the surfaces in the two-dimensional view should be established. The Top (**T**), Front (**F**), and Right (**R**) surfaces are clearly identified for the player (see again Fig. 1(b)). This hint will automatically disappear after a few moments. The arrows shown at the bottom of the stage are used for rotating the cube. The Player rotates the cube using these arrows, identifies the color of a specific surface on the cube, selects the color from the dropdown menu, and changes the color of the corresponding surface on the two-dimensional shape. The **Hint** button is used to invoke assistance while playing the game. When the player clicks on this button, the surfaces in the two-dimensional shape with the wrong colors are highlighted (see Fig. 1(c)). The **Reset** button is used for restarting the current level. The **Quit** button gracefully ends the game. Finally, Fig. 1(d) shows the screen displayed at the end of level one. A level ends if the colors of the corresponding surfaces on the two shapes match. The player can then move to the next level by clicking on the **Next Level** button.

The game has five levels. Figure 2(a)-(d) show level two to level five, respectively. Each level is characterized by the number of cells on every surface of the cube. Each cell has its own color. In the current version of the game, colors are randomly generated from a specific set of distinguishable colors. Similar to level one, a player will complete each subsequent level if she successfully copies the colors from the cells on the cube surface to the corresponding cells in the two-dimensional shape. Clearly, as the player progresses through the levels, matching the cells becomes more harder.

Fig. 2. Levels two to five in the game. In level k, there will be $k \times k$ colored cells on every surface of the cube.

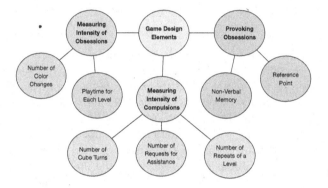

Fig. 3. Three categories of game design elements. These elements are embodied in the mechanics of the game and its entities.

5 Game Design Elements

The main goal of the game is to raise the anxiety level of the player by putting her in a continuous state of uncertainty. In this way, the player will be pushed to perform the compulsive actions. Therefore, to achieve this goal, three sets of design elements have been identified and implemented in our game. Figure 3 shows a mindmap of the proposed game elements. There are three categories of game design elements: (1) elements that provoke obsessions, (2) elements that measure the intensity of obsessions, and (3) elements that measure the intensity of compulsions.

The first element in the first category is referred to as the **Reference Point**. This new design concept is inspired by a tactic employed by OCD muslim

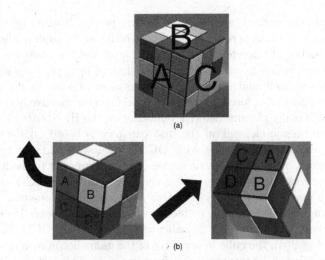

Fig. 4. Two levels of reference points that rotate as the cube is rotated: (a) The whole surface can be used as a reference point in level one. (b) Every cell on a surface can be used as a reference point in level two. Arrows represent rotations.

patients during prayers[1]. Such people with OCD use the reference point to control their anxiety. For example, when a person with OCD performs a prayer[2], she mostly feels unsure about the number of bowings and prostrations she has performed. In this case, some people use a pen as a reference point. When the patient performs the first prostration, she rotates the pen to the right. Also, when she prostrates again, she rotates the pen in a different direction. So, in this case, the pen, which acts as a reference point, helps the patient to control her anxiety.

Similarly, in our game, when the player rotates the cube, she has to identify a cell on every surface as a reference point for the easy identification of other cells and their colors. In the first level of the game, every surface contains only one cell (see Fig. 1(b)). Hence, there will be only one reference point on each surface. However, as the player progresses through the levels, the number of cells increases on every surface. Consequently, the number of potential reference points also increases. For example, as shown in Fig. 2(a), there are four potential reference points on each surface. Thus, for the kth game level, there are k^2 potential reference points on each surface. This combinatorial increase in the number of reference points and the resulting visual patterns are going to have a profound impact on OCD patients who cannot tolerate uncertainty.

There are two levels of reference points (see Fig. 4). In the first level, the surface itself is used as a reference point. In the second level, however, the indi-

---

[1] Based on interviews with actual OCD muslim patients. This design concept is general and applicable to different types of tasks such as prayers and checking.

[2] A physical activity referred to as *Salah*. It involves a set of movements like bowing and prostration.

vidual cells on the surface are used as reference points. Both types of reference points rotate as the cube is rotated (see Fig. 4(b) for an example). The gradually increasing number of reference points in each level and the continuous rotation of the reference points provoke anxiety and doubts in a person with OCD. It partly causes an intimidating image (i.e., a source of fear) in her mind [16]. This intimidating image forces the player to perform compulsive actions such as checking and seeking reassurance (e.g., clicking on the Hint button).

The second game element in the first category is based on the concept of non-verbal memory [17]. People with OCD have low confidence toward non-verbal resources, such as geometric shapes, when compared to healthy people. A connection was found between the increasing severity of OCD and the low confidence in non-verbal memory [17]. Our game contains geometric shapes: the cube itself and the cells on each surface along with their colors. These are non-verbal resources. They represent a challenge for people with OCD. For example, as shown in Fig. 2(d), the cube in level five of the game becomes very complex in terms of maintaining the two types of reference points. This is due to the increase in the number of cells on each surface, the greater variation in the cell colors, and the different distribution of colors on each surface. Clearly, it is challenging for a person with OCD to confidently remember the surface color patterns as well as the locations of the reference points on every surface in the cube.

As for the second category of design elements, the playtime for each level can be used as a measure of the intensity of obsession. A person with OCD is expected to take a longer time in performing each level. It should be noted that doubts increase when a player takes a longer time to finish a level. In other words, we expect a positive correlation between the length of playtime and the level of anxiety in the player. The second design element in this category is the number of color changes. A patient searches for ways to cope with the intimidating images in her mind (i.e., internal fears). Therefore, she is expected to change colors again and again. The number of color changes is directly proportional to the level of anxiety in the player.

Finally, the third category of design elements focuses on measuring the intensity of compulsions. The first element involves the number of times each level is repeated. The increase in the magnitude of the intimidating images (i.e., the number of cells and colors on every surface) leads to increasing doubts in the player's non-verbal memory and puts the player in a severe state of anxiety that causes her to restart the level. Hence, the number of times a player repeats a level is directly proportional to the severity of the player's compulsions. The second element in this category is about the number of times the player asks for assistance in identifying places of conforming and/or non-conforming cells. This element simulates the mental state of a person with OCD when she tries to ignore concerns through rational thinking. Rationalizing is a technique to control anxiety. Therefore, the number of times the player asks for assistance is directly proportional to the severity of the player's compulsions. The last element in this category involves the number of cube turns performed by the player. This element simulates the mental state of a person with OCD when she tries to fight

Table 1. Questionnaire for reviewing the proposed game design elements by experts in psychiatry. For each statement, the expert has to select one of four options: absolutely appropriate, appropriate, inappropriate, or unrelated.

No.	Statement
1	The reference point represents a tool that assists the patient in controlling herself. Therefore, losing track of the reference point provokes doubts and anxiety in a patient with OCD
2	Multiplicity of cells and their colors on a single surface causes a patient's low confidence in her ability to store the correct pattern in her memory
3	A patient with OCD takes a longer time to finish every level in the game. This is due to the challenges resulting from the other elements in the game, such as the absence of the reference point and the low confidence in non-verbal memory
4	The patient tends to change colors to cope with the anxiety that feeds the intimidating pictures in her mind
5	The increase in the magnitude of the intimidating image effect in the mind of an OCD patient leads to an increase in her anxiety. This can cause the patient to restart the level again to get rid of anxiety
6	While playing, a patient with OCD requests assistance in identifying conforming and non-conforming cells. In this way, the patient will control her anxiety and ensure that the gameplay goes well
7	A patient with OCD tends to rotate the cube more when compared with the number of rotations made by a healthy person
8	The proposed game induces doubts into an OCD patient
9	The proposed game causes an OCD patient to engage in a compulsive behavior
10	The proposed game can be used in detecting and measuring OCD
10*	**The proposed game can be used in detecting and measuring the likelihood of some OCD symptoms**

* Statement 10 has been revised based on the recommendations of the psychiatric experts.

obsessive thoughts through rumination. Rumination is a mental compulsion in which an OCD patient engages with her obsessive thoughts in an effort to figure them out [18]. Therefore, the player is expected to rotate the cube to ensure conformity and thus control her doubts. As a result, the number of times the cube is rotated is directly proportional to the severity of the player's compulsions.

6   Review of Game Design Elements by Experts in Psychiatry

A design review session was conducted remotely by the first author with two practicing psychiatrists. Both psychiatrists were present in the session and they decided to give a common opinion. The two psychiatrists were not involved in the design of the game. In the fist half of the session, a PowerPoint presentation was given. In this presentation, the goal of the game was clearly stated. Also, an overview of our research methodology was given. Further, some relevant approaches and games in the literature were highlighted. After that, the game, its rules, and how it is played were described. Finally, the proposed game design elements were explained in detail. At the end of the presentation, time was allocated for clarification and discussion.

In the second half of the session, the two psychiatrists were asked to rate the statements in the questionnaire shown in Table 1. For statements 1–9, both psychiatrists reported them as *appropriate*. As for statement 10, it was reported by both as *inappropriate*. Both psychiatrists agreed that statement 10 needed to be re-written. They recommended the new statement shown in bold at the end of Table 1. The overall outcome of the design review session was that the proposed game can provoke obsessions in OCD patients and make them engage in compulsive behaviors. Also, the game can measure the intensity of the resulting obsessions and compulsions. Hence, the game can detect and measure the likelihood of some OCD symptoms.

7   Future Works

The current implementation of the game is a proof-of-concept available in the form of a desktop application. In order to evaluate the effectiveness of the game, we plan to conduct experiments with real OCD patients. Furthermore, to expand our user base, we plan migrate the game to the Cloud and offer it as a Software as a Service (SaaS). In this way, the game becomes available to end consumers (such as patients and psychiatrists) via Web browsers and Cloud services. We also plan to use artificial intelligence to generate proper cubes for different types of OCD patients and to build predictive models using the data generated from the game.

8   Conclusion

OCD involves doubts that can evolve into obsessions, which eventually lead to compulsive actions. Serious games based on the concept of cognitive gameplay are essential in the study of OCD. This paper has proposed a set of game design elements for the purpose of detecting and measuring OCD symptoms. A game embodying the proposed design elements have been successfully developed.

Acknowledgements. Ameera Alajlan would like to acknowledge the support received from KFUPM via the summer research program for high school students (Hxplore 2021). Also, she would like to thank Dr. Samah Al-Khawashki and Dr. Ahmed Al-Madani from the Department of Psychiatry at King Saud university in Riyadh for reviewing the game design elements. Ahmed Alqunber and Yahya Osais would like to acknowledge KFUPM for support.

References

1. American Psychiatric Association: Diagnostic and statistical manual of mental disorders, 5th edn. American Psychiatric Association Publishing Inc., Washington, D.C (2022)
2. World Health Organization: Depression and other common mental disorders - Global health estimates. World Health Organization, Geneva (2017). https://apps.who.int/iris/bitstream/handle/10665/254610/WHO-MSD-MER-2017.2-eng.pdf. Accessed 11 July 2022
3. Rialda Kovacevic: Mental health - lessons learned in 2020 for 2021 and forward. World Bank Blogs, https://blogs.worldbank.org/health/mental-health-lessons-learned-2020-2021-and-forward. Accessed 11 July 2022
4. Yang, W., et al.: The cost of obsessive-compulsive disorder (OCD) in China - a multi-center cross-sectional survey based on hospitals. Gen. Psychiatry **34**(6), BMJ Journals (2021)
5. Burr, C., et al.: Digital psychiatry - risks and opportunities for public health and wellbeing. Trans. Technol. Soc. **1**(1), 21–33 (2020)
6. Vajawat, B., Varshney, P., Banerjee, D.: Digital gaming interventions in psychiatry - evidence, applications and challenges. Psychiatry Res. **295**, 113585 (2021)
7. Brezinka, V.: Ricky and the spider - a video game to support cognitive behavioral therapy treatment of children with obsessive-compulsive disorder. Clin. Neuropsychiatry **10**(3), 6–12, Giovanni Fioriti Editore (2013)
8. Kim, K., et al.: Anxiety provocation and measurement using virtual reality in patients with obsessive-compulsive disorder. CyberPsychol. Behav. **11**(6), 637–641, Mary Ann Liebert, Inc. (2008)
9. Kim, K., et al.: Development of a computer-based behavioral assessment of checking behavior in obsessive-compulsive disorder. Compr. Psychiatry **51**(1), 86–93 (2010)
10. Van Bennekom, M.J., et al.: A virtual reality game to assess obsessive-compulsive disorder. CyberPsychol. Behav. Soc. Netw. **20**(11), 718–722, Mary Ann Liebert, Inc. (2017)
11. van Bennekom, M.J., et al.: A virtual reality game to assess OCD symptoms. Front. Psychiatry **11**. Frontiers Media SA, Lausanne, Switzerland (2021). https://www.frontiersin.org/articles/10.3389/fpsyt.2020.550165/pdf. Accessed 11 July 2022
12. Kartberg, E.: OCD and empathy games - using empathy games to inform the public about OCD. MS thesis. University of Skövde, Skövde, Sweden (2019). https://www.diva-portal.org/smash/get/diva2:1367393/FULLTEXT01.pdf. Accessed 11 July 2022
13. Haworth, R.: An investigation of cognitive implications in the design of computer games. Doctoral dissertation. University of Western Ontario, Ontario, Canada (2015)
14. Muller, J., Roberts, J.E.: Memory and attention in obsessive compulsive disorder - a review. Anxiety Disord. **19**(1), 1–28 (2005)

15. Sedig, K., Parsons, P., Haworth, R.: Player-game interaction and cognitive gameplay - a taxonomic framework for the core mechanic of videogames. Informatics 4(4), MDPI (2017). https://www.mdpi.com/2227-9709/4/1/4/pdf?version=1484303273. Accessed 11 July 2022
16. Haase, M.T.: The lived experience of obsessive compulsive disorder. Doctoral dissertation. University of Alberta, Edmonton, Canada (2003)
17. Cha, K.R., et al.: Nonverbal memory dysfunction in obsessive-compulsive disorder patients with checking compulsions. Depression Anxiety 25(11), E115–E120 (2008)
18. Stacy Quick: The rumination trap. https://www.treatmyocd.com/blog/the-rumination-trap. Accessed 11 July 2022

The Role of Games in Overcoming the Barriers to Paediatric Speech Therapy Training

Charlotta Elo[1]([⊠]) [iD], Mauri Inkinen[1], Eveliina Autio[1], Tanja Vihriälä[1] [iD], and Johanna Virkki[1,2] [iD]

[1] Faculty of Medicine and Health Technology, Tampere University, Tampere, Finland
charlotta.elo@tuni.fi
[2] Tampere Institute for Advanced Study, Tampere University, Tampere, Finland

Abstract. In addition to training at the therapists', an important part of paediatric speech therapy is home practice with parents. The purpose of this study was to investigate the barriers in home practice from the perspective of speech-language pathologists (SLP). Another goal was to gather an understanding on the role of games in speech therapy and how games could be used to overcome the above barriers. Participants were 26 SLPs in Finland who participated in an online questionnaire. Our findings indicate that successful speech therapy home practice is affected by multiple factors, such as resources, motivation and commitment, but also by multiple stakeholders. According to our results, SLPs are active users of games. The games SLPs use in their clinical work are self-made, speech therapy-targeted games (board games, digital games, functional games), commercial board games, and commercial digital games. SLPs commonly use games as platforms that they modify for different purposes. The games are used to make the speech therapy training itself playful, and playing a game is used as a reward after training. Based on our results, the supporting role of games in speech therapy is recognized by SLPs but there is still great unused potential.

Keywords: Gamification · Paediatric speech therapy · Serious games · Survey

1 Introduction

Speech-language pathologists (SLPs) work with children of all ages with challenges in speech, language, oral motor skills, breathing, or eating. Children with challenges in speech motor skills, such as childhood dysarthria or childhood apraxia of speech, make up a large proportion of the caseloads of most paediatric SLPs [1]. Studies [2] indicate that a higher dose or higher dose frequency of a specific intervention results in more effective outcomes compared to lower dose or lower dose frequency, meaning that rehabilitating requires a lot of repetition. Thus, speech therapy practice is often intensive, consisting of many repetitions, and can continue daily for months or even years. This kind of persistent training requires a lot from the children, as they must find motivation to keep up the exercises. Subsequently, SLPs must be able to motivate the children for training repeatedly.

© The Author(s), under exclusive license to Springer Nature Switzerland AG 2022
K. Kiili et al. (Eds.): GALA 2022, LNCS 13647, pp. 181–192, 2022.
https://doi.org/10.1007/978-3-031-22124-8_18

Empirical evidence confirms that with adequate training, parents can provide effective interventions compared to no treatment; in many cases, such interventions can even be as effective as traditional SLP-delivered therapy while being more cost-effective [3–6]. Despite empirical support for (and widespread SLP recognition of) the importance of parental engagement for successful home practice [7–9], ensuring adequate parental involvement is difficult. Unfortunately, parents in prior studies have described home practice as not fun and a chore to get over with [10] and indicated that sustaining their motivation is hard and stressful [11]. Thus, another major motivation challenge of SLPs is to be able to motivate the children and their parents for home training.

Serious games are games used for "serious", non-entertainment purposes [12, 13]. These purposes include, for example, learning and education, rehabilitation, and health promotion. The use of serious games in rehabilitation, including speech therapy, has been studied [12], and they have been recognized as one way of maintaining motivation. Still, there is no previous research data on which games are used by SLPs in their clinical work and in which ways these games are used. Thus, in our publication we study 1) what are the barriers SLPs perceive as preventing the successful implementation of home practice and 2) what is the role of games in paediatric speech therapy?

2   Method

2.1   Study Design and Participants

The data collection was conducted using an online questionnaire. A voluntary participation request and a link to our study's online questionnaire was sent to various social media communities for Finnish SLPs in December 2021. All 26 responses were appropriate and thus included in the data. No additional demographic details (i.e., besides occupation) were collected to maximize anonymity.

The questionnaire was developed iteratively, first among the research team, then tested on an external SLP. Based on this external feedback, item wording was honed, and the questionnaire was tested again on a different external SLP. This version was accepted as final. The content (translated from Finnish) analyzed for the study was in response to the following prompts: (1) How have you made speech motor exercises motivating for a child? Give at least three concrete ideas, (2) Give at least three concrete examples of tasks that motivate to practice speech motor skills at home, (3) In your experience, what practical factors prevent the implementation of home practice? and (4) Free comments on the topic.

2.2 Analysis

Analysis of the Barriers. All research team members concurrently discussed initial data classification of each segment of data that was as small as possible while forming a complete, coherent singular concept. During subsequent phases of thematic organization [14], identified codes were checked against these segments to ensure the codes represented the original meanings in the data. These codes were analyzed and categorized further by two researchers resulting in a codebook version containing 4 major themes with a total of 10 subthemes. This codebook version was tested to achieve intercoder reliability by conducting an intercoder agreement to 100% of the data. The agreement with an external researcher, not involved in the research, was 72.6%. After that, all researchers discussed the data and codes, making changes to the codebook. Following that, with the external researcher, another intercoder agreement test by coding 100% of the data was done with the agreement of 87.6%. The researchers conducting the second intercoder agreement discussed the differences until they reached a conclusion. Finally, the codebook was reviewed again and agreed upon by all researchers. The final version of the codebook consisted of 4 major themes and 11 subthemes.

Analysis of the Games. The research team collected and analyzed all the answers, for questionnaire questions 1 and 2, where SLPs reported on how they use games in their clinical work. First, two researchers went through the data, independently thematizing the responses. Following that, they compared the themes they had formed and discussed the differences until they reached a conclusion about the themes, resulting in a codebook containing 5 major themes and 4 subthemes. During subsequent phases of thematic organization, the identified codes were checked to ensure the codes represented the original meanings in the data. Next, an external researcher, not involved in the research, went through the data to check that all game-related responses had been identified. The external researcher reviewed and commented on the two researchers' codebook. Finally, the codebook was reviewed again and agreed by the two researchers and the external researcher. The final version of the codebook consisted of 4 major themes and 5 subthemes.

3 Results and Discussion

3.1 Barriers to Children's Speech Therapy

As seen in Table 1, the four major themes were: (1) family life, (2) parents, (3) challenges in working with the child, and (4) the SLP. The themes are in the table in order of magnitude. Most of the respondents mentioned more than one barrier.

Table 1. Themes and subthemes related to barriers identified from the data, with examples mentioned by SLPs and the percentage of respondents who mentioned the theme or subtheme.

Theme	Subtheme	Examples of the barriers mentioned (with respondent ID in parentheses)	By (%)
Family life			76.9
	Resources	"Busy everyday life" (SLP10) "Families are strained." (SLP 2)	69.2
	Siblings	"In families with many kids, who sometimes have other special needs kids too, practice tends to be rare." (SLP 9) "Multiple special needs children in the family" (SLP 20)	19.2
Parents			73.1
	Commitment	"Parents don't commit to practicing." (SLP 22) "Parental indifference toward practicing" (SLP 3)	38.5
	Not understanding the importance	"Thinking that therapy is for practice" (SLP 2) "Parents don't prioritize home practice because they feel that since the child is understood at home, it's not a big problem that less familiar people don't understand their speech." (SLP 24)	34.6
	Motivation	"Parents lacking motivation has to be the biggest factor." (SLP 13) "Poor parent motivation" (SLP 8)	34.6

(*continued*)

Table 1. (*continued*)

Theme	Subtheme	Examples of the barriers mentioned (with respondent ID in parentheses)	By (%)
	Feeling incompetent	"The family is unsure whether they know how to guide practice properly." (SLP 2) "Experience of not being able to do the job" (SLP 12)	15.4
	Parent language/communication/cognition challenges	"Parents 'don't know how' to do exercises despite guidance, as in parents have poor cognitive or everyday-life management skills." (SLP 14) "The parents' own speech-motor problems [and] bi- or multilingualism can be a hurdle or even a barrier." (SLP 17)	11.5
Challenges in working with child			57.7
	Motivation	"The child won't do it, because practice without a fun motivator or game just isn't fun." (SLP 5) "Paper tasks being 'boring' and unmotivating." (SLP 21)	38.5
	Child-parent interaction problems	"Parenting difficulties, in which case I may not even guide toward home practice if the parent is critical or shaming when guiding the child" (SLP 15) "Problems in the child-parent interactive relationship; the child refuses to practice with the parent" (SLP 6)	23.1

(*continued*)

Table 1. (*continued*)

Theme	Subtheme	Examples of the barriers mentioned (with respondent ID in parentheses)	By (%)
SLP			34.6
	Guidance	"Insufficient guidance: if the speech-language pathologist just "throws homework at the family" without sufficient guidance, the parents may think that, e.g., they don't have time to sit down and practice with the child. The SLP must give parents guidance [on] how practice can be implemented amid everyday life: during car trips, or attaching the routine to brushing teeth or playing games, etc." (SLP 10) "I always take speech-motor clients' parents along for sessions, so they see what and how to practice." (SLP 13)	34.6
	Collaboration	"Motivating and encouraging parents is the most important thing, so that we can reach a good collaborative relationship." (SLP 3) "There's no time to see parents and thus I can't motivate/guide them." (SLP 25)	15.4

Family Life. The most often mentioned family life subtheme was resources, meaning general strain or stress and difficulties finding time for and scheduling home training. This was unsurprising given the theme's prevalence in previous studies [11, 15–17]. For example, all six parents interviewed by Sugden et al. [11] mentioned how being busy makes it challenging to fit home practice into their schedule. Importantly, at least one parent report from a study by Davies et al. [18] explicitly links the tension of competing family and home time demands to decreased motivation. As more free time is typically difficult to come by, ways around this barrier are likely to be found primarily in more efficient organization of training schedules. For instance, one of our respondents identified evenings as an often-impractical time for training, as the child may be tired, suggesting that practice at day care may be more opportune.

Families' other children were mentioned as another family life barrier for home practice, especially when several children in the same family have special needs or similar challenges, which has also come up in previous studies [11, 17]. None of our respondents went into further detail, but prior studies (e.g., [17]) indicate that siblings wanting to be part of the practice activity can be distracting. Suggested solutions to this barrier include having another caretaker distract the siblings during practice or practicing with an older child while younger ones are asleep [17].

Parents. The second largest major theme was parent-related barriers. Our results regarding parental feelings of incompetence have also been raised in past studies (e.g., [10, 15]. Mothers interviewed by Goodhue et al. [17] inversely connected the severity of the child's problem with their confidence in administering home practice. This is unfortunate, because similar parental uncertainty has been linked to a desire for a less personally active approach in their child's therapy [18]. Such uncertainty may also explain much of what the SLPs perceive as miscellaneous or unexplained parental noncommitment in our data and past studies (e.g., [19]).

Our results suggest many parents don't understand the importance of parental involvement and home practice, often expecting the SLP alone to take responsibility for their child's treatment. These results mirror those of several prior studies, including SLP -surveys [15, 16] and parent interview studies [11, 17, 18]. In these, parents have often expressed uncertainty about what speech-language therapy and their role in it consist of as well as an initial assumption that the SLP would carry out the intervention primarily alone.

Many respondents described parental motivation as vital for home practice. A factor conceptually close to motivation—parental lack of commitment—was among the most-reported barriers in our data. This result mirrors a survey study by Lim et al. [7], in which lack of parent engagement was the second-most common SLP-service delivery barrier. Some respondents did causally link parents without motivation to other factors: namely, parental expectations that practice won't help anyway, a belief that their child won't be able to concentrate on practice in the home setting, or the idea that the child being understood at home is enough and thus speech practice isn't necessary. These rationales relate to other themes identified in our data, particularly insufficient understanding of home practice importance and challenges in working with the child.

The final parent-related subtheme arising from our data was parental challenges in language, communication, or cognition. One SLP described lacking a common language with the parents as sometimes leading to communication falling short. Parents may also have their own speech-motor challenges or not share (all) languages with the child, making it harder to support the child's home practice. One respondent also attributed parents' not knowing how to do home exercises to poor cognitive skills or everyday life management skills. Past studies have not typically mentioned these types of barriers arising from individual parental traits and abilities, more often focusing on shared difficulties (e.g., time and scheduling), as discussed above.

Challenges in Working with the Child. The third largest major theme was the challenges in working with the child. In a study by Watts Pappas et al. [20], negative child emotions evoked by therapy caused strong reactions in parents as well, including discontinuing therapy. Thus, child and parent motivations toward therapy are clearly tightly linked. When children enjoy the practice, they are likely to actively remind the parent to practice with them [17], thus helping overcome many family life or parent barriers.

Our finding of general parent-child relationship features hampering home practice have also come up in past studies, though the importance of this dynamic has rarely been highlighted as a major finding. One example is a study by Thomas et al. [10], wherein parents described how emotionally difficult it can be for them to have to provide negative feedback (as instructed by the intervention) to their child. Many parents also reported that their child expressed fewer negative, had better emotion regulation skills, and generally "worked better" at the clinic with an SLP than with them at home. These findings underscore how vital it is to get parents actively involved during training sessions to properly instruct and practice skills.

SLP. The fourth major theme of barriers to speech therapy home training consisted of challenges related to the SLP. Collaboration barriers cited included misunderstandings and being unable to keep in touch regularly enough, either because of too little time or the lack of a shared language with parents. Guidance barriers included insufficient explanations of how and why to do practice, not fully motivating and encouraging parents, not helping parents figure out how to fit practice into busy family schedules, giving the child too many exercises for them to remember, and not including parents in session so they can learn how to practice at home. These results mirror prior findings by Sugden et al. [11] in which parents indicated SLP support in guiding home practice and reassuring parents of their ability to carry it out has been crucial but is still sometimes inadequate.

3.2   Role of Games in Paediatric Speech Therapy

Types of Games. Although games were not mentioned in the questionnaire, altogether 18 out of 26 (69.23%) respondents mentioned a game at least once. In the analysis about the role of games in speech therapy, 3 major themes about game types one of which had a total of 3 subthemes were identified. The themes were (1) self-made (the respondent or another SLP), speech therapy-targeted games (board games, functional games and digital games), (2) commercial board games and (3) commercial digital games. The games were

(1) used during the exercises to make the exercises playful and thus motivating and (2) as a reward, where the child was allowed to play a game (in most cases a tablet game) after speech therapy training. The themes and subthemes, as well as examples of the games mentioned are seen in Table 2.

In a recent study, Saaedi et al. [12] reviewed the use of digital games for children with speech disorders. According to the work, digital games are actively designed specifically for versatile speech therapy purposes and the use of games increased children's motivation and concentration during training. In our results, it is interesting that many SLPs use (commercial) games as platforms that they modify for different purposes, for example by adding parts or functions or just by taking advantage of a game board that is related to child's interests and using it for something else than playing the game itself. Further, it is notable that board games were more often mentioned than digital games, whereas the most often mentioned games were self-made, speech therapy-targeted games (board games, functional games, digital games). SLPs mentioned that fast-paced and surprising games are the most motivating.

The identified parent-related barriers, such as lack of motivation and engagement and feeling of incompetence, were the major themes identified from the responses in this study. These are also supported by an SLP survey by Lim and colleagues [7], where the most-often reported strategy for overcoming the barriers was training parents to conduct therapy at home. The authors in [7] concluded that SLPs could likely benefit from better tools for training and engaging parents. This seems reasonable, as parents can hardly be expected to learn about SLP -service importance without education (or "training"), and without the motivation arising from that understanding, why would they be engaged? Also, many parents in a study by Davies et al. [18] explicitly expressed a desire for the SLP to teach them better techniques for training (and interacting) with their child to replace methods that weren't working. Based on these findings, use of specifically designed games that guide and monitor the home practice could reduce parents' feelings of incompetence and thus increase their motivation for their child's speech therapy practice.

Saaedi and collegues [12] also stated that most of the games they reviewed had been designed so that they are suitable for home practicing when parent, who has been instructed by a SLP, plays games together with the child. As parental challenges in language, communication, or cognition also showed up as identified barriers in our responses, games that engage the parents to speech therapy training could offer support, for example in forms of games in different languages and instructive games, to the parents as well. Further, as the other children in the family were seen as a barrier to training, social games that involve the whole family could be an interesting option. Especially the use of functional games, such as car tracks and playing tag, which were mentioned by the respondents, seem a potential way to bring the speech therapy training as part of the family life in a playful way.

Table 2. Themes and subthemes related to role of games identified from the data, with examples mentioned by SLPs and the percentage of respondents who mentioned the theme.

Theme	Sub theme	Examples of the games mentioned (with respondent ID in parentheses)	By (%)
Self-made, Speech therapy-targeted games			53.9
	Board games	"I have crafted a fishing game." (SLP 4) "A dice game where several moving characters in parallel compete to see who can finish first" (SLP 20)	
	Functional games	"Playing tag outside while practicing the /r/." (SLP 13) "A car track, where you drive around and under the road you can see task cards that you have to collect." (SLP 24)	
	Digital games	"I have created an electronic game, e.g., on Keynote or in my workplace's own online rehabilitation environment." (SLP 4) "Animated games made with Power point" (SLP 12) "PowerPoint exercises found from Ideas for remote speech therapy -Facebook group." (SLP 4)	
Commercial board games		"Use of different games e.g., dice games, memory games, board games." (SLP 20) "The most motivating games have been fast-paced and surprising games (e.g., Slap the Ghost, Bomb Game or Pop-Up Pirate)." (SLP 8)	38.5
Commercial digital games		"Digital exercises: speech motor exercises can easily be added to a theme that motivates the child, e.g., a Minecraft game." (SLP 10) "Games on the abcya -site (first task, then decorate e.g., muffins, then task-decorate again…)" (SLP 4)	19.2
Role of games			50.0
	Make training playful	"Tasks Combined with Different Activities: Games, Playing, Building, Etc." (SLP 2) "GAme Boards Related to the Child's Interests E.G., Frozen, Paw Patrol, Etc." (SLP 12)	
	Training rewarded by playing	"FIrst a Speaking Task, then Favorite Game on the Ipad" (SLP 25) "REwards, Such as Playing on an iPad" (SLP 19)	

Our study contained some limitations that future studies could remedy. Firstly, the respondents were all from Finland, and a more international viewpoint would make the results more generalizable. Further, this study consisted of the views of SLPs only, while studying the views of parents and children themselves is important, because their views of the same situation can provide insights SLPs can't detect, such as how parent and child feelings affect motivation for the intervention (e.g., [20]). We also concur with Lim and colleagues' [7] assessment that parental variables, such as socioeconomic status and mental health may moderate how effectively they can implement home practice for their child, warranting further study. As paediatric speech therapy training is associated with many types of interventions, depending, for example, on the severity of the child's impairment, the barriers may also be experienced differently. Thus, future studies should also investigate how factors, such as age of the children and type of the intervention, affect to the barriers perceived, as those factors were not at the focus of this study.

4 Conclusions

There are several barriers, such as resources, motivation and commitment, associated with paediatric speech therapy home practice according to SLPs in Finland. The barriers identified in this study seem to be comparable to the barriers identified in previous international studies (see, e.g., [17, 19]). SLPs use board games, functional games, and digital games to make the training playful, and playing a game is used as a reward after training. SLPs often see games as platforms that can be modified to support speech therapy training in versatile ways.

Based on our results, the supporting role of games in speech therapy is recognized by SLPs but there is still great unused potential. We feel that utilizing the data collected, the barriers identified, and the current and potential role of games recognized in this study, support the development of games and playful solutions to address especially those challenges related to paediatric speech therapy home practice. Next, our goal is to connect game designers and SLPs to create design guidelines to provide specific indications to serious game designers.

References

1. Baker, E., McLeod, S.: Evidence-based practice for children with speech sound disorders: part 1 narrative review. Lang Speech Hear. Serv. Schools 42(2), 102–122 (2011)
2. Kaipa, R., Peterson, A.M.: A systematic review of treatment intensity in speech disorders. Int. J. Speech Lang. Pathol. 18(6), 507–520 (2016)
3. Tosh, R., Arnott, W., Scarinci, N.: Parent-implemented home therapy programmes for speech and language: a systematic review. Int. J. Lang. Commun. Dis. 52(3), 253–269 (2017)
4. Roberts, M., Kaiser, A.P.: The effectiveness of parent-implemented language interventions: a meta-analysis. Am. J. Speech Lang. Pathol. 20(3), 180–199 (2011)
5. Lawler, K., Taylor, N.F., Shields, N.: Outcomes after caregiver-provided speech and language or other allied health therapy: a systematic review. Arch. Phys. Med. Rehabil. 94(6), 1139–1160 (2013)

6. Roberts, M., Kaiser, A.P., Wolfe, C., et al.: Effects of the teach-model-coach-review instructional approach on caregiver use of language support strategies and children's expressive language skills. J. Speech Lang. Hear. Res. **57**(5), 1851–1869 (2014)

7. Lim, J., McCabe, P., Purcell, A.: Challenges and solutions in speech-language pathology service delivery across Australia and Canada. Eur. J. Per. Cent. Heal. **5**(1), 120 (2017)

8. Melvin, K., Meyer, C., Scarinci, N.: What does "engagement" mean in early speech pathology intervention? A qualitative systematised review. Disabil. Rehabil. **42**(18), 2665–2678 (2020)

9. Tambyraja, S.: Facilitating parental involvement in speech therapy for children with speech sound disorders: a survey of speech-language pathologists' practices, perspectives, and strategies. Am. J. Speech-Lang. Pathol. **29**(4), 1987–1996 (2020)

10. Thomas, D., McCabe, P., Ballard, K.J., et al.: Parent experiences of variations in service delivery of rapid syllable transition (ReST) treatment for childhood apraxia of speech. Dev. Neurorehabil. **21**(6), 391–401 (2018)

11. Sugden, E., Munro, N., Trivette, C.M., et al.: Parents' experiences of completing home practice for speech sound disorders. J. Early Interv. **41**(2), 159–181 (2019)

12. Saeedi, S., Bouraghi, H., Seifpanahi, M.-S., et al.: Application of digital games for speech therapy in children: a systematic review of features and challenges. J. Healthc. Eng. 4814945–20 (2022)

13. Djaouti, D., Alvarez, J., Jessel, J.-P., Rampnoux, O.: Origins of serious games. In: Ma, M., Oikonomou, A., Jain, L.C. (eds.) Serious Games and Edutainment Applications, pp. 25–43. Springer, London (2011). https://doi.org/10.1007/978-1-4471-2161-9_3

14. Guest, G., MacQueen, K.M., Namey, E.E.: Applied Thematic Analysis. SAGE Publications, Thousand Oaks (2012)

15. Sugden, E., Baker, E., Munro, N., et al.: An Australian survey of parent involvement in intervention for childhood speech sound disorders. Int. J. Speech Lang. Path. **20**(7), 766–778 (2018)

16. Watts Pappas, N., McLeod, S., McAllister, L., et al.: Parental involvement in speech intervention: a national survey. Clin. Linguist. Phon. **22**(4–5), 335–344 (2008)

17. Goodhue, R., Onslow, M., Quine, S., et al.: The Lidcombe program of early stuttering intervention: mothers' experiences. J. Fluency Disord. **35**(1), 70–84 (2010)

18. Davies, K., Marshall, J., Brown, L., et al.: Co-working: parents' conception of roles in supporting their children's speech and language development. Child Lang. Teach. Ther. **33**(2), 171–185 (2017)

19. Mandak, K., Light, J.: Family-centered services for children with complex communication needs: the practices and beliefs of school-based speech-language pathologists. Augm. Alt. Commun. **34**(2), 130–142 (2018)

20. Watts Pappas, N., McAllister, L., McLeod, S.: Parental beliefs and experiences regarding involvement in intervention for their child with speech sound disorder. Child Lang. Teach. Ther. **32**(2), 223–239 (2016)

Ludic Didactics
For an Inspired, Motivating and Playful Education

Mela Kocher(✉)

Zurich University of the Arts, 8005 Zurich, Switzerland
mela.kocher@zhdk.ch

Abstract. The pandemic-related, rapid transformation of learning environments and scenarios into digital spaces gave new urgency to the differentiation of digital didactics. Many new didactic opportunities, but also major technological, social and methodological challenges, emerged. In the phase of exclusively online teaching in 2020, it became quickly evident that the sole transfer from analog to digital teaching was not effective: New designs for motivational learning scenarios were called for. This articles discusses art- and design-based experiments and methods in higher education learning scenarios, where a ludic sophistication of digital didactics was further developed. "Ludic didactics" encompass playful, game-based approaches, methods and settings that support and inspire teachers and learners in education. Thus, ludic didactics are understood more as a form of "playification" than "gamification": Their playful mechanics and methods go beyond the still prevailing use of points, badges and leaderboards which are applied for learning incentives and feedback. In this paper we give examples and propose PHEW (Play/Hybrid/Easy/Walkabout), a set of "superpower" methods for ludic didactics.

Keywords: Ludic didactics · Playification · Education · Serious games · Gamification · Digital didactics

1 Games and Play in Education

1.1 Gamification as Negative Learning Conditioning

Education is gamified, even if it is not always recognized and intended as such. Grading is a numerical or alphabetical feedback system, which in itself is effective at most as extrinsic motivation, but not infrequently puts more pressure on learners than it motivates to learn. It is a high-score system in which one competes against oneself (previous grades) and against others; not infrequently, one is rewarded (e.g., with money) or punished (e.g., with withdrawal of media time, if you are a child) for good or bad grades. Other positive or negative incentive or feedback systems such as stickers or badges, sweets, joker days, leaving early or detention, reward and punish social behavior at school. When teachers

Supplementary Information The online version contains supplementary material available at https://doi.org/10.1007/978-3-031-22124-8_19.

K. Kiili et al. (Eds.): GALA 2022, LNCS 13647, pp. 193–201, 2022.
https://doi.org/10.1007/978-3-031-22124-8_19

aim to be a bit playful, they usually use the format of quizzes or contests, which again are forms of competitive assessments [23].

However, these didactical mechanics have very little to do with "play" and not much to do with "game" either. They are based on the common, nowadays frequent, use of gamification, which handles and conditions with basic game elements in a short-term, superficial way [4]. That kind of "pointsification" might even be harmful, e.g. creating anxiety. "What is important now is to understand that even gamification has a meaning. Gamification, like pointsification, does not simply increase the use and intensity of an activity; instead it transmits precise values related to competition, hierarchy, and predation" [16]. Also, it has long been observed that extrinsic motivation does not automatically turn into intrinsic motivation, but that, on the contrary, "[...] once gamification is used to provide external motivation, the user's internal motivation decreases." [19, p.1].

Scholars have since been "rethinking gamification" in a constructive and critical way [12], and radical concepts like "school without grades" counter pointsification in school and strive for more transparency and commitment in feedback, through dialogic discussions between teachers and learners instead [20].

1.2 Games and Learning

Yet there is still so much room for games and play in education. Well-designed awareness or educational games, such as "Papers, please" [21] or "Dragonbox" [27], have shown us that games are an excellent way to learn, especially when game mechanics and rule sets are interwoven with the message they aim to carry out. In their multimodal way, games can be meaningful for different types of learners.

Accordingly, it is widely acknowledged that (educational) games can or should be used in the classroom [7], but only if they are embedded in an adequate didactic scenario [15]. Engaged discussions [24] and mindful approaches are being taken on how to achieve this [13]. The anthology "Didaktik des digitalen Spielens" (Didactics of Digital Games), for example, discusses in detail the use of different games for teacher's education in the subject German, or for sports and history classes [17]. In summary, mere gaming alone or incoherent edutainment do not work as simple learning bait. It is therefore a matter of didactics, the methodological know-how of the inclusion of digital games in education.

Educational institutions could go a giant step further by not only incorporating new teaching materials – applied games – but thinking more intensively about how education could become more playful overall, how to use game-based, playful methods to create engaging and motivating learning scenarios. What is needed, is to reach beyond the current gamification approach: We need to differentiate the "ludic didactics" – the art and science of embracing playful and game-based approaches to reinvigorate teaching and learning.

In the following, we will elaborate on the challenges and opportunities for such a didactic approach that have opened up in the last two years, since the outbreak of the Covid pandemic.

2 Ludic Didactics

2.1 Differentiation of (Digital) Didactics

When, effectively from one day to the next, teaching was unavoidably shifted from the analog to the digital space, it posed a huge challenge for numerous teachers. Digital didactics, or rather, a multitude of digital didactics [18], were striving to develop state-of-the-art, digitally supported forms of teaching and learning. While the development of technical enhanced teaching and learning has begun many years before the outbreak of the pandemic, studies show that teachers had often struggled with online teaching due to technical, social and motivational factors [26]. The shift to digital education in 2020 meant therefore a great boost to the development digital of didactics. At first, and during the lock-down of the universities, many teachers pursued the strategy of a 1:1 translation or transfer of teaching from the analog to the digital space, and used the digital space either as an asynchronous repository (material collection), or held face-to-face lessons via video conferencing.

In many surveys conducted at universities in 2020/2021, it became clear that often learners and teachers in this situation showed motivational difficulties[1]. The interpersonal communication in the discursive digital forms of teaching were susceptible to disruption, due to technology, but also due to the teaching formats of the "digital university", such as a "removal of physicality" ("Enthebung der Körperlichkeit") could be observed [22, p. 47].

New approaches had to be created in order to make room for the interpersonal spaces, for a new spatiality, for a new way of working collaboratively. In particular, the artistic and design-oriented disciplines, which did not function with large theoretical university lectures, were challenged to find new experimental approaches. Here, many smaller and bigger playful interventions emerged, and the differentiation of digital didactics thus also gave a great developmental impulse to the ludic didactics.

2.2 Playful Interventions

Particularly in higher education, didactic innovations were made, and the e-learning and teaching development centers were in great demand to find digital solutions for the various disciplines and departments. Quick interdisciplinary methods for engagement and presence in virtual spaces, e.g. "check-in" and "check-out" methods emerged to capture the personal moods of participants and to functionally begin and end the virtual classroom, i.e., to frame it. These were often play-based, and activating questions and tasks to participants in videoconferences represented small interventions, and sometimes shook the comfort zones. Whether one designed one's screen background thematically to the subject, brought something from one's apartment into the frame, invented or narrated a story together – countless examples showed an immense amount of imagination (Fig. 1).

Numerous business ideas emerged. One particularly successful example is the "Goats on Zoom" project where you can book the presence of a British goat for a video call.

---

[1] Even though many of those surveys are internal and unpublished, see for some discussion and exchange between Swiss university members the hub of the "LeLa Learning Lab for Higher Education Didactics for Digital Skills" [14].

Fig. 1. Surprise intervention with goat Lola, in a higher education team meeting on Zoom

At a set time, the goat shows up (ideally bursts in the virtual room as a surprise guest), stays for 5 min in the video chat and even writes in the text chat [6].

Other playful mechanics soon became standard in online meetings, such as the use of chance (to nudge collaboration in video conferences), the use of wheels of fortunes to gamify decision-making, or the use of online bingo for following (and disrupting) online seminars and lectures – among many other innovative approaches.

3   PHEW

3.1   A Ludic-Didactic Experimental System

In order to capture, systematize and discuss (as well as deconstruct) these smaller and larger experiments within a ludic didactics, we have created PHEW, a discursive and deconstructive set of methods in the E-Learning faculty at the Zurich University of the Arts (ZHdK) [29]. "PHEW is a ludic, design-based, agile and inclusive 'superpower' concept that builds on basic elements of artistic, design and cultural practice of action as a starting point for new teaching-learning concepts and social issues." [2, p. 129]. The "superpower" concept with the acronym PHEW stands for game-based scenarios (Play) in analog, digital or hybrid spaces (Hybrid), is designed to be low-threshold and inclusive (Easy) and pursues an active reflection dimension (Walkabout). Let's take a closer look at two examples of a PHEW application for higher education: First, the element of a walkabout in various applications, and second, a playfully structured, more complex, two-day seminar on educational playgrounds.

3.2 The "Walkabout" as an Activating Tool for Reflection

The walkabout is a learning journey about connecting, randomizing and reflecting. Favorably, the journey happens while going outside, following a free-style adaptation of the rite of passage in Australian Aboriginal society [1]. Also, in the science of strollology, walking is seen as an aesthetic practice [5].

The "walkabout module" can be used very well at conferences where different people come together and where it can be helpful to move outside the conference rooms and take a different spatial perspective. For example, it can be employed to discuss the digital transformation which teaching and learning has been undergoing in the past years. In that sense it was used at the online ELIA Biennale 2020 "Expanding the Arts" and at the Eduhub Days 2021 "Shaping the future of teaching and learning in higher education" where it was both conducted as a 1.5 h session [9, 10].

After a welcome and thematic embedding in the Zoom plenary room, participants were randomly assigned to breakout sessions in groups of two. They walked together outside and had audio and/or video modes activated. Using a custom-built web-based randomized question generator, they asked each other questions about digital learning and teaching and made references to their physical environments [28]. Afterwards, each person individually had time to reflect on the experience alone, giving everyone's individual experience its meditative value.

An offline variation of this module was designed in 2022 as a "Peer Learning Gamification" for a continuing education program for teachers. As part of the LeLa Learning Lab for Higher Education Didactics for Digital Skills, the students go for a walk together, while they can express a constructive project critique with random question cards [14].

The "walkabout" is thus a very straightforward didactic method that moves participants from the screen or classroom outside into the fresh air and into a new spatial, social and cognitive perspective. It works analogue and digital/hybrid and can be blended with more or less ludic elements.

3.3 Playgrounds in Education

A more complex example of ludic didactics is represented by the seminar "Playgrounds in Education", which was held for two hours on each of two consecutive days in February 2022 in the ELIA Future Arts series [11]. The international event, attended by about 50 participants, took place on Zoom and on Miro. The structure of the meeting format was, in some way, a hero's journey with different stations. The goal of the seminar was to gain more knowledge about play mechanics in education and to share and reflect on one's own experience – be it one's own roles, didactic methods, the school as a play system, artistic approaches as play elements, etc. The participants were asked to prepare themselves for the event by taking the "Bartle Test" [3] and then to name themselves on Zoom with their first name and their player type, e.g. Galit (Killer). Graphically displayed on the Miro was then the "rabbit hole" and thus the didactic entrance to the visual setting, which for Day 1 was in the form of a koi, and for Day 2 of a turtle (the latter in reference to Terry Pratchett's Discworld fantasy novels). The individual stations of the conference then took place on the individual fish scales or turtle shells – dramatically zooming in

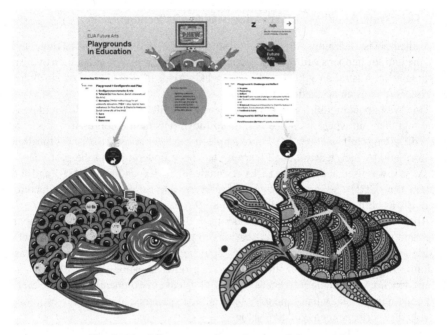

Fig. 2. Playfully structured two days' workshop on Miro.

and out of various topics and questions was thus not only represented cognitively, but also visually (Fig. 2).

The circles or stations, which the participants zoomed in one after the other, presented together a journey, a digital walkabout. They were: a) Configure, b) Tutorial, c) Gameplay, d) Save, e) Quest, f) Game Over. At the beginning of the seminar those stations were all visually covered by blank circles and then, one for one, unveiled by a digital assistant, to create a sense of excitement and anticipation. As an initiation in "configure", participants first had to choose a superhero with a specific superpower to support and inspire them for the day. In a short "tutorial", theoretical basics and concepts about game studies and game mechanics were conveyed in order to provide an informative framework for the participants who were not game-savvy. In "gameplay", everyone was asked to share their own experiences and expand on their understand of ludic didactics, by the help of the PHEW framework. They were acoustically together in Zoom in groups of two, and also visually observing the other contributions on Miro. During a short break, people could then either opt out or play the multi-player browser game paper.io [25] together. In the "save" part, existing questions and feedbacks were collected and discussed, and in the "quest" section the mission for the next day was given: to be a game designer and invent a mini-game for Zoom or Miro. In "game over", the superhero roles were reflected upon and on Zoom the individual take-away messages were adopted in waterfall mode (all participants write in the chat window and then press send simultaneously) (Fig. 3).

The next day in "turtle mode", the participants' games were tested and reflected, and the focus was more on game-related feedback, challenge and immersion in the classroom,

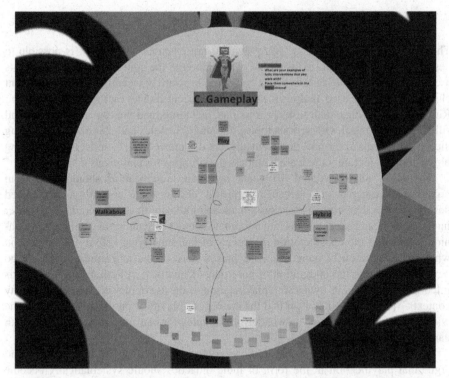

Fig. 3. Group brainstorming about everyone's ludic activities in higher education

with input from a master's student from Art Education, and again with different stations and missions to complete together, in pairs and alone – this time with the inspirational help of a superhero's sidekick.

3.4 Lessons Learned

The concept and set-up of the "Playgrounds in Education" Workshop aimed at very consistently to use game and play elements to structure, name and infuse every moment of this educational scenario, from the preparation, the roles, the activities up to the framing, the communication, the break and the feedback. To discuss playgrounds in education, it needed to be done via a playful approach, if it wanted to be meaningful. This is a complex example of ludic didactics since not only the form, but also the content of the workshops were game-related.

The oral feedback that we received, in evaluating the different ludic didactic interventions that this paper discusses, showed clearly the appreciation of the participants and their motivation to think further in this direction and conduct own experiments. To us it was important to understand that ludic didactic interventions must be designed in an inclusive way: not only addressing the playful and extroverted participants, but also the more observing and calmer learning types – this can be done by structuring groups, allowing different ways of engagement and allowing to scale the playful activities.

4 Playification for Teaching and Learning

The playful walkabout and the Miro seminar are examples for how it is possible to design towards playification instead of gamification in the education sector. No points are awarded, there is no leaderboard or badges as an award or incentive. Instead, different elements of play are used, making meaningful didactical choices for the learning content. Rituals, role-playing, small tasks or missions, including randomness, using humor and silly elements to deal with serious topics, flipping schedules and classrooms, throwing dice, using wheels of fortune, going outside on a discursive stroll or subversively playing bingo during a lecture – there are countless possibilities for playification!

Nicholson already stated 10 years ago that Gamification should turn from organization-centered or mechanism-centered design more towards user-centered design: "Rather than using a point system, meaningful gamification encourages a deeper integration of game mechanisms into non-game contexts. Meaningful gamification techniques focus on the consideration of aspects of the underlying activity to understand where an integration of game elements makes sense. Even more intriguing is to go beyond games into the integration of pure play elements. […] Perhaps this concept is important enough for its own term: 'playification' is the use of play elements in non-play contexts." [19, p. 6]. Nicholson tied the concept of playification to the example of the widely known "Piano Stairs", a wonderful example of urban art, public play and health game.

We will take this shift from gamification towards playification a step further and argue that playification in the form of ludic didactics should systematically become an integral part of education, especially when it comes to the digitization of teaching. Our proposed system of methods and analysis called PHEW (for play, hybrid, easy and walkabout) is one possible example for this. It is now a matter of further systematizing, expanding, and advancing such ludic didactics for motivated, curious, and challenging learning and teaching.

References

1. Ancient Origins. https://www.ancient-origins.net/history-ancient-traditions/walkabout-coming-age-0012191. Accessed 19 July 2022
2. Axelsson, C., Kocher, M.: Playful times – experiencing world: a ludic strategy in arts & education. In: Loffredo, A.M., Wenrich, R., Axelsson, C., Kröger, W. (eds.) Changing Time – Shaping World. Changemakers in Arts & Education. Transcript, Bielefeld [in press]. ISBN: 9783839461358
3. Richard, B.: The Bartle test of gamer psycholog. https://matthewbarr.co.uk/bartle/index.php. Accessed 19 July 2022
4. Bauer, R., Kocher, M.: Spiele – radikale lehr- und lernmittel. In: SwissFuture 01/2020. https://www.swissfuture.ch/de/wp-content/uploads/sites/2/2021/03/sf_120.pdf. Accessed 19 July 2022
5. Burckhardt, L.: Why is landscape beautiful? The science of Strollology. Birkhäuser, Berlin, München, Boston (2015). https://doi.org/10.1515/9783035604139
6. Cronkshaw Fold Farm. https://www.cronkshawfoldfarm.co.uk/goatsonzoom. Accessed 19 July 2022

7. De Luca, V., Rossini-Drecq, E., Ascolese, A.: Turning fun into learning: how serious games inspire new educational frameworks. In: IATED Academy. INTED 2018 Conference Proceedings (2018). ISBN: 9788469794807
8. Edmunds, T., Lauricella, S.: Ludic pedagogy: schooling our students in fun, faculty focus (2021). https://www.facultyfocus.com/articles/philosophy-of-teaching/ludic-pedagogy-schooling-our-students-in-fun/. Accessed 20 July 2022
9. Eduhub Days 2021. Shaping the Future of Teaching and Learning in Higher Education. https://www.eduhub.ch/events/eduhub-days-2021/. Accessed 20 July 2022
10. ELIA Biennial 2020. Expanding the Arts. https://elia-artschools.org/page/2020BiennialConferenceZurich. Accessed 19 July 2022
11. ELIA Future Arts 2022. https://elia-artschools.org/page/ELIAFutureArtsPlaygroundsinEducationProgramme. Accessed 19 July 2022
12. Fuchs, M., Fizek, S., Ruffino, P., Schrape, N.: Rethinking Gamification. Meson press, Lüneburg (2014). ISBN: 9783957960016
13. Huang, W., Soman, D.: A Practitioner's Guide To Gamification Of Education. University of Toronto, Rotman School of Management (2013)
14. LeLa. Lernlabor Hochschuldidaktik für digitale Skills. https://lela.ch/. Accessed 19 July 2022
15. Lorber, M., Schutz, T.: Gaming für Studium und Beruf. Warum wir lernen, wenn wir spielen. hep, Bern (2016). ISBN: 9783035504668
16. Mosca, I.: +10! Gamification and deGamification. In: GAME. The Italian Journal of Game Studies, 1/2012 (2012). https://www.gamejournal.it/plus10_gamification-and-degamification/. Accessed 19 July 2022
17. Möring, S., et al.: Didaktik des Digitalen Spielens, vol. 9. Universitätsverlag Potsdam (2021)
18. Muuss-Meerholz, J.: There is No Digital Didactics. Compendo – Digital Toolbox (2014)
19. Nicholson, S.: A User-Centered Theoretical Framework for Meaningful Gamification. Games+Learning+Society 8.0, Madison, WI (2012). https://scottnicholson.com/pubs/meaningfulframework.pdf. Accessed 19 July 2022
20. Nölte, B., Wampfler, P.: Schule ohne Noten. Neue Wege zum Umgang mit Lernen und Leistung, hep, Bern (2021)
21. Pope, Lucas. Papers, please. 3909 LLC (2013)
22. Ruf, O.: Die Digitale Universität. Passagen, Wien (2021)
23. Spanjers, I.A., Könings, K.D., Leppink, J., Verstegen, D.M., de Jong, N., Czabanowska, K., et al.: The promised land of blended learning: quizzes as a moderator. In: Educational Research Review, vol. 15, pp. 59–74 (2015)
24. Universität Halle. Deutsch-Didaktik-Digital. Schule als Spielfeld. Podium. https://d-3.germanistik.uni-halle.de/event/schule-als-spielfeld/. Accessed 19 July 2022
25. Voodoo. Paper-io. https://paper-io.com/. Accessed 19 July 2022
26. Watson, K., McIntyre, S.: "Too hard, too busy": a case study in overcoming these barriers to online teaching. In: ICEL 2012–7th International Conference on E-Learning (2012)
27. WeWantToKnow AS, DragonBox Algebra (2012)
28. Zurich University of the Arts. https://learning.zhdk.ch/walkabout/. Accessed 19 July 2022
29. Zurich University of the Arts. https://www.zhdk.ch/learning/e-learning. Accessed 19 July 2022

Out of the Maze: Investigating Fluid Intelligence and Numeracy as Predictive Factors of Planning Skills Using Video Games

Gianluca Guglielmo[1](✉) ⓘ, Elisabeth Huis in 't Veld[1,2] ⓘ, Michał Klincewicz[1,3] ⓘ,
and Pieter Spronk[1]

[1] Department of Cognitive Science and Artificial Intelligence, Tilburg University, Warandelaan 2, 5037 AB Tilburg, The Netherlands
G.Guglielmo@tilburguniversity.edu
[2] Sanquin, Department of Donor Medicine Research, Plesmanlaan 125, 1066 CX Amsterdam, The Netherlands
[3] Institute of Philosophy, Department of Cognitive Science, Jagiellonian University, Grodzka 52, 31-048 Krakow, Poland

Abstract. The aim of this study was to test whether an online video game can be used to investigate planning ability and whether fluid intelligence, objective numeracy, and subjective numeracy are predictive of game performance. Our results demonstrate that fluid intelligence is particularly important, which is in line with previous non-game-based studies that show a relationship between classical planning tests and fluid intelligence. Video games have been previously used for research into cognitive processes and taking them online facilitates data collection on a larger scale. Online video games also afford data collection without the expense and stress of a laboratory environment. For these reasons, using online video games to investigate human cognition is a promising alternative to the classic cognitive paradigms used in laboratories.

Keywords: Cognitive skills · Numeracy · Fluid intelligence · Planning capabilities · Video games

1 Introduction

The ability to plan is useful in all areas of life. Individuals that are especially good at planning are typically faster in coming to a decision. Planning, defined as "the predetermination of a course of action aimed at achieving some goals" [1], is often operationalized as sequential decision-making and prediction of an optimal, or at least satisfying, course of action. According to previous research, planning skills are associated with better occupational outcomes, including income [2], and additionally, planning performance is also likely to be associated with more foundational skills, such as numeracy and fluid intelligence [2, 3]. Fluid intelligence and objective numeracy are involved in problem-solving, including calculations and mental rotation of objects. Subjective numeracy is a measure of confidence in one's ability to solve problems that involve numbers, including calculations. Subjective numeracy also measures the preference that one has to deal either with the information presented as numbers or in prose [4, 5].

However, pen and paper versions of psychometric tests are more difficult to use in experimentation. Digital versions of these tests could facilitate the automatic, large-scale assessment of these skills in an easy and remote way. Additionally, video games could be suited for this purpose, as they have been shown to be effective for cognitive skills measurement [6] and could therefore provide a useful tool able to facilitate the study of individual differences in planning skills outside the lab, for non-academics and businesses. Video games have already successfully been used to test cultural differences [7], introduce new business concepts [8], and hire new employees [9], just to name a few. The idea of introducing a planning test as a sort of game was already introduced by [3]. However, no online video game was developed yet to directly measure planning tasks in an online fashion. The aim of this study is to develop an online game able to measure planning skills; in doing so we would like to suggest that online video games can be used to track specific skills and their relationship with more fundamental skills such as fluid intelligence or numeracy We do this by using a game specifically created to engage the planning process. Additionally, we hypothesize that fluid intelligence and numeracy are significant predictors of performance in the game.

2 Related Works

2.1 Planning Tests and Gamification

Several tasks have been developed and used to measure planning capabilities, the most famous of which are the Tower of London (TOL) [10] and the Tower of Hanoi (TOH) [11]. In these tasks, participants have to reorder either balls (in case of the TOL) or disks (in case of the TOH) given certain constraints. Both have been extensively used in different domains such as in child and adult neuropsychology to test, for example, the effect of obsessive-compulsive disorders [12], ADHD [13], and autism [14] on planning capabilities. Other existing planning tasks involve grids or mazes; e.g. the Porteus Maze Test [15] in which the subject has to draw the correct path through as many mazes as possible while avoiding touching the walls of the mazes or the errands-task [1] where participants have to stop by shops, represented as points on a grid, in a fictitious town center. The goal is to find the path with the shortest distance from a starting point to the endpoint while at the same time being able to visit all the shops present on the grid.

Tests, implemented using grids or mazes, and tasks that involve the optimization of the distance traveled, can be used to create a video game to investigate planning skills. In this study, we designed and implemented a video game incorporating the aforementioned features with the intention to investigate the players' capability to plan ahead.

2.2 Effect of Numeracy and Fluid Intelligence

Individual differences in planning skills are sometimes due to differences in the level of (fluid) intelligence, which is defined as the ability to solve novel problems by reasoning and is typically measured by the performance of mental operations, such as solving geometrical puzzles. This may be why fluid intelligence has been identified as a strong predictor of planning performance [3] and more specifically on the TOL and the TOH [16] tasks. Differences in planning ability are also sometimes due to individual differences in numeracy, which is sub-divided into subjective numeracy and objective numeracy. Objective numeracy, often referred to as statistical numeracy, refers to the ability to deal with numerical problems involving probability and statistics. Subjective numeracy refers to the motivational aspect of decision-making and the willingness of the subject to engage in tasks concerning risk appraisal and in general numerical problems. Participants with high scores in subjective numeracy tend to have a more positive attitude toward numerical problems and adopt more complex strategies and fewer heuristics while making decisions [17]. Moreover, when combined, numeracy skills and fluid intelligence are predictors of avoiding decisions with negative consequences and optimizing monetary outcomes [17].

3 Methods

3.1 Sample and Procedure

A total of N = 78 participants were recruited from the University of Tilburg (Netherlands) and received course credits. The sample consisted of 23% (n = 18) men, 75.6% (n = 59) women, and n = 1 refused to provide their biological sex. The participants were $M = 21.27$ ($SD = 3.23$) years old and had $M = 13.64$ ($SD = 4.10$) years of education. The sample size obtained was a posteriori analyzed to evaluate the level of power reached considering the number of predictors and the outcomes used in this study (both conveyed in Sect. 4.3). Such analysis was performed considering a medium Cohen's f-squared effect size of 0.29 calculated using the correlation among predictors and between predictors the outcome [18]. The analysis, performed with the G*Power software yielded an approximated total power of 0.95.

The experiment was run during the Covid-19 pandemic, for this reason, data were collected online avoiding direct contact between participants and experimenters. Participants started the experiment with an online questionnaire in Qualtrics filling in demographic information, after which they completed the cognitive skills tasks. After having completed these tests, participants were directed to play the video game using the link specified in Appendix A. To enter the game, all participants had to first enter a unique identifier and a password and then read instructions and complete a practice level of the game. Afterward, their scores were directly sent to the experimenters via an email created for the purpose.

3.2 Cognitive Skills

Fluid Intelligence. Raven's standard progressive matrices (RPM) was used to measure fluid intelligence. The test consists of 60 patterns (and thus a maximum score of 60), where the participants are asked to complete the pattern by choosing the missing tile. The participants had 20 s to solve each of the patterns, with a total of 20 min for the whole task [19]. This resulted in a good internal consistency of Cronbach's alpha of 0.89 whereas other studies suggested an expected alpha between 0.86 and 0.92 [20].

Numeracy Skills. Objective numeracy was tested using a digitized version of the Berlin Numeracy test (BNT). Participants were asked four numeracy-related questions (with a maximum score of 4), to be completed in 5 min, requiring the participants to be able to work with percentages and proportions (they were allowed to use pencil and paper for calculations). An internal consistency of $\alpha = 0.54$ was obtained (slightly lower than the expected 0.60 [17]). Subjective numeracy was investigated using the Subjective Numeracy Scale (SNS), assessing the attitude that a subject has towards numerical problems. The SNS is composed of 8 questions, scoring on a Likert scale ranging from 1 to 6. The first 4 questions of the SNS are used to measure how confident a participant is in dealing with numerical information (self-efficacy or confidence) [4]. The last 4 are used to measure the participants' preference for information to be presented numerically or in prose. Cronbach's α in this sample was 0.74 (a bit lower than the expected 0.86) [17]. The time it took to complete all cognitive skills tasks was also recorded.

3.3 Videogame Design and Rules

The video game was implemented in Unity and was made available online (Appendix A). Its objective is to move a small yellow circle across a grid to the exit. Each grid contains 40 obstacles (red triangles) arranged in a different order, and 5 targets (green circles) to collect before reaching the end. All grids are drawn using tools provided at: https://www.theedkins.co.uk/jo/maze/design/index.htm.

We set up each game session with two conditions. In the first condition, participants were instructed to minimize the total distance to the end. In the second, they had to minimize the number of obstacles walked on (red triangles). In both conditions, participants were asked to finish the tasks as quickly as possible and could see the elapsed time displayed during the game. The novelty in this game, compared to other paradigms [1, 15], is the use of obstacles in the second condition used to evaluate the planning task. These details, to a certain extent, may be similar to real-life tasks where people have to plan the best course of action considering the presence of obstacles that may occur along the way (e.g. in logistics).

Each participant's session consisted of 6 games with 3 grids per condition where the same grid was never presented twice in a row. All the participants were presented with the same grids for both the triangles and the distance domain in the same order, in both conditions, lower scores represented higher performance. The game provided participants with real-time feedback about their performance in the game measured in terms of time needed and either distance or number of triangles (see Fig. 1). The participants were either asked to minimize the number of obstacles hit (the red triangles) or the total distance to reach the end while collecting the tasks (the green dots). In our game, lower scores represent better performance since in theory, proficient participants manage to reach the end, collecting the tasks, hitting fewer triangles, and walking a shorter distance. The Cronbach's alpha for both triangle and distance conditions (calculated on 78 participants) was equal to 0.70.

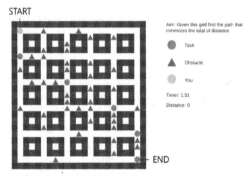

Fig. 1. An example of a game grid. The green dots are targets that the participant has to 'collect' by moving the yellow dot over them and the red triangles are obstacles to avoid (only applicable in condition 2). The instruction and performance are shown on the right of the maze (Color figure online).

3.4 Data Pre-processing

The demographic data and the results of the administered tests were extracted from .csv files obtained via Qualtrics. The pre-processing was performed using the Pandas, and NumPy libraries available in Python.

During the stage of the analysis, the participant not providing their biological sex was discarded. The biological sex information was encoded as 0 = female, and 1 = male. Scores on the cognitive skills tasks were calculated according to the scoring instructions of each task, and then standardized (standardization is a process that rescales the data between 1 and −1 where the mean is around 0). Such a process was performed in order to avoid the effect of data having a different magnitude on the outcome variable [17]. The performance in the game was measured as the total distance in the first condition, and the total number of obstacles hit in the second condition. Hence, a higher score indicates a lower performance. These scores were also standardized to a range between −1 and 1 and combined into one score to assess the overall score of the participants.

4 Results

After having performed the pre-processing, descriptive information was provided to evaluate the potential correlations between predictors. Afterward, we run analyses to evaluate if the two biological sexes differed in their score on the predictors used. Eventually, a regression analysis was run using the cognitive skill scores as predictors (adding age, biological sex, and years of education to the model as control variables) and the total score on the planning game as the dependent variable. The analyses in this section were run using the SciPy and the Statsmodels library in Python.

4.1 Descriptive Information

Participants had an average fluid intelligence score of 43.52 ($SD = 4.76$). Furthermore, the participants scored $M = 1.32$ ($SD = 1.06$) on objective numeracy and $M = 33.7$

($SD = 5.12$) on subjective numeracy. Our results show moderate and weak correlations among subjective and objective numeracy ($r = 0.29, p = .01$), between fluid intelligence and objective numeracy ($r = 0.42, p < .001$), and between subjective numeracy and fluid intelligence ($r = 0.28, p = .01$). However, an analysis to evaluate multicollinearity in the data, showed a variance inflation factor below 2 for all the predictors, including control variables, chosen for this study. Such results suggest a lack of multicollinearity in the data [21].

4.2 Independent Variables and Differences Between Biological Sexes

No gender differences were found in age ($t(34.62) = 1.85, p = .07$), years of education ($t(48.76) = 0.46, p = .65$), objective numeracy ($t(25.09) = -0.61, p = .55$) or fluid intelligence ($t(25.07) = -0.55 p = .59$). However, women ($M = 33.02, SD = 5.27$) scored lower on subjective numeracy than men ($M = 35.8, SD = 5.27; t(36.01) = 2.37$, $p = .02$) and therefore, an interaction term accounting for the effect of biological sex on subjective numeracy was added in the regression model. Given the homogenous (student) sample, age and years of education were not used as a term for potential interactions.

4.3 Predictors of Planning Performance

To assess the effect of fluid intelligence, objective numeracy, and subjective numeracy on the score obtained in the game, a multiple linear regression was run. These predictors explained 23% of the variance obtained in the combined planning game score ($F(7,69) = 2.9, p = .01$). But only fluid intelligence significantly predicted performance in the planning game (See Table 1).

Table 1. The results obtained using a multiple linear regression.

	B	SD	β	U	L	t	p
Biological sex (ref: Female)	−0.04	0.08	−0.06	0.27	−0.46	−0.52	.603
Age	0.08	0.08	0.13	0.23	−0.07	1.13	.263
Years of education	−0.04	0.07	−0.06	0.10	−0.18	−0.51	.615
Fluid intelligence	−0.24	0.08	−0.38	−0.09	−0.40	−3.10	.003*
Objective numeracy	−0.04	0.08	−0.06	0.12	−0.19	−0.49	.627
Subjective numeracy	−0.06	0.08	−0.15	0.07	−0.26	−1.14	.256
Subjective numeracy x Biological sex	0.07	0.09	0.10	0.57	−0.26	0.75	.458

4.4 Planning Game Score

Figure 2 shows the distribution of the total scores of both conditions on the planning game, by fluid intelligence scores. On average, in the first condition, the mean distance was equal to 84.05 ($SD = 26.98$) and in the second condition, $M = 9.02$ ($SD = 2.00$) triangles were hit across the 3 grids. The optimal distance and number of triangles across the 3 grids were respectively 56.67 and 6.00. 26 participants managed to reach the optimal distance score while only 2 managed to obtain the optimal triangles score. No participant obtained optimal performance on both domains. Also, significant correlations between fluid intelligence and the scores ($r = -0.23$, $p = .04$ and $r = -0.29$, $p = .01$) were found across the 2 conditions.

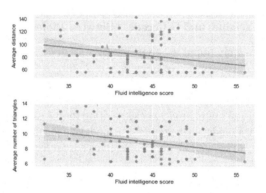

Fig. 2. Scatter plots showing the relationship between fluid intelligence and the scores obtained in condition 1 (minimizing the distance; top) and condition 2 (minimizing number of obstacles hit).

4.5 Relationship of Time Variations in Planning Game and Predictors

The participants required an average of 117.99 s to complete all the 6 proposed grids ($SD = 43.41$), where males took on average 114.41 s to fulfill all the grids ($SD = 49.96$) while females took 119.09 s ($SD = 41.14$); this difference was not statistically significant ($t(24.15) = -0.35$, $p = .73$). On average, participants significantly required more time to complete the triangles domain ($M = 63.03$ s, $SD = 23.49$) than the distance domain ($M = 54.97$ s, $SD = 25.02$) ($t(152) = 2.05$, $p = .04$).

Time-related analyses were also run on the time the participants required to fulfill the tests related to predictors measuring performance in Fluid intelligence and Objective numeracy; such time was based on the last click registered by Qualtrics on the test pages. Participants required 660.47 s ($SD = 130.47$) to complete the RPM where females took 650.26 s ($SD = 130.50$) and males 693.23 s ($SD = 125.10$); however, this difference was not statistically significant ($t(28.72) = -1.25$, $p = .22$). For what concerns the BNT, participants took 237.72 s ($SD = 53.13$) to complete the test; where males and females took respectively 251.05 s ($SD = 44.58$) and 233.66 s ($SD = 54.83$) to complete the task. Such a difference was not significant having a $t(33.49) = 1.34$ and a $p = .19$.

5 Discussion

The planning game we developed for the study reported here required players to plan and optimize their moves through a grid and avoid obstacles. Sequences of player moves displayed a wide range of variability, reflecting the planning and optimization processes at work. We found that higher fluid intelligence scores predict a better-planned and more optimized sequence of moves on the route through a grid to a goal. Fluid intelligence involves processes responsible for manipulating information in real-time, abstraction, and general reasoning, which suggests that these are important mechanisms for planning ahead and optimizing during gameplay. This is not surprising since fluid intelligence has previously been shown to be important to planning [3] and a wide range of complex behaviors and skills [20, 22].

Previous studies showed that numeracy is a predictor of superior decision-making in problems with uncertain and probabilistic outcomes [17]. Our game involved some uncertainty since the grids were complex enough to make it impossible for players to plan their entire route before making their first move. Unexpectedly, we did not find any significant relationship between numeracy and performance. While we found that males tend to have higher subjective numeracy scores compared to women, which means that they are more confident about their ability to solve numerical problems, they did not perform better in the game compared to women. Our results, also suggested that participants required longer to fulfill the triangles domain. Such results, together with the fact that only two participants found the optimal path for the triangles domain, suggest that the triangles domain may be harder than the distance domain.

We also found no effect of age and years of education on performance. This is surprising since previous research showed that age and years of education predict performance in solving mazes, but measures of intelligence do not [15]. Our study points in the other direction. That said, our sample was relatively young and homogenous with respect to age and years of education, as they were all students in the same University, so we remain cautious about just how significant this may be.

One limitation of our study is that it does not use a validated measure of planning performance. This means that we cannot draw strong conclusions about the extent the game we developed captures planning ability. We assumed that it does, because of its similarity to mazes widely used in psychology research to study spatial and social cognition [23], and especially those used to investigate planning, such as the Porteus Maze Test [15], or the more recently developed Electric Maze Test [3]. Our work gamifies these tests by adding extra mechanics at the expense of introducing potential confounds. We are confident about validity since previous work demonstrates that planning skills are important in video games that involve strategy [24].

Our work also makes a methodological contribution. We showcase how video games created using widely-accessible tools can be used to study human cognitive processes. Playing video games online requires little time and affords data to be sent automatically to the experimenter, which facilitates data collection significantly and has the added benefit of being outside of a laboratory setting. Furthermore, an online game like ours can be combined with non-invasive psychophysiological measures based on webcam recordings. This affords an opportunity to investigate the connection between behaviors and psychophysiological reactions to make inferences about psychological processes. Given all this, our paper demonstrates the potential of video games to tap into the same processes, constructs, and behaviors that are engaged in laboratory experiments, and real-life situations.

Acknowledgments. The research reported in this study is funded by the MasterMinds project, part of the RegionDeal Mid- and West-Brabant, and is co-funded by the Ministry of Economic Affairs and Municipality of Tilburg.

Appendix A

Planning game link: https://play.unity.com/mg/other/my-new-microgame-4526.
Identifier: Test2022, Password: logistics.

References

1. Garling, T.: Processing of time constraints on sequence decisions in a planning task. Eur. J. Cogn. Psychol. **6**(4), 399–416 (1994)
2. Fernandez, F., Liu, H.: Examining relationships between soft skills and occupational outcomes among US adults with—and without—university degrees. J. Educ. Work. **32**(8), 650–664 (2019)
3. Sheppard, K.W., Cheatham, C.L.: Validating the electric maze task as a measure of planning. J. Cogn. Dev. **18**(2), 309–322 (2017)
4. Peters, E., Shoots-Reinhard, B.: Numeracy and the motivational mind: the power of numeric self-efficacy. Med. Decis. Making, 729–740 (2022)
5. Zikmund-Fisher, B.J., Smith, D.M., Ubel, P.A., Fagerlin, A.: Validation of the subjective numeracy scale: effects of low numeracy on comprehension of risk communications and utility elicitations. Med. Decis. Making **27**(5), 663–671 (2007)
6. Kokkinakis, A.V., Cowling, P.I., Drachen, A., Wade, A.R.: Exploring the relationship between video game expertise and fluid intelligence. PLoS ONE **12**(11), e0186621 (2017)
7. NorouzzadehRavari, Y., Strijbos, L., Spronck, P.: Investigating the relation between playing style and national culture. IEEE Trans. Games (2020)
8. Buiel, E., et al.: Synchro mania-design and evaluation of a serious game creating a mind shift in transport planning. In: 46th International Simulation and Gaming Association Conference, ISAGA, pp. 1–12 (2015)
9. Allal-Chérif, O., Bidan, M.: Collaborative open training with serious games: relations, culture, knowledge, innovation, and desire. J. Innov. Knowl. **2**(1), 31–38 (2017)
10. Phillips, L.H.: The role of memory in the Tower of London task. Memory **7**(2), 209–231 (1999)
11. Kotovsky, K., Hayes, J.R., Simon, H.A.: Why are some problems hard? Evidence from the Tower of Hanoi. Cogn. Psychol. **17**(2), 248–294 (1985)
12. Delorme, R., et al.: Shared executive dysfunctions in unaffected relatives of patients with autism and obsessive-compulsive disorder. Eur. Psychiatry **22**(1), 32–38 (2007)
13. Riccio, C.A., Wolfe, M.E., Romine, C., Davis, B., Sullivan, J.R.: The Tower of London and neuropsychological assessment of ADHD in adults. Arch. Clin. Neuropsychol. **19**(5), 661–671 (2004)
14. Robinson, S., Goddard, L., Dritschel, B., Wisley, M., Howlin, P.: Executive functions in children with autism spectrum disorders. Brain Cogn. **71**(3), 362–368 (2009)
15. Krikorian, R., Bartok, J.A.: Developmental data for the Porteus maze test. Clin. Neuropsychol. **12**(3), 305–310 (1998)
16. Zook, N.A., Davalos, D.B., DeLosh, E.L., Davis, H.P.: Working memory, inhibition, and fluid intelligence as predictors of performance on Tower of Hanoi and London tasks. Brain Cogn. **56**(3), 286–292 (2004)

17. Sobkow, A., Olszewska, A., Traczyk, J.: Multiple numeric competencies predict decision outcomes beyond fluid intelligence and cognitive reflection. Intelligence **80**, 101452 (2020)
18. Faul, F., Erdfelder, E., Buchner, A., Lang, A.G.: Statistical power analyses using G*Power 3.1: tests for correlation and regression analyses. Behav. Res. Methods **41**, 1149–1160 (2009)
19. Hamel, R., Schmittmann, V.D.: The 20-minute version as a predictor of the Raven Advanced Progressive Matrices Test. Educ. Psychol. Measur. **66**(6), 1039–1046 (2006)
20. Al-Bokaia, H., Al-Subaihib, A.A.: Standard Progressive Matrices (SPM): validity and reliability. Int. J. Innov. Creativity Change **15**(4), 276–293 (2021)
21. Akinwande, M.O., Dikko, H.G., Samson, A.: Variance inflation factor: as a condition for the inclusion of suppressor variable(s) in regression analysis. Open J. Stat. **5**(07), 754 (2015)
22. Kulikowski, K., Orzechowski, J.: All employees need job resources: testing the" Job Demands-Resources Theory" among employees with either high or low working memory and fluid intelligence. Medycyna Pracy **69**(5) (2018)
23. Dudchenko, P.A.: 'A history of 'maze' psychology', Why People Get Lost: The Psychology and Neuroscience of Spatial Cognition (2010)
24. Gabbiadini, A., Greitemeyer, T.: Uncovering the association between strategy video games and self-regulation: a correlational study. Pers. Individ. Differ. **104**, 129–136 (2017)

A Virtual Ship Evacuation Serious Game: Assessment of Data and Passenger Training

Anastasios Theodoropoulos[1](✉) ⓘ, George Kougioumtzoglou[2],
and George Lepouras[2] ⓘ

[1] Department of Performing and Digital Arts, University of Peloponnese, Tripoli, Greece
ttheodor@uop.gr
[2] HCI-VR Laboratory, University of Peloponnese, Tripoli, Greece
https://hci-vr.dit.uop.gr/

Abstract. A considerable loss of life at sea is attributed to maritime accidents in passenger ships. Crew and passenger training with evacuation drills is a challenging and costly process while the complexity and size of ships affect negatively the outcomes in most evacuations. A proposed solution is the development of an evacuation serious game simulator, to improve the repeatability and realism of evacuation drills. To this end, a novel prototype multiplayer serious game was developed. The Ship Evacuation Simulator (SES) allows the simultaneous participation of computer-controlled bots and human-controlled avatars in ship evacuation scenarios. In this paper, numerous sets of scenarios were conducted, with and without the participation of human users, in order to assess SES in terms of training level, evacuation time, survival rate and user immersion. The evaluation process incorporated elements such as fire, smoke, day/night rotation, etc. This paper presents the SES game and then discusses the outcomes of the evacuation sessions. Future research aims to assess the influence of virtual reality technology with SES, in order to achieve higher immersion levels.

Keywords: Serious game · Evacuation · Ship evacuation simulator

1 Introduction

The evacuation of a passenger ship is considered one of the most catastrophic and deadly processes. A series of accidents have occurred worldwide with high numbers of casualties. Previous research highlights the importance to this research field, with many marine accidents [1–4]. Maritime accidents impose high numbers of casualties even nowadays and the main goal here is to reduce the loss of life at sea by training the passengers. The evacuation drills approach provides valuable scientific data, but it is not suitable for passenger training, while it demands high maintenance, and detailed preparation and may cause serious accidents. Moreover, it is considered unsuitable for evacuation training, as it is impossible for an evacuation drill to include high numbers of untrained passengers.

The proposed solution is a serious game simulator, where the passengers will join and play before their journey starts and improve their evacuation skills, while they will

K. Kiili et al. (Eds.): GALA 2022, LNCS 13647, pp. 212–222, 2022.
https://doi.org/10.1007/978-3-031-22124-8_21

familiarize themselves with the ship's structure. In order to implement a realistic and credible evacuation environment, where the users will be immersed and trained, the Ship Evacuation Simulator (SES) was developed [5]. This paper presents the results from the assessment process of the SES. More specifically, the evacuation game, how credibly it simulates evacuation scenarios and how the users improve their performance, after participating in virtual scenarios. Hopefully, this approach may provide a knowledge that passengers can use during real evacuation incidents.

2 Related Work

Evacuation Serious Games (ESG) are usually, used to safely test the evacuability of an area or structure. Availability is a term that derives from the shipping industry evacuation and is defined as the various elements that affect the evacuation of a passenger ship such as the spatial elements, the module layout, the life-saving appliances the crew training, etc. [6]. ESGs may assess the behavior and movement of evacuees and the evacuation rules. Research on ESGs focuses on different areas. e.g., human crowd movement, structural improvement, and human behavior. Examples of ESG include the Serious Human Rescue Game [7], the EVI [8], the VELOS [9], the EVA [10] and the VR Serious Game [11].

Furthermore, concerning immersion in games, a proposed approach is the measurement of the user's ppresence. Presence is the psychological perception that the user is part of the virtual environment, while perception is a function of system characteristics and possible user actions [12]. A Presence of 100% indicates a high level of Immersion, while 0% points out a lack of Immersion [13].

3 SES: A Serious Game for Evacuation Training and Evaluation

SES is a multiplayer serious game, with elements of simulation [5]. The simulation element derives from the ship movement and the behavior of the computer-controlled bots, which have been both implemented within the environment.

3.1 Development

Unreal Engine is considered one of the most popular and successful game engines for this purpose [14]. It supports the importation of high-quality external models, the design of realistic graphics, the flexibility of Blueprint, C++ development, or a combination of both, a reliable physics engine and an advanced AI design system. The Human characters were created and animated with Mixamo and its client Aero for parameterizing the assets. The modification of the graphical assets (desks, tables, chairs, etc.) and their settings, such as the pivot point and physical properties, were completed in 3D Studio Max.

3.2 Evacuation Areas

The scenery of the evacuation scenarios is the model of the Passenger Ferry Express Samina, which sunk in 2000, in one of the most renowned marine accidents in Greece.

The ship model is composed of two compartments (Fig. 1), the Upper and the Lower passenger decks. The two levels are connected by stairwells internally and externally. The Lower deck hosts the cabin area and a small gathering area at the front. The Upper Deck combines the airplane seat area, the main restaurant at the front, and three balconies one at the restaurant and two at the sides. The different areas within the compartments are connected with doors.

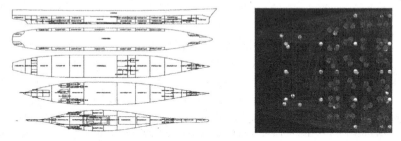

Fig. 1. Express Samina compartments (left) and front top-down view (right).

3.3 Gameplay

The evacuation scenarios may start immediately or afterwards, based on the scenario implemented by the administrator. Administrators can participate as evacuees, or they can choose to just monitor the scenarios. The users start at a random location within the ship and when the evacuation starts, they should move to one of the exits (balconies). The players have the freedom to help others or to focus on their own escape. In parallel, various events may spawn in the area, such as a fire, smoke, ship listing, etc. (Fig. 2). If a player is trapped or killed by one of the hazardous elements, exits the simulation and receives feedback.

Fig. 2. Evacuees avoiding a fire element

If a player successfully reaches an exit, should remain in the area and receives different feedback (optional) and a positive message. The general evacuation feedback is displayed only to the administrator, after the completion of the scenario, indicating the number of casualties and injuries by cause and the total evacuation time. The setup of the serious game allows the collection of spatial, behavioral and numerical data. Spatial elements such as congestion and bottlenecks can be identified, specific behaviors can be also observed, while a detailed report with the casualties and injuries sorted by instigator type and evacuees' type, as well as the total Survival Rate and the total time of the evacuation.

4 Experimental Setup and Results

The evacuation area is the upper and lower decks of the model in Fig. 1. The users control their avatars, and the administrator sets up the scenarios. Each scenario has a specific setup. The number of evacuees, fires, smoke sources, the day/night circle, the ship movement, etc. can be parameterized. The administrator can allow the participation of human users or may choose to conduct an exclusively bot-based evacuation scenario. The evaluation was based on data collected after testing the SES in scenarios with the participation of computer-controlled bots and scenarios with the combination of bots and human testers. During the evacuation new element may be spawned by the administrator. For the bot-only scenarios, several bots are spawned without any human participant (Bot Scenarios). For the scenarios that allow human-users several users participate simultaneously with computer-controlled bots (Hybrid Scenarios). In both types of scenarios, the data was logged after the completion of each session. This feature of the simulator collects data about the Initial number of evacuees, the total casualties, the casualties by type of evacuees and instigator (e.g., fire), the total injuries and the injuries by evacuees' type and instigator, and the total evacuation time.

The human-user/testers were college students, aged from 19 to 22 years old, with a good understanding of the gameplay and the nature of computer games. Based on their declaration, they used to play computer games almost daily for at least the last decade, therefore they are described as experienced gamers. None of the testers had traveled with a passenger ship before, a fact that creates a clear template as they could not transfer any previous knowledge in the simulation. Therefore, the collection of the experimental data was based on the results extracted by the simulator as logs and the feedback provided by the testers after the completion of the experimental sessions. An exception was the measurement of user immersion, where the students were asked to turn a page from the green to the red side when felt that they were not immersed in the virtual environment and the supervisor had to confirm the time.

4.1 Results Without Human Users

Scenarios Set 1. An important process before the conduction of more sophisticated experiments is the validation of SES. Several scenarios with conditions like the Express Samina disaster were conducted. In these experiments, the results of the SES have been evaluated to validate the fidelity of every given set of scenarios. Results completely different from the ones provided by the original incident should indicate some revisions to the application and/or the methodology. Five Scenarios were conducted for Scenarios Set 1 (Table 1).

The total survival rate stands to $SR = 88\%$, 85%. 86%, 88% and 83%, for a corresponding Casualties Rate of $C_i = 12\%$, 15%, 14%, 12% and 17% (Fig. 3).

Table 1. Ship evacuation simulator validation, Express Samina accident (September 2000).

Evacuation time	Number of evacuees (n)	Evacuation time limit (in minutes) (ETL)	Survival rate (SR)
Scenario 1.1 - Express Samina	472	45	88%
Scenario 1.2 - Express Samina	472	45	85%
Scenario 1.3 - Express Samina	472	45	86%
Scenario 1.4 - Express Samina	472	45	88%
Scenario 1.5 - Express Samina	472	45	83%

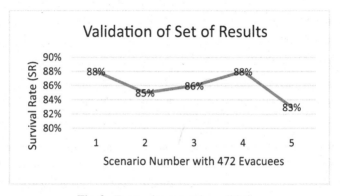

Fig. 3. Evacuation scenarios validation

The evacuation settings define the total number of evacuees to $k = 472$ and the Evacuation Time Limit to ETL = 45 min, which is the number of evacuees and the total time from the sounding of the alarm until the sinking of the ship, during the real accident. Taking into consideration the casualties of $C_i = 15\%$ of the real incident and the similarity of the result after five evacuation sessions, the validation can be verified. The mathematical verification of a set of SRs is shown in the formula below (1):

$$M_s = \frac{1}{k} \sum_{i=1}^{k} C_i \qquad (1)$$

and

$$\min(C_i) < M_s < \max(C_i) \qquad (2)$$

where M_s: The Arithmetic Median of the set of SRs, k: The index of the scenario, C_i: The Casualties in each scenario.

If the M_s value is higher than the lowest C_i and less than the highest C_i, then the value is verified. Subsequently, the $M_s = 14$ of the current set of Scenarios, satisfies the equation of formula (2) $(\min(C_i) = 12 < M_s = 14 < \max(C_i) = 17)$.

Scenarios Set 2. The Set of Scenarios 2 studies alternative conditions based on the original ones. The Express Samina disaster occurred at night. In this set the scenarios asset the impact of a daytime disaster with the same conditions. Afterward, more elements are introduced such as the total absence of illumination, increased capacity, and lower ETL.

Table 2. Alternative scenarios, Express Samina accident.

Evacuation scenario	Number of evacuees (n)	Evacuation time limit (in minutes) (ETL)	Survival rate (SR)
2.1 – Daylight	472	45	88%
2.2 – Daylight	472	45	89%
2.3 – No Lights	472	45	55%
2.4 – No Lights	472	45	44%
2.5 – No Lights, Increased Capacity, Limited Time	600	30	12%
2.6 – No Lights, Increased Capacity, Limited Time	600	15	14%

In the above table (Table 2), the application of Daytime conditions improved the SR rate to 88% and 89% and increase of up to 6% compared to Set of Scenarios 1. During the Express Samina disaster, the electrical power malfunctioned, and the power was lost after the water from the gush entered the engine room. Scenarios 2.3, 2.4 examine the outcome if the power has been cut off in the entire incident. The results show that the SR drops dramatically to SR = 55%, 43%, and 44%, an increased Ci by 50%. The last part of this Set of Scenarios increases the number of passengers (n) from 472 to 600 and sets the ETL to 30 and then to 15 min. A limit in the evacuation time reduces the Casualties/Survivors Ratio CSR, significantly. The impact of the ETL on the Ratio of the Casualties (Ci) and the SR is calculated with the below formula (3).

$$\lim_{ETL \to 0} \left(\frac{C_i}{SR_n} \right) = CS_R \tag{3}$$

where ETL: the Evacuation Total Time, C_i: the total casualties, SR_n: the number of survivors and CS_R: the Casualties/Survivors Ratio.

Scenarios Set 3. An important factor in Evacuation is the measurement of Evacuability which is calculated by the below function [15].

$$E = \text{function}\{\text{env}, d, r, \delta(ni); t\}. \tag{4}$$

where E: the Evacuability factor, Env: the environment (geometry, topology, semantics), r: the Response Time, d: τhe spatial distribution of the evacuees, δ: τhe walking speed.

Instead of just calculating separate scenarios using their Evacuability, we propose the calculation of the difficulty of a scenario before its conduction and then the comparison with the outcome. Thus, the third Set of Scenarios studies the impact of Instigator on evacuation scenarios. An Instigator is an element introduced into the evacuated area that affects the process. In this set, the instigators are Fire, Smoke, and Light Ship Movement (Table 3).

Table 3. Survival rate introducing instigators (bots)

Evacuation scenario	Time (TLS) (m)	Survival rate (SR)	Number of evacuees (n)	Instigator
3.1	No Time Limit	90%	472	Fire
3.2	No Time Limit	86%	472	Fire & Smoke
3.3	No Time Limit	83%	472	Fire, Smoke & Light Ship Movement
3.4	15	47%	472	Fire
3.5	10	30%	472	Fire

The modification of the evacuation factor (TLS, n etc.) affects the SR, as its drops when new elements are added to the equation. This provides the opportunity to mathematically calculate the Severity (S_E) of an evacuation scenario. S_E is used to predict the difficulty of a given scenario and would help the Administrators to design more effective Sets of Scenarios. S_E of an evacuation scenario is calculated by the below formula (5).

$$|S_E| = \frac{\frac{\varepsilon_n}{n}f + \sum_{I_{fire}=0}^{I_{firen}} \varepsilon I_{firen} + \sum_{I_{smoke}=0}^{I_{smoken}} \varepsilon I_{smoken} + \sum_{I_{ShipM}=0}^{I_{ShipMn}} \varepsilon I_{ShipMn}}{TLS} \tag{5}$$

where $|S_E|$: the absolute Severity Evacuation value, ε_n: the maximum passenger capacity, n: the number of evacuees, f: the ship type coefficient (10 for RO-RO Passenger ships, lower for bigger ships and higher for smaller ships and boats), ε: the phenomenon intensity (low, medium, high), $I_{firen}, I_{smoken}, I_{shipMn}$: the minimum number of instigators of a given category, $I_{fire}, I_{smoke}, I_{smoke}$: the final number of instigators, TLS: the total L.

If the TLS is not defining or it is limitless can be replaced with 600 as the maximin evacuation time. If additional instigators appear, they are added to the bracket as shown in formula (5). Two factors that have been included in SES are the internal illumination status of the ship (described as Ship Illumination) and the Daytime conditions, which describes the Day/Night circle. To include these two elements, the formula is updated with the Ship Illumination and Daytime variables.

For the Severity evaluation of a given scenario the calculated S_E is compared with the value ranges in Table 4. A scenario with expected low casualties and evacuation of most evacuees should get a score between 0.0 and 0.3, and a scenario with medium casualties and some casualties should get a score between 0.3 and 0.9. Most severe cases should get scores of more than 0.9.

Table 4. Severity evacuation index

S_E	Severity
<0.3	Low
>0.3 and <0.9	Medium
>0.9 and <1.8	High
>1.8	Very High

4.2 Results with Human Users

Scenarios Set 4. From this Set of Scenarios, human users have been introduced to the simulation. The scenarios 4.1(m) And 4.2(m) are differentiated for testing purposes and thus the number of computer-controlled bots is lower (14 and 44). The rest of the scenarios correspond with the scenarios in Table 4.

Table 5. Survival rate introducing instigators (humans)

Evacuation scenario	Time (TLS) (m)	Survival rate (SR)	Number of human evacuees (n_h)	Number of evacuees (n)	Instigator
4.1(m)	No Time Limit	94%	6	14	Fire
4.2(m)	No Time Limit	95%	6	44	Fire & Smoke
4.3(m)	No Time Limit	91%	6	466	Fire, Smoke & Light Ship Movement
4.4(m)	15	42%	6	466	Fire
4.5(m)	10	22%	6	466	Fire

Table 5 indicates that the results are like the bot-only scenarios with no significant deviations. The mathematical verification of the differentiation between the bot-only and multiplayer scenarios is shown below in formula 6.

$$\Delta R = SR1 : SR2 \tag{6}$$

where Δ_R: the ratio between the casualties of two evacuation scenarios, SR_1: the casualties' ratio of the bots-only scenario, SR_2: the casualties' ratio of the multiplayer scenario.

The above formula indicates the ratio between the casualties of two simulation sessions, with similar conditions. This means that if two scenarios include different numbers and types of instigators, different time limits and conditions as well as different ship types, in the formula should not be used.

Scenarios Set 5. Set of Scenarios 5 evaluates the user immersion of the human users and the level of experience and knowledge in good evacuation practices, they acquired. After five scenarios, Table 6 was created for the assessment of User Immersion. There are two columns that measure the Full Immersion and the Immersion elements. The Full Immersion measures the level of immersion of the testers and the Immersion element is the length of immersion after this state was achieved.

Table 6. Training level sequence

Evacuation scenario	Time (TLS) (m)	Full Immersion	Immersion (average time in m)	Survival rate	Injured
5.1(m)	No Time Limit	100%	3	66%	50%
5.2(m)	No Time Limit	100%	3	66%	50%
5.3(m)	No Time Limit	100%	5	83%	50%
5.4(m)	No Time Limit	100%	6	83%	33%
5.5(m)	No Time Limit	83%	7	100%	33%

The second crucial element is the increased survival rate while the users keep participating to evacuation sessions. To validate the results, the evacuation conditions have stayed unchanged for all the scenarios of Set 5. The users participate in consecutive sessions, while the Survival and Injured ratio are measured. If the Survival Rate keeps increasing, the conclusion is that the users have been trained or have acquired more detailed information about good evacuation practices. For increment acceptance evaluation, a simple arithmetic progression, on the SR of both scenarios, can be used. Then this is compared to the minimum value in Table 6. An increase of 10% (6.6%) is considered the baseline increase to validate the training of the testers. The below formula has been used for the evaluation of user training.

$$x_n = SR_1 + d_n(nSR - 1) \tag{7}$$

where X_n: Increase of SR in each session, SR_1 = the value of SR of the first session of the set, d_n: The difference between consecutive sessions, nSR: the total number of sessions of the set.

$$d_n > nSRn \qquad (8)$$

Based on the results of the formula in formula (7), we compare the progression for all the sessions, and then we compare if the value is higher to the corresponding results from the simulator passing the values to formula (8). Therefore, a baseline is set, based on an arithmetic sequence with a common difference of 10% and if the SR_n value of each corresponding session is higher than the baseline, then the Set of Session is validated and indicates the users have acquired substantial knowledge of the evacuated area and learned good evacuation practices.

5 Conclusions

In this work, several experiments, conducted in SES evacuation serious game, were demonstrated. In parallel, the evaluation and assessment of the results were validated with the mathematical formulas designed for that purpose. SES results have been validated with the results from the Express Samina disaster, while exceeding the expected accuracy, with very similar outcomes. The casualty's deviation from the original accident is less than 10% on average and in every simulation session. The upcoming results indicated that the inclusion of more elements affects negatively or positively the outcome of an evacuation. A simulation without a time limit or a daylight session improves the Evacuability and the SR. On contrary, at nighttime, the absence of internal illumination and the introduction of hazardous elements (fire, smoke, etc.) decrease the Evacuability and SR. After the technical verification of SES, the second stage included human testers. This introduction of human users that impersonate evacuees did not disrupt the process and the outcome of the simulation, providing results similar to the ones with bot-only scenarios. Finally, the human users stated that Immersion was achieved and maintained, while they improved their performance, in every consecutive evacuation session, an indication that they were trained in good evacuation practices.

SES is a prototype and subject to future improvements. Upcoming iterations will include, a complete virtual reality setup, to improve user immersion and gameplay, machine learning for the computer-controlled bots, multiple Ship Models, and different categories of ships (Cargo, Tankers, etc.) and a non-ship-related component for building evacuation.

Acknowledgment. This work was supported by the National Contribution for University of the Peloponnese European Research Projects (years 2016–17) - CrossCult (Grant Number 84329).

References

1. Vassalos, D., Hamamoto, M., Molyneux, D., Papanikolaou, A.: Contemporary Ideas on Ship Stability. Elsevier (2000)

2. Onsongo, S.K.: Analysis of the domestic passenger ferry safety in Kenya (2017)
3. Hänninen, H.: Negotiated risks: the Estonia accident and the stream of bow visor failures in the Baltic ferry traffic. Helsinki School of Economics (2007)
4. Kee, D., Jun, G.T., Waterson, P., Haslam, R.: A systemic analysis of South Korea Sewol ferry accident–Striking a balance between learning and accountability. Appl. Ergon. **59**, 504–516 (2017)
5. Kougioumtzoglou, G., Theodoropoulos, A., Lepouras, G.: Design and development of a game-engine-based simulator specialised on ships evacuation. Int. J. Hum. Factors Model. Simul. **7**(3–4), 301–328 (2022)
6. Vassalos, D., Christiansen, G., Kim, H.S., Bole, M., Majumder, J.: Evacuability of passenger ships at sea. Safety at Sea and Marine Equipment Exhibition (SASMEX) (2002)
7. Rüppel, U., Schatz, K.: Designing a BIM-based serious game for fire safety evacuation simulations. Adv. Eng. Inform. **25**(4), 600–611 (2011)
8. Pennycott, A., Hifi, Y.: Evacuability of a flooded passenger ship (2010)
9. Ginnis, A.I., Kostas, K.V., Politis, C.G., Kaklis, P.D.: VELOS: a VR platform for ship-evacuation analysis. Comput. Aided Des. **42**(11), 1045–1058 (2010)
10. Silva, J.F.M., Almeida, J.E., Pereira, A., Rossetti, R.J., Coelho, A.L.: Preliminary experiments with EVA-serious games virtual fire drill simulator. arXiv preprint arXiv:1304.0726 (2013)
11. Ha, G., Lee, H., Lee, S., Cha, J., Kim, S.: A VR serious game for fire evacuation drill with synchronized tele-collaboration among users. In: Proceedings of the 22nd ACM Conference on Virtual Reality Software and Technology, pp. 301–302 (2016)
12. Skarbez, R., Brooks, F.P., Whitton, M.C.: Immersion and coherence: research agenda and early results. IEEE Trans. Vis. Comput. Graph. **27**(10), 3839–3850 (2020)
13. Chen, S., Pan, Z., Zhang, M., Shen, H.: A case study of user immersion-based systematic design for serious heritage games. Multimed. Tools Appl. **62**(3), 633–658 (2013)
14. Kougioumtzoglou, G., Theodoropoulos, A., Lepouras, G.: A guide for the development of game-based evacuation simulators. In: Auer, M.E., Rüütmann, T. (eds.) ICL 2020. AISC, vol. 1328, pp. 554–566. Springer, Cham (2021). https://doi.org/10.1007/978-3-030-68198-2_51
15. Kim, N.-S.: Successful deriving evacuation factors of the Korean aged. Indian J. Sci. Technol. **9**(40) (2016)

High-Level Decision-Making Non-player Vehicles

Alessandro Pighetti, Luca Forneris, Luca Lazzaroni⬛, Francesco Bellotti$^{(\boxtimes)}$,
Alessio Capello⬛, Marianna Cossu, Alessandro De Gloria, and Riccardo Berta

Department of Electrical, Electronic and Telecommunication Engineering (DITEN),
University of Genoa, Via Opera Pia 11a, 16145 Genoa, Italy
{luca.lazzaroni,franz,alessio.capello,
marianna.cossu}@elios.unige.it, {alessandro.degloria,
riccardo.berta}@unige.it

Abstract. Availability of realistic driver models, also able to represent various driving styles, is key to add traffic in serious games on automotive driving. We propose a new architecture for behavioural planning of vehicles, that decide their motion taking high-level decisions, such as "keep lane", "overtake" and "go to rightmost lane". This is similar to a driver's high-level reasoning and takes into account the availability of ever more sophisticated Advanced Driving Assistance Systems (ADAS) in current vehicles. Compared to a low-level decision making system, our model performs better both in terms of safety and average speed. As a significant advantage, the hierarchical approach allows to reduce the number of training steps, which is critical for ML models, by more than one order of magnitude. The developed agent seems to show a more realistic behaviour. We also showed feasibility of training models able to differentiate their performance in a way similar to the driving styles. We believe that such agents could be profitably employed in state of the art SGs for driving, improving the realism of single NPVs and overall traffic.

Keywords: Reinforcement learning · Automotive driving · Serious games · PPO · Autonomous agents · ADAS · Driving games · Racing games

1 Introduction

Driving a car is a key activity for several people around the world both in personal and in social terms, and it can be effectively supported by tools aimed at improving performance, for instance in terms of safety and fuel consumption (e.g., [1, 2]).

Some (not many) serious games (SGs) have been developed (e.g., [3]), exploiting their appeal and ability to provide different features such as fun, narrative, engagement, realism, abstraction. A significant issue is learning transfer, since playing a game is very different from driving a 1+ ton. Vehicle with several lives continuously at stake. However, some concepts/aspects may be learnt, and it is important that SGs are well designed to meet their specific instructional target. One key aspect in this context is

K. Kiili et al. (Eds.): GALA 2022, LNCS 13647, pp. 223–233, 2022.
https://doi.org/10.1007/978-3-031-22124-8_22

given by the modelling of non-player vehicles (NPVs), that constitute the traffic around the ego vehicle (i.e., the vehicle driven by the player).

A key technology for decision making is given by deep reinforcement learning (DRL). Decision making is necessary for behavioural planning of a vehicle, which includes path/trajectory planning and tracking (e.g., [4, 5]). DRL consists in using deep neural network (DNN) models to improve reinforcement learning (RL) [6, 7]. Highway-env is a collection of simple 2D bird-eye view environments for training RL agents in automated driving and tactical decision-making tasks, particularly in highway settings [8]. Highway-env is one of the environments provided within OpenAI gym, an open-source Python library for developing and comparing RL algorithms by providing a standard API to communicate between learning algorithms and environments [9]. An RL agent learns by interacting with the environment in which it is immersed. Interactions consists of observations and actions. An action is the decision taken by the agent based on the latest observation provided by the environment.

Highway-env looks like a significant tool to implement NPVs [10]. It provides two alternative types of low-level input interface to a RL model: one based on discrete actions (faster, slower, left, right, idle) and one based on continuous actuators (throttle level, with negative values indicating the braking, and steering angle). To the best of our knowledge, state of the art decision making agents are designed at this level of control (e.g., [11–13]). However, we argue that human-like decisions could concern a higher level. Low level control, in fact, can be deferred to advanced driving assistance systems (ADAS), such as the adaptive cruise control (ACC), also in current vehicles. Thus, in this work we are interested in exploring the behaviour of NPVs driven by a higher-level RL-based decision maker. Through the design choice of targeting higher-level decision making, we expect not only to achieve a more realistic behaviour of the vehicles, but also to get benefits in terms of model training, which is the most critical aspect of any machine learning (ML) algorithm, particularly in DRL.

2 Related Work

While a lot of games have been developed in the racing area, serious games to specifically support specific aspects of automotive driving are much rarer.

The Good Drive game [3] presents players with the major sequences that cover the entire French driving licence training programme. The scenes involve passing and overtaking, in rural and urban areas, and different time of the day and weather conditions. The player must control his vehicle, follow the road rules and adapt to what is happening in the environment. The presentation website stresses that Good Drive "does not aim to replace traditional methods for learning to drive; instead, it serves to support these". [14] is a popular 3D commercial game for driving training before going on road, with the main goal of learning to respect traffic laws, use turn signals, etc.

[15] presents the implementation of an educational game on traffic behaviour awareness through the main stages of analysis, design, development, and evaluation. Reported results reveal that a properly developed educational game could enhance traffic awareness through experiential and mediated learning. [16] presents a virtual reality SG providing players the knowledge on the basic rules before they drive a real car on the real road.

User tests revealed that the game can combine enjoyment with learning basic driving elements. [17] investigates the effects of the use of SG in eco-driving training. The results demonstrate that the serious game influences positively the behaviour of inexperienced drivers in ecological driving.

[18] presents a set of fuzzy logic models that process signals from basic vehicular sensors (e.g., speed and throttle position) in order to estimate fuel consumption, which is then usable in different ways in reality-enhanced SGs. As a complementary tool, Edgine supports smart configuration of limited-resource edge devices in order to send the proper information to a cloud-based measurement management system [19].

[20] is an important general resource, as it provides a comprehensive overview of artificial intelligence (AI) for serious games. Particularly, it presents a set of advanced game AI components that enable pedagogical affordances and that can be easily reused across game engines and platforms. All components have been applied and validated in serious games that were tested with real end-users.

In the specific area of driving games, [21] describes at high level the requirements, architecture, and best practices for high-speed vehicle racing AI. [22] exploits the WRC6 rally game, with realistic physics and graphics, to train an Asynchronous Actor Critic (A3C) reinforcement learning (RL) model in an end-to-end fashion. The authors also propose an improved reward function to learn faster. [23] is a blog post presenting a Deep Q-Network (DQN) [24] developed for driving a car in a simple racing game.

3 Reinforcement Learning and the Highway-env Environment

RL is one of the three main paradigms of Machine Learning, beside Supervised and Unsupervised Learning. The goal of RL is to train an Agent that learns a policy to maximize the outcome of its actions applied on an uncertain dynamic system. Since the true outcome between actions and state of the dynamic system is unknown, the Agent is trained with an empirically approximated outcome function called Reward Function (RF). The training consists in a MonteCarlo trial-and-error approach, usually in a simulated environment, where the Agent can explore different strategies and get the corresponding outcome with the RF. When a model is learnt using a Neural Network, this paradigm is called Deep Reinforcement Learning (DRL) [24].

A variety of algorithms have been developed for training RL models. They can be roughly divided in three classes:

- Value-based methods (e.g., Q learning [25] and DQN [24]), that chooses the next action of an agent by estimating the cumulative benefit of each possible action.
- Policy-based methods, including policy gradient methods (e.g., Proximal Policy Optimization (PPO) [26]), that optimize a performance objective (typically the expected cumulative reward) through gradient ascent [27].
- Model-based methods which provide a model of the environment to predict how it responds to the agent's actions [28].

As anticipated, we have chosen highway-env as our highway decision-making environment [8]. Regarding the DRL algorithms (e.g., DQN, PPO, etc.), we deployed the state of the art Stable-Baselines3 implementations [29] on the proposed environment[29]. The environment represents a multi lane highway (Fig. 1), where the Ego Vehicle (EV) is driven by the autonomous agent and has the goal of covering as much distance as possible, avoiding collisions with Non Player Vehicles (NPV). NPVs follow a heuristic behaviour, with some randomness applied in order to avoid over-fitting on the agent's part. To increase scenario variability, we modified the kinematic model to set different values to several vehicle parameters, such as max acceleration, brake intensity, etc. We also added number of vehicle randomization at each episode.

The agent behaviour is detailed in the next section. Here we stress that, for a SG application, the goal is to employ one or more trained agents (i.e., EVs) as NPVs in the target SG, in order to create a suited environment for the SG (where the EV will be driven by a player).

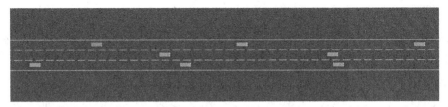

Fig. 1. Snapshot from highway-env. The EV is coloured in green; NPVs are light-blue (Color figure online)

4 High-Level Decision-Making Model

As anticipated, the core innovation is given by the definition of a high-level decision maker (DM) module, which is the model (to be trained through RL) that controls the EV. Also taking into account state of the art systems in vehicles (e.g., the Adaptive Cruise Control, ACC), we defined the following actions for the DM decisions:

- Keep lane: the ACC is activated. If a vehicle is present ahead in the lane, the EV keeps a safe time headway. Otherwise, it goes at the max speed.
- Overtake: change lane to the left so to make an overtake if a vehicle is present in the ego lane ahead. Otherwise, the Cruise Control is activated.
- Go to the rightmost lane: change lane to the right, wait one or two seconds and repeat this, until the rightmost lane is reached.

Figure 2 shows the vehicular behaviours enacted by these actions. Figure 3 provides a complete system overview. In our design, the EV includes two serial subsystems, as in [30]: the Decision Maker (DM) and the Behaviour Executor (BE). The DM gets the observations from the environment and selects the appropriate high-level action accordingly. The observations are the basic ones defined in highway-env: presence (whether a vehicle is present or not), and longitudinal and lateral position and velocity, for the EV and the $N = 4$, in our case, closest vehicles.

The high-level actions are received by the BE, which implements the appropriate behaviour in a series of low-level settings (throttle levels and steering angles). Such values are clipped by a clipper module, that enforces physical feasibility before feeding the environment (whose interface is left unchanged).

Each behaviour is executed in an infinite loop, which is terminated as soon as the DM chooses a different action than the previous one. The BE implementation simulates the behaviour of state of the art on-board ADAS through simple proportional integrative derivative (PID) controllers in a closed loop control schema.

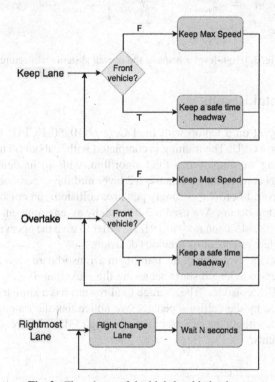

Fig. 2. Flowcharts of the high-level behaviours

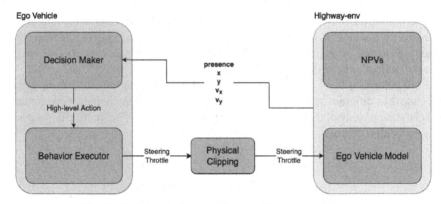

Fig. 3. High-level schema of the overall system architecture

5   Experimental Results

We trained the agent on a laptop with Intel Core i7-10750H CPU, 16 GB of RAM, NVIDIA RTX 2060 GPU. The training is completed within about 60 min.

For the training we employed a PPO algorithm, with all its default values [31], including the DNN configuration, which is a 2 layer multilayer perceptron (MLP), with 64 neurons per layer. In order to strongly penalize collisions, an episode is terminated whenever a collision occurs. We used a 3-lane highway environment (Fig. 1), setting policy frequency (i.e., decision rate) to 1 Hz, in order to give the agent sufficient time to observe the complete effects of its previous decision.

Figure 4 shows the evolution of the training in a Tensorboard view [32]. We can see that the average episode length starts achieving the maximum (i.e., with no collisions at all) at around 60K episodes. The average total reward has a similar shape since it is strongly influenced by the collision penalty. We notice that the training is quite rapid, smooth and stable, without the catastrophic forgetting [33], which frequently affects the training of RL agents.

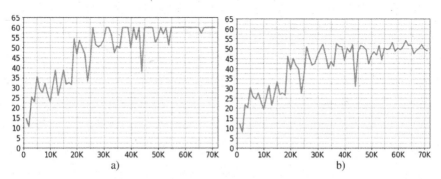

Fig. 4. Training metrics a) episode length in seconds and b) total reward as a function of the number of training iterations.

Table 1. Performance comparison over sixty 60-s episodes

Model	Total collisions	Km per episode	Training steps
High-level DM agent	0	1.83	70K
Low-level agent [10]	2	1.76	1.75M

Table 2. Environment settings

Model	Speed levels [m/s]	No. Vehicles per episode	Traffic density	No. Reward functions
High-level DM agent	[20, 25, 30]	10	0.5	3
Low-level agent [10]	Cont(20, 36)	Uniform(10–20)	0.4	11

Table 1 compares the performance of the resulting policy with that of an agent [10] which outputs the five highway-env low-level discrete actions: faster, slower, left, right, idle. The comparison considers the number of collisions and kilometres travelled in 60 episodes of 60 s each.

Results show that the high-level agent performs better under all the dimensions. It is important to highlight that the training of the higher-level agent took more than one order of magnitude less steps than the lower-level agent. This is due to the idea of pairing high-level decisions with lower level exploitation of We argue that this reduction is motivated by a simpler agent training due to our idea of abstracting higher-level decisions, while exploiting state of the art ADASs for the lower-level longitudinal and lateral motion control. An expert assessment also noticed a more realistic behaviour by the high-level agent. A quantitative indicator for this is given by the reduction to 0 of the number of collisions.

Some details must be mentioned on the comparison, as the environments are not exactly the same, as reported in Table 2. An episode in [10] has fewer total vehicles (ego + NPVs) but slightly more concentrated (density factor 0.5 vs 0.4). [10] was specifically developed with a large number of rewards compared to the original highway-env (11 vs 3), in order to better enforce traffic law and safer behaviour (e.g., penalties for right overtake, unsafe distance to the front vehicle, hazardous lane change, steering angle). In this work we kept the three original highway-env reward functions: penalty for collisions, positive rewards for right-lane and high-speed.

Finally, we investigated the feasibility of differentiating DM agents by driving styles (e.g., aggressive, conservative, normal). This would be useful in a SG, for instance to differentiate scenarios, with particular reference to the difficulty level. For instance, a higher-difficulty level could be crowded with aggressive vehicles. We explored this by specifying different values for the rewards and penalties (Table 3) with which an agent is trained, leading to different agent behaviour. In all cases the training episode was interrupted at the occurrence of a collision, thus preventing the agent to get any further reward for that episode. Results in the previous tables refer to the "normal" agent. The total reward is normalized between 0 and 1 as per the highway-env implementation [8], which creates some distortion in the values reported in Table 3. Particularly, the effect of the speed reward is strongly amplified in the "aggressive" style training, because of the lack of the other two rewards. Results (Table 4) show that the "conservative" model performs quite similarly to the "normal" one, in spite of the strong increase in the collision penalty value. On the other hand, the "aggressive" model drives quite faster (15% more than the "normal"), being able to almost always travel at the 130 km/h maximum possible speed. However, it also collides with other vehicles in some episodes. This is the reason why the average number of travelled kms drops with respect to both the other models (because an accident terminates an episodes).

Table 3. Reward values for training three different driving styles (negative rewards are penalties).

Driving style	Collision	Speed	Right lane
Conservative	−5	0.4	0.2
Normal	−1	0.4	0.2
Aggressive	0	0.4	0

Table 4. Performance of the different driving styles

Model's style	Avg. Episode length [s]	Tot. Collisions	Avg. km travelled	Avg. Speed [km/h]
Conservative	60	0	1,79	108
Normal	60	0	1,83	110
Aggressive	46	18	1,65	127

6   Conclusions and Future Work

We have proposed a new, hierarchical architecture for behavioural planning of vehicles, that decide their motion taking high-level decisions, such as "keep lane", "overtake" and "go to rightmost lane". This is similar to a driver's high-level reasoning and takes into account the availability of ever more sophisticated ADAS in current vehicles. Compared to a low-level DM system, our model performs better both in terms of safety and average speed. As a significant advantage, the proposed approach allows reducing the number of training steps, which is critical for ML models, by more than one order of magnitude. The developed agent seems to show a behaviour more similar to that of a real car. We also showed feasibility of training models able to differentiate their performance in a way similar to the driving styles. We believe that such agents could be profitably employed in state of the art SGs for driving, improving the realism of single NPVs and overall traffic.

We argue that future work could aim at further improving the achievements through two main directions: the study of different DRL models and training policies, and the use of more accurate dynamic models inside highway-env, overcoming the limits of the kinematic model. The dynamic model may allow more realistic vehicle behaviour. Also, it will be very interesting to assess the effect of the developed models on player fun and engagement inside a SG.

References

1. Massoud, R., Berta, R., Poslad, S., De Gloria, A., Bellotti, F.: IoT sensing for reality-enhanced serious games, a fuel-efficient drive use case. Sensors. **21**, 3559 (2021). https://doi.org/10.3390/s21103559
2. Nousias, S., et al.: Exploiting gamification to improve eco-driving behaviour: the GamECAR approach. Electron. Notes Theor. Comput. Sci. **343**, 103–116 (2019). https://doi.org/10.1016/j.entcs.2019.04.013
3. The Good Drive, a serious game for learning to drive - Renault Group. https://www.renaultgroup.com/en/news-on-air/news/the-good-drive-a-serious-game-for-learning-to-drive/. Accessed 22 July 2022
4. Leurent, E., Mercat, J.: Social Attention for Autonomous Decision-Making in Dense Traffic (2019). https://doi.org/10.48550/arXiv.1911.12250
5. González, D., Pérez, J., Milanés, V., Nashashibi, F.: A review of motion planning techniques for automated vehicles. IEEE Trans. Intell. Transp. Syst. **17**, 1135–1145 (2016). https://doi.org/10.1109/TITS.2015.2498841
6. Francois-Lavet, V., Henderson, P., Islam, R., Bellemare, M.G., Pineau, J.: An introduction to deep reinforcement learning. Found. Trends® Mach. Learn. **11**, 219–354 (2018). https://doi.org/10.1561/2200000071
7. Arulkumaran, K., Deisenroth, M.P., Brundage, M., Bharath, A.A.: A brief survey of deep reinforcement learning. IEEE Signal Process. Mag. **34**, 26–38 (2017). https://doi.org/10.1109/MSP.2017.2743240
8. GitHub - eleurent/highway-env: A minimalist environment for decision-making in autonomous driving. https://github.com/eleurent/highway-env. Accessed 11 July 2022
9. Brockman, G., et al.: OpenAI Gym. (2016). https://doi.org/10.48550/arXiv.1606.01540
10. Campodonico, G., et al.: Adapting autonomous agents for automotive driving games. In: de Rosa, F., Marfisi Schottman, I., Baalsrud Hauge, J., Bellotti, F., Dondio, P., Romero, M. (eds.) GALA 2021. LNCS, vol. 13134, pp. 101–110. Springer, Cham (2021). https://doi.org/10.1007/978-3-030-92182-8_10
11. Rana, A., Malhi, A.: Building safer autonomous agents by leveraging risky driving behavior knowledge. In: 2021 International Conference on Communications, Computing, Cybersecurity, and Informatics (CCCI), pp. 1–6 (2021). https://doi.org/10.1109/CCCI52664.2021.9583209
12. Rais, M.S., Boudour, R., Zouaidia, K., Bougueroua, L.: Decision making for autonomous vehicles in highway scenarios using Harmonic SK Deep SARSA. Appl. Intell. (2022). https://doi.org/10.1007/s10489-022-03357-y

13. Zhang, S., Wu, Y., Ogai, H., Inujima, H., Tateno, S.: Tactical decision-making for autonomous driving using dueling double deep Q network with double attention. IEEE Access. **9**, 151983–151992 (2021). https://doi.org/10.1109/ACCESS.2021.3127105

14. SL, UT: Car Driving School Simulator (Android). https://car-driving-school-simulator.en.upt odown.com/android. Accessed 22 July 2022

15. Gounaridou, A., Siamtanidou, E., Dimoulas, C.: A serious game for mediated education on traffic behavior and safety awareness. Educ. Sci. **11**, 127 (2021). https://doi.org/10.3390/edu csci11030127

16. Likitweerawong, K., Palee, P.: The virtual reality serious game for learning driving skills before taking practical test. In: 2018 International Conference on Digital Arts Media Technology, ICDAMT (2018). https://doi.org/10.1109/ICDAMT.2018.8376515

17. Hrimech, H., et al.: The effects of the use of serious game in eco-driving training. Front. ICT. **3** (2016)

18. Massoud, R., Poslad, S., Bellotti, F., Berta, R., Mehran, K., Gloria, A.D.: A fuzzy logic module to estimate a driver's fuel consumption for reality-enhanced serious games. Int. J. Serious Games **5**, 45–62 (2018). https://doi.org/10.17083/ijsg.v5i4.266

19. Lazzaroni, L., Mazzara, A., Bellotti, F., De Gloria, A., Berta, R.: Employing an IoT framework as a generic serious games analytics engine. In: Marfisi-Schottman, I., Bellotti, F., Hamon, L., Klemke, R. (eds.) GALA 2020. LNCS, vol. 12517, pp. 79–88. Springer, Cham (2020). https://doi.org/10.1007/978-3-030-63464-3_8

20. Westera, W., et al.: Artificial intelligence moving serious gaming: presenting reusable game AI components. Educ. Inf. Technol. **25**(1), 351–380 (2019). https://doi.org/10.1007/s10639-019-09968-2

21. Tomlinson, S.L., Melder, N.: An architecture overview for AI in racing games. (2015). https://doi.org/10.1201/b16725-44

22. Perot, E., Jaritz, M., Toromanoff, M., De Charette, R.: End-to-end driving in a realistic racing game with deep reinforcement learning. In: 2017 IEEE Conference on Computer Vision and Pattern Recognition Workshops (CVPRW), pp. 474–475 (2017). https://doi.org/10.1109/CVPRW.2017.64

23. Fakhry, A.: Applying a Deep Q Network for OpenAI's Car Racing Game. https://toward sdatascience.com/applying-a-deep-q-network-for-openais-car-racing-game-a642daf58fc9. Accessed 22 July 2022

24. Mnih, V., et al.: Human-level control through deep reinforcement learning. Nature **518**, 529–533 (2015). https://doi.org/10.1038/nature14236

25. Watkins, C.J.C.H., Dayan, P.: Q-learning. Mach. Learn. **8**, 279–292 (1992). https://doi.org/10.1007/BF00992698

26. Schulman, J., Wolski, F., Dhariwal, P., Radford, A., Klimov, O.: Proximal Policy Optimization Algorithms (2017). https://doi.org/10.48550/arXiv.1707.06347

27. Sutton, R.S., McAllester, D., Singh, S., Mansour, Y.: Policy gradient methods for reinforcement learning with function approximation. In: Advances in Neural Information Processing Systems. MIT Press (1999)

28. Wang, T., et al.: Benchmarking Model-Based Reinforcement Learning (2019). https://doi.org/10.48550/arXiv.1907.02057

29. Raffin, A., Hill, A., Gleave, A., Kanervisto, A., Ernestus, M., Dormann, N.: Stable-Baselines3: reliable reinforcement learning implementations. J. Mach. Learn. Res. **22**, 1–8 (2021)

30. Mirchevska, B., Pek, C., Werling, M., Althoff, M., Boedecker, J.: High-level decision making for safe and reasonable autonomous lane changing using reinforcement learning. In: 2018 21st International Conference on Intelligent Transportation Systems (ITSC), pp. 2156–2162 (2018). https://doi.org/10.1109/ITSC.2018.8569448

31. PPO—Stable Baselines3 1.6.1a0 documentation. https://stable-baselines3.readthedocs.io/en/master/modules/ppo.html. Accessed 23 July 2022
32. Abadi, M., et al.: TensorFlow: Large-Scale Machine Learning on Heterogeneous Distributed Systems (2016). https://doi.org/10.48550/arXiv.1603.04467
33. Kirkpatrick, J., et al.: Overcoming catastrophic forgetting in neural networks. Proc. Natl. Acad. Sci. **114**, 3521–3526 (2017). https://doi.org/10.1073/pnas.1611835114

Influence of a Mixed Reality Game on Students' Personal Epistemology. An Empirical Study

Simon Morard$^{(\boxtimes)}$ ⓘD, Eric Sanchez ⓘD, and Catherine Bonnat ⓘD

TECFA, University of Geneva, 40 bd du Pont d'Arve, 1211 Geneva 4, Switzerland
simon.morard@unige.ch

Abstract. This paper deals with an empirical study about the way information is used by 12–15 years students when they play Geome, a mixed reality game dedicated to museum school visits. With Geome, the students solve ill-structured problems about environmental issues and they deal with fake news or rumors. The playful learning experience is analyzed from the players' perspective based on the dimensions of personal epistemology, i.e. thinking and beliefs about the nature of knowledge and knowing. Experiments in the museum have been conducted with 3 classes, and mixed data (audio, video and game interactions) were collected from specific moments of the gameplay and analyzed according to the epistemological dimensions. The verbatim analysis shows that the combination of an ill-structured problem and a ludic scenario may encourage students to actively process information and to develop critical thinking. Thus, we discuss the characteristics of the game's influence on students' personal epistemology.

Keywords: Students' personal epistemology · Game-based learning · Mixed reality game · Museum school visits

1 Introduction

The introduction of digital-game-based-learning inside museums should not only engage and motivate players through the direct experiences with the game world and the scenography but also provides possibilities for reflectively exploring phenomena and testing hypotheses [1]. Our research aims to understand the subjectivity of the learning experience from the player's perspective using theoretical frameworks from game-based-learning and epistemological theories i.e. the nature and justification of human knowledge [2].

Our research field is a nature museum, for which we developed a mixed reality learning game for middle school students (12–15 years old). The players play the game Geome and interact with the museum exhibition with a digital tablet. A quick introduction by the game master sets the universe and challenge of the game. Due to bad weather conditions, players find themselves stuck in a valley. Divided into teams (2–3 students)

Supplementary Information The online version contains supplementary material available at https://doi.org/10.1007/978-3-031-22124-8_23.

they must gather resources to survive. Scanning the different stuffed animals allows them to obtain various resources, depending on the choice they make: to hunt, to protect, to domesticate or to escape from animals. Once they get enough resources, they may trade them with other teams. This frantic search for resources leads to the depletion of a «Tree of life», a metaphor for the quality of the environment. This metaphor describes an abstract concept (the quality of the environment) in a more comprehensible and concrete way by providing analogies from familiar domains (the health of a tree) [3].

This first part of the game lasts between 10 to 15 min. The game is set up in such a way that it is, at this stage, impossible to succeed. Players are then called as wildlife experts, they deal with fake news, rumors and polemics related to the natural environment. As they make their way through the museum, they discover new areas, they find clues and elements of the museum exhibition allowing them to address the issues and to make visible the complexity of the natural ecosystem interactions. Their discoveries allow them to complete an ecosystemic map listing and connecting animals according to their interdependence. The resolution of their investigation depends on an evaluation of the information obtained and their ability to identify relationships between animals. The enigmas are ill-structured problems that cannot be solved with a high degree of certainty. Goals are unclear, information is incomplete and there is not a single solution (e.g. suspicious tree deaths are reported in the media) [4]. The game aims to foster student's capacity to understand the concerns of the Anthropocene as a new geological epoch subject to biodiversity decrease and major climate changes. At a metacognitive level, the game allows students to question themselves about the nature of knowledge and the way it is produced [5–7].

Our work is grounded on the framework of personal epistemology, considered as beliefs and theories that individuals develop in relation to knowledge and its acquisition [5, 7]. This framework allows us to study the players' ability to process information during a museum school visit. Student's personal epistemology shapes their perceptions of a given task, as well as the way they approach it [6]. When a student faces a complex problem, he needs to critically evaluate the relationship between theory and evidence. Thus, information processing involves argumentation skills, critical thinking, and the capacity to understand the underlying arguments and epistemology [7]. We aim to develop a methodology dedicated to characterizing epistemology based on audio and video recordings. In a previous work we identified key moments of the gameplay during which students may express their personal epistemology [8]. In the following we present the theoretical background, the research questions, the methodology and we discuss the results in the final part.

2 Personal Epistemology and Game Experience

2.1 Players as Problem Solvers

Games often provide a meaningful environment for problem-based learning [1]. Critical thinking and the ability to address complex problems are considered to be important human skills [9, 10]. Problems generally restrict a player's progression in the game world [1], as rules and game mechanics influence player's behavior [11]. Geome's enigmas deal with media education, and socio-scientific and environmental issues linked to the

Anthropocene (climate change, depletion of biodiversity, see Table 1). Real life problems are usually ill-structured problems [4]. Solutions depend on the available information, and the player's ability to evaluate them and to identify the complexity of the relationships within an ecosystem [8].

Table 1. Enigma about the suspicious death of trees.

Excerpt of an enigma from Geome	Thematic/Subject
An article has just been published in a scientific journal. We could not have access to it directly, but the information was taken up by several newspapers and Internet sites in Valais. Here is the summary that was made and spread	Media education and critical thinking
«In Valais, the trees are dying. It is the fault of the Great Capricorn beetle which attacks the young oak forests. This wood-feeding insect likes young trees and makes them sick by digging galleries»	Anthropocene and environmental issues
The foresters, who work directly in the forest, find this story astonishing. So they went to the site to observe young oak trees. They were able to observe traces on oaks ready to be cut down	Anthropocene and environmental issues
Go to the location and report your observations. Can we trust what has been published by the media?	Media education and critical thinking

We study the game experience in the light of research conciliating the game (the artifact used to play) and the play (the situation experienced by the player) [11, 12]. Play may be considered as an epistemic experience as the player explores the museum exhibition and uses his creative thinking to solve a problem. Mixed reality games based on the use of tangible and digital elements such as Geome allow developing knowledge in a playful setting based on investigation and discussion. Indeed, during the game, knowledge may be experienced as a performance [13] as players are in a constant state of action and reflection, thinking and doing [12]. Geome provides a structured and immersive playful problem-solving experience that enables the development of both knowledge and "way of knowing" to be transferred to real life situations. The way players acquire knowledge and think about knowing could be characterized from the perspective of the personal epistemology framework [5–7].

2.2 Students' Personal Epistemology and Critical Thinking

Critical thinking depends on a broad use of different types of knowledge [14] and the relationship between critical thinking, knowledge and knowing, is complex and reciprocal. First, students must have knowledge about a specific domain before they can critically think about it (propositional knowledge). They also need to possess the needed skills to evaluate that knowledge (procedural knowledge). The concept of knowledge and knowing are therefore substantial aspects of conceptualizing critical thinking [10, 15]. We consider museum and in-game information as the premise of a propositional knowledge, the ability to process, link and connect this information are related to student's personal epistemology, allowing them to develop procedural knowledge [15]. Prior research on personal epistemology has found that the ability to think critically is embedded in a progression of epistemological beliefs [16, 17]. Scholars suggest that students with poor critical thinking skills have an absolute view of knowledge. When students move on to the most developed epistemological level, their critical thinking tends to improve as well [14, 17]. Students' personal epistemology therefore has an important role for their ability to evaluate the credibility of competing claims [17].

Student's epistemological beliefs, or alternatively personal epistemology, are premises of critical thinking. Critical thinking can be considered as a tool for understanding and determining the reliability and relevance of knowledge. Student's personal epistemology and beliefs are indissociable to their critical thinking [15]. Personal epistemology is defined as an individual's view of the nature of knowledge and knowing, including one's personal beliefs as a knower [3, 7, 18]. Organized as a system of beliefs, called dimensions [2], personal epistemology has four dimensions (certainty, simplicity, source, justification) organized by two axes: the nature of knowledge and the act of knowing. The first axis concerns an individual's beliefs about what knowledge is. The second relates to the way in which the individual comes to know something [2]. The first dimension, certainty, is the degree to which one sees knowledge as fixed or fluid. Simplicity, the second dimension, refers to knowledge viewed as a continuum of an accumulation of facts to highly interrelated concepts. The dimension source indicates the origin of knowledge, outside of oneself, from an external authority to an awareness of being a potential meaning maker. The fourth dimension, justification, refers to how individuals evaluate evidence, authority, and expertise. The dimensions expand along a continuum, extending from less sophisticated (naive) to sophisticated ways of knowing. Over time, personal epistemology develops toward more relativistic beliefs [2, 5]. Critical thinking and epistemological beliefs are embodied in social practices [7, 17] and students are expected, according to their personal epistemology, to assess the reliability and relevance of evidence, to identify arguments, to analyze information and to deal with opposing viewpoints. Students' personal epistemology, beliefs and critical thinking might vary within the same discipline [15].

In order to characterize the personal epistemology induced by the playful experience in the museum, we address the following research questions: How do the dimensions of students' personal epistemology manifest themselves through their reasoning and critical thinking during the game? In particular we want to know (1) What dimensions of epistemology can be inferred from their responses? (2) Where do they reside on a continuum from naive to sophisticated?

3   Research Method

This chapter describes our methodology, the data collected and the established indicators to characterize a player's personal epistemology. Thanks to a Design-based-research method, Geome evolved according to an iterative process [19]. The *a priori* analysis [8] allowed us to hypothesize about specific moments in the game when students' personal epistemology is likely to be solicited. These moments are now recorded by adding audio recording functionality to the game interface.

This study was conducted in a nature museum. 3 classes accompanied by their teachers participated in game-based museum school visits. The teachers were also involved in the design of the game, the enigmas, and the debriefing. Three experiments took place, with 7th, 8th and 9th grade students, student's ages varied from 12 to 15. They share a homogenous cultural background. Students from 2 classes speak French, the other one are bilingual (French-German). 19 teams composed of 2 to 3 students took part in the games. For each experimentation, a member of each teams was equipped with an on-board camera placed on a shoulder.

Thanks to an *a priori* analysis, we know that specific moments of the game may solicit specific dimensions of student's personal epistemology. Indeed, based on the different clues collected during the game, the player may doubt its reliability (*certainty* dimension). The identification of the relationships between the elements collected from the museum exhibition and the drawing of an ecosystemic map have the potential to make the student aware that knowledge is interrelated (*simplicity* dimension). Since the players gather information and propose different solutions, he is expected to identify himself as a meaning maker (*source* dimension) while being confronted with authority figures (e.g., the media, scientific information from the museum). The success of the mission depends on a good appreciation of the quality of the available information, as well as on a certain resistance to the discourses from authority. It is therefore expected that the game will mobilize the students' personal epistemology on the *justification* dimension and that they will succeed in questioning information not supported by strong arguments [8]. The present study should allow us to verify, through the analysis of in-game students' responses and their interactions with each other, whether these dimensions are really solicited during the game.

The data collected consists of audio recorded with the digital tablet. The first collection occurs when players are asked to answer the following question regarding the information provided: *Do you think that you can trust what has been published by the media?* Once they have obtained enough information and scanned all the elements related to the enigma (2 clues and 7 elements of the museography, spread throughout the museum) they are then asked to answer 2 other questions: *After investigation, do you think the article that accused the Great Capricorn beetle was reliable? Who could be responsible for these holes/marks on the oaks?*

87 audio files were collected, some of which were incomplete (e.g., the student laughed, could not find his words, or indicated that he/she wanted to formulate another message). A total of 66% of the voice recordings (N = 58) are usable and transcribed to characterize a personal epistemology. In addition, on-board cameras placed on the shoulders of 9 students recorded 405 min of video data (an average of 45 min per group). In some cases, the access to the video allowed us to avoid server errors and to monitor the students' answers. More importantly, for the groups with these cameras, we had access to the exchanges preceding the audio recording, allowing us to assess whether the answers were the result of a consensus within the group, or whether they emerged from the personal decision of the leader of the team.

Prior research on critical thinking and personal epistemology are generally based on quantitative multiple-choice questionnaires, test, or qualitative interviews [20]. Researchers have discussed the adequacy and validity of self-report questionnaires [7] and concluded that there is a need to directly assess students' performance [5, 7]. Our research methods aim to get access to how players' interactions and how they deal with ill-structured problems, likely to solicit their critical thinking and personal epistemology. The data were analyzed using a qualitative approach, more specifically a categorical analysis, based on indicators of personal epistemology. We selected this method as a means to characterize the students' personal epistemology with a set of indicators that allow us to identify whether the statements made by the students are related to the nature of knowledge or to the act of knowing. They range from naive (na) to sophisticated (so), with a midpoint labeled intermediate (in) [2]. The indicators were identified in similar previous work and adapted from the given definitions of the main dimensions [3]. They have been used to facilitate the debriefing at the end of the game and tested with students during focus groups. For this study we focus on the qualitative difference in critical thinking and personal epistemology, categorized with our indicators, by examining student's reactions and exchanges when they address an ill-structured problem during the game. Their answers were transcribed. We coded the verbatims based on specific indicators.

4 Results

The categorical analysis of the audio records (verbatims) allows us to: (1) Categorize students according to their personal epistemology when they face potential fake news; (2) identify an improvement of their personal epistemology when they manage to propose a solution for the enigma; (3) characterize players' personal epistemology evolution during the game. Results are presented below. When the players take note of the enigma (Table 1) they discuss media reliability. Their responses allow us to classify the different teams of players (N = 19) into the following 4 groups.

(a) Players who question the information provided by the media, based on personal opinions sometimes argued, sometimes selected in an arbitrary way by indicating that they want to verify this information by themselves (thus perceiving themselves as potential producers of knowledge - *source* intermediate, *justification* naive to intermediate). Their argumentation towards the information is based on the importance of getting evidence, and thus additional information linked to what the enigma states (information connected to each other, *simplicity* intermediate). The students express a possibility of alternative truth than the one suggested by the media, thus translating an intermediate epistemology for the *certainty* dimension. We call them *Verifiers* (N = 2).

(b) Players who express doubt about the information coming from the media, considered as an external authority (*source* - intermediate). Their *justification* is based on personal opinions with little argumentation, or by arbitrarily selecting certain information (naive according to our indicators). They nevertheless indicate the need to get evidence, without specifying by who (thus not perceiving themselves as potential legitimate producers of knowledge, *source* naive) nor where (source, by whom?

what? i.e. elements of the museum) this evidence will be obtained. They indicate possibilities of alternative truths compared to those presented in the media (*certitude* - intermediate). We classify them as *Doubters* (N = 11).

(c)   Players who consider the media as a reliable source of information, despite indications that should have warned them against the possible diffusion of fake news. The *justification* for considering the media as a reliable source of information thus depends on individual opinions (naive). According to them, the media, based on scientific articles, are considered as an external authority producing reliable information (naive *source*). We classify them as *Believers* (N = 3).

(d)   Those who do not know and are not able to argue their choices and decisions (naive *Justification*) to which we include the group for whose audio records are not usable. We classify them as the *Undecided* (N = 3) Those four groups share a relatively poor argumentation induced by a naive justification. This is at this stage explicable as they have not yet been able to gather information related to the enigma in the museum. They are expected to justify their opinions later on during the game, when they manage to get enough information. Except for the *Verifiers*, they do not perceive themselves as knowledge producers, whereas they are supposed to take the role of a nature expert. We see that the most solicited dimensions are source and justification, while there are few mentions to the certainty and simplicity dimensions

Once the players have collected enough clues, information and completed an ecosystemic map, they are questioned and recorded about the reliability of the media and about a potential solution to the initial problem of the enigma. The collected audio records and traces allow us to classify their answers, according to indicators of personal epistemology and sorted into groups.

(a') The enigma has multiple solutions and players perceive the complexity of the Anthropocene by indicating open ended solutions (N = 8). The insect incriminated by the media is seen as a member of the ecosystem and not as the unique responsible for the death of the oaks. They express a systemic understanding of the ecosystem presented by the museum exhibition. Thus they demonstrate a sophisticated *simplicity* dimension. (b') Players indicate *a unique solution* to the enigma (N = 4) different from the one initially stated by the media. These answers are interpreted as the existence of absolute truth related to the naive dimension of *certainty*. This new answer is the result of the capacity to link the information provided by the museum and to take the context into account (intermediate *simplicity*). (c') Players propose a *unique solution*, identical to the one initially proposed by the media (N = 1). They believe that valid information comes from an external authority (naive *source*) and that an absolute truth is possible (naive *certainty*). (d') Players who did not manage to complete the game and for which data are missing (N = 6). The reasons for missing data result from software issues during the first experiment (3 teams did not play the second part of the game) or from teams not having enough time to complete the game.

As expected by the *a priori* analysis [8] players provide solutions for the enigma. Regardless of the relevance of the provided solution, students are likely to identify themself as meaning makers (*source* intermediate). Therefore, most players identify the complex relationships among the information provided by the museum exhibition (*simplicity*). Their beliefs evolved whether they propose a unique or complex solution. Thus, knowledge can change based on new evidence (*certainty*) [5]. Concerning the *justification* dimension, players must argue their decision according to their own representation of knowledge and collected information. Their justification was mostly naive when they first faced the enigma. Since the game is over, their answers are more constructed and argued, by an arbitrary choice of solution, from an evaluation of the information in their possession (*intermediate* justification). Figure 1 shows the evolution of students' personal epistemology from the beginning to the end of the game and the resolution of the enigma, according to the analysis of the messages recorded. All *Believers*, who initially considered the information as credible (in reality, a fake news) suggest new solutions by stepping back from this authority figure. The *doubters* who completed the game converge towards the idea that media information is inaccurate.

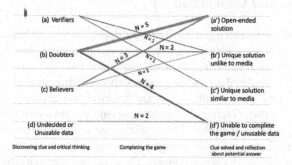

Fig. 1. Categorization of the player's according to their ability to process information

Since we recorded 9 teams of players equipped with onboard cameras, we got specific information related to personal epistemology and how the game was played. Teammates share opinions before recording a common response. This is particularly the case at the beginning of the game when the information displayed by the media must be evaluated. For some teams, we observe disagreements followed by negotiation or rereading of the enigma to reach a consensus. This consensus reflects a personal epistemology shared by members from the same team. In one team, a player took the lead by formulating an answer without consulting his teammates. That same team didn't answer the last question of the enigma and therefore should belong to the category (d'). Based on the data collected with the on-board camera it appears that they completed the game but they skipped the recording because they wanted to complete the ecosystemic map. Then, they were involved in a long discussion about the relationships between animals in the museum (sophisticated simplicity) which allows us to categorize them into (a'). This type of situation could be avoided in future experiments by making sure that the game-master (the museum member in charge of the school visit) reminds the players to fill-in the final questionnaire.

Figure 1 shows that one team of *Verifiers* ends up with answering that the media were right (i.e. the worst way to solve the enigma) even though their personal epistemology was assessed as sophisticated. The analysis of the data recorded with the onboard camera revealed that only one of the 3 players was really engaged in the game. All the clues needed to solve the enigma were collected, but the information provided was not taken into account. This team shifted from a problem-solving game where the players face conflicting information and express critical thinking, to a quest game where the player collects clues that provide no specific information. This result is in line with previous research on the subjectivity of the game experience, where the game as intended by the game designer is interpreted by the players [11].

Lately, regarding our data collection method, players have sometimes seemed embarrassed by recording an audio note, nevertheless we observe more elaborate responses than in the first iteration where they answered by writing. The on-board cameras did not disturb the students' visit and allowed us to have a discreet and complete follow-up of their interactions.

5 Discussion and Conclusion

The current work shows that a game offering the opportunity to address an ill-structured problem may encourage students to actively process information and to develop critical thinking. Nevertheless, their ability to process information is under the influence of their previous personal epistemology. Some players express their willingness to verify media information by themselves, while others are doubtful and express personal opinions without arguing for them. During the game, these students are confronted with evidence and express doubt about the reliability of this information. As a result, their personal epistemology evolves regarding the *certainty* dimension. However, the results show that the game has no influence for some students. They still consider that reliable information comes from external authorities and do not consider that they are capable of producing knowledge by themselves. This lack of resistance to authority figures is characteristic of a naive vision of the source of knowledge [5] and we consider that it is a major issue for educators. The game consists of an authentic and complex situation that confronts students with an ill-structured and non-deterministic problem that challenges their personal epistemology. Nevertheless, for some students, their naive epistemology is an obstacle to the resolution of the game. Although for some players, the game does not influence their personal epistemology, we consider that playing is nevertheless of great interest. Indeed, the experience that led them to make bad decisions can be discussed during the debriefing that follows the game. Thus, the question of how information can and should be evaluated can still be addressed by referring to a lived experience that makes sense to the players. These results lead us to revise our ambitions downwards. It is difficult to get students to develop their personal epistemology in a game situation, as the information presented in the game may be considered playful, or non-serious, and thus be treated with little attention. Nevertheless, we consider this critical attention to information to be of primary importance for learning. It is as if the act of playing, the adoption of this playful attitude, would lead students to accept the risk of failure and not to use their critical thinking skills, as they would do in a more formal learning situation.

We identify the following limits to our research: the nature of the personal epistemology is contextual, it also results from a negotiation between teammates, and the epistemology expressed by the group results from this discussion. Moreover, it is difficult to access the personal epistemology on the sole basis of the analysis of the verbatim. Post-game interviews are needed. We also see the need to consider the capacity of the game to arouse emotions to create engaging situations likely to challenge the student's personal epistemology. Connections with current research on epistemic emotions will be undertaken in this sense [22]. We mainly used the on-board camera data in moments temporally close to those of the audio recordings, these data could be more exploited to further characterize the epistemology of the players. Finally, it must be taken into consideration that debriefing can have an influence and that personal epistemology can evolve, not just by playing, but by reflecting on one's play experience.

References

1. Kiili, K.: Digital game-based learning: towards an experiential gaming model. Internet High. Educ. **8**(1), 13–24 (2005)
2. Hofer, B.K., Pintrich, P.R.: The development of epistemological theories: beliefs about knowledge and knowing and their relation to learning. Rev. Educ. Res. **67**(1), 88–140 (1997)
3. Lakoff, G.: The neural theory of metaphor. In: The Cambridge Handbook of Metaphor and Thought, pp. 17–38. Cambridge University Press (2008)
4. Jonassen, D.H.: Toward a design theory of problem solving. Educ. Tech. Res. Dev. **48**(4), 63–85 (2000)
5. Hofer, B.: Epistemological understanding as a metacognitive process: thinking aloud during online searching. Educ. Psychol. **39**, 43–55 (2004)
6. Hofer, B., Sinatra, G.: Epistemology, metacognition, and self-regulation: musings on an emerging field. Metacogn. Learn. **5**, 113–120 (2010)
7. Hammer, D., Elby, A.: On the form of a personal epistemology. In: Personal Epistemology: The Psychology of Beliefs About Knowledge and Knowing, pp. 169–190. Lawrence Erlbaum Associates Publishers (2002)
8. Bonnat, C., Oliveira, G., Morard, S., Paukovics, E., Sanchez, E.: Rapport au savoir en contexte muséal: Le cas du jeu Geome. In: 10e Conférence sur les Environnements Informatiques pour l'Apprentissage Humain, pp. 381–384 (2021)
9. Holyoak, K.J.: Symbolic connectionism: toward third-generation theories of expertise. In: Toward a General Theory of Expertise: Prospects and Limits, pp. 301–335. Cambridge University Press
10. Halpern, D.F.: Thought and Knowledge: An Introduction to Critical Thinking, 5th edn., p. xvi, 637. Psychology Press (2014)
11. Suovuo, T., Skult, N., Joelsson, T.N., Skult, P., Ravyse, W., Smed, J.: The game experience model (GEM). In: Bostan, B. (ed.) Game User Experience and Player-Centered Design. ISCEMT, pp. 183–205. Springer, Cham (2020). https://doi.org/10.1007/978-3-030-37643-7_8
12. Venegas, R.S.: Digital play as an epistemic experience. In: Play, Philosophy and Performance. Routledge (2021)
13. Squire, K.: From content to context: videogames as designed experience. Educ. Res. **35**(8), 19–29 (2006)
14. Bok, D.: Our Underachieving Colleges: A Candid Look at How Much Students Learn and Why They Should Be Learning More, p. viii, 429. Princeton University Press (2006)
15. Hyytinen, H., Holma, K., Toom, A., Shavelson, R., Lindblom-Ylänne, S.: The complex relationship between students' critical thinking and epistemological beliefs in the context of problem solving. Frontline Learn. Res. **6**, 1–25 (2014)
16. King, P.M., Kitchener, K.S.: Reflective judgment: theory and research on the development of epistemic assumptions through adulthood. Educ. Psychol. **39**(1), 5–18 (2004)
17. Kuhn, D.: A developmental model of critical thinking. Educ. Res. **28**(2), 16–46 (1999)

18. Pintrich, P.R.: The role of metacognitive knowledge in learning, teaching, and assessing. Theory Pract. **41**(4), 219–225 (2002)

19. Anderson, T., Shattuck, J.: Design-based research: a decade of progress in education research? Educ. Res. **41**(1), 16–25 (2012)

20. Heijltjes, A., Gog, T., Leppink, J., Paas, F.: Improving critical thinking: effects of dispositions and instructions on economics students' reasoning skills. Learn. Instr. **29**, 31–42 (2014)

21. Crahay, M., Fagnant, A.: À propos de l'épistémologie personnelle: Un état des recherches anglo-saxonnes. Revue française de pédagogie, pp. 79–117 (2007)

22. Muis, K.R., Chevrier, M., Denton, C.A., Losenno, K.M.: Epistemic emotions and epistemic cognition predict critical thinking about socio-scientific issues. Front. Educ. **6**, 121 (2021)

Taxonomies and Evaluation Frameworks

Experts' Evaluation of a Proposed Taxonomy for Immersive Learning Systems

Khaleel Asyraaf Mat Sanusi[1,2(✉)] [ID], Deniz Iren[2] [ID], and Roland Klemke[1,2] [ID]

[1] Cologne Game Lab, TH Köln, Cologne, Germany
ks@colognegamelab.de
[2] Open University of the Netherlands, Heerlen, The Netherlands

Abstract. Immersive learning systems (ILSs) allow the recreation of an idealized world in virtual environments, providing experiences that can help learners in learning skills realistically. These environments are typically supported by immersive technologies to improve immersion and provide real-time feedback. However, designing an ILS is a strenuous process due to its wide selection of technologies, design practices, and pedagogical interventions. In this paper, we evaluate the unified taxonomy of ILS by conducting a qualitative analysis with 42 experts from various backgrounds. The evaluation covers the ILS strengths, ILS weaknesses, reusable ILS components, and additional ILS components.

Keywords: Immersive learning systems · Taxonomy · Expert evaluation

1 Introduction

Immersive environments allow the modeling of virtual and custom-made worlds to create near to realistic experiences [1]. In the learning domain, learning scenarios can be created to rival the real world, making the learning sessions more relevant, effective, challenging, and fun [2].

ILSs use augmented (AR), virtual (VR), and mixed (MR) reality to enhance the immersive experience and provide real-time feedback to the learner [3]. Studies show that immersive systems are suitable for training in multiple domains and may have a positive impact on learning outcomes [4]. Sensor technologies are being used for tracking learners' behavior and performance with the help of artificial intelligence (AI) [5,6]. Instructions and feedback can be given in a timely manner to ensure that the desired learning goal can be achieved faster [7]. Multimodal instruction and feedback components convey more and richer information in communication using multiple input and output modalities [8].

Supplementary Information The online version contains supplementary material available at https://doi.org/10.1007/978-3-031-22124-8_24.

K. Kiili et al. (Eds.): GALA 2022, LNCS 13647, pp. 247–257, 2022.
https://doi.org/10.1007/978-3-031-22124-8_24

ILSs show that different characteristics such as technological support, learning objectives, and modalities can coalesce to form effective systems and provide meaningful learning experiences [9]. Designing an ILS comprises a selection of suitable components. However, the wide selection of ILS technologies, design practices, and pedagogical interventions makes it strenuous to design such systems effectively.

In this paper, we report on findings of how experts from multiple domains evaluate ILSs and their respective components by conducting a qualitative analysis. The experts involved are teachers, students, and researchers, from learning science, computer science, game design, TEL, and management. They were presented with concepts of ILSs, the unified ILS taxonomy (see Sect. 3), and five prototype examples (see Sect. 4). A survey was subsequently given for the experts' valuable contribution. We lay out our research questions as follows:

- **RQ1** - What are the strengths and weaknesses of ILSs based on experts from different backgrounds?
- **RQ2** - Which ILS components from the unified taxonomy received more requests and can be used for future development of ILSs?
- **RQ3** - What are additional ILS components that were suggested by the experts for improving the unified taxonomy of ILS?

The paper is structured as follows. Section 2 provides an overview of the related work on taxonomies of ILS development. Section 3 introduces the unified taxonomy of ILS. Section 4 describes our research method. Section 5 shows the results of our study. Section 6 covers a discussion about how we address our research questions, theoretical and practical contributions, limitations, future work, and finally, concludes the paper.

2   Related Work

In various studies, ILS characteristics such as interaction technology, game design, pedagogical modeling, or purpose, are grouped to form taxonomies. A combination of such taxonomies would benefit the ILS developers when defining the scope of their projects and selecting design trajectories to explore.

De Freitas and Oliver [10] introduced a four-dimensional framework for teachers to evaluate the potential of simulation-based learning. The dimensions include pedagogic considerations, mode of representation, contextual factors, and learner. Hertel et al. [11] focus on task and modality dimensions in their taxonomy of AR interaction techniques. Motejlek and Alpay [12] suggest a taxonomy that includes three sub-categories for immersive learning using AR and VR. The dimensions cover; purpose, user experience, delivery technology, gamification, and interaction. In their review, Menin et al. [2] categorize the literature on immersive learning using the dimensions; display devices, immersion level, interaction, feedback, serious purpose, and target participants.

Bloom's taxonomy covers learning objectives in three dimensions, namely cognitive, affective, and psychomotor [13]. Kovács et al. [14] claimed that existing multimedia systems limit the potential efficiency and effectiveness of learning, as such systems mostly address two modalities (visual and audio channels). By presenting a survey on existing technical opportunities for the development of an immersive learning environment, the authors described four components of such an environment, namely visual, audio, olfactory, and haptic.

3   Unified Taxonomy of ILS

In this section, we introduce our unified taxonomy of ILSs (see Fig. 1). The categories and entries are gathered and partly adopted from multiple sources in the literature. The objective of this taxonomy is to provide an overview of various components of ILSs, laying out potential design decisions and explorations when defining the scope of an ILS development project. Therefore, we recommend ILS developers use this taxonomy as initial guidance and tailor it by adding, removing, or improving components for the modification of their projects.

The unified taxonomy of ILS consists of three dimensions; *technology*, *pedagogy*, and *modality*. We categorize the technology dimension into two sub-categories; *experience* that enable users to experience immersion, and *interaction* that recognize different modalities and collect user inputs [11,12]. The second dimension, pedagogy, is segregated into two; *learning objectives* [13], and *interventions* that describe the frame of interaction and when the informative actions are taken by the ILSs. Finally, the modality dimension is classified into multiple sensory channels and interaction modes that can be used by the ILSs [2].

4   Methods

4.1   Research Design

The presentation slides were prepared with the following contents: a definition of ILSs, the introduction of our proposed taxonomy, and video demonstrations of five ILS prototypes that were selected from the project portfolio of our research group. In doing so, we provide concrete examples to the participants.

The first two prototypes focus on the psychomotor aspect of the learner [6]. Flowmotion (Fig. 2a) is a webcam-based game with a body-tracking feature that helps the learner to train in the basics of yoga poses. Yu & Mi (Fig. 2b) is an AR game that teaches the learner to interact with a virtual robot for the assembly of a sensor case procedurally. The next two prototypes concentrate on the cognitive aspect of the learner. The Big Banger (Fig. 2c) is an AR physics-based game that focuses on the laws of motion. Sir Kit's Solar Power Trip (Fig. 2d) is an AR card game that offers an overview of solar power through playful experimentation. The fifth prototype, MPITT (Fig. 2e), is a toolbox for instruction and feedback components that can be used in both domains.

The presentation was given in four different sessions; Session 1 an online training program for teachers and students with different backgrounds, Session 2 an on-site plenary meeting amongst the learning scientists, Session 3 an internal

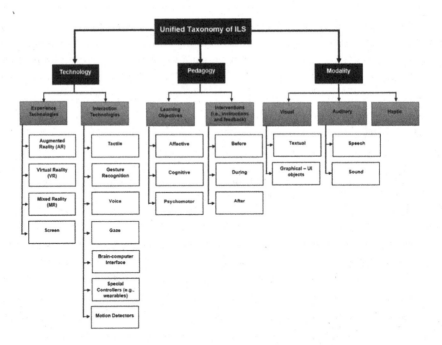

Fig. 1. Overview of the unified ILS taxonomy

online meeting amongst the game development experts, and Session 4 an online meeting amongst the AI, social science, and management experts.

An online survey was created consisting of 13 items and open-ended questions with the following sections; (1) demographic information, (2) ILSs' strengths and weaknesses, and (3) ideal components for future ILSs development. The survey was left open to participants for one week, providing them sufficient time to answer the questions. Meanwhile, the presentation materials were shared with the participants. For the data analysis, the Atlas.ti tool was used to code and analyze transcripts, create network diagrams, and visualize data.

4.2 Participants

A total of 42 people participated in the survey. However, five responses had to be excluded due to the lack of detail, or insufficiently following instructions, leaving 37 responses to be analyzed. There were 39% students, 34% teachers, 2% with two roles (teacher and researcher), and 2% with three roles (teacher, researcher, and manager). The backgrounds consist of; computer science (CS) (43%), educational technology (ET) (16%), game design (GD) (9%), physics (PH) (7%), science and technology (ST) (7%), psychology (PS) (5%), management (MGMT) (5%), art (5%), mathematics (MT) (2%), and language (LG) (2%). Nearly half of the participants (45.2%) have never experienced or tried ILSs before our study, while the rest either have (35.7%) or are unsure (19%).

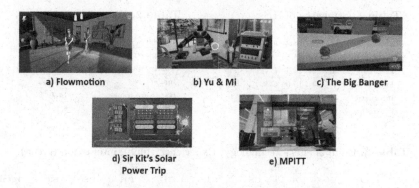

a) Flowmotion   b) Yu & Mi   c) The Big Banger

d) Sir Kit's Solar   e) MPITT
Power Trip

Fig. 2. Screenshots of the prototypes

In Session 1, 30 participants (CS, PH, MT, GD, CS, LG, A, and ST) answered the survey. Following the session, several participants raised a common issue in which the design of the survey was overwhelming and confusing, particularly the diagram of the unified ILS taxonomy, and the images of the prototypes with their respective ILS components. Hence, we excluded the images but kept the unified taxonomy of ILS as it is an essential component of the survey and to ensure the consistency of the collected data for the next sessions.

In Session 2, five participants from the TEL background answered the survey. The distribution of the survey had to be altered due to the on-site session. Hence, a QR code was created for the participants to access the survey. Sessions 3 and 4 were conducted remotely. Five participants (A, CS, and GD) from Session 3 and three participants (PS and MGMT) from Session 4 answered the survey.

4.3   Instrument

Qualitative data were gathered by asking 11 open-ended questions which are segregated into two sections. The first section focuses on the participants' general view of ILSs by describing the strengths and weaknesses of ILSs, whereas the second section consists of questions for participants to select the needed ILS components for their ILS development projects based on the unified taxonomy of ILS. Follow-up questions asked the participants to suggest any additional components and improvements for tailoring the taxonomy.

5   Results

5.1   Strengths and Weaknesses of ILSs

Tables 1 and 2 shows the strengths and weaknesses of ILSs based on the responses. For strength, we report that "Innovative" (35.85%) has the highest percentage, along with "Engaging/Immersive" (24.53%) in second place, and "Fun" (15.09%) in third place. For weaknesses, we report that "Complexity" (34.69%) has the highest percentage, followed by "Costly/Hardly accessible" (22.45%) in the second place, and "Ineffective" (20.41%) in the third place.

Table 1. Strengths of ILSs.

Strength	Percentage
Innovative	35.85%
Engaging/Immersive	24.53%
Fun	15.09%
Interactive	13.21%
Flexibility	11.32%

Table 2. Weaknesses of ILSs.

Weakness	Percentage
Complexity	34.69%
Costly/Hardly accessible	22.45%
Ineffective	20.41%
Hardware issues	14.29%
Inconvenient	8.16%

Table 3. Components - technology; Experience (blue), interaction (green).

	A	CS	ET	GD	PH	PS	ST	Totals
AR	-	6 (13.64%)	2 (4.55%)	2 (4.55%)	2 (4.55%)	1 (2.27%)	2 (4.55%)	15 (34.09%)
VR	1 (2.27%)	2 (4.55%)	-	2 (4.55%)	-	-	-	5 (11.36%)
MR	-	2 (4.55%)	1 (2.27%)	1 (2.27%)	-	-	-	4 (9.09%)
Screen	-	1 (2.27%)	-	-	-	-	-	1 (2.27%)
Brain-computer interface	-	1 (2.27%)	-	-	-	-	-	1 (2.27%)
Gaze	1 (2.27%)	1 (2.27%)	-	-	-	-	-	2 (4.55%)
Gesture recognition	1 (2.27%)	1 (2.27%)	-	2 (4.55%)	1 (2.27%)	-	1 (2.27%)	4 (9.09%)
Motion detectors	-	1 (2.27%)	-	-	-	-	-	3 (6.82%)
Tactile	-	-	1 (2.27%)	-	-	-	-	1 (2.27%)
Voice	1 (2.27%)	2 (4.55%)	1 (2.27%)	2 (4.55%)	1 (2.27%)	-	-	7 (15.91%)
Wearables	-	-	-	-	-	-	1 (2.27%)	1 (2.27%)
Totals	4 (9.09%)	17 (38.64%)	5 (11.36%)	9 (20.45%)	4 (9.09%)	1 (2.27%)	4 (9.09%)	44 (100.00%)

5.2   Components from the Unified Taxonomy of ILS

A total of 44 entries were reported in Table 3, addressing the ILS components for the technology dimension of the taxonomy. The "AR" entry recorded the highest percentage (34.09%) for the experience technology. The "Voice" entry has the highest percentage (15.91%) for the interaction technology. CS has the highest number of counts with 17 (38.64%) for selecting the components, followed by GD with 9 (20.45%) and ET with 5 (11.36%).

The selected components from the pedagogy dimension are reported in Table 4 with 29 counts. In the learning objectives, the "Cognitive" aspect recorded the highest percentage value (58.62%). For the intervention technique, the highest count recorded was "Feedback: During" with a percentage of 10.34%. Similarly to Table 3, CS has the highest number of counts with 8 (27.59%), but in this case, followed by ET with 6 (20.69%) and GD with 4 (13.79%).

Table 4. Components - pedagogy; Learning objectives (blue), intervention (green).

	A	CS	ET	GD	MT	PH	PS	ST	Totals
Affective	-	1 (3.45%)	-	1 (3.45%)	-	-	-	-	2 (6.90%)
Cognitive	1 (3.45%)	6 (20.69%)	3 (10.34%)	2 (6.90%)	1 (3.45%)	2 (6.90%)		2 (6.90%)	17 (58.62%)
Psychomotor	-	1 (3.45%)	1 (3.45%)	1 (3.45%)	-	-	1 (3.45%)	-	4 (13.79%)
Instructions: Before	1 (3.45%)	-	-	-	-	-	-	-	1 (3.45%)
Feedback: During	1 (3.45%)	-	1 (3.45%)	-	-	-	1 (3.45%)	-	3 (10.34%)
Feedback: After	1 (3.45%)	-	1 (3.45%)	2 (6.90%)	-	-	-	-	2 (6.90%)
Totals	4 (13.79%)	8 (27.59%)	6 (20.69%)	4 (13.79%)	1 (3.45%)	2 (6.90%)	2 (6.90%)	2 (6.90%)	29 (100.00%)

For the modality dimension, we report a total number of 16 counts in Table 5. This dimension has fewer components than the previous two, hence the number of counts was low. We observed that the "Graphical" (31.25%) and "Speech" (37.50%) were the most preferred visual and audio modalities, respectively.

Table 5. Components - modality; Visual (blue), auditory (green)

	A	CS	ET	GD	PH	PS	ST	Totals
Textual	-	-	-	-	1 (6.25%)	-	-	1 (6.25%)
Graphical	-	1 (6.25%)	1 (6.25%)	1 (6.25%)	1 (6.25%)	-	1 (6.25%)	5 (31.25%)
Sound	-	1 (6.25%)	1 (6.25%)	-	-	1 (6.25%)	1 (6.25%)	4 (25.00%)
Speech	1 (6.25%)	2 (12.50%)	1 (6.25%)	1 (6.25%)	1 (6.25%)	-	-	6 (37.50%)
Totals	1 (6.25%)	4 (25.00%)	3 (18.75%)	2 (12.50%)	3 (18.75%)	1 (6.25%)	2 (12.50%)	16 (100.00%)

5.3 Additional ILS Components and Refinement

In this subsection, we report the findings on the additional ILS components suggested by the participants and which of the existing components can be improved for refining our taxonomy. The exclusion criteria were necessary as several participants selected the same components from the proposed taxonomy. Therefore, we excluded these answers to avoid redundancy.

For the technology (Fig. 3), several participants proposed that the audio technology (e.g., speakers, headphones) should be added to the experience technology. Several sensors such as emotion, temperature, eye-tracking, and odor were suggested for the interaction technology. AI technology was also recommended for personalized learning, which could potentially be a sub-category for this dimension. As for the modality dimension, only one ILS component was suggested by several participants, namely the olfactory.

Some additional ILS components for the pedagogy dimension can be observed in Fig. 4. Several participants suggested that the learning domains should be divided into smaller sub-categories. Precisely, the psychomotor domain should include sub-types of skills that focus on specific (fine skills) and generic (gross skills) human muscles. Critical thinking and social learning were mentioned as the sub-types of the cognitive domain. The refinement of feedback was suggested, namely formative evaluation and tactile (real-life tangible objects). We observed a new sub-category that can be added to our taxonomy, which is the collaboration among the learners to recreate the traditional classroom experience.

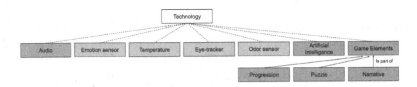

Fig. 3. Technology; Experience (blue), interaction (green), sub-category (gray). (Color figure online)

6   Discussion and Conclusion

We evaluate the unified ILS taxonomy by conducting a qualitative analysis with multiple experts from various backgrounds. A definition of ILSs, an introduction of the unified ILS taxonomy, and demonstrations of ILS prototypes were presented to the experts in four different sessions. A survey consisting of open-ended questions was provided. The experts performed the evaluation of ILSs that cover: (1) strengths and weaknesses, (2) reusable components, and (3) additional components for refining the taxonomy. Below, we reflect on how our study contributes to answering the research questions.

RQ1: *Strengths Reported:* Participants think that ILSs have the needed and sufficient technologies to replicate an authentic learning setting in a virtual environment and design it in a way that can be more engaging and fun. They reflect on how such technologies can help learners train skills independently and serve as a supporting tool to help teachers with their learning sessions. *Weaknesses reported:* The most notable one is the complexity of the technology, particularly when developing the virtual environment or setting up the device/s for a learning session as technical specialties are needed. Special equipment is also needed for the ILSs and these devices are hardly accessible as they are costly. Moreover, the teachers are skeptical about the effectiveness of the ILSs, questioning the potential of such technologies in classroom settings.

RQ2: AR technology was the most prominent component in the experience technology. A plausible explanation would be that the technology itself is ideal and feasible for developing cognitive skills, and progressively used in such a domain [3]. Smartphones and tablets are commonly owned and most of these devices have built-in AR functionality. In the interaction technology, voice input was the most selected component [9]. This could be the emergence of the voice-based AI-powered digital assistant (e.g., Alexa, Siri) in which speech is used as an input to control smart devices. Meanwhile, some participants might be unfamiliar with these technologies, thus no counts were recorded within these groups. In the pedagogy dimension, the cognitive domain was the most chosen component, possibly due to the background details of most participants. Real-time feedback was the most popular intervention technique which is typically effective when mistakes can be corrected immediately [5,7].

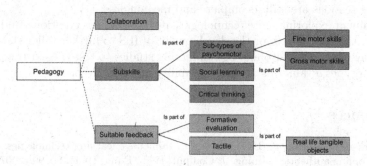

Fig. 4. Pedagogy; Learning objectives (blue), intervention (green), sub-category (gray). (Color figure online)

RQ3: Based on the survey results, the participants think that audio technology can be used as a fundamental tool to provide instructions and feedback [5]. AI technology was suggested to track the learner's performance and provide personalized feedback during a learning session [6]. A sub-category of game elements was proposed to enable gamified experiences as part of the ILSs to make them more fun and engaging. In the pedagogy dimension, the participants think that psychomotor and cognitive domains need to be narrowed to specific skills that can be learned within the ILSs. The refinement of feedback was suggested due to more than 30% of the participants being educators, and such a component should be crucial. A collaboration practice is needed in the ILSs to avoid the risk of learners learning things unassisted and enhance team-building skills.

In summary, our paper offers the following contributions. The evaluation of the experts from different backgrounds provides insights into how they perceive the ILSs in terms of usability, strengths, and weaknesses, which can be a crucial step before designing or improving future ILS projects in the related domain. Our unified taxonomy of ILS covers various aspects of ILS, initiating a systematic way of exploring possible design choices and guiding the ILS developers with the implementation of their projects. The unified taxonomy of ILSs allows researchers and developers to explore comprehensively and therefore, could potentially build a solid foundation in ILS development projects.

Limitations and Future Work

Several shortcomings were encountered during the study. Primarily, a combination of physical and remote sessions has restricted our objectives in allowing the participants to test the prototypes practically, resulting in us presenting the prototypes. The use of the QR code to access the survey during the physical session introduced some inconveniences with the need to answer the survey (including open-ended questions) by using their smartphones. Some of the questions were not answered sufficiently and properly. As explained in Sect. 4.2, the refinement of the survey design was necessary. Even so, some answers retrieved from the following sessions are still incomplete and meaningless.

We aim at exploring more technologies, pedagogical interventions, and design practices that are suited for the development of ILS to further tailor the unified taxonomy of ILS. We also aim at conducting studies to test the existing or new ILS prototypes, evaluating systems' usability and effectiveness.

References

1. Herrington, J., Reeves, T.C., Oliver, R.: Immersive learning technologies: realism and online authentic learning. J. Comput. High. Educ. **19**(1), 80–99 (2007)
2. Menin, A., Torchelsen, R., Nedel, L.: An analysis of VR technology used in immersive simulations with a serious game perspective. IEEE Comput. Graph. Appl. **38**(2), 57–73 (2018)
3. Mat Sanusi, K.A., Majonica, D., Künz, L., Klemke, R.: Immersive training environments for psychomotor skills development: a student driven prototype development approach. In: 2021 Multimodal Immersive Learning Systems, pp. 53–58. CEUR (2021)
4. Limbu, B., Vovk, A., Jarodzka, H., Klemke, R., Wild, F., Specht, M.: WEKIT.One: a sensor-based augmented reality system for experience capture and re-enactment. In: Scheffel, M., Broisin, J., Pammer-Schindler, V., Ioannou, A., Schneider, J. (eds.) EC-TEL 2019. LNCS, vol. 11722, pp. 158–171. Springer, Cham (2019). https://doi.org/10.1007/978-3-030-29736-7_12
5. Di Mitri, D., Schneider, J., Trebing, K., Sopka, S., Specht, M., Drachsler, H.: Real-time multimodal feedback with the CPR tutor. In: Bittencourt, I.I., Cukurova, M., Muldner, K., Luckin, R., Millán, E. (eds.) AIED 2020. LNCS (LNAI), vol. 12163, pp. 141–152. Springer, Cham (2020). https://doi.org/10.1007/978-3-030-52237-7_12
6. Mat Sanusi, K.A., Mitri, D.D., Limbu, B., Klemke, R.: Table tennis tutor: forehand strokes classification based on multimodal data and neural networks. Sensors **21**(9), 3121 (2021)
7. Ericsson, K.A., Prietula, M.J., Cokely, E.T.: The making of an expert. Harv. Bus. Rev. **85**(7/8), 114 (2007)

8. Di Mitri, D., Schneider, J., Specht, M., Drachsler, H.: From signals to knowledge: a conceptual model for multimodal learning analytics. J. Comput. Assist. Learn. **34**(4), 338–349 (2018)
9. Schneider, J., Börner, D., Van Rosmalen, P., Specht, M.: Can you help me with my pitch? Studying a tool for real-time automated feedback. IEEE Trans. Learn. Technol. **9**(4), 318–327 (2016)
10. De Freitas, S., Oliver, M.: How can exploratory learning with games and simulations within the curriculum be most effectively evaluated? Comput. Educ. **46**(3), 249–264 (2006)
11. Hertel, J., Karaosmanoglu, S., Schmidt, S., Bräker, J., Semmann, M., Steinicke, F.: A taxonomy of interaction techniques for immersive augmented reality based on an iterative literature review. In: 2021 IEEE International Symposium on Mixed and Augmented Reality (ISMAR), pp. 431–440. IEEE (2021)
12. Motejlek, J., Alpay, E.: A taxonomy for virtual and augmented reality in education. arXiv preprint arXiv:1906.12051 (2019)
13. Bloom, B.S.: Taxonomy of Educational Objectives: The Classification of Educational Goals. Cognitive Domain (1956)
14. Kovács, P. T., Murray, N., Rozinaj, G., Sulema, Y., Rybárová, R.: Application of immersive technologies for education: State of the art. In: 2015 International Conference on Interactive Mobile Communication Technologies and Learning (IMCL), pp. 283–288. IEEE (2015)

A Design Space of Educational Authoring Tools for Augmented Reality

Mohamed Ez-zaouia[1]([✉]), Iza Marfisi-Schottman[1], Maysa Oueslati[1],
Cendrine Mercier[2], Aous Karoui[3], and Sébastien George[1]

[1] Le Mans Université, LIUM, Le Mans, France
{mohamed.ez-zaouia,iza.marfisi,maysa.oueslati,
sebastien.george}@univ-lemans.fr
[2] Nantes Université, CREN UR 2661, Nantes, France
cendrine.mercier@univ-nantes.fr
[3] University for Teacher Education, 1700 Fribourg, Switzerland
aous.karoui@edufr.ch

Abstract. Recently, numerous *authoring tools* for Augmented Reality
(AR) have been proposed, in both industry and academia, with the aim
to enable non-expert users, *without programming skills*, to scaffold educational AR activities. This is a promising authoring approach that can
democratize AR for learning. However, there is no systematic analysis
of these emerging tools regarding *what AR features and modalities they
offer (RQ1)*. Furthermore, little is known as to *how these emerging tools
support teachers' needs (RQ2)*. Following a two-fold approach, we first
analyzed a corpus of 21 authoring tools from industry and academia
and formulated a comprehensive **design space** with four dimensions:
(1) *authoring workflow*, (2) **AR modality**, (3) **AR use**, and (4) **content and user management**. We then analyzed two workshops with
19 teachers to understand their needs for AR activities and how existing
tools support them. Ultimately, we discuss how our work can support
researchers and designers of educational AR authoring tools.

Keywords: Design space · Augmented reality · Education · Design
process

1 Introduction

Augmented Reality (AR) is now used by thousands of users for formal and non-
formal learning and training [5]. Because AR offers an immersive medium for
representing and interacting with content [14], it is increasingly put forward
to support active and experiential learning in many disciplines, including art,
science, technology, engineering, mathematics, and medicine [2,9]. AR engages
users by combining real and virtual worlds [13] and by creating authentic experiences through motion, sight, touch, sound, and haptic, which is essential for

Supplementary Information The online version contains supplementary material
available at https://doi.org/10.1007/978-3-031-22124-8_25.

K. Kiili et al. (Eds.): GALA 2022, LNCS 13647, pp. 258–268, 2022.
https://doi.org/10.1007/978-3-031-22124-8_25

multisensorial learning [15]. Further, AR feels meaningful to users because it transforms real-world into a playground with a prominent game factor [10]. Research has advocated that educators should integrate AR in their curricula to create sensory-rich and engaging activities, increase dwell-time, and facilitate comprehension of content and phenomena [3].

However, recent reviews have underlined that creating AR experiences that fit pedagogical needs remains a salient challenge because of (i) the complexity of authoring AR and (ii) lacks of evidence-based methods to integrating AR in everyday classrooms [1,5,16]. Currently, authoring AR experiences requires significant technical knowledge and skills [12]. The vast majority of AR applications are created using advanced programming and complex toolkits, such as Unity3d, Unrealengine, Vuforia, ARCore, Threejs, to name a few. The programming approach has two main limitations. First, it is only accessible to a small group of people with advanced programming skills. Second, toolkits have limited "built-in" support for helping teachers use AR to its full pedagogical capacities [5,6]. Such limitations make it harder for teachers to harness this new learning medium for their everyday classrooms.

To lower the barriers to creating AR experiences in educational settings, recent research and industry have been empowering non-expert end-users to create AR applications with **authoring tools**. Such tools offer user-friendly interactions, such as taking a photo of an object (*e.g.,* poster, book cover, drawing, QRCode) and adding augmentations (*e.g.,* texts, images, 3D models). This AR activity can then be saved and shared with other users who will be able to view the augmentations via their devices (*e.g.,* phones, tablets, glasses) (see Fig. 1-(b)-T8,T17).

Recently, many authoring tools have emerged in both academia and industry. Each tool has unique design elements, affordances, features and modalities. There are significant differences between existing tools, which make it difficult for researchers and designers to grasp a holistic view of the rapidly-growing AR authoring research and practice. The few studies that have analyzed authoring tools [5,11,12] focused mostly on (i) technical aspects and (ii) tools that require programming (i.e., toolkits), (iii) including non-educational tools. Therefore, we still lack a characterization of existing educational AR authoring tools that do not require programming. In this view, we aim to address two research questions:

– **RQ1:** *What AR features and modalities do emerging educational AR authoring tools offer, mainly tools that are suitable for non-expert users?*
– **RQ2:** *How do emerging authoring tools support teachers' needs?*

In the following, we first present previous studies on AR authoring tools. Then, in Sect. 3, we present our method to fill the gap. In Sect. 4, we propose the first **design space of educational AR authoring tools**. In the field of Human-Computer Interactions, the term "design space" is a conceptual metaphor for knowledge that "enables us to investigate how a design solution emerges" [7]. Design spaces aim at formulating a comprehensive view of design dimensions and options underlying an area of interest. We distilled our design space based on the analysis of 21 recent authoring tools from industry and academia. In addition, we conducted two workshops with 19 teachers to identify their needs and how existing tools might support them, presented in Sect. 5. Ultimately, in Sect. 6, we show how our work can provide insights, as well as practical guidance, for researchers, educators and technology designers to engage with the design and use of AR authoring tools.

2   Background and Related Work

Recently, a dozen systematic reviews have been conducted to reveal trends, benefits, and challenges of educational AR [1,2,5,6,8,9,13]. For example, Radu [13] analyzed 26 studies that compare AR to non-AR-learning. Garzón et al. [6] reviewed the impact of pedagogical factors on AR learning, such as approaches, intervention duration and environment of use. Ibáñez and Delgado-Kloos [9] reviewed AR literature in STEM fields and characterized AR applications, instructional processes, research approaches and problems reported. However, these systematic reviews were silent on authoring tools and their underlying design considerations and functionalities.

Very few studies reviewed design aspects underlying AR authoring tools. Nebeling and Speicher [12], classified existing authoring tools relevant to rapid prototyping of AR/VR experiences in terms of four main categories: screens, interaction (use of camera), 3D content, and 3D games. Mota et al. [11] discussed authoring tools under the lens of two main themes: the authoring paradigms (stand-alone, plug-in) and deployment strategies (platform-specific, platform-independent). Dengel et al. [5] reviewed 26 AR toolkits that are mostly cited in scientific research. However, the authors found only five authoring tools that do not require programming. While the aforementioned studies provided insights into the design and use of AR authoring tools, they focused mainly on (i) technical aspects of AR, (ii) programming toolkits, (iii) including non-educational ones. In addition, to the best of our knowledge, no study has yet analyzed authoring tools from industry, even-thought a vast majority of teachers might use commercial tools because they are advertised.

Yet, systematic reviews have raised several design challenges, such as usability difficulties, lacks of ways to customize the experiences, inadequacy of the technology for teachers, difficulty to design experiences, expensive technology, and lack of design principles for AR [5,6,9,13]. A further study of the functionalities offered by AR authoring tool and their adequacy with teachers seems necessary. Inspired by design space [e.g., 7,16], we conduct this type of analysis to (i) identify design dimensions and options of educational AR authoring tools, that do not require programming, from both academia and industry, and (ii) link them to the AR activities that teachers aspire for.

3   Method

We conduct this work in the context of a design-based research project that involves end-users (teachers and learners). To tackle our two research questions, we followed four main steps:

1) Defining AR Authoring Tools: We established a working definition as a frame of reference to build a corpus of tools for our analysis. We define an *"AR authoring tool" as a tool that enables non-expert users to scaffold AR experiences without the need for programming code* [5,11,12].

2) Building the Corpus: We aimed to build a representative corpus of most recent tools. We searched in bibliographic hubs (i.e., ACM Digital Library, Google Scholar, Science Direct, Springer) (using keywords: "education", "learning", "authoring tool", "augmented reality") and identified 9 tools from academia. The inclusion criteria was: resent research papers (published after 2019) and active research projects. Similarly, we searched for tools from industry in Google search and identified 12 tools (five of them were also cited in Dengel et al. [5] systematic review). We looked for tools and papers with varying modalities to capture the extent of variability of design space.

3) Analyzing Authoring Tools (RQ1): We followed a thematic design space analysis [4,7]. We tested, read papers, documentations, and watched videos of the 21 tools. We met several times to discuss and iteratively formulate the dimensions and options of design space by following six steps of thematic analysis [4]. Figure 1 summarizes the results of the coding.

4) Analyzing Teachers' Needs (RQ2): We recruited 19 teachers via a partnership with CANOPE, a public network that offers professional training for teachers in France. Teachers were from various disciplines: [Gender: $(women = 8, men = 11)$, Teaching_Years: $(min = 2, max = 40)$, School_Level: $(elementary = 5, middle = 11, high = 2, university = 1)$]. They also have various technology-use expertise in classrooms, AR_Use: 26.3% and Smartphone_Use: 63.2%. We conducted two 3-hour co-design sessions where teachers paper-prototyped AR activities they wanted to use.

4   Design Space of AR Authoring Tools

We identified four main design dimensions of AR content authoring: (1) *authoring workflow,* (2) *AR modality,* (3) *AR use* and (4) *content and user management.* Each dimension identifies categories and options [4,7]. Figure 1 summarizes the results of our design space analysis (also online as supplementary materials: https://bit.ly/3B2Rvxl).

4.1   Dimension 1: Authoring Workflow

The authoring workflow involves *production style, content sources, collaboration* and *platform.*

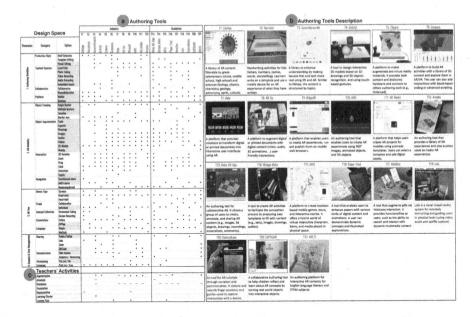

Fig. 1. (a) Overview of design space and how 21 authoring tools span its dimensions (we highlight in green essential options that emerged from the teachers study). (b) Overview of 21 analyzed authoring tools. (c) The seven AR activities that we identified from the teachers study and how existing tools enable creating these activities ("●": full support by a tool, "—": limited support). We provide supplementary materials on google drive with references of the corpus: https://bit.ly/3B2Rvxl.

Production Style: *Shelf selection* provides users with pre-made experiences that cannot be customized. *Template editing* allows users to scaffold experiences based on customizable templates. *Visual editing* allows users to produce AR experiences using user-friendly interactions, such as drag-and-drop and configuration menus.

Content Sources: *Local files* allow users to import files from their devices, such as images, 3D models and videos. *Photo taking, audio* and *video recording* allow users to take photos, record video/audio directly from their device. *Embedded assets* provide users with pre-made assets and resources (e.g., 3D models).

Collaboration: Enables *a/synchronous* collaborative authoring.

Platform: *Mobiles* allow authoring AR experiences using mobile devices (i.e., native apps or mobile browsers). *Desktops* allow authoring AR using browsers.

4.2 Dimension 2: AR Modality

The AR modality involves four main categories, namely, *object tracking, object augmentation, interaction,* and *navigation.*

Object Tracking: *Single marker* allows users to track a single image in a scene. *Multiple markers* allows users to track two or more images in a scene. *Location* allows users to track real-world coordinates (GPS). *Marker-less* allows users to track flat surfaces in a scene (e.g., floor, wall, table) in order to project augmentations.

Object Augmentation: *Texts* provide general information. *Legends* provide information about specific elements of objects. *Drawings* support free-form writings and annotations of objects. *Images* show pictorial information on objects. *Videos & Audios* associate visual and auditory media to objects. *3D models* illustrate objects in 3D format. Finally, *modals* provide interactive details and contextual information, such as pop-up information sheets.

Interaction: *3D rotation* allows users to rotate AR objects in the three-dimensional space. *Zoom* allows users to change the scale and explore AR objects in more detail. *Drag* allows users to change AR objects' positions. *Click* allows users to change the augmentations state or transition to another state in an AR experience. *Haptic* provides users with kinesthetic feedback, using touch sense (e.g., vibrations). *Animation* allows users to explore animated content.

Navigation: *Coordinated-views* involves multiple views showing information that is both simultaneous and separate in an AR experience. For example, in Fig. 1-(b)-T1, when a user clicks on the left view (menu) it updates the model view in the center. *Multi-scene* allows users to navigate in multiple scenes (e.g., Fig. 1-(b)-T3).

4.3   Dimension 3: AR Use

We identified four categories in relation to how end-users use AR: *device type, usage, content collection, connectivity,* and *language.*

Device Type: *Hand-held* allows users to view augmentations, either using desktop browsers or mobile apps. *Head-held* allows users to view content using AR headsets/glasses. *Screens* allow users to view content outside AR/VR, e.g., in browsers.

Usage: In contrast to *individual*, *collaborative* usage simultaneously engages a group of users interacting with AR objects and with one another.

Content Collection: *Screenshot taking* and *screen recording* allow users to capture cameras' field of view, such as 3D models projected in the real world —mainly to document moments of AR experiences (e.g., Fig. 1-(b)-T6).

Connectivity: In contrast to *offline*, *online* tools require the internet to use AR.

Language: In contrast to *single*, *multiple languages* offers content in several languages.

4.4 Dimension 4: Content and User Management

Content and user management relates to handling content access. We identified three main categories: *sharing, administration,* and *licensing*.

Sharing: *Public publish* allows publishing AR activities in open access. *Links* allow generating clickable links that can be given to students. *Codes* allow generating simple access codes. *QRCodes* allow generating scannable QRCodes.

Administration: *User access* involves granting/revoking access to users, for example, removing an access link or code. User *analytics and monitoring* provides teachers with analytics on how users interacted with AR experiences.

Licensing: Involves providing *free* or *paid* content.

5   Teachers' Needs: AR Functionalities and Activities

A) Elicitation and ideation: We conducted two co-design sessions. They started with a 30-minute elicitation phase, during which the 19 teachers explored 11 AR educational applications[1]. We then asked them to paper-prototype (to remove technical constraints) one or more AR activities for their course. We provided them with a toolkit (large paper worksheet, markers, tablet screens printed out on paper) and guidelines to help them describe (i) the context in which the AR activity is used (ii) the objects they wanted to augment, (iii) the augmentations they wanted to add, and (iv) the interactions they wanted their students to have access to via the tablet's screen. After the paper-prototyping, we asked the participants to present their prototypes to the group. We videotaped the workshops. We collected the recordings and 24 worksheets. The collected data is being published as a data paper. Three authors analyzed the recording and the worksheets to identify teachers' needs.

B) Teachers' Needs and AR activities: We identified five types of pedagogical AR activities and two ways of grouping these activities. The most common type of activity (18 out of 24) is **image augmentation** that allows teachers to add media resources to an image. The teachers wanted to add various types of resources, such as text, images, videos, 3D models, audio, videos, as well as modals to open multimodal information sheets or external links. A primary school teacher, for example, wants to augment the pages of a book with an audio recording of her saying specific vocabulary (e.g. "The reindeer has four hooves and 2 antlers") and an image of the real animals so kids can compare it to the book illustrations. Another teacher wants to augment the ID photos of his high-school students with the 3D models they created in technology class. The second type of activity is **image annotation** in which teachers want to

---

[1] Foxar, SpacecraftAR, Voyage AR, DEVAR, ARLOOPA, AnatomyAR, ARC, Le Chaudron Magique, SPART, Mountain Peak AR, SkyView Free. P.S. These were not part of our corpus because they are applications not authoring tools.

associate information (e.g., legends) to specific points of an object. For example, a teacher wants to indicate the names of the specific areas on a photo of a theater (e.g. stage, balconies). The third type of activity is **image validation**. Teachers want to create activities that students can complete on their own by using AR to automatically validate if the chosen image is correct. For example, a middle school science teacher wants to ask students to assemble the pieces of a map correctly. Another wants students to identify a specific part of a machine (e.g. motor) by scanning QRCodes on it. The fourth type of activity is **image association**. For example, a primary school teacher wants children to practice recognizing the same letter, written in capital and small letters. The fifth type of activity is **superposition of layers on an image**. For example, a university geology teacher wants students to be able to activate or deactivate layers showing various types of rock on a photo of a mountain. Finally, teachers want to group activities into a **learning cluster** or into a **learning path** as ordered activities.

6   Discussion

A) Possibilities and limitations of existing AR authoring tools: Looking at the four dimensions of design space (Fig. 1-(a)), it is clear that existing authoring tools provide many possibilities. Platforms vary from pre-made content (e.g. Lifeliqe) to pre-made templates (e.g., Assemblrworld) and visual editing (e.g. Grib3d, AWE). Most platforms provide ways to blend different media types in AR experiences, which can support experiential learning and a deeper understanding of complex topics [9]. Different media can provide multiple perspectives and make abstract concepts more concrete and engaging [3,14]. Furthermore, interaction and navigation modalities are also provided and might allow users to interact with content and control of what and how information is presented in a scene. Such modalities can aid learning because users explore and learn information from different perspectives by changing display parameters, using kinesthetic sense and by physically enacting concepts and phenomena (motor activity), which can support cognition [13,15].

However, there are limitations. Shelf selection and template editing platforms provide limited customization, which corroborate previous findings [13]. In addition, while some authoring tools enable users to create and import contents directly from device' sensors, which can be important because it reduces the burden of using other external tools, they provide very limited editing functionalities. Also, only six tools provide collaborative authoring, even though collaboration can be important for content educators and learners —to collectively create and share AR activities [3]. Similarly, only six tools allow users to engage in AR collaboratively even though a meta-analysis [6] found that collaborative AR has the highest impact on learners. Another important aspect that is lacking in most analyzed tools (16/21) is learning analytics (e.g., dashboards [18]), which can provide teachers with feedback about learners' experience, such as emotional state, progression and engagement.

B) How do existing authoring tools support teachers' needs? The functionalities, wanted by teachers and highlighted in green in Fig. 1-(a)), are more or less covered by the existing authoring tools. In particular, eight tools seem to cover the functionalities required to create the activity **image augmentation** (see Fig. 1-(c)). Two tools (Assemblrworld and Meta-AR-App) can partially create **image annotations** because they only allow text-based annotations, whereas teachers wanted to add rich-text annotations. While all the maker-based tools can recognize an image and show augmentations, none of them fully support **image validation** since teachers wanted to customize the augmentations of the outcome of a validation. **Image association** requires tracking multiple markers, which only a few tools support. In addition, even if these tools detect multiple markers, they do not provide ways to show an augmentation when multiple markers are simultaneously present in a scene. Lifeliqe provides coordinated views to navigate in layers of 3D models, which is similar to **image superposition**. However, the content is limited to 3D models and not customizable (shelf selection) and the coordinated views are only possible in *screen* mode (browser) not in AR. Assemblrworld allows creating multi-scenes without a specific order, which can support **learning clusters**. Similarly, Cospace allows creating multi-scenes with a specific order, which can support **learning paths**. However, the tool is marker-less, so teachers can not add markers for the activities. In general, most of these tools are commercial, that provide mainly limited free accounts which is a notable limitation because teachers highlighted that it would be difficult for them to secure funding. Only five tools provide activities that can be done offline even though teachers highlighted that their schools have limited access or no internet. In addition, the tablets they use do not have access to mobile data. This makes it impossible to access online outdoor AR activities, which are shown to have a positive impact on AR learning [6]. Teachers also wanted to record audio for their AR activities and most tools allow video recording but not audio. Also, most teachers raised the need for modals, e.g., interactive menus and buttons, that show contextual multimodal information and only three tools support modals.

C) Recommendations on how to design educational AR activities: While existing tools provide several modalities, we found little guidance on how to design effective educational AR activities, beyond technical tutorials. Based on literature, we provide three recommendations. First, we recommend that designers incorporate pedagogical approaches, such as collaborative learning, project-based learning, inquiry-based learning, situated learning, and multimedia learning to support educators in creating pedagogy-based AR activities [6]. Second, we recommend that designers engage with teachers to uncover pedagogical activities to support [e.g., 17]. For example, our teacher study revealed seven activities. Authoring tools can provide scaffolds for such activities. And finally, because authoring tools are targeting non-expert users (not professional designers), it seems important to accompany such tools with guidance to design AR content best. Guidance might cover multimedia, contiguity, coherence, modality, personalization, and signaling principles [16].

D) Implication for design and research: Our work can be useful for future research in four main ways. First, current design space synthesizes important dimensions and options of authoring AR activities. This work can inform researchers and designers about emerging interactive authoring technologies for AR from industry and academia. Second, we provide a characterization of teachers AR activities, which can inform researchers and designers about teachers' pedagogical needs for AR in ecological settings. Third, as highlighted above, existing tools provide little support for teachers' AR activities and the proposed design space can help setting up an authoring tool that leverages ideas from existing tools to support pedagogically-driven AR activities. Finally, future studies can use our work as a framework to design comparative studies that investigate the impact of different modalities of AR applications [1].

E) Limitation: We recognize that a keyword-based search could omit papers or tools that might be relevant to our work. However, our goal was not to find all the tools and papers fitting our definition but to build a representative corpus for analysis. The teachers who participated in the co-design workshops were self-selected, which might represent self-motivated teachers. Furthermore, we did not cover the gamified factors of educational AR authoring tools as well as immersive AR, which might require another study.

7 Conclusion

We analyzed 21 educational authoring tools from academia and industry and formulated a comprehensive design space of four dimensions: (1) authoring workflow, (2) AR modality, (3) AR use, and (4) content and user management. In addition, we analyzed two co-design workshops with 19 teachers and uncovered seven AR activities to support teachers. While existing tools provide a wide range of modalities, they provide limited support for authentic and pedagogical activities. We hope our work provides design-based insights and practical guidance to educators, researchers, and technology designers to inform the design and use of educational AR authoring tools.

References

1. Akçayır, M., Akçayır, G.: Advantages and challenges associated with augmented reality for education: a systematic review of the literature. Educ. Res. Rev. **20**, 1–11 (2017)
2. Arici, F., Yildirim, P., Caliklar, Ş., Yilmaz, R.M.: Research trends in the use of augmented reality in science education: content and bibliometric mapping analysis. Comput. Educ. **142**, 103647 (2019)
3. Billinghurst, M., Duenser, A.: Augmented reality in the classroom. Computer **45**(7), 56–63 (2012)
4. Braun, V., Clarke, V.: Using thematic analysis in psychology. Qual. Res. Psychol. **3**, 77–101 (2001)

5. Dengel, A., Iqbal, M.Z., Grafe, S., Mangina, E.: A review on augmented reality authoring toolkits for education. Front. Virtual Reality **3** (2022)
6. Garzón, J., Kinshuk, Baldiris, S., Gutiérrez, J., Pavón, J.: How do pedagogical approaches affect the impact of augmented reality on education? A meta-analysis and research synthesis. Educ. Res. Rev. **31**, 100334 (2020)
7. Halskov, K., Lundqvist, C.: Filtering and informing the design space: towards design-space thinking. ACM Trans. Comput.-Hum. Interact. **28**(1), 1–28 (2021)
8. Hincapie, M., Diaz, C., Valencia, A., Contero, M., Güemes-Castorena, D.: Educational applications of augmented reality: a bibliometric study. Comput. Electr. Eng. **93**, 107289 (2021)
9. Ibáñez, M.-B., Delgado-Kloos, C.: Augmented reality for STEM learning: a systematic review. Comput. Educ. **123**, 109–123 (2018)
10. Laato, S., Rauti, S., Islam, A.N., Sutinen, E.: Why playing augmented reality games feels meaningful to players? The roles of imagination and social experience. Comput. Hum. Behav. **121**, 106816 (2021)
11. Mota, R.C., Roberto, R.A., Teichrieb, V.: [POSTER] Authoring tools in augmented reality: an analysis and classification of content design tools. In: IEEE International Symposium on Mixed and Augmented Reality 2015, pp. 164–167 (2015)
12. Nebeling, M., Speicher, M.: The trouble with augmented reality/virtual reality authoring tools. In: 2018 IEEE International Symposium on Mixed and Augmented Reality Adjunct (ISMAR-Adjunct), pp. 333–337 (2018)
13. Radu, I.: Augmented reality in education: a meta-review and cross-media analysis. Pers. Ubiquit. Comput. **18**(6), 1533–1543 (2014)
14. Roopa, D., Prabha, R., Senthil, G.: Revolutionizing education system with interactive augmented reality for quality education. Mater. Today: Proc. **46**, 3860–3863 (2021)
15. Shams, L., Seitz, A.R.: Benefits of multisensory learning. Trends Cogn. Sci. **12**(11), 411–417 (2008)
16. Yang, K., Zhou, X., Radu, I.: XR-Ed framework: designing instruction-driven and learner-centered extended reality systems for education. arXiv:2010.13779 [cs] (2020)
17. Ez-Zaouia, M.: Teacher-centered dashboards design process. In: 2nd International Workshop on eXplainable Learning Analytics, Companion Proceedings of the 10th International Conference on Learning Analytics & Knowledge LAK20 (2020)
18. Ez-Zaouia, M., Tabard, A., Lavoué, E.: EMODASH: a dashboard supporting retrospective awareness of emotions in online learning. Int. J. Hum.-Comput. Stud. **139**, 102411 (2020)

The Effectiveness of Adaptive Digital Games for Learning: Calling for a Broader View on Assessment

Stefanie Vanbecelaere[1,2,3](✉) ⓘ, Febe Demedts[1,2,3] ⓘ, Bert Reynvoet[3] ⓘ, and Fien Depaepe[1,2] ⓘ

[1] Itec, Research Group of Imec, KU Leuven, Kortrijk, Belgium
`stefanie.vanbecelaere@kuleuven.be`
[2] Centre for Instructional Psychology and Technology, KU Leuven Kulak, Kortrijk, Belgium
[3] Brain & Cognition, KU Leuven Kulak, Kortrijk, Belgium

Abstract. Digital games for learning have been introduced as a motivating way for children to learn as they can provide immediate feedback, embed the learning content in an attractive narrative, and adapt item difficulty to learners' performance in the game. Although studies showed positive benefits of using digital educational games compared to other teaching methods, a systematic assessment of the effectiveness of digital games for learning is lacking. In this paper, we reflect on two intervention studies in which we investigated the effectiveness of digital games for learning with integrated adaptivity. Based on this work, we propose an extension of the framework of All and colleagues [5] for assessing digital games for learning including cognitive, noncognitive, and efficiency outcomes. We added aspects of study design that need to be considered such as learner, intervention, and measurement characteristics. The validation and adoption of this framework may contribute to more standardized procedures to assess the effectiveness of digital games for learning.

Keywords: Digital games for learning · Effectiveness · Methodologies

1 Introduction

The development of math and reading is an important goal during primary education. Early numerical skills and reading skills have been shown predictive for children's future academic performance and it has been argued that the training of these skills at a young age prevents children from later difficulties in math and reading [1, 2]. However, many children still experience difficulties acquiring these fundamental skills and a tendency toward more inclusive education strengthens the need for the development of appropriate interventions. Over the past years, the use of technology in education has increased, and consequently also the number of technological interventions available for schools.

Supplementary Information The online version contains supplementary material available at https://doi.org/10.1007/978-3-031-22124-8_26.

Especially *digital games for learning*, which refer to games 'with some learning goals in mind' [3, p 2], are introduced as a way for children to learn these fundamental skills [4].

Studies investigating the effectiveness of digital games for learning often did so in a "narrow sense", as they focused only on immediate cognitive effects (i.e. assessing whether trained skills were gained after gameplay). The need for a broader and more considerate investigation of the effectiveness of games is also echoed in a recent meta-analysis of Dondio et al. [25]. To evaluate the effectiveness of digital games for learning in a broader way, All and colleagues [5] developed a framework including learning, motivational, and efficiency outcomes. Regarding learning outcomes, not only improvement in performance is considered as evidence of the effectiveness of a game, but also increased interest in the trained topic. Furthermore, one should also examine whether the trained skills are transferred to tasks similar to the ones being trained in the game (i.e., the so-called 'near transfer'), or whether they are also generalized to other tasks (i.e., 'far transfer'). With regard to the motivational outcomes, when evaluating the effectiveness of educational games the motivation and enjoyment of the game experience need to be considered. Finally, also efficiency outcomes should be considered: "if a game helps in reducing the time needed to teach a certain subject matter, resulting in similar learning outcomes, it is considered as effective" [5, p 34].

In what follows, we elaborate on the method and results of two exemplary studies examining the effectiveness of two digital games for learning. To design these studies we relied on the framework of All and colleagues [5] to investigate the effectiveness in a broad and consistent way. In the discussion, we reflect on the feasibility of the framework and consequently propose an extension of the framework of All and colleagues [5] to study the effectiveness of digital games for learning more comprehensively.

2   Methodology

Two intervention studies were conducted to investigate the effectiveness of two digital games for learning early math and reading skills. Instead of a media comparison approach, which compares a game condition to a non-game condition, we applied a value-added approach, which enables the evaluation of the effectiveness of one specific game feature (in this case adaptivity).

Intervention study A includes children in the third grade of Kindergarten ($N = 191$, age range 5–6 years) in which we investigated the effect of an adaptive version of the reading game (RG, developed by Pelckmans in collaboration with Martine Ceyssens) compared to a nonadaptive version of the RG and an active control group, on young children's learning and motivational outcomes. Participating classes were randomly assigned to either an experimental or control condition and subjects were randomized within the adaptive and nonadaptive game condition. In the active control condition, children received similar tasks as in the RG, but these tasks were not embedded in a digital game, and thus, there was no feedback or attractive narrative and all children received the same number and difficulty of exercises. The children played the RG during four weeks, two times per week for 30 min. Near (phonological awareness and letter knowledge) and far (reading ability) transfer skills were indexed with standardized tests during both pre- and posttest. Concerning motivational outcomes, children's interest in reading and self-concept were assessed with a questionnaire administered one-on-one. Prior knowledge, home language, and socioeconomic status (SES) were taken into account to investigate how these variables moderated the effectiveness of the intervention. More information about the design and procedures of this study can be found in Vanbecelaere and colleagues [6].

Intervention study B studied the effects of an adaptive and nonadaptive version of the number sense game (NSG, developed by KU Leuven – GOA2012/010, coordinator Lieven Verschaffel) on learners' outcomes. Children ($N = 84$, age range 6–7 years) in first grade of primary education were randomly assigned to a condition in which children trained early numerical skills with an adaptive version of the NSG, or to a condition in which they trained with a nonadaptive version. The training took place over a period of three weeks resulting in six training sessions in total. Near (number line estimation and digit comparison) and far transfer (math ability) outcomes were assessed with standardized tests before, immediately after the training, and delayed after two weeks. Math anxiety was assessed with a questionnaire administered one-on-one before and two weeks after the training. Efficiency outcomes were operationalized in two ways: 1/based on pretest-posttest outcomes and registering the training time needed to achieve particular learning gains [7] and 2/based on the log data learning efficiency was modeled [8]. Furthermore, it was examined whether the effect of the intervention was moderated by the children's prior knowledge. More information about the design and procedures of the study can be consulted in Vanbecelaere and colleagues [7].

The adaptive and nonadaptive versions of the NSG and RG adapt for children's cognitive variables and more specifically their ability as continuously measured based on the individual performance during gameplay. Inspired by the Elo-rating system [9], a rating of the learners' ability was constantly updated and adjusted after each item response. Psychometric modeling techniques (i.e. Item Response Theory, IRT) were adopted to determine the difficulty of the tasks based on the performance of the children. This method -a combination of IRT and the Elo-rating method- showed to be very effective for managing adaptivity within an online game [10]. In the nonadaptive version of the NSG and the RG, the levels were presented with theoretically-assumed increased difficulty. The games were nonadaptive in the sense that children could always proceed to the next level regardless of their performance.

3   Results

In what follows, we discuss the results of intervention studies A and B. Regarding children's learning outcomes, first, children showed improved scores on all trained skills (i.e. phonological awareness, letter knowledge, digit comparison, number line estimation) from pre- to posttest, with no observed differences between the adaptive, non-adaptive, and active control conditions immediately after the intervention (study A, study B). Second, we observed no differences regarding transfer skills between the adaptive, nonadaptive, and active control condition on general reading fluency (study A) or mathematical competence (study B). Third, we distinguished between the effects of the intervention immediately after the intervention and delayed after a few weeks.

Delayed posttest results showed significant improvements compared to the pretest in all conditions (study B). With regard to math, results revealed no differences between the conditions immediately after the intervention and delayed after a few weeks (study B). Fourth, regarding the effects in terms of individual differences, the results revealed evidence that children who did not speak Dutch at home equally benefited from an adaptive, nonadaptive, or active control condition in terms of cognitive reading outcomes as children who spoke Dutch at home (study A). Also, children with high/low prior knowledge or children with different SES backgrounds equally benefited from the adaptive or nonadaptive condition (study B).

No differences were observed between the adaptive, nonadaptive, and active control condition for interest in reading and self-concept toward reading (study A). Furthermore, the results revealed that children's math anxiety scores decreased from pre- to posttest, but no differences between the adaptive and nonadaptive condition were determined (study B).

Efficiency outcomes were operationalized in two ways. First, based on the pretest-posttest outcomes and the time children needed to finish the game, the results indicated that children assigned to the adaptive condition needed significantly less time compared to the nonadaptive condition to achieve the same learning goals (study B). Interestingly, for number line estimation tasks, a significant interaction between prior knowledge (score on number line estimation task) and condition was obtained: children with high prior knowledge benefited more from the adaptive game condition, in the sense that they needed less time to obtain the learning goals compared to children with high prior knowledge in the nonadaptive condition. By contrast, children with low prior knowledge needed significantly more time in the adaptive condition to reach the learning goals compared to children with low prior knowledge in the nonadaptive condition (study B) [7]. Second, a more fine-grained operationalization of 'time' was obtained by using log data collected during gameplay. We found that the children made progress both in the nonadaptive and the adaptive version of the NSG, but that children learned more efficiently within the adaptive version of the game (study B) [8]. The implemented adaptivity increased learning efficiency across, but not within a game-playing session.

4   Discussion and Conclusions

In what follows, we will first reflect on the adopted methodology in the two presented studies. Based on these reflections, we propose a comprehensive framework to investigate the effectiveness of digital games for learning.

4.1   Reflections on the Adopted Methodology

A first reflection is related to the study design and more specifically the characteristics of the intervention. In line with the value-added approach, we specifically investigated the effectiveness of one characteristic of the game, namely adaptivity. This enabled us to gain insights into which specific game features encourage learning. The results pointed out that the adaptive training was equally effective as the nonadaptive training in terms of children's performance on tests measuring what they trained in the games and on tasks that required transfer. Compared to previous research, a recent review by Ninaus and Nebel [11] reported that five out of ten studies reported positive significant findings in favor of adaptive game training in terms of learning outcomes. One study reported mixed findings and four studies reported no statistically significant outcomes. Other meta-analyses investigating the effect of adaptivity (but not necessarily in games) also showed mixed effects [12, 13]. The variation in results across studies may be caused by how the adaptivity is operationalized [11]. Comparing the results of a study to previous intervention studies is only possible if the game features are clearly described [14].

A second reflection is related to which outcomes were measured in the two studies. In this research, it was hypothesized that training of children's number comparison, number line estimation, phonological awareness, letter knowledge, and word reading would foster these outcomes and possibly would lead to transfer to more advanced mathematical and reading outcomes. Theoretically, it is more likely to observe higher learning gains on trained skills compared to transfer skills [15, 16].

A third reflection is related to how the outcomes in these studies were measured. The intervention studies we conducted only included standardized tests to measure trained skills and transfer effects. However, prior intervention studies often measure near transfer with self-developed tests [16]. On the one hand, self-developed tests often more closely resemble the tasks children received during gameplay and are therefore more sensitive to detecting differences in children's learning. On the other hand, they are less reliable/valid than standardized tests and these studies are also more difficult to reproduce. Concerning noncognitive measures, we used individual interviews with the children (study A, study B). Previous research has often used self-report questionnaires administered in groups to measure math and reading anxiety [17]. When self-report pen-and-paper questionnaires are administered in groups, social desirability plays an important role [18]. Although one-on-one administration is much more time-consuming, we experienced that the experimenter could better estimate whether the child fully understands the question and we believe that the child considers his/her answer more compared to taking a test with all children simultaneously. Nevertheless, reliability scores of the self-report questionnaire administered in groups were acceptable [17] whereas the reliability of the self-report responses administered during individual interviews was rather questionable (study A, study B). Measures to evaluate children's learning efficiency have not been frequently included in empirical studies so far. In study B, we relied on pretest-posttest results and data collected during gameplay (log data) was used to operationalize learning efficiency. We experienced several benefits of using log data to assess children's learning efficiency. First, traditional assessments are taken at a single point in time (e.g. pretest-posttest designs) and therefore might result in an over- or underestimation of the child's actual skill, while skills are dynamic and constantly changing in nature [19]. By making use of log data this dynamic character of learning can be taken into account. Second, the collection of log data is unobtrusive which contrasts with the sometimes extensive assessment batteries young children have to complete. Third, log data typically consists of detailed information about children's actions during gameplay allowing to determine small differences between learners or between groups of learners. Fourth, detailed information about learners' accuracy, differences in learners' ability, and differences in the difficulty of items can be taken into account. As such, learning efficiency can be modeled, and not just the speed at which students finish the game.

A fourth reflection is related to when children were assessed. Children's noncognitive outcomes were assessed before and after the intervention (study B) while the individual interviews only took place after the intervention (study A). To obtain a more complete picture of how children's noncognitive factors vary between conditions and from pre- to posttest, the additional use of unobtrusive (e.g., physiological) measures providing data about children's noncognitive factors during gameplay may be an interesting avenue for further investigation [20, 21]. Relying on posttests only as in study A is methodologically not recommended because a lack of baseline measurement disables the researcher to derive whether differences in children's noncognitive outcomes between the conditions already existed before the intervention [22].

A fifth reflection is related to the learner characteristics we took into account when studying the effectiveness of the intervention. We observed that individual differences such as prior knowledge, home language, and SES did not moderate the effectiveness of the intervention. Previous research reported mixed evidence. Some studies found that adaptive tools were more effective than typical instruction for students with low prior knowledge [12, 23]. This result is explained by the fact that children with low prior knowledge need more guidance to master the content than they are able to receive in a typical classroom. On the contrary, Faber and colleagues [24] found that an adaptive tool was more effective for high-performing students compared to high-performing students in business-as-usual settings. They argue that high-performing students are offered more exercises in the adaptive learning environment enabling them to obtain higher results on performance tests. Teachers have fewer opportunities to provide individual practice to high-performing children in a business-as-usual setting and/or are often more focused on keeping up with the low-performing children.

4.2   Toward a Comprehensive Assessment Framework

Based on the reflections in the previous section, we propose a comprehensive framework to assess the effectiveness of digital games for learning. We have adapted and extended the framework of All and colleagues [5] in four ways. First, instead of making a distinction between learning, motivational and efficiency outcomes, we think it is more comprehensive to discern cognitive outcomes, noncognitive outcomes and efficiency outcomes. Second, we specified how the outcomes can be measured (i.e. "when" and "how" to measure learning outcomes). Third, we added intervention characteristics which are typical choices researchers need to make when designing a game intervention. Fourth, we added learner characteristics which are factors that may influence the effectiveness of the game intervention. Figure 1 presents the extended framework.

First, regarding the *outcomes*, All and colleagues [5] distinguish only between achieving the learning goals of the game and the ability to transfer the learned content, in terms of cognitive outcomes. However, also for noncognitive outcomes, a similar distinction can be made. For example, emotions, motivation and enjoyment to complete the tasks during gameplay can be considered as noncognitive in-game outcomes. However, if playing the game leads to increased motivation for a certain subject (e.g. mathematics), which is also observable during other (offline) class activities, we consider this a noncognitive transfer effect. To the best of our knowledge, this distinction between in-game and transfer effects regarding noncognitive outcomes has not been made in intervention studies. Future empirical research can show whether this is a useful categorization.

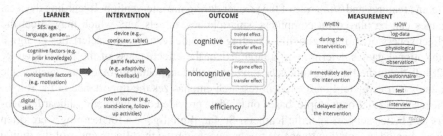

Fig. 1. Framework for assessing the effectiveness of DGBL

Second, *"when"* to assess learners is important to consider. Depending on the research question(s), instruments can be administered before, during, immediately after and delayed a few weeks/months after the intervention. Different conclusions can be derived depending on when the instruments are administered. Pretests are important to examine whether there were differences between the conditions prior to the intervention and need to be taken into account when analyzing children's learning gains [22]. Posttests are crucial to determine whether children obtained the targeted learning goals, and delayed tests are important to gain insight into the sustainability of the intervention effects [26]. Also during the intervention cognitive and non-cognitive outcomes can be measured. Benefits are that this data can give a more fine-grained idea about how children's knowledge and skills develop [27]. Dynamic assessment of cognitive, noncognitive, and efficiency factors during gameplay is unobtrusive and can reduce the time that is necessary for assessing children, leaving more time for learning. Although a long tradition exists in using pre- and posttest assessments to examine the effectiveness of adaptive digital games, we believe that when combined with the use of data collected during learning (i.e. log data, physiological data), additional light on children's cognitive and noncognitive factors can be shed.

Furthermore, *"how"* the outcomes are measured is an important consideration. In our framework, we included a list of possible instruments that can be used to measure cognitive, noncognitive and efficiency outcomes. Tests and questionnaires have been widely adopted to measure the effects of a game intervention. Standardized instruments might be less sensitive to observing differences between conditions compared to self-developed instruments, but the former are more reliable and foster comparing results across studies that used the same measures [15, 16]. In recent years, the possibility to collect and store large amounts of data (i.e. log data) provides objective data about events or actions taking place during gameplay [27]. For example, in-game cognitive (e.g., accuracy scores to measure performance) and noncognitive (e.g. time on task to measure effort) outcomes can be measured. Also, physiological data such as heart rate and skin conductance can be used to capture for example learners' emotions [27]. Which instrument to use depends on many factors such as among others the type of research (quantitative versus qualitative), the characteristics of participants (e.g. attention span, age) and how complex it is to measure the variable (e.g. physiological data of learners' states need to be combined with observational data derived from video recordings).

Third, regarding the *intervention*, it is important that the intervention is clearly described. The intervention can be described based on the following categories: 1/device, 2/game features and 3/the role of the teacher during the intervention. Regarding devices, games can be played on computers, smartphones, tablets, etc. which may affect the effectiveness of an intervention. Regarding the game features, characteristics of digital educational games determine to a large extent the effectiveness of the game. Prensky [28] distinguished among others adaptivity, feedback, social involvement, agency, the game's narrative etc. Finally, recent research emphasizes the importance of the role of the teacher [29]. For example, based on the data provided on a teacher dashboard, teachers can better support specific learners. So far, digital games for learning were often implemented in isolation to enable researchers to derive the effectiveness of the digital tool itself. Depending on the research question(s) at stake, intervention studies take a media comparison or value-added approach to investigate the effectiveness of the intervention. In both approaches, a game condition is compared to a control condition. In media comparison studies, the control condition entails for example a pen-and-paper condition or a 'business-as-usual' condition, while in value-added studies the conditions only differ on one characteristic of the intervention.

Fourth, researchers should take into account learners' background characteristics such as gender, SES, age, school etc. which may influence learning. In line with the Opportunity-Propensity model of Byrnes and Miller [30], these characteristics are present early in a child's life. Furthermore, there are other cognitive (e.g. prior knowledge, executive functions) and noncognitive (e.g. motivation, anxiety) factors which can directly influence how much children benefit from the game intervention.

In conclusion, intervention studies investigating the effectiveness of digital games for learning to date are very heterogeneous in terms of research design and used instruments. Furthermore, the effectiveness is often investigated in a narrow sense, meaning that the effect of the training is assessed only in terms of learners' progress on the trained skills. We propose an extension of the framework of All and colleagues [5] which is more comprehensive, not only in terms of outcomes but also in terms of how and when the outcomes can be measured. We believe that the adoption of this framework by researchers can guide the design of intervention studies and ultimately can lead to a broader and more standardized examination of the effects of digital games for learning.

References

1. Nelson, G., McMaster, K.L.: The effects of early numeracy interventions for students in preschool and early elementary: a meta-analysis. J. Educ. Psychol. **111**(6), 1001–1022 (2019)
2. Piasta, S.B., Wagner, R.K.: Developing early literacy skills: a meta-analysis of alphabet learning and instruction. Read. Res. Q. **45**(1), 8–38 (2010)
3. Becker, K.: What's the difference between gamification, serious games, educational games, and game-based learning? Acad. Lett. (2021)
4. Wouters, P., van Nimwegen, C., van Oostendorp, H., van der Spek, E.D.: A meta-analysis of the cognitive and motivational effects of serious games. J. Educ. Psychol. **105**(2), 249–265 (2013)

5. All, A., Castellar, E.P.N., Van Looy, J.: Towards a conceptual framework for assessing the effectiveness of digital game-based learning. Comput. Educ. **88**, 29–37 (2015)
6. Vanbecelaere, S., Cornillie, F., Sasanguie, D., Reynvoet, B., Depaepe, F.: The effectiveness of an adaptive digital educational game for the training of early numerical abilities in terms of cognitive, noncognitive and efficiency outcomes. Br. J. Edu. Technol. **52**(1), 112–124 (2021)
7. Vanbecelaere, S., Van den Berghe, K., Cornillie, F., Sasanguie, D., Reynvoet, B., Depaepe, F.: The effectiveness of adaptive versus non-adaptive learning with digital educational games. J. Comput. Assist. Learn. **36**(4), 502–513 (2020)
8. Debeer, D., Vanbecelaere, S., Van Den Noortgate, W., Reynvoet, B., Depaepe, F.: The effect of adaptivity in digital learning technologies: modelling learning efficiency using data from an educational game. Brit. J. Educ. Technol. **52**(5), 1881–1897 (2021)
9. Elo, A.E.: The Rating of chessplayers, past and present. Arco Publishing, Inc. (1978)
10. Park, J.Y., Cornillie, F., van der Maas, H.L., Van Den Noortgate, W.: A multidimensional IRT approach for dynamically monitoring ability growth in computerized practice environments. Front. Psychol. **10**, 620 (2019)
11. Ninaus, M., Nebel, S.: A systematic literature review of analytics for adaptivity within educational video games. Front. Educ. **5**, 611072 (2021)
12. Gerard, L., Matuk, C., McElhaney, K., Linn, M.C.: Automated, adaptive guidance for K-12 education. Educ. Res. Rev. **15**, 41–58 (2015)
13. Liu, Z., Moon, J., Kim, B., Dai, C.-P.: Integrating adaptivity in educational games: a combined bibliometric analysis and meta-analysis review. Educ. Tech. Res. Dev. **68**(4), 1931–1959 (2020). https://doi.org/10.1007/s11423-020-09791-4
14. Clark, D.B., Tanner-Smith, E.E., Killingsworth, S.S.: Digital games, design, and learning: a systematic review and meta-analysis. Rev. Educ. Res. **86**(1), 79–122 (2016)
15. Graham, L.J., De Bruin, K., Lassig, C., Spandagou, I.: A scoping review of 20 years of research on differentiation: investigating conceptualisation, characteristics, and methods used. Rev. Educ. **9**(1), 161–198 (2020)
16. Swanson, E., Stevens, E.A., Scammacca, N.K., Capin, P., Stewart, A.A., Austin, C.R.: The impact of tier 1 reading instruction on reading outcomes for students in grades 4–12: a meta-analysis. Read. Writ. **30**(8), 1639–1665 (2017)
17. Vanbecelaere, S., Van den Berghe, K., Cornillie, F., Sasanguie, D., Reynvoet, B., Depaepe, F.: The effects of two digital educational games on cognitive and non-cognitive math and reading outcomes. Comput. Educ. **143**, 103680 (2020)
18. Schrader, C., Brich, J., Frommel, J., Riemer, V., Rogers, K.: Rising to the challenge: an emotion-driven approach toward adaptive serious games. In: Ma, M., Oikonomou, A. (eds.) Serious Games and Edutainment Applications, pp. 3–28. Springer, Heidelberg (2017). https://doi.org/10.1007/978-3-319-51645-5_1
19. Thomson, J.M., Foldnes, N., Uppstad, P.H., Njå, M., Solheim, O.J., Lundetræ, K.: Can children's instructional gameplay activity be used as a predictive indicator of reading skills? Learn. Inst. **68**, 101348 (2020)
20. Singh, N., Aggarwal, Y., Sinha, R.K.: Heart rate variability analysis under varied task difficulties in mental arithmetic performance. Heal. Technol. **9**(3), 343–353 (2018). https://doi.org/10.1007/s12553-018-0272-0
21. Verkijika, S.F., De Wet, L.: Using a brain-computer interface (BCI) in reducing math anxiety: evidence from South Africa. Comput. Educ. **81**, 113–122 (2015)
22. Gliner, J.A., Morgan, G.A., Harmon, R.J.: Pretest-posttest comparison group designs: analysis and interpretation. J. Am. Acad. Child Adolesc. Psychiatry **42**(4), 500–503 (2003)
23. Borleffs, E., Glatz, T.K., Daulay, D.A., Richardson, U., Zwarts, F., Maassen, B.A.M.: GraphoGame SI: the development of a technology-enhanced literacy learning tool for Standard Indonesian. Eur. J. Psychol. Educ. **33**(4), 595–613 (2017). https://doi.org/10.1007/s10212-017-0354-9

24. Faber, J.M., Luyten, H., Visscher, A.J.: The effects of a digital formative assessment tool on mathematics achievement and student motivation: results of a randomized experiment. Comput. Educ. **106**, 83–96 (2017)

25. Dondio, P., Santos, F.H., Gusev, V., Rocha, M.: Do games reduce maths anxiety? a review of the current literature. In: Fotaris, P. (ed.) ECGBL 2021. Proceedings of the 15th European Conference on Game Based Learning, pp. 287–292. ACI (2021)

26. Suggate, S.P.: A meta-analysis of the long-term effects of phonemic awareness, phonics, fluency, and reading comprehension interventions. J. Learn. Disabil. **49**(1), 77–96 (2016)

27. Noroozi, O., Pijeira-Díaz, H.J., Sobocinski, M., Dindar, M., Järvelä, S., Kirschner, P.A.: Multimodal data indicators for capturing cognitive, motivational, and emotional learning processes: a systematic literature review. Educ. Inf. Technol. **25**(6), 5499–5547 (2020). https://doi.org/10.1007/s10639-020-10229-w

28. Prensky, M.: The games generations: how learners have changed. In: Prensky, M. (ed.) Digital game-based learning, pp. 35–51. McGraw-Hill, New York (2001)

29. Baker, R.S.: Stupid tutoring systems, intelligent humans. Int. J. Artif. Intell. Educ. **26**(2), 600–614 (2016)

30. Byrnes, J.P., Miller, D.C.: The relative importance of predictors of math and science achievement: an opportunity–propensity analysis. Contemp. Educ. Psychol. **32**(4), 599–629 (2007)

Gamification in Work Teams: A Q Study on How Team Members Experience Gamification

Jerry B. Stolte, Lise A. van Oortmerssen$^{(\boxtimes)}$ ⓘ, and Bé Albronda

Faculty of Management, Open Universiteit, PO Box 2960, 6401 DL Heerlen, The Netherlands
lise.vanoortmerssen@ou.nl

Abstract. Gamification relates to the application of game elements in a non-game context. Recently, the concept receives increasing acknowledgement as a tool for achieving motivational or behavioural goals. The effects of gamification in education, on an individual level, have been the topic of academic research for some time. However, until now, only few academic studies have addressed the implementation of gamification in teams in organizational contexts. Using Q methodology, this study combines quantitative and qualitative data to explore how team members experience gamification in work teams. The results show two main perspectives on gamification in organizational work teams. The first perspective, described as the eager team gamer, is predominantly positive. It reveals an experience of increased enjoyment, collaboration, creativity, and productiveness among team members. The second perspective, labelled as the critical player, is much more demanding. It acknowledges the potential positive influences of gamification in certain contexts, but feels strongly about possible inappropriateness in serious tasks or environments, and is adverse towards competitive elements. The results of this Q study add to our understanding of how and why team members in organizations may variously perceive gamification of team tasks.

Keywords: Gamification · Teams · Q methodology

1 Introduction

Gamification is the application of game elements in a non-game context, usually employed to affect motivation and human behaviour in a positive manner. The use of game elements in a serious context is a phenomenon that has become more widespread during the last decade. Gamification is applied most commonly within the domains of education, health and crowdsourcing [1]. Less often, but increasingly, gamification is applied within the domain of work. Research has shown that gamification in the work domain may improve employee engagement [e.g., 1, 2], social interaction among employees [e.g., 1, 3, 4] and performance [1, 4]. However, as shown by a comprehensive review of gamification research, only a small percentage of gamification studies regards a work context [1]. The implementation of gamification in organizations may be targeted at individual level outcomes as well as at team level outcomes. Although we know that gamification may induce social interaction, few studies have investigated the benefits

© The Author(s), under exclusive license to Springer Nature Switzerland AG 2022
K. Kiili et al. (Eds.): GALA 2022, LNCS 13647, pp. 279–287, 2022.
https://doi.org/10.1007/978-3-031-22124-8_27

of gamification of work team tasks. Our study explores experiences with gamification in work-place teams, addressing the following research question: *What perspectives on gamification of team tasks exist among team members in organizations?* Applying Q methodology, this study reveals and describes two different perspectives on gamification of team tasks. The results of this Q study add to our understanding of how and why team members in organizations may variously perceive gamification of team tasks.

2 Theoretical Background

Gamification refers to the employment of a design approach in order to simulate game characteristics and affect participants' psychological and behavioural outcomes. Since around 2010, gamification has attracted attention of both practitioners and scholars [1]. Drawing on the tenets of self-determination theory, gamification appeals to basic human needs and (potentially) affects users' intrinsic and extrinsic motivations related to autonomy, competences, and relatedness [2–4]. Examples of outcome elements that may induce intrinsic motivation are fun and learning experiences. Outcome elements that may raise extrinsic motivation encompass, for example, rewards and recognitions. Gamification designs mostly focus on progress and achievement-oriented affordances, for example by introducing points, badges, or leaderboards. Immersion-related affordances, such as narratives and avatars, currently appear less frequently [1]. This observation resonates with Meske et al.'s statement that current gamification designs are predominantly tailored to extrinsic motivations and that intrinsic motivations are largely overlooked [4]. Hence, the current state of gamification developments do not yet do justice to the wide variety of motivations of users that may be involved [1].

The implementation of gamification is generally targeted at influencing motivation and behaviour in positive ways, especially in terms of commitment and perseverance [5]. For example, activities that are burdensome, once gamified, may be easier to perform. The majority of studies on gamification show that gamification has beneficial effects [1]. Nevertheless, also a considerable number of studies show mixed findings. Adverse effects of gamification may include, among others, discouraging of users due to a competitive environment [1], diminishing of creativity due to (too) strictly defined paths of action [1], or diminishing of the team output due to discussion about rules and mandatory game behaviour [6]. Counterproductive effects of gamification may be evoked by perceived inappropriateness, for example of the reward system in a gamification design [7]. According to Meske et al., extrinsic motivation through gaming elements like points, badges and leaderboards could even decrease users' primary intrinsic motivation [4].

Research has shown that teamwork may benefit from gamification by increasing motivation and supporting team tasks, thereby boosting team performance [2, 3, 6]. Patricio et al. suggest that gamification is a way to make team tasks more enjoyable and a way to tackle collaboration issues [2]. Their case study of innovation teams reveals that game rules and time constraints provide a structure that can enhance team members' engagement, coordination, and conflict management. Gamification of the team task helps team members to remain focused and avoid dispersion. Patricio et al. also point out that playfulness of a gamified team task might counter stress and fatigue among team members, thereby supporting a team's collaborative efforts and collective creativity [2, see also 4]. For different team members, different motivations for engaging in a gamified team task may apply. This is illustrated by the findings of a study conducted by Fodor and Barna, involving a gamified team building application that promotes joint sport activities [8]. Their findings show that engaged users might be primarily motivated by very different drivers of behaviour: achieving long-term goals; achieving victory over others; or enjoying interacting with others [8]. In the present study, the focus is on attitudes and experiences of employees who have been confronted with gamified team tasks. In the next section of this paper, we outline the applied method.

3 Method

3.1 Q Study Design

Following an abductive approach, combining quantitative and qualitative data, Q methodology transforms individual viewpoints into a limited number of coherent perspectives on a specified topic [9–12]. The data for a Q factor analysis derives from a set of statements (Q set) regarding the research subject, sorted from least agree (-5) to most agree (+5) by a number of participants (P set). By using ranking of the different statements (Q sorting), the researcher forces a respondent to not only agree or disagree with an opinion, but to distinguish and compare ideas in relation to each other, rather than in isolation [9–12]. In Q methodology, the Q set, and not the participants, constitute the study sample. The participants are the variables. In addition to the Q sorts, qualitative data are gathered through interview questions in order to gain deeper insights into respondents' sortings. All collected Q sorts are compared with each other [9–12]. Q sorts that tend to be similar will form a factor, a cluster of viewpoints representing a shared way of thinking on the subject matter. A Q study results in a limited number of thorough, nuanced perspectives [9–12].

3.2 Instruments

The Q set is a set of straightforward and easy to understand statements that are subjected to ranking by the participants [9–12]. The set of 45 items used in this study is based on a literature review of gamification and more in particular of gamification in work team settings. The Q set (see Table 1) was designed with the aim of providing a good coverage of themes in relation to the research question [10, 12]. Statements were derived from generally accepted views as well as critical notes. They represent a wide range of opinions about the research subject. Items were included regarding social interaction and teamwork, competition, gamification design, effectiveness, and appropriateness.

For reasons of user-friendliness, the Q set items were translated into Dutch so it would be easier for respondents to sort the statements from disagree to agree and to discuss them afterwards. In addition to the Q set, a brief accompanying questionnaire was composed, consisting of demographic questions and a question regarding what type(s) of gamification the participant was acquainted with. Finally, a topic list for additional interviews was prepared.

Table 1. Q set

No	Statement
1	Gamified tasks are easy to work on
2	Due to the use of gamification, the teamwork or collaboration was more pleasant in my opinion
3	When the layout or the design is not attractive and inviting, I am not inclined to participate
4	Gamification increases my own contribution to the team output
5	Gamification increases the contributions of other team members to the team output
6	Because of gamification, collaboration during assignments is advantageous
7	Due to the application of gamification, there is more criticizing of one another's contributions
8	Due to the application of gamification, there is more complementing of one another's contributions
9	During the execution of gamified tasks, team members tend to ignore one another's contributions
10	During the execution of gamified tasks, team members tend to take notice of one another's contributions
11	While working on the gamified task, I experienced fun in collaborating with my colleagues
12	I noticed an increased involvement in an assignment on my part
13	I noticed an increased involvement of others in an assignment
14	Due to gamification, my feeling of responsibility towards the outcome of the assignment has increased
15	Due to gamification, my team members' feelings of responsibility towards the outcome of the assignment have increased
16	The use of gamification has a positive effect on the progress of an assignment
17	Using gamification in work is an appropriate way to reach certain (organizational) goals
18	Using gamification feels inappropriate
19	Gamification adds value to the experienced teamwork
20	I notice an increase of attention and focus to the assignment when gamification is applied
21	The solidarity of the group during the (gamified) assignment is positive
22	Gamification is distracting from actual organizational goals
23	When game elements are implemented in work, it has a positive effect on creativity
24	Gamification in work has no significant effect on any results or outcomes
25	Due to the implementation of gamification in my work I have discovered (new) qualities in my colleagues
26	Gamification results in equal contributions from all team members to the assignment and results

(continued)

Table 1. (*continued*)

No	Statement
27	The process of gamification is boring
28	Gamification is appropriate for children, not for adults in their work
29	It is demotivating to work on a gamified task
30	Gamification makes no (significant) contribution to the experience of my work
31	I prefer working alone on a gamified task
32	Earning coins/medals/winning is not of any importance to me
33	Because me and my colleagues differ from one another, gamification causes a gap between team members
34	I make an effort to reach the highest level or achieve the highest score
35	Competition in work creates negative sentiments towards colleagues
36	I think gamification is more suitable for people younger than me
37	It is unnecessary to give scores or to add competition to the work process
38	Gamifying elements in my work have a negative effect on my enthusiasm
39	I am pleased to participate in a task with gamification
40	It is an unnecessary obligation to participate in gamification or gamified tasks
41	Games and game elements do not belong in a serious context
42	A competitive environment alienates me from the actual work task
43	I put forth better ideas together with my colleagues thanks to playfulness
44	Gamification makes me feel like I am (or my work is) not being taken seriously
45	Storytelling attributes to the experience of the gamified task

3.3 Participants and Procedure

The P set consisted of people who have had recent experiences with gamification, specifically in their team and thus with co-workers. A P set should include a heterogeneous group of respondents holding defined viewpoints to express, and should not be composed randomly but composed based on theoretical grounds [10, 12]. Therefore, we included invited participants with expected positive attitudes towards games as well as participants with expected negative or cynical attitudes towards games. Literature suggests that younger generations are more likely to enjoy games, especially when digital media or design are involved [13]. Therefore, we selected participants from various ages. Q studies do not require large numbers of participants [10, 12]. The number of participants is less important than who the participants are [9]. For a Q set of 45 statements, Webler et al. suggest a minimum of 15 participants, conform a 3:1 ratio [11].

Invitations were sent to 59 candidates who work in various organizations in the Netherlands and have experience with gamification in their work team. Of these candidates, 15 participants completed the Q sort. Five respondents also participated in an additional interview. Prior to the Q sorting, the participants were asked to fill out the short questionnaire. Several reported job titles were head of department, team leader, psychologist, innovation manager, IT specialist and chief creative officer. Of the 15 participants, seven were male and eight female. The ages of the participants varied from 27 to 59. One participant worked in the private sector, all others worked in the public sector, for example in healthcare. The selected participants had various experiences with gamification, ranging from stand-alone brainstorm sessions with team members to gamified assignments with colleagues that lasted for a longer period of time.

The QMethod Software application was used. This research tool allows for the entire Q study to be executed in a digital and online environment. With this tool, the researcher can create the Q set, add a questionnaire, and invite the participants to participate in the study. The tool also has built-in factor analysis functionalities. All participants received a link to the portal. With their unique participant code, they were able to log into their own Q sort environment. In the application, they were first informed about the research, methodology and instructions. This part also included an informed consent. The next steps were marked as levels, like in games: Level 1 included the instructions to guide the player through the Q sort. Level 2 consisted of presorting the statements, and level 3 was the actual Q sort. After finalizing level 3, the player reached the finish. Afterwards, all participants were rewarded with a prize in the form of a local food product.

3.4 Analytical Strategy

Factor extraction was executed in the online QMethod Software application. The correlation matrix of all Q sorts was calculated, after which the matrix was subjected to factor extraction. Then, factor rotation was applied in order to examine the spheres of opinion from different angles [10]. After the quantitative stage of the data analysis, the qualitative stage followed. The meanings of the Q sorts were explored, with a special focus on the statements placed at the extremes of the Q sorts. The qualitative data derived from the interviews were applied to help interpret the results. Finally, the demographic information retrieved by the short survey was analysed in relation to the factors.

4   Results

4.1 Factor Extraction and Rotation

For the factor extraction, the application of Centroid Factor Analysis and Principal Component Analysis produced similar results. Factor extraction resulted in seven factors. Table 2 shows the eigenvalue and explained variance of the seven factors after Centroid Factor Analysis.

Following factor extraction, as a generic rule, it is best to reduce the number of factors to a minimum while explaining as much study variance and as many Q sorts as possible [10]. There is no one correct number of factors to retain. A factor is considered reliable for interpretation when it has an eigenvalue above 1.0. A total explained variance of 35–40% or more for all included factors together is considered acceptable [10]. Only Factor 1 and 2 complied with the requirements of an eigenvalue above 1 and a sufficient cumulative variance. Therefore, these two factors were retained and examined more closely. The

Table 2. Eigenvalue and (cumulative) explained variance per factor

	Eigenvalue	% Explained variance	Cumulative variance
Factor 1	6.7602	45.0680	45.0680
Factor 2	1.1175	7.4502	52.5182
Factor 3	0.4327	2.8846	55.4028
Factor 4	0.4899	3.2662	58.6690
Factor 5	0.4280	2.8534	61.5224
Factor 6	0.2563	1.7087	63.2311
Factor 7	0.2747	1.8314	65.0625

application of factor rotation to examine the spheres of opinion from different angles did not result in additional insights. An analysis of the demographic data showed no consistent patterns across the two factors.

4.2 Factor 1. The Eager Team Gamer

The first generally shared point of view, Factor 1, can be described as the eager team gamer. It highlights the positive effects of gamification in work teams. The eigenvalue for Factor 1 is 6.76 and the factor explains slightly over 45% of the total variance. It is clear that this perspective includes most participants in this study. According to this point of view, creativity, teamwork experience and productiveness are positively influenced by the implementation of gamification. For these people, the use of gamification will undoubtedly have a beneficial impact on their work experience. The way team members experience gamification, has a clearly constructive outcome for Factor 1. From Factor 1's point of view, gamification has a positive effect on the progress in a work task. Factor 1 feels like game elements can increase fun, creativity and productiveness in teamwork. Factor 1 experiences positive stimuli from competitiveness. Storytelling adds to a positive experience in gamification. Factor 1 feels that both their own as well as their team members' contributions to a task can be improved using gamification. Gamification can have a beneficial effect on how employees experience working in a team. For Factor 1 gamification is not considered inappropriate or demeaning, nor does it cause the feeling of not being taken seriously at work.

4.3 Factor 2. The Critical Player

The second viewpoint, Factor 2, will be described as the critical player. The eigenvalue for Factor 2 is 1.12. The factor explains 7.45% of the total variance. According to Factor 2, competitiveness has a negative effect on teamwork and it even alienates the employee from his or her actual work. Gamification, if successfully designed and implemented, can have a positive impact on collaboration and work experience. However, this player is much more demanding. If the design or construction of the gamified task is not attractive, the interest to participate is already lessened. Using storytelling does not necessarily make gamification more attractive in Factor 2's opinion. In most cases, Factor 2 will not feel comfortable with gamifying certain serious tasks for it might decrease the earnestness of their work. It might feel disrespectful or childish. In the case of certain serious tasks, Factor 2 will encounter a decrease in involvement and even a loss of solidarity within a team. The outcome for solidarity within a team is usually negative in the opinion of Factor 2. For Factor 2, gamification is something to be considered carefully before implementing within a team. Gamifying certain serious tasks and adding game elements in a professional collaboration can have a counterproductive outcome. It might come across as demeaning or inappropriate and can actually have a negative impact on solidarity within a team.

5 Discussion

Our Q study investigated perspectives on gamification of team tasks among team members in organizations who have experience with one or more types of gamified team tasks. The findings of our study reveal two distinct perspectives. The first perspective, described as the eager team gamer, is predominantly positive. It reveals an experience of increased enjoyment, collaboration, creativity, and productiveness among team members. The second perspective, labelled as the critical player, is much more demanding. It acknowledges the potential positive influences of gamification in certain contexts, but feels strongly about possible inappropriateness in serious tasks or environments, and is adverse towards competitive elements. Both perspectives have in common that gamification in teamwork needs to be carefully put together. A badly constructed gamified task will not capture the interest of either perspective. It is also clear that gamification, when being made mandatory, loses its appeal for most employees.

This explorative study is subject to at least two limitations. First, the sample is relatively small and consists predominantly of employees in the public sector. Future studies may involve more respondents and may focus on variations among different sectors and work environments. Second, in the Q set, we could not include the full range of design elements, as this would make the Q set too large. For more insights into the attitudes among team members regarding different gamification designs, more research is needed. Especially the experiences regarding narrative designs may be worthwhile exploring in more detail, since these seem to be able to add considerable value to team members' appreciation of gamification.

The results of this study confirm the notion that gamification of team tasks, by appealing designs, has the potential to enhance enjoyment, collaboration, creativity and productiveness in work teams [2–4, 6]. However, the results also confirm that a competitive dimension does not generally induce beneficial psychological effects for all team members [1]. Moreover, the results underline that gamification of team tasks may have adverse effects if design and implementation do not correspond with the unique demands of the task and work environment. To conclude, gamification does not constitute a simple and straightforward management solution. Nevertheless, gamification of team tasks has the potential to engage team members and boost interaction and performance – bringing the team in a state of flow [1, 2, 4].

References

1. Koivisto, J., Hamari, J.: The rise of motivational information systems: a review of gamification research. Int. J. Inf. Manag. **4**, 191–210 (2019)
2. Patricio, R., Carrizo Moreira, A., Zurlo, F.: Gamification in innovation teams. Int. J. Innov. Stud. **6**, 156–168 (2022)
3. Muñoz, M., Pérez Negrón, A.P., Mejia, J., Piedad Gasca-Hurtado, G., Gómez-Alvarez, M.C., Hernández, L.: Applying gamification elements to build teams for software development. IET Softw. **13**(2), 99–105 (2019)
4. Meske, Ch., Brockmann, T., Wilms, K., Stieglitz, S.: Social collaboration and gamification. In: Stieglitz, S. et al. (eds.) Gamification, Progress in IS, pp. 93–109. Springer International Publishing Switzerland (2017)
5. Muszynska, K.: Gamification of communication and documentation processes in project teams. Procedia Comput. Sci. **176**, 3645–3653 (2020)
6. Vegt, N., Visch, V., Vermeeren, A., de Ridder, H., Hayde, Z.: Balancing game rules for improving creative output of group brainstorms. Int. J. Des. **13**(1), 1–19 (2019)
7. Diefenbach, S., Müssig, A.: Counterproductive effects of gamification: an analysis on the example of the gamified task manager Habitica. Int. J. Hum.-Comput. Stud. **127**, 190–210 (2019)
8. Fodor, S., Barna, B.: An empirical study on factors affecting user engagement in a gamified team building environment. Int. J. Serious Games **7**(3), 81–95 (2020)
9. Van Exel, N.J.A., de Graaf, G.: Q methodology: a sneak preview(2005). https://qmethod.org/portfolio/van-exel-and-de-graaf-a-q-methodology-sneak-preview/
10. Watts, S., Stenner, P.: Doing Q methodological Research: Theory, Method and Interpretation. SAGE Publications Ltd., London (2012)
11. Webler, T., Danielson, S., Tuler, S.: Using Q Method to Reveal Social Perspectives in Environmental Research. Social and Environmental Research Institute, Greenfield (2009)
12. Brown, S.R.: Political Subjectivity: Applications of Q Methodology in Political Science. Yale University Press, New Haven (1980)
13. Bittner, J.V., Shipper, J.: Motivational effects and age differences of gamification in product advertising. J. Cons. Mark. **31**(5), 391–400 (2014)

Posters

Flow in a Game-Based Learning Platform Design for K-12

Lionel Alvarez[1,2] , Aous Karoui[1,3(✉)] , Quentin Brumeaud[1],
and Thierry Geoffre[1]

[1] University for Teacher Education, 1700 Fribourg, Switzerland
lionel.alvarez@unifr.ch, {aous.karoui,quentin.brumeaud,
thierry.geoffre}@edufr.ch
[2] University of Fribourg, 1700 Fribourg, Switzerland
[3] University of Grenoble Alpes, 38400 Grenoble, France

Abstract. Designing a learning platform for K-12 students implies didactic foundations translated into an IT solution. GamesHUB is an example where an interdisciplinary team combined their theoretical backgrounds to think, design, and create with a clear view to learning. After several assessments of teachers' perceptions that helped to design GamesHUB in an iterative and agile process, this paper finally presents the first documented tests of the learning platform in four K-12 classrooms (N = 76). An adapted *E-gameFlow*—simplified for 8- to 10-year-old students—was used to evaluate the learning experience and satisfaction. Results indicate that self-reported concentration, perceived challenge, autonomy, and immersion were considered high. The reported experience through drawings and keywords adds to the hypothesis that GamesHUB is generating flow. However, these results need to be expended to confirm the impact and help the next steps of development. It invites the designing team to keep a similar layout and a similar student experience in the future development and tests of GamesHUB.

Keywords: Game-based learning · e-learning · Flow assessment

1 The Learning Platform Foundations

Founded in 2020, project GamesHUB aims to design and develop a Web learning platform for K-12 learners with or without learning disabilities that is, as much as possible, evidence-based and targeting a Universal Design for Learning (UDL) [1] ambition. Computer science, speech therapy, and second language acquisition skills joined the research unit within the PEAPL project, thanks to a European Erasmus + fund[1].

1.1 The Didactic Foundations

GamesHUB provides access to different games and game levels, all being linked to educational goals. In a basic experience, the student can browse through games and

---

[1] Erasmus + KA201-302DDA9 (2020–2023, 449'923€). https://peapl.eu/

different levels of difficulty, organized by tags, school topics and school grades. The teacher may either give the tablet to the student for free play to learn or assign lists of game levels.

However, short tests with teacher students in 2020 indicated the necessity of allowing a more articulated progression of the learning experience, close to a didactic sequence frame as could be proposed in an ordinary classroom. Therefore, learning pathways can now be developed by the teacher using games and game levels as resources that are chosen and organized to target a specific learning objective. Selecting different levels is made possible using a series of filters (element of the competency framework [2] that is targeted, difficulty, tags) and a visualization of the pathway created is shown as a chain of "bricks", each brick being a game level. A pathway may also integrate links to online resources or instruction to go on with an unplugged activity (for instance, work in a group, use of a paper resource, or check with the teacher).

For a created learning path, remediations can be anticipated and added to the path as an optional brick only sent to the learner according to the score obtained to one or several previous steps (in evaluation mode). This allows to add bricks to help to recover understanding or target a weak prerequisite according to the competency framework. Once the pathway is fully created, it can be addressed to one or several students.

1.2 The Design of the Platform

To ensure that every learner, whatever his/her learning difficulties, can benefit from being engaged on GamesHUB learning paths or games—if s/he can interact with a tablet or computer—, the platform was initiated with UDL in mind [1]. Accordingly, two guidelines were chosen from the very beginning to respect this ambition in the development: reduction of barriers, and diversity (of learning experiences, of mediations, and of ways of expressing the skills). The first can be found on GamesHUB with the digital assistive tools that are additional features made accessible to every learning situation [3], like contrast or font adaptations, as well as text-to-speech, writing pads or visual dictionary. In addition to that, the implementation of an adaptive learning system that recommends games or game levels is also on its way [4], so the barriers like the absence of prerequisites will also be taken care of. The latter—diversity—exists in a variety of ways in GamesHUB:

- Every game is developed in four taxonomy levels [5];
- The experience can be self-guided play or personalized learning pathways [6].
- Every game exists in several difficulty levels.
- A variety of cultural backgrounds are explicitly chosen.
- Alternating between online learning and unplugged activities is promoted and made possible with simple steps within the learning pathways.
- Embedding external resources allows a wider diversity of mediations.

2 Testing the Flow and the Learning Experience

The assessment of flow in education when using a digital interface is relatively common [7]. The flow is usually defined as an optimal learning experience or a "psychological mental state of a person who is immersed in an activity with energized concentration, optimal enjoyment, full involvement, and intrinsic interests, and who is usually focused, motivated, positive, energized, and aligned with the task at hand" [8].

2.1 The Adapted Questionnaire: *EgameFlow* for Children

EgameFlow consists in eight criteria measured by a Likert scale. However, in our context, we assumed that it would be hard for children to provide pertinent answers for every question (42 in total). Therefore, we created an adapted version of *EgameFlow*[2]. This one includes the four following *EgameFlow* dimensionsconcentration, challenge, autonomy, and immersion. As the learning pathways are individual, the social interaction criteria were intentionally dropped. Other criteria such as knowledge improvement perceived, and feedback were dropped because we cannot be sure about the relevance of the answers to be given by the children. The seven Likert scale was reduced to five, and the numbers were replaced by smileys. Some of the assertions were restated to make it more understandable for children. For example, the assertion "I become unaware of my surroundings while playing the game" was restated to "I forgot the teacher and my friends when I was doing the exercises". At the end, the children were asked to provide their global feeling about using the platform, with a drawing and keywords.

2.2 The Learning Experience Designed

Two learning pathways have been created in GamesHUB to allow these first test sessions, according to the two different classroom curriculums implied. We used progressive articulations of the most advanced games levels currently available on the platform:

- *Par ici ou par-là* (PCPL) which implies a text and a map, giving instructions to the reader to move around the map (specific objectives: reading and understanding of verbs of motion and prepositions/adverbs of location);
- *Orthodyssée des Gram* (Gram) which implies to use syntactic clues to build grammatical sentences.

As *Par ici ou par-là* is an in-built game of GamesHUB, we wanted to assess how children would deal with the game, but also with the regular framework [9] of the platform. On the opposite, *Orthodyssée des Gram* is a game that has been developed previously, independently, then integrated to the platform, so we wanted to check how the students would cope with a pathway alternating those two games with different layouts and design. Remediations (*cf.* Sect. 1.1) were added to check if they were correctly sent when required.

2.3 The Classrooms and the Data Collection

Schools where GamesHUB was implemented were in Romandie, the French-speaking region of Switzerland. Typically, classrooms are composed of around 20 pupils, and the teacher's practice is driven by a curriculum called Plan d'Etudes Romand[3]. IT equipment

---

[2] https://blog.hepfr.ch/create/gameshub/k12-EgameFlow/
[3] www.plandetudes.ch

is very diversified and unequal from one school to another, because computers or tablets are paid by the city/village, not by the state. Four classrooms of 8- to 10-year-old students (N = 17 in one 4th grade, N = 22 in one 5th grade, and N = 37 in two 6th grades) with enough tablets for each pupil (N = 76, 37 girls and 39 boys) were available for GamesHUB implementation and testing.

First, a short presentation was given about why the researcher is present. After that, students could ask questions about GamesHUB and the included features. Then, they used it on tablets. Students had one specific learning path adapted to their curriculum, before they had to fill out the adapted *EgameFlow* scale, printed on paper. To ensure that students understood the questions, which could be challenging, especially for 4th grade pupils, we first explained the questions to them during a short plenum session. Support was then available for children who had some issues with French, like the allophone students.

3   The Flow Reported

3.1   Results

This section presents the data in Tables 1 and 2. The descriptive statistics were made with JASP 0.16.3[4], as well as the correlation between each *EgameFlow* dimension.

Table 1. Descriptive statistics about flow documented with *EgameFlow*.

Variables	N	Mean	Std. deviation	Min.	Max.
A. Concentration	76	4.40	0.68	2	5
B. Challenge	76	4.33	0.62	1.5	5
C. Autonomy	76	4.47	0.79	2	5
D. Immersion	76	4.08	0.84	1	5

Table 2. Pearson's correlations between each *EgameFlow* dimension.

Variable		A-Concentra.	B-Challenge	C- Autonomy
B-Challenge	r (p-value)	0.546*** (< .001)	–	–
C-Autonomy	r (p-value)	0.230* (0.023)	0.508*** (< .001)	–
D-Immersion	r (p-value)	0.373*** (< .001)	0.551*** (< .001)	0.374*** (< .001)

Note. All tests one-tailed, for positive correlation, with heatmap. * $p < .05$, ** $p < .01$, *** $p < .001$.

---

[4] https://jasp-stats.org/download/

3.2 Discussions

The four dimensions assessed by our adapted *EgameFlow* scale are high, as shown on Table 1, with an average of 4.4 (SD = 0.68) for the reported concentration, of 4.33 (SD = 0.62) for the reported challenge, of 4.47 (SD = 0.79) for the reported autonomy, and of 4.08 (SD = 0.84) for the reported immersion. This might indicate a relatively intensive flow experienced by the 8- to 10-year-old students while working on GamesHUB. This can be due to several factors. Indeed, playing on iPads and experiencing a new learning environment make it more difficult to separate the motivational factors related to the material and the setting from the motivation related to the platform and the learning games themselves. However, we feel that the current design of the GamesHUB platform as well as the design of the *Gram* and *PCPL* games have contributed to this overall feeling of satisfaction.

On the other hand, these results might also indicate social desirability bias [10], with pupils indicating what could want the researcher present to collect data. The correlation between each dimension is also high, systematically significant (p < 0.5 for correlation between concentration and autonomy, p < .001 for every other correlation) as shown on Table 2. This might also indicate the *EgameFlow* dimensions are generally correlated, as stated by Fu et al. [11].

However, the social desirability bias hypothesis is rather to be discarded because we asked the students to deliberately conclude their answers to the questionnaire with their overall feeling, following this experience. They were asked to submit in their learning experience drawing what they remembered about the games they liked best and writing down short words that reflected their state of mind at the time.

The drawings that the 8- to 10-year-old students made after playing and learning with GamesHUB sometimes represent the pleasure of using a tablet, but usually show that they appreciated the games *PCPL* and *Gram* embedded in the learning paths. The fact that learning is game based seemed like a motivating factor.

The keywords show that students experienced learning and fun thanks to the tablet and the designed games (PCPL and Gram). Some indicated the interest of being able to redo simple tasks within a progression.

The teachers present at the experiments also stated that the students were more motivated because they were certainly attracted by this way of learning.

4 Conclusion

GamesHUB is a game-based learning Web platform designed with UDL in mind. An interdisciplinary team is designing and developing it. Implementations and tests in real setting (4 classrooms, 76 students) were conducted to assess ecological validity thanks to our adapted version of the *EgameFlow* scale for children use. The results report a very positive flow experienced by the pupils, in each of the four dimensions.

We welcome these first results with caution due to the possible social desirability bias. However, direct returns while observing the students' activity, and reported experience through drawings and keywords, were also good and motivating to go on with an iterative process of development and tests.

More investigations are needed to clearly document the student learning experience, the teacher experience, and if the ambition—UDL perspective—is explicitly implemented. A new test session is planned by the autumn 2022 with teachers' interviews, before a larger and more ambitious implementation, including adaptive learning, planned during the beginning of year 2023 in project PEAPL agenda.

References

1. Meyer, A., Rose, D.H., Gordon, D.: Universal Design for Learning: Theory and practice. CAST incorporated, Wakefield (2014)
2. Karoui, A., et al.: Adaptive pathways within the european platform for personalized language learning PEAPL. In: Adjunct Proceedings of the 29th ACM Conference on User Modeling, Adaptation and Personalization, pp. 90–94. ACM, Utrecht (2021). https://doi.org/10.1145/3450614.3464480
3. Alvarez, L., Karoui, A., Geoffre, T., Rodi, M., Dherbey-Chapuis, N.: Promoting universal design for learning through digital assistive tools in GamesHUB. In: Hilliger, I., Muñoz-Merino, P.J., De Laet, T., Ortega-Arranz, A., Farrell, T. (eds.) Educating for a New Future: Making Sense of Technology-Enhanced Learning Adoption: 17th European Conference on Technology Enhanced Learning, EC-TEL 2022, Toulouse, France, September 12–16, 2022, Proceedings, pp. 421–426. Springer International Publishing, Cham (2022). https://doi.org/10.1007/978-3-031-16290-9_31
4. Karoui, A., et al.: Towards an automated adaptive learning web platform through personalization of language learning pathways. In: EC-TEL (2022)
5. Anderson, L.W., Krathwohl, D.R.: A Taxonomy for Learning, Teaching, and Assessing : A Revision of Bloom's Taxonomy of Educational Objectives. Longman, London (2001)
6. Karoui, A., et al.: Adaptive pathways within the european platform for personalized language learning PEAPL. In: UMAP 2021 - Adjunct Publication of the 29th ACM Conference on User Modeling, Adaptation and Personalization, pp. 90–94 (2021). https://doi.org/10.1145/3450614.3464480
7. Alvarez, L., Carrupt, R., Audrin, C., Gay, P.: Self-reported flow in online learning environments for teacher education: a quasi-experimental study using a counterbalanced design. Educ. Sci. **12**, 351 (2022). https://doi.org/10.3390/educsci12050351
8. Bonaiuto, M., et al.: Optimal experience and personal growth: flow and the consolidation of place identity. Front. Psychol. **7**, 1–12 (2016). https://doi.org/10.3389/fpsyg.2016.01654
9. Karoui, A., Alvarez, L., Ramalho, M., Geoffre, T.: Parcours adaptatifs au sein de la Plateforme Européenne d'Apprentissage Personnalisé des Langues PEAPL (2021). https://doi.org/10.5281/ZENODO.4673080

10. Krumpal, I.: Determinants of social desirability bias in sensitive surveys: a literature review. Qual. Quant. **47**, 2025–2047 (2013). https://doi.org/10.1007/s11135-011-9640-9
11. Fu, F.L., Su, R.C., Yu, S.C.: EGameFlow: a scale to measure learners' enjoyment of e-learning games. Comput. Educ. **52**, 101–112 (2009). https://doi.org/10.1016/j.compedu.2008.07.004

Gamification for Spatial Digital Learning Environments in Higher Education: A Rapid Literature Review

Sanghamitra Das[1], Margarita Osipova[1], Sri Vaishnavi Nakshatram[1], Heinrich Söbke[1]([✉]), Jannicke Baalsrud Hauge[2,3], and Christian Springer[4]

[1] Bauhaus-Universität Weimar, Goetheplatz 7/8, 99423 Weimar, Germany
{sanghamitra.das,margarita.osipova,srivaishnavi.nakshatram,
heinrich.sobke}@uni-weimar.de
[2] BIBA GmbH, Hochschulring 20, 28359 Bremen, Germany
baa@biba.uni-bremen.de
[3] Royal Institute of Technology, Kvarnbergagatan 12, Södertälje, Sweden
jmbh@kth.se
[4] FH Erfurt, Altonaer Street 25, 99085 Erfurt, Germany
christian.springer@fh-erfurt.de

Abstract. Digital learning environments exhibit spatial dimensions, such as virtual labs, virtual worlds, or 360° models. This usage increased during the pandemic, and heterogeneous motivation was found in the target audiences. Gamification is seen as enhancing the motivation of heterogeneous audiences to more homogeneous levels. Consequently, the question arises, which options are available for the gamification of spatial digital learning environments? This article presents the results of a rapid literature review addressing what is known regarding a) which mechanisms of gamification support engagement and motivation, b) which mechanisms of gamification support spatial learning, and c) why and when gamification should be used. The three databases ACM, IEEE and Scopus were examined, and 25 relevant articles were found. Qualitative results regarding the application domains, the type of digital environment, the gamification mechanisms, and the influence of gamification are compiled. Overall, the results reveal that gamification elements applied in spatial digital learning environments have so far been little adapted to spatiality.

Keywords: 360-degree · Virtual lab · Spatiality · Education · Virtual field trips · Virtual reality

1 Introduction

As technology advances, new digital learning environments are emerging. Digital learning environments with spatial dimensions have been increasingly implemented in classes.

Supplementary Information The online version contains supplementary material available at https://doi.org/10.1007/978-3-031-22124-8_29.

Several benefit from technologies capable of representing spatial dimensions, such as virtual reality (V.R.). Examples include virtual labs [1, 2], virtual worlds [3], or 360°VR models that support, for example, virtual field trips [4]. Evaluation indicates that such spatial digital learning environments (SDLE) support learning processes effectively, e.g., by enabling explorative learning in authentic environments [4]. However, it has also been mentioned that not all learners are equally addressed; some, for example, feel overwhelmed by free exploration, while others consider free exploration an essential stand-alone feature of SDLEs. Thus, this diverging motivation among the users induces heterogeneous engagement levels. This is challenging since motivation and engagement are prerequisites for learning outcomes [5] and must be considered in the design of SDLEs [6]. An established method for increasing motivation in traditional digital learning environments, such as learning management systems, is using gamification [7–9], i.e., using game elements to enhance learning activities [10]. Beyond the already established gamification mechanisms in digital learning environments, our research concerns gamification mechanics specifically addressing the spatial component, like getting rewarded for being in a physical or virtual place. Related to spatiality is embodied cognition, which summarizes learning processes accompanied by movement of the body or moving the body in space [11]. Embodied cognition is an inspiring cue that spatiality might be meaningful for gamification mechanisms. For example, game mechanics from location-based games, such as check-in at locations [12], might be transferred into SDLEs, benefiting from spatiality. Therefore, we conducted a literature review identifying already known gamification mechanisms for SDLEs related to a) gamification mechanisms that support engagement and motivation, b) gamification mechanisms that support spatial learning, and c) overall guidance on using gamification in SDLEs. Specific gamification mechanisms for SDLEs are currently only conjectured. Consequently, the study is designed as a *rapid review* [13], i.e. we look for clues and qualitatively analyze potential articles to target a more comprehensive review later.

2 Method

The study followed the basic structure of PRISMA [14]. Databases used were IEEE, Scopus, and ACM. We aimed to include all articles containing gamification in connection with an SDLE used for learning purposes and revealing motivation and engagement (Digital Appendix A describes the search term). In Step 4, we observed that some articles present gamification approaches, and SDLEs targeted a younger audience than our target group, so we excluded articles unrelated to higher education. Finally, we identified 25 articles that met the inclusion criteria (Digital Appendix B). Of note, we could not obtain access with reasonable effort to 10 articles in the IEEE database, and due to the nature of the *rapid review* [13], we excluded these articles. The information from the articles is qualitatively extracted. The complete list of articles is in Digital Appendix C. These are referenced using the prefix "R". We consider a learning environment spatial if the learner can take different positions in this learning environment and can experience the environment immersive, e.g., operating it via V.R. glasses. Thus, we excluded all articles referencing desktop spatial environments.

3 Results

Based on the reviewed articles, we specified the list of topics discussed that concern gamification in spatial learning environments: The topics *Application Domains, Types of SPLEs, Gamification Mechanisms* and *Learning Outcomes* are presented in this section. We have chosen the first two topics for characterizing the environments and their application domains. In comparison, the last two topics are intended to answer the research questions a) to c) posed above.

Application Domains in Education. Spatial environments give the ability to interact with the surroundings in three dimensions. Most of the articles were related to the application domains that initially had a spatial component, such as body anatomy and chemical molecules, or interaction with real-world 3D objects [R5, R8, R10]. Further, we identified environments that do not represent any physical object in the real world yet represent essential concepts in education. A V.R. environment for teaching affinity transformation in mathematics is an example where the object has abstract nature [R15]. Another application domain is collaborative V.R. spaces, such as [R19], in which formal and informal learning scenarios are organized. Visualizations are often an important topic for these domains because one of the primary benefits of spatiality is the capability to visualize objects in detail [R10, R20]. Accordingly, urban studies and architecture were application domains, for example [R20], modelling urban areas of a major city [R20].

Furthermore, multi-sensory interaction was also deployed in other environments, like spatial V.R. environments, allowing the integration of haptic technology. It provides physical feedback for activities such as grabbing or training complex procedures, such as cardiopulmonary resuscitation [R1, R7]. A general observation of SDLEs described in the articles was that the activities supported could be split into learning, training, and assessment activities. For learning activities, the reason for using spatial environments was to introduce learners to 3D representations of learning objects. Training activities allowed the exploration of procedures related to represented real-world objects but augmented with additional information, such as prompts and explanatory texts. Noticeably, the environments for training abstract concepts like mathematics were based on desktop V.R. In contrast, tasks practising technical tools demanded spatially representation of the tool, allowing the learners to explore immersively. For assessment tasks, motivations for using SDLEs were "immersion and motivation", but spatial environments were frequently used for doing classical quizzes, just with the questions and answers placed in the space [R22]. However, assessment activities were sometimes implemented as a part of SDLEs, originally aiming at training activities for evaluating training results [16] [R1, R10].

Types of SDLEs. Most articles presented SDLEs based on V.R. technologies. However, further articles discussing learning motivation, spatiality, and gamification mentioned immersion based on augmented reality (A.R.). Although AR has limited applicability to online learning, we included these articles in the literature review because the gamification mechanisms used might be transferable to SDLEs [R6, R24].

Gamification Mechanisms. Mainly, basic gamification mechanics were employed, such as points, badges, and leaderboards. For example, [R13] used level and leaderboards, whereas [R4] employed leaderboards and achievements in a serious V.R. game teaching assessment of medical images. In further studies, gamification was reported to raise previously relatively low levels of student engagement. Another example of a serious V.R. game used exploration in a building as a game mechanic [R12]. The focus is less on describing individual mechanics than on a game experience. One of the few examples of a spatially oriented gamification mechanism is an anatomic 3D puzzle [R17].

Learning Outcomes. Most articles agreed on the positive impacts of gamification on motivation and engagement and thus indirectly on learning outcomes. Especially learning scenarios regarding abstract concepts, such as molecular genomics and cyber security, seems to benefit from the immersive nature of SPLEs. For example, the *Cell Explorer*, an interactive V.R. journey into the nucleus of a human cell, received in an early prototype "extremely positive feedback" [R16]. Nevertheless, another case study of a V.R.'s experience on cybersecurity-related issues *has two limitations*: First, the evaluation is not related to isolated mechanisms, and second, an entire serious game was evaluated. For the case study of a 3D anatomic puzzle, rather than assessing the learning effectiveness, the usefulness of different operating metaphors was evaluated [R17]. Also, not the learning effectiveness but the motivation was investigated in the case study of modelling a large city [R9]. Here, an increase in motivation was demonstrated as soon as the learners understood the underlying concepts. Positive effects on motivation are demonstrated in various studies on social V.R. platforms. Further, [R19] reported a positive assessment of a new social V.R. learning environment.

4   Discussion and Conclusion

The study provided an initial understanding of gamification in spatial environments and presented a relatively young research area that deserves further exploration. However, for potentially extending the study, several limitations need to be resolved. For example, we used the terms *spatial environment*, *360-degree*, *virtual reality* and *virtual lab* to find articles about spatial environments. These terms are not comprehensive and need to be supplemented. A similar non-completeness applies to the term *gamification*. The choice of databases may need to be reconsidered since *Scopus* claims to cover a large portion of the articles in *IEEE* and *ACM*. This claim contradicts the number of articles found and still needs to be clarified.

Nevertheless, the review is still applicable, given more articles found in ACM. Further, we excluded articles that examined desktop V.R. environments. Nevertheless, desktop V.R. environments can be included in a comprehensive review by assuming that desktop V.R. environments could be ported to immersive V.R. environments and vice versa. The gamification mechanisms in desktop V.R. can inform immersive V.R. The differences between games and gamification would require a proper definition to trace the exclusion and inclusion criteria. In the articles presented here, the article authors interpret the terms differently at times.

Furthermore, the efficacy of gamification is subject to uncertainties since findings on gamification are inconsistent. There is a gap between theory and practice regarding the effect of gamification on motivation and engagement [18]. Adverse effects are reported [19], for example, for essential gamification elements such as points, badges, and leaderboards [20]. However, integrating gamification mechanics meaningfully into learning processes may be powerful [21]. Further exciting study results are the non-findings, pointing to potential research activities. For example, we did not find any articles that examined spatial audio and haptics–phenomena related to spatiality–regarding effects on motivation and engagement.

Spatial digital learning environments (SDLEs) typically encounter heterogeneous audiences of varying motivations and different engagement levels. Gamification is generally seen to compensate for motivation deficits. Accordingly, in this rapid literature review, we searched gamification approaches for SDLEs. Among the results of the 25 articles identified, we found that gamified SDLEs support technical application domains that involve real-world objects, such as medicine, and abstract application domains, such as mathematics (R.Q. c). Mainly V.R. technology is used to develop the SDLEs.

Furthermore, besides common points, badges, and leaderboard gamification (R.Q. a), only a few gamification mechanisms specific to SDLEs could be found, such as an anatomic 3D puzzle (R.Q. b). Regarding learning outcomes, it became apparent that the evaluation status mainly relates to prototypes, or learning-related constructs, such as motivation. Accordingly, it is concluded that specific spatial gamification mechanisms have not been developed, and their effectiveness in motivation and engagement is still to be validated.

Acknowledgement. This work has been partly funded by the German Federal Ministry of Education and Research (BMBF) through the projects DigiLab4U (No. 16DHB2113) and AuCity2 (No. 16DHB2131) and EU projects Unilog (CB743), Includeme (No. 621547-EPP-1–2020-1-RO-EPPA3-IPI-SOC-IN),

References

1. Bogusevschi, D., Muntean, C.H., Muntean, G.-M.: Teaching and learning physics using 3D virtual learning environment: a case study of combined virtual reality and virtual laboratory in secondary school. J. Comput. Math. Sci. Teach. **39**, 5–18 (2020)

2. Pfeiffer, A., Uckelmann, D.: Open digital lab for you-laboratory-based learning scenarios in education, research and qualification. In: Proceedings 2019 5th Experiment International Conference Experiment at 2019, pp. 36–41 (2019). https://doi.org/10.1109/EXPAT.2019.8876560

3. Tilhou, R., Taylor, V., Crompton, H.: 3D virtual reality in K-12 education: a thematic systematic review. In: Yu, S., Ally, M., Tsinakos, A. (eds.) Emerging Technologies and Pedagogies in the Curriculum. BHMFEI, pp. 169–184. Springer, Singapore (2020). https://doi.org/10.1007/978-981-15-0618-5_10

4. Wolf, M., Wehking, F., Montag, M., Söbke, H.: 360°-based virtual field trips to waterworks in higher education. Computers **10** (2021). https://doi.org/10.3390/computers10090118

5. Blumenfeld, P.C., Kempler, T.M., Krajcik, J.S.: Motivation and cognitive engagement in learning environments. In: Sawyer, R.K. (ed.) The Cambridge handbook of the learning sciences, pp. 475–488. Cambridge University Press, Cambridge, NY (2006)
6. Peters, D., Calvo, R.A., Ryan, R.M.: Designing for motivation, engagement and wellbeing in digital experience. Front. Psychol. **9**, 797 (2018). https://doi.org/10.3389/fpsyg.2018.00797
7. Dicheva, D., Irwin, K., Dichev, C.: OneUp : supporting practical and experimental gamification of learning. Int. J. Serious Games. **5**, 5–21 (2018). https://doi.org/10.17083/ijsg.v5i3.236
8. Chen, C.C.B., et al.: Gamify online courses with tools built into your learning management system (Lms) to enhance self-determined and active learning. Online Learn. J. **22**, 41–54 (2018). https://doi.org/10.24059/olj.v22i3.1466
9. de Sousa, B., et al.: A systematic mapping on gamification applied to education. In: Proceedings 29th Annual ACM Symposium Application Computer - SAC 2014, pp. 216–222 (2014). https://doi.org/10.1145/2554850.2554956
10. Deterding, S., Dixon, D., Khaled, R., Nacke, L.: From game design elements to gamefulness: defining gamification. In: Proceedings of the 15th International Academic MindTrek Conference, pp. 9–15. ACM, New York (2011)
11. Skulmowski, A., Rey, G.D.: Embodied learning: introducing a taxonomy based on bodily engagement and task integration. Cogn. Res. Principles Implicat. **3**(1), 1 (2018). https://doi.org/10.1186/s41235-018-0092-9
12. Laato, S., Inaba, N., Hamari, J.: Convergence between the real and the augmented: experiences and perceptions in location-based games. Telemat. Informatics. **65**, 101716 (2021). https://doi.org/10.1016/j.tele.2021.101716
13. Tricco, A.C., et al.: A scoping review of rapid review methods. BMC Med. **13** (2015). https://doi.org/10.1186/s12916-015-0465-6
14. Moher, D., Liberati, A., Tetzlaff, J., Altman, D.G.: Preferred reporting items for systematic reviews and meta-analyses: the PRISMA statement. Int. J. Surg. **8**, 336–341 (2010). https://doi.org/10.1016/j.ijsu.2010.02.007
15. Tiefenbacher, F.: Evaluation of gamification elements in a vr application for higher education. In: Yilmaz, M., Niemann, J., Clarke, P., Messnarz, R. (eds.) EuroSPI 2020. CCIS, vol. 1251, pp. 830–847. Springer, Cham (2020). https://doi.org/10.1007/978-3-030-56441-4_63
16. Araiza-Alba, P., et al.: The potential of 360-degree virtual reality videos to teach water-safety skills to children. Comput. Educ. **163**, 104096 (2021). https://doi.org/10.1016/j.compedu.2020.104096
17. Tsai, W. Te, Chen, C.H.: The use of augmented reality to represent gamification theory in user story training. In: ACM International Conference Proceeding Series, pp. 265–268. ACM (2019). https://doi.org/10.1145/3345120.3345131
18. Alsawaier, R.S.: The effect of gamification on motivation and engagement. Int. J. Inf. Learn. Technol. **35**, 56–79 (2018). https://doi.org/10.1108/IJILT-02-2017-0009
19. Hernandez, A.: How Safe Are You Playing Ingress?. http://techaeris.com/2015/06/24/editorial-how-safe-are-you-playing-ingress/
20. Toda, A.M., Valle, P.H.D., Isotani, S.: The dark side of gamification: an overview of negative effects of gamification in education. In: Cristea, A.I., Bittencourt, I.I., Lima, F. (eds.) HEFA 2017. CCIS, vol. 832, pp. 143–156. Springer, Cham (2018). https://doi.org/10.1007/978-3-319-97934-2_9
21. Söbke, H.: A case study of deep gamification in higher engineering education. In: Gentile, M., Allegra, M., Söbke, H. (eds.) GALA 2018. LNCS, vol. 11385, pp. 375–386. Springer, Cham (2019). https://doi.org/10.1007/978-3-030-11548-7_35

MMORPGs as Serious Games: Learning and Developing Social Skills Through MMORPGs

Matteo Curcio[(✉)]

Defence Research and Analysis Institute, Center for Higher Defence Studies, 00165 Roma, Italy
curcio.dottorando@casd.difesa.it

Abstract. Massively multiplayer online role-playing games (MMORPGs) are complex environments created for entertainment where the goals are set to be achieved by many players and/or groups. Therefore, playing MMORPGs requires the users to possess different social skills, build communities, and coordinate to face the challenges ahead. Recent literature suggests that these video games further help the learning process of a second language and can be used as a tool to develop practical skills. This article argues that given the complex structure of MMORPGs, users who play these video games develop new social skills, improve their previous and learn new ones applicable in real life. To understand if MMORPGs enhance social skills and produce real-life benefits like serious games, the research has been conducted with a netnography approach in (N = 1) MMORPGs and (N = 400) users involved in (PVE) and (PVP) activities. The findings illustrate that most users, from the early playtime stage of the game to the late one, have improved their social skills and, in some cases, learned new ones.

Keywords: MMORPG · Social Skills · Serious games · Netnography · Mixed-Methods · Video Games

1 Introduction

MMORPGs[1] are complex virtual worlds that differ from other video games type because they require online cooperation between users to achieve the best results. In other words, the players must gather and collaborate to defeat the challenges the video games pose[2], and they cannot do that alone. Therefore, in these games, it is common to form guilds, groups, friends, and teams to participate in the game contents. These steps require user

---

[1] An example of common MMORPGs: Word of Warcraft, Guild Wars 2, Black Desert.

[2] Players must participate in a series of activities with their character previously created, such as Raids, which is a coordinated attack against a boss, farming experience and items to increase the character's power, fight against other players (PVP) and participate in events.

Supplementary Information The online version contains supplementary material available at https://doi.org/10.1007/978-3-031-22124-8_30.

K. Kiili et al. (Eds.): GALA 2022, LNCS 13647, pp. 304–309, 2022.
https://doi.org/10.1007/978-3-031-22124-8_30

interactions, time, and a communicative approach to build relationships and trust. Recent research has examined the complexity of these MMORPGs, and some studies illustrated that these video games could improve skills and offer social advantages. For example, in the linguistic domain, language skills can be enhanced by real-time online interaction with peers and game narratives or instructions embedded in the MMORPGs [1], or it is possible to learn new languages [2, 3]. In addition, different academics have also argued that they could be used as a tool for motivation [4, 5], a way to improve cognitive capabilities [6], learning social skills [7, 8], and improving performance at a young age [9]. Although other studies on this matter exist in addition to the ones previously cited, this research differs in methodology because it outlines a possible new approach to studying social skills in this environment, as well as identifying which social skills have been learned - developed and how the MMORPG has contributed to their improvement.

2   Methodology

The research has been conducted with a mixed method approach divided into two steps: Netnography was applied to gather all the relevant data, and consequently, a survey was administered to the users to consolidate the findings. As netnography requires direct observations and respect for the ethical codes, all the participants were made aware of the research, gave their informed consent, and agreed to participate in an anonymous form. The research was carried out for three years inside the MMORPG - Guild Wars 2 and involved the participation of 400 users. The reason for selecting that video game is because the researcher had spent more than 3500 h of gameplay inside it and could access a more extensive pool of users. The research envisaged an active involvement of the researcher in the daily activities of the community to observe dialogues, user behaviors, and interactions. The time spent inside the video game within the community was equally distributed in activities involving PVE[3] and PVP[4] environments. This distinction has been made because not every player plays PVP, the interactions that occur are different, and PVP activities are fundamentally distinct from PVE.

2.1   Data Collection and Assessment

As the participants were involved in the MMORPG daily activities, the researcher actively participated with the community to gather information. To observe and correctly assess the social skills of the users, the following steps have been taken:

- The observation has been carried out in all environments and daily activities of the game by participating with the community.
- Public chats messages and conversations inside Guilds and discord servers have been collected manually
- To determine each user's starting level of social skills, a score was assigned after one month of observations, following Table 1 criteria. The scores range from 0, meaning that the users do not possess any social skills listed, to 1, representing very poor, and 5 representing very good.

---

[3] Player Versus Environment - Players compete/fight against the game's artificial intelligence.
[4] Player Versus Player – Players compete/fight against other players.

- Observations and data collected were used to modify the score of each user to determine whether there had been any changes, according to Table 1. This step occurred every two weeks, and a summary for each user was made at the end of each year.
- To determine if a user has developed or learned that specific social skill, the ending score was the determining factor. (e.g., if a user had 0 points in collaboration in the first stage but reached a score of 3 at the end of the three years, it means that he has learned that skill because he did not possess it before. Consequently, if a user had 2 points in collaboration in the first stage but reached 5 at the end of the three years, it means he developed those skills). Therefore, social skills were considered learned only when the score went from 0 to 1+.
- The score was assigned based on the feedback gathered during the observations and data collected on the users.

Table 1. Social skills observed and standards for the observation

Collaboration: The user actively collaborates with other users to complete quests, dungeons, or in-game events and offer his help to newcomers
Leadership: The user can lead a guild/clan or a team of players under challenging situations and environments. Can form allies, mediate disputes, communicate effectively with all members, and make fast-paced decisions
Problem Solving: The user can solve complex quests and dynamics and make fast decisions to overcome game problems. Can identify and prioritize his character's needs and develop solutions and implement them
Personal Growth: The user has developed soft skills and learned skills through gaming that can implement in real life. This includes the mental, emotional, and physical domains
Decision Making: The user has made important decisions for his in-game character and others and has improved his cognitive skills by learning which objectives must first be achieved
Time Management: The user can organize and plan what to do first in his daily gaming adventure. Have been able to organize real-life commitments with game one and is always showing up in time for events
Teamwork: The user can accomplish challenging quests with a team of friends and can help their teammates
Being social: The user can interact, share his feelings with others, and socialize with users from different cultures. It does not have toxic behavior and actively answers in the game chat
Attitude: The user has improved his attitude towards something or someone after Playing MMORPGs
Communication: The user can communicate effectively with every user, has improved his way of exposing his feelings and problems, and has developed active listening
Cooperation: The user actively cooperates with all of the game's community. It does not only play or interact with his friends or guild mates but develops a relationship with others
Coordination: The user can listen to directives and coordinate with other gaming users effectively

To complete this research and confirm the validity of the collected data, an online survey of 19 questions has been administered to users to determine whether the MMORPG interaction process has contributed to the change in their social skills.

3 Findings

The findings obtained during the observation period are summarized as follows (Table 2):

Table 2. Percentage of users who learned and developed social skills

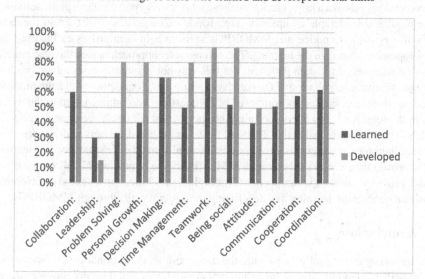

Table 3. Example of conversation collected in game and analyzed

Anonymous User says: Mmorpgs and games in general have certainly taught me some tricks that can be applied in real life. Example: binding your long cooldown skills to a button less accessible, and binding skills you use often to buttons that are easiest to press. You can apply this to real life: in the kitchen with pots, pans utensils, dishes, spices... To the garage or work for tools. Its a general system of organization where things you use often are conveniently placed close to the workspace and thing less often used are tucked away in a storage area as to not clutter your everyday workspace

Anonymous User says: For the first year, the game didn't really affect my life. But when I started Playing group content that required cooperation and voice channels (like raiding) I did gain more social skills, and upon getting leadership positions in guilds and leading raids myself, I can definitely say I gained confidence and leadership skills

As reported in Table 2[5], the material gathered and analyzed for the learning process suggests that most users learn coordination, cooperation, and teamwork, which are the basis of MMORPGs. Surprisingly decision-making was also a skill many users·have learned, along with collaboration. Moreover, leadership has only been observed in a few users, most of whom were guild leaders. In the development process, the observations and data gathered suggest that this is the real advantage of Playing MMORPGs. An improvement in social skills has been observed in almost all users, while data regarding leadership and attitude indicate similar outcoming to the learning process. In this case, learning is more complex than developing; leadership can only be learned if the users practice it (by becoming guilds leaders or in competitive teams), while it can be easily developed if a user is already a leader. Another interesting information obtained is that the users who have shown a higher score are those who actively participate in game activities that require considerable complexity (e.g., Raids - Competitive PVP). From the data, it is also possible to notice that MMORPGs seem to help both processes favoring the development rather than the learning. The netnography approach helped the observation and the analysis of the data gathered, but this was not enough to assess their validity. The qualitative interpretation of the data had to find some foundation with a quantitative method; therefore, the survey composed of 19 questions was administered to the users. From the total pool, 344 users compiled the survey, and the results were analyzed with SPSS. The analysis revealed that 27.3% of the users provided answers with a score of 3[6] or less; therefore, the users disagreed or were neutral about the idea that they had learned or improved their social skills through MMORPGs. The remaining 72.7%, on the other hand, provided answers with a score of 3 or higher, thus reflecting a neutral or favorable position concerning learning and developing their social skills through MMORPGs.

4 Conclusions

The serious game's goal is to provide the users with an educational experience, while MMORPGs intend to offer an entertainment environment that does not provide educational content. This dichotomy in the last decade has become consistently more subtle as different scientific literature is proving that these video games can be used as a tool for many purposes. The findings gathered and analyzed during these three years offer a broader view of alternative use of these video games and suggest that MMORPGs could assist the development and learning of social skills. Therefore, as the growing literature demonstrates the benefits of Playing these video games, MMORPGs could also be considered and valued as serious games. The findings of this study open up the possibility of future research and insights to better grasp the potential of these platforms.

References

1. Zhang, Y., Song, H., Liu, X., Tang, D., Chen, Y., Zhang, X.: Language learning enhanced by massive multiple online role-playing games (MMORPGs) and the underlying behavioral

---

[5] The results are reported with a 10% deviation, as some players stopped playing during the three years or there was insufficient data. Furthermore, the accuracy is + - 5%.

[6] The score of 3, representing "neutral," has been calculated as it is an uncertain answer that, in any case, expresses a value that can be further interpreted.

and neural mechanisms. Front. Hum. Neurosci. **11**, 95 (2017). https://doi.org/10.3389/fnhum.2017.00095

2. Kongmee, I., Strachan, R., Pickard, A., Montgomery, C.: A case study of using online communities and virtual environment in massively multiplayer role playing games (MMORPGs) as a learning and teaching tool for second language learners. Int. J. Virtual Pers. Learn. Environ. (IJVPLE) **3**(4), 1–15 (2012). https://doi.org/10.4018/jvple.2012100101

3. Peterson, M.: Massively multiplayer online role-playing games as arenas for second language learning. Comput. Assist. Lang. Learn. **23**(5), 429–439 (2010). https://doi.org/10.1080/09588221.2010.520673

4. Bawa, P., Watson, W., Watson, S.L.: To game or not to game? how using massively multiplayer online games helped motivation and performance in a college writing course: a mixed methods study. **3**(1), 26 (2017)

5. Voulgari, I., Komis, V., Sampson, D.G.: Player motivations in massively multiplayer online games. In: 2014 IEEE 14th International Conference on Advanced Learning Technologies, Athens, Greece, pp. 238–239 (2014) https://doi.org/10.1109/ICALT.2014.75

6. Campello de Souza, B., de Lima e Silva, L.X., Roazzi, A.: MMORPGS and cognitive performance: a study with 1280 Brazilian high school students. Comput. Human Behav. **26**(6), 1564–1573 (2010) https://doi.org/10.1016/j.chb.2010.06.001

7. Siang Ang, C., Zaphiris, P.: Social learning in MMOG: an activity theoretical perspective. Interact. Technol. Smart Educ. **5**(2), 84–102 (2008). https://doi.org/10.1108/17415650810880754

8. Ducheneaut, N., Moore, R.J.: More than just "XP": learning social skills in massively multiplayer online games. Interact. Technol. Smart Educ. **2**(2), 89–100 (2005). https://doi.org/10.1108/17415650580000035

9. Suh, S., Kim, S.W., Kim, N.J.: Effectiveness of MMORPG-based instruction in elementary English education in Korea: effectiveness of MMORPG-based instruction. J. Comput. Assist. Learn. **26**(5), 370–378 (2010). https://doi.org/10.1111/j.1365-2729.2010.00353.x

Constructing Gamified Learning Experiences

Ioana Andreea Stefan[(✉)], Ancuta Florentina Gheorghe, Jannicke Baalsrud Hauge, Antoniu Stefan, and Catalin Radu

Research and Innovation Department of Advanced Technology Systems, ATS Research, 137395 Razvad, Dâmbovița County, Romania
ioana.stefan@ats.com.ro

Abstract. Educational games are usually delivered as ready-to-use tools, with little to no customization features, and meeting specific needs of learners, as well as of learning contexts remains a key issue. The emergence of authoring tools in the last decade aimed to address this challenge, and to provide teachers means to improve the use of games in education. In spite of that, bridging games and education, especially inclusive education, is yet to reach momentum. In creating serious games, teachers are to follow the rigors of game design processes, and attempt to meet the learner expectations that are shaped by a decades-old, successful entertainment industry. In this context, the authors discuss the challenges associated with gamified and game-based authoring processes, and present the rationale behind the design of an authoring tool that aims to provide teachers with a richer inventory of assets and tools to facilitate the creation of engaging learning experiences in support of inclusive education.

Keywords: Game design · Inclusive education · Authoring tools

1 Introduction

Technology-enriched contexts [1–6] provide teachers new opportunities to create captivating learning experiences [7] able to build long-term motivation. Tools that enable teachers to add stimuli across the learning experiences can be more effective in provoking students to learn through exploration [8]. Research [9–13] has shown the capabilities of serious games to nurture learning in different contexts, and for various target groups, including disadvantaged learners, as well as learners with special needs [14] and disabilities [15]. However, in order to bring a significant and sustainable contribution to the construction of engaging learning experiences adapted to specific learner needs, while maintaining cost efficiency and promoting quality [16], teachers should be provided easy-to-use authoring tools that explore existing learning resources and applications, and do not require advanced programming skills. Moreover, related work shows it is necessary to consider that the development of gamified experiences from scratch remains challenging for teachers [17, 18]. Therefore, authoring processes should be scaffolded by providing customizable, pre-designed templates. Also, gamified learning experiences should not compromise the promise of fun game bring to learning settings. Adding too much content to a gamified experience might severely hinder the desired outcome [19],

© The Author(s), under exclusive license to Springer Nature Switzerland AG 2022
K. Kiili et al. (Eds.): GALA 2022, LNCS 13647, pp. 310–315, 2022.
https://doi.org/10.1007/978-3-031-22124-8_31

and learners might give up. The amount of learning and assessment content a gamified learning path should be mitigated carefully to balance the achievement of the desired learning outcomes and the provision of engaging activities.

This paper focuses on these challenges and discusses the rationale behind the design of the INCLUDEME Authoring Tool for Gamified Lesson Path (AT-GLP). A case study that drove the design processes is presented along with several learning sequences available in the authoring tool. The group of Ukrainian refugees was inhomogeneous, and the level of English proficiency varied. Communication was challenge, especially being able to read and write using the Latin alphabet. The aim of the experiment was to analyze specific learner needs, in order to improve content modelling and authoring processes.

The work presented in this work-in-progress paper can be seen as an extension of previous work we have carried out on authoring tools [20], and it is part of an Erasmus+ project, the INCLUDEME Project that aims to deliver an authoring tool that will enable teachers to create gamified learning activities without support from developers. The main target group of the project is disadvantaged learners.

The paper first presents the case study in Sect. 2, then explains the transposing of the findings into the design process, with examples in Sect. 3. Section 4 discusses lessons learned and next steps.

2   Case Study

The main objective of this case study was to analyse content models of various lengths and intensity and determine which models are most suitable to be integrated into gamified experiences, and which can conduct to the best outcomes. The case study involved 20 Ukrainian immigrants that came to Romania after the war started at the beginning of 2022. The group enrolled in an English course that lasted for two months. The testing group consisted of 4 were males and 16 females with ages between 16 and 54. All of them were able to communicate in English.

2.1   Learning Content Models

The course consisted of 16 sessions that integrated gamified synchronous learning modules, and asynchronous (self-regulated learning) modules. These modules integrated H5P tool templates [21, 22] that provide various options to present learning content and assessment units (minigames).

The learning content was structured based on the following models [23]:

1. *The bulk learning approach*: four learning sessions (two synchronous and two asynchronous) comprising detailed information provided on a specific grammar topic. For example, for the simple present learning module, the information included the present form of the verb to be, the rules to form the simple present, spelling rules, adverbs associated with the present tense simple.
2. *The atomic learning approach*: four learning sessions were broken down to small learning units, presenting only one specific item, e.g. adverbs associated with the present tense simple.

3. *Joint atomic learning approach*: four learning sessions were constructed as paired learning units, where similar topics were presented in parallel, e.g. the present tense simple and the simple past.

The gamification system included points and rewards (objects such as pens, pencils, notebooks, etc.), which were given based on the number of exercises a learner completed. A leader board was set up, listing the learners that had the best results, and that attended all courses.

2.2 Lessons Learnt

A set of exercises was prepared for each session to be able to evaluate the learning outcomes. Two focus groups were organised for formative and summative evaluation: one for formative evaluation [24] after eight learning sessions (mid-term), and one for summative evaluation [25] at the end of the two months (after 16 sessions) to discuss the proposed approaches, and identify the best ways to construct future leaning units. The evaluation was based on open assessment. The participants were able to use all the available resources during the evaluation, and they had access to Internet.

The evaluations have revealed that:

- The bulk synchronous learning approach (scenario 1) was the least effective. The evaluations have shown that the number of mistakes per exercise was very high, with 72% of learners making four to five mistakes per a ten-item exercise. The discussions in the focus groups showed that, even if the learners were aware of the rules, and even if they checked the resources they were given, they were not able to apply the rules efficiently. The conclusion was that too much information was provided, and it was difficult to navigate through all of it, and thus this cognitive overload lead to the low learning outcome.
- 64% of learners did not read the entire material that was provided. Only 38% of the participants completed the exercises associated with the first bulk asynchronous learning session, and only 17% of them filled in the exercises in the second bulk asynchronous learning session.
- The synchronous atomic learning session showed an increase in the learning outcomes, with less than 10% of the participants making mistakes during the evaluations. The synchronous joint atomic learning session showed a significant increase in the learning outcomes. The number of mistakes has been reduced substantially, with only one and rarely two mistakes per a ten-item exercise.
- The asynchronous atomic learning session was more successful than the bulk session, with more participants doing their homework. 39% of the learners did of their homework, while 53% of them completed it partly. The asynchronous atomic learning sessions were most successful, 83% of learners completing their tasks. The number of mistakes per exercise was again very low, with only one and rarely two mistakes per a ten-item exercise.

3   Learning Paths: A Gamification Story

The experience presented in the case study above was used to inform the design processes of the INCLUDEME Authoring Tool for Gamified Lesson Paths. The AT-GLP enables the creation of gamified learning activities from scratch or based on predefined templates. Teachers can integrate H5P tools and games into the GLPs.

The main reference point for the design extracted from the case study was the difference between the types of learning content models that were part of the experiment. The key AT-GLP templates implemented the atomic learning content approach that was proven to be more effective in a game-based setting (Fig. 1).

Fig. 1. Atomic content examples

The templates include a limitation on the maximum number of characters (250 characters) that a screen or a text placeholder can accommodate, supporting only highly granular atomic content. There is no limitation on the number of screens that a GLP can contain. Also, the teachers can opt to create their own templates from scratch, opting to integrate larger content units.

4   Discussion and Conclusions

The core of delivering successful learning experiences to disadvantages learners is providing the right content, in the right format and at the right time, considering the fact that demand for content extends or contracts with the fall or rise in learning rhythm and knowledge intensity. The authoring tool will allow the creation of different digitally-supported learning scenarios to address specific learning needs.

To enable this approach, the atomic learning model was applied [21], where a Learning Atom is a unit of knowledge that contains information about a particular topic or concept, with the property that the atom contains all the key information related to the subject and can be dispensed to the learner independently or together with other linked atoms. The authoring tool enables the management of the entire lifecycle of such a learning content unit, from creation, validation, mixing, reuse, to syndication.

Teachers will have access to a distributed atomic content management workflow, which allows them to create new content, integrate existing content from other repositories and track new versions, and at the same time have very clear mechanisms for validating the final version that is made available to students.

This paper focused on understanding how to better the learning outcomes of disadvantaged learners through gamified experiences. An atomic model was experimented against a classical teaching approach, where content would be provided in bulk. The case study has revealed that the atomic model is most suitable for learners that do not and/ or cannot follow a regular learning pattern. Increasing the granularity of learning content to an atomic level increased the learner motivation, the learning outcomes, and it matched the game-based approach. Atomic content can be copied and pasted as such into simple game structures, such as the quizzes that were integrated into the GLPs. The atomic approach also facilitates learning content reuse, and eases the authoring process for teachers.

While the atomic learning approach is adequate to construct gamified experiences, the current approach is limited by the availability of content pre-structured as atomic content. Moreover, atomic learning units need to be validated through further testing to assess their capability to deliver the desired learning outcomes.

Future work will focus on the expansion of the atomic content library, the validation of the atomic content unit in relation to specific learning objectives and outcomes, and the validation of the adequacy of the atomic content units for specific disabilities, such as dislexia, autism, etc.

References

1. Dağ, F., Durdu, L., Gerdan, S.: Evaluation of educational authoring tools for teachers stressing of perceived usability features. Proc. Soc. Behav. Sci. **116**, 888–901 (2014)
2. Layona, R., Yulianto, B., Tunardi, Y.: Authoring tool for interactive video content for learning programming. Proc. Comput. Sci. **116**, 37–44 (2017)
3. Obie, H.O., Chua, C., Avazpour, I., Abdelrazek, M., Grundy, J., Bednarz, T.: Authoring logically sequenced visual data stories with gravity. J. Comput. Lang. **58**, 100961 (2020)
4. Metikaridis, D., Xinogalos, S.: A comparative analysis of tools for developing location based games. Entertain. Comput. **37**, 100403 (2021)
5. Edmond, C., Bednarz, T.: Three trajectories for narrative visualisation. Vis. Inform. **5**(2), 26–40 (2021)
6. Zogopoulos, V., Geurts, E., Gors, D., Kauffmann, S.: Authoring tool for automatic generation of augmented reality instruction sequence for manual operations. Proc. CIRP **106**, 84–89 (2022)
7. Huang, Y.M., Chiu, P.S.: The effectiveness of a meaningful learning-based evaluation model for context-aware mobile learning. Br. J. Edu. Technol. **46**(2), 437–447 (2015)
8. Hwang, G.J.: Definition, framework and research issues of smart learning environments-a context-aware ubiquitous learning perspective. Smart Learn. Environ. **1**(1), 4 (2014)
9. Rodríguez López, F., Arias-Oliva, M., Pelegrín-Borondo, J., Marín-Vinuesa, L.M.: Serious games in management education: an acceptance analysis. Int. J. Manag. Educ. **19**(3) 100517 (2021)
10. Robinson, G.M., Hardman, M., Matley, R.J.: Using games in geographical and planning-related teaching: serious games, edutainment, board games and role-play. Soc. Sci. Human. Open **4**(1), 100208 (2021)
11. Urgo, M., Terkaj, W., Mondellini, M., Colombo, G.: Design of serious games in engineering education: an application to the configuration and analysis of manufacturing systems. CIRP J. Manuf. Sci. Technol. **36**, 172–184 (2022)

12. Allal-Chérif, O., Lombardo, E., Jaotombo, F.: Serious games for managers: creating cognitive, financial, technological, social, and emotional value in in-service training. J. Bus. Res. **146**, 166–175 (2022)

13. Sajjadi, P., Ewais, A., De Troyer, O.: Individualization in serious games: a systematic review of the literature on the aspects of the players to adapt to. Entertain. Comput. **41**, 100468 (2022)

14. Antunes, A., Neves Madeira, R.: PLAY - model-based platform to support therapeutic serious games design. Proc. Comput. Sci. **198**, 211–218 (2022)

15. Hassan, A., Pinkwart, N., Shafi, M.: Serious games to improve social and emotional intelligence in children with autism. Entertain. Comput. **38**, 100417 (2021)

16. Dai, W., Liu, J.J., Korthaus, A.: Dynamic on-demand solution delivery based on a context-aware services management framework. Int. J. Grid Util. Comput. 26, **5**(1), 33–49 (2014)

17. Gheorghe, A.F., Stefan (Stănescu), I.A., Stefan, A., Crintescu, M., Beligan, D., Cirnu, C.E.: Prototyping digital educational games. In: Proceedings of the 13th International Scientific Conference eLearning and software for Education (eLSE 2017), Bucharest, Romania (2017)

18. Stefan (Stănescu), I.A., et al.: Blending context-aware challenges into learning environments. In: 12th European Conference on Games Based Learning, Sophia Antipolis, France (2018)

19. Stefan A., et al.: Story-oriented learning, in new technology and redesigning learning spaces. In: Proceedings of the 15th International Scientific Conference "eLearning and Software for Education" Bucharest, 11–12 April 2019, vol. 1, pp. 30–38 (2019)

20. Baalsrud Hauge, J.M., Stefan, I.A., Baalsrud Hauge, J., Stefan, A., Gheorghe, A.F.: Redesign with accessibility in mind. In: Joint Conference on Serious Games 2021 (2021)

21. Stefan (Stănescu), I.A., Stefan, A., Gheorghe, A.F., Roceanu, I., Baalsrud Hauge, J.M.: Changing the fabric of learning content through the atomic learning approach. In: The Interservice/Industry Training, Simulation and Education Conference (I/ITSEC) (2016)

22. Killam, L.A., Luctkar-Flude, M.: Virtual simulations to replace clinical hours in a family assessment course: development using H5P, gamification, and student co-creation. Clin. Simul. Nurs. **57**, 59–65 (2021)

23. Dong, H.: Adapting during the pandemic: a case study of using the rapid prototyping instructional system design model to create online instructional content. J. Acad. Librariansh. **47**(3), 102356 (2021)

24. Krystyna, K., Matusiak, K.K.: Evaluating a digital community archive from the user perspective: the case of formative multifaceted evaluation. Libr. Inf. Sci. Res. **44**(3), 101159 (2022)

25. Opdecam, E., Everaert, P.: Effect of a summer school on formative and summative assessment in accounting education. J. Account. Educ. **58**, 100769 (2022)

Gamifying JupyterLab to Encourage Continuous Interaction in Programming Education

Annabell Brocker[✉], Sven Judel, Rene Roepke, Nikol Mihailovska, and Ulrik Schroeder

Learning Technologies Research Group, RWTH Aachen University, Aachen, Germany
{a.brocker,judel,roepke,schroeder}@cs.rwth-aachen.de,
nikol.mihailovska@rwth-aachen.de

Abstract. With the advancements in research and development of virtual learning environments, Learning Analytics provides access to extensive learning experiences and can provide meaningful analyses to be used for gamification. In the context of programming education, programming platforms like JupyterLab present an immersive, interactive environment in which learners spent valuable time of their learning process. As such, capturing the learners' activities when programming allows to reflect on how learners solve assignments, what challenges they face and how gamification influences their behavior. This paper presents a data-driven gamification approach utilizing Learning Analytics in the interactive programming environment JupyterLab. Future work entails the application of gamification in programming courses and evaluating how data-driven gamification supports learners in gaining programming skills.

Keywords: Programming · Jupyter · Gamification · Learning analytics

1 Introduction

When using virtual learning environments, e.g. for programming education, Learning Analytics (LA) can be used to analyze learners' activities and gain insights on how learners interact with educational materials. LA can also be used to implement gamification in order to foster motivation and engagement, e.g. in introductory programming courses where novices perceive learning how to code as hard and high dropout rates can be reported [2,5]. JupyterLab presents an interactive programming environment in which learners can work actively with program code when solving assignments, thus, offering valuable data for LA and gamification. This way, learners can already be supported during code development, however, JupyterLab does not support gamification to engage learners in continuously using the programming environment for practice.

To this end, the following paper presents a data-driven gamification approach which automatically analyzes learning activities in JupyterLab and allows to

K. Kiili et al. (Eds.): GALA 2022, LNCS 13647, pp. 316–322, 2022.
https://doi.org/10.1007/978-3-031-22124-8_32

enrich the programming experience with game elements to foster engagement and continuous interaction by answering the research questions *How can Learning Analytics be applied on game elements in Jupyter?* as well as *What data is necessary to allow the support of continuous interactivity?*.

2   Background and Related Work

The project **Jupyter**[1] offers extendable, open source solutions for interactive programming environments supporting various programming languages. The basis is provided by a notebook, i.e. a JSON file that contains different types of cells (e.g., code cells or markdown cells). Notebooks can be edited and executed in JupyterLab, a web application which includes a notebook editor, file browser, window manager, terminal emulator, and an extension manager. JupyterLab presents an immersive, interactive programming environment which allows for easy access and use, e.g. in introductory programming courses, since no installation on learners' devices is required. It is therefore a suitable system to use with programming beginners or novices. Further, to reduce course failures and dropout rates [2], gamification can be applied [6].

Gamification is an approach to encourage users' interest and involvement in a non-game-based environment by adding game elements [6]. While it can be used in various contexts, gamification is often applied to the educational domain [14,18]. A popular application area is programming education, e.g. using game elements in introductory programming courses to motivate learners [9, 18]. While some game elements provide learners with further opportunities for interaction (e.g., challenges), other game elements visualise the learners progress (e.g., badges) [13,19]. Both types of game elements can be integrated into an environment using statistics from LA [13]. In contrast to [9,13,18] the approach presented in our paper can give students feedback in the form of game elements already during the programming process and not only at the end of a learning process. That way, for example, badges for the use of certain constructs could already be awarded during coding.

To capture learners' activities within JupyterLab and support LA for data-driven gamification, extensive logging functionality is needed. **Juxl** (JupyterLab xAPI Logging Interface) [3] is a JupyterLab extension to collect interaction and learning activities in a Learning Record Store (LRS) as xAPI statements[2], an LA data standard that allows data collection across multiple platforms. It allows three different logging variants: anonymous, pseudonym or personalised logging with information potentially stored in the system (by the users) [3]. As Juxl does not provide analyses through methods of LA itself, collected learner activities need to be processed further to be used for gamification.

Here, **Excalibur LA** [12] as a central and modular infrastructure for the integration of LA processes in various platforms can be used. As such, a rights engine, a data warehouse, procedures carrying out different analyses, a result

---

[1] https://jupyter.org, accessed 30.06.2022.
[2] https://xapi.com, accessed 24.06.2022.

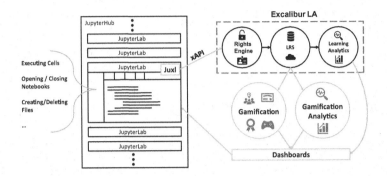

Fig. 1. Architecture for integrating gamification into JupyterLab.

store as well as a result store API are provided, as visualized in Fig. 1. Although the infrastructure was initially developed for LA, it can also be used for other applications such as gamification, as the integration of game elements is based on analyses such as how long participants have interacted with a learning unit. In this paper, Juxl and Excalibur LA are used to provide a data-driven gamification approach to be applied in JupyterLab.

3   Gamification in JupyterLab

Compared to summative evaluation of learners' submissions, in JupyterLab, code examination can already take place during the learners' coding process when working on learning materials. In the field of gamification, these immediate, real-time analyses can be used to support the learner with appropriate game elements and, thus, increase motivation and learner engagement. An example is the promotion of learners' continuous interaction with learning materials.

Continuous Interaction is defined as "the process by which individual learning [...] is fostered on an ongoing basis" [17, p. 438] and has shown to be an important factor concerning user engagement [7]. In order to measure the learners' engagement with learning materials or their activity within the environment overall, different metrics can be used, e.g., overall time spent in the course [16], activity type, start and end time of learning sessions [15] and the frequency and duration of interactions [11]. User engagement is thus examined through *frequency* of using JupyterLab, the *duration* of learning sessions and the *activities* during each learning session. All metrics are made accessible to learners using three game elements: *Redeemable points, experience points* and *badges*. Table 1 summarizes metric usage to increase learner engagement and learners' continuous interaction in programming education. Especially in beginner's programming courses, a permanent active involvement with the learning materials is necessary in order to gain an overall understanding of the concepts of programming [1].

The integration of data-driven game elements is based on various events within JupyterLab. In a first step, the events to be captured for the correspond-

Table 1. Gamification elements to encourage continuous interaction with learning materials in JupyterLab.

Metric	Game Element	Explanation
Frequency	Redeemable points	Obtained by streak of consecutive logins. Online currency that can be used to unlock additional material or badges
Duration	Experience points	Obtained by each interaction within the JupyterLab environment. Denote the level of progress
Activities	Badges	Obtained by reaching predefined activity requirements. Visualize the successful completion of tasks or accomplishment of goals

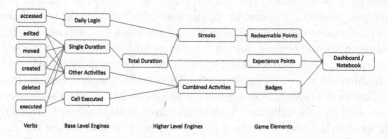

Fig. 2. Necessary data and analyses to integrate the three metrics for encouraging continuous interaction.

ing game element must be identified and converted into an xAPI statement and stored within an LRS using Juxl. In the second step, corresponding analytics engines must be designed and implemented within the Excalibur LA setting, on which the generation of the identified game elements is based. In order to measure the frequency of learners working on learning materials, it is necessary to know if learners are logged in and how much time they spent during a session. As such, one redeemable point can be achieved by daily use of at least x specified minutes. Those redeemable points may be used, for example, for an extension of the exercise submissions or for bonus percentage points in the final examination. The total duration of learners activity in the environment is rewarded by experience points. Here, all interaction data of learners' with the system are evaluated. Different experience points are achieved for different duration's with learning materials. An important factor in this context is the time of no measured interactions, as student engagement can be inferred from the inactive time [8]. Finally, all the learners' activities are to be examined in more detail in order to enhance them further. Badges will represent the learners' various successes with the content. Figure 2 visualizes which activities (in form of verbs) from JupyterLab are needed to integrate different game elements.

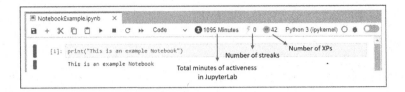

Fig. 3. Example showing how the results of the analyses including the experience points can be displayed directly in a notebook.

Currently, Excalibur LA only supports the analyses of logged statements every 24-h. In case of LA, this time period is usually sufficient, but in the field of data-driven gamification, **direct analyses and immediate feedback** will be necessary in order to inform the learner about his progress in a timely manner. For example, awarding redeemable points every 24-hours would be sufficient, as this is a one-time message at the beginning of the login. In contrast, by receiving experience points and badges, learners should be notified immediately. Therefore, the infrastructure will be extended by an option to do real-time analyses.

A **dashboard** serves to permanently display the learner's current progress, such as how many redeemable/experience points he has received so far or which badges he has already collected. To individualise the dashboard, learners should be able to switch game elements on/off independently and adjust the arrangement of the individual graphics. Furthermore, the dashboard provides more detailed information, in this case on interactions with the learning materials/notebooks, and combines the data-driven game elements with further LA visualisations to constantly keep learners' interest up [4,10]. Teachers also have access to a teacher-only dashboard that visualises LA results and shows how learners are using game elements (Gamification Analytics).

In addition, individually selected game elements or results of analyses can be made available to participants in each notebook in order to increase direct feedback. An example can be found in Fig. 3. Here, users can see how long they have been active in JupyterLab, how often they have logged consecutively (streaks) and how many experience points they have earned so far.

4   Conclusion and Future Work

This paper presents a data-driven approach to implement gamification in JupyterLab using LA. By collecting learners' actions in the interactive programming environment, e.g. when interacting with code cells in JupyterLab, LA can provide valuable insights on how learners solve assignments and what challenges they face. Based on LA, gamification can be applied to foster motivation and engagement. While this work introduces game elements like points and badges to encourage continuous interaction, the modular approach allows for more game elements to be integrated in the future (e.g. *leaderboards* or *progress bars*). Prospectively, a user interface in JupyterLab itself is intended for easy configuration of game elements, e.g. configuring thresholds for achieving a redeemable point or receivable badges. Furthermore, using Excalibur LA as a centralized infrastructure allows to combine learner data from JupyterLab with learner data from other systems, like a learning management system. This enables more comprehensive analyses as all learning activities can be evaluated across platforms. Overall, capturing learner activities and enabling gamification in programming environments like JupyterLab could reduce the high dropout rates in novices programming courses.

References

1. Berssanette, J.H.: Active learning in the context of the teaching/learning of computer programming: a systematic review. Inf. Technol. Educ. Res. **20**, 201–220 (2021)
2. Bosse, Y., Gerosa, M.A.: Why is programming so difficult to learn?: Patterns of difficulties related to programming learning mid-stage. In: SIGSOFT Software Engineering Notes, vol. 41, pp. 1–6. ACM (2017)
3. Brocker, A., Judel, S., Schroeder, U.: Juxl: JupyterLab xAPI logging interface. In: International Conference on Advanced Learning Technologies, pp. 158–160 (2022)
4. Cassano, F., Piccinno, A., Roselli, T., Rossano, V.: Gamification and learning analytics to improve engagement in university courses. In: Di Mascio, T., et al. (eds.) MIS4TEL 2018. AISC, vol. 804, pp. 156–163. Springer, Cham (2019). https://doi.org/10.1007/978-3-319-98872-6_19
5. Derus, S.R.M., Ali, A.Z.M.: Difficulties in learning programming: views of students. In: International Conference on Current Issues in Education, pp. 74–79 (2012)
6. Deterding, S., Dixon, D., Khaled, R., Nacke, L.E.: From game design elements to gamefulness: defining "gamification". In: MindTrek (2011)
7. Dixson, M.D.: Measuring student engagement in the online course: the online student engagement scale (OSE). Asynchronous Learn. Netw.**19** (2015)
8. Edwards, J., Hart, K., Warren, C.: A practical model of student engagement while programming. In: Technical Symposium on Computer Science Education, pp. 558–564. ACM (2022)
9. Fotaris, P., Mastoras, T., Leinfellner, R., Rosunally, Y.: Climbing up the leaderboard: an empirical study of applying gamification techniques to a computer programming class. Electron. J. e-Learn. **14**, 94–110 (2016)
10. de Freitas, S., et al.: How to use gamified dashboards and learning analytics for providing immediate student feedback and performance tracking in higher education. In: International Conference on World Wide Web Companion, pp. 429–434 (2017)
11. Growth Engineering: Measuring user engagement on your learning management system (2016). https://www.growthengineering.co.uk/measuring-user-engagement-on-lms/
12. Judel, S., Schroeder, U.: EXCALIBUR LA - an extendable and scalable infrastructure build for learning analytics. In: International Conference on Advanced Learning Technologies, pp. 155–157 (2022)
13. Klock, A.C.T., Ogawa, A.N., Gasparini, I., Pimenta, M.S.: Integration of learning analytics techniques and gamification: an experimental study. In: International Conference on Advanced Learning Technologies, pp. 133–137 (2018)

14. Koivisto, J., Hamari, J.: The rise of motivational information systems: a review of gamification research. Inf. Manage. **45**, 191–210 (2019)
15. Moubayed, A., Injadat, M., Shami, A., Lutfiyya, H.: Relationship between student engagement and performance in e-learning environment using association rules. In: World Engineering Education Conference, pp. 1–6 (2018)
16. Rodgers, T.: Student engagement in the e-learning process and the impact on their grades. Cyber Soc. Educ. **1**(2), 143–156 (2008)
17. Tannenbaum, S.I.: Enhancing continuous learning: diagnostic findings from multiple companies. Hum. Resour. Manag. **36**, 437–452 (1997)
18. Venter, M.I.: Gamification in STEM programming courses: state of the art. In: Global Engineering Education Conference, pp. 859–866 (2020)
19. Yampray, K., Inchamnan, W.: A method to visualization data collection by using gamification. In: International Conference on ICT and Knowledge Engineering (2019)

Enhancing Information Literacy Skills: A Game Design for Seeking Information and Making Queries

Paavo Arvola[✉] and Tuulikki Alamettälä

Tampere University, Tampere, Finland
`paavo.arvola@tuni.fi`

Abstract. Information literacy is an essential skill in today's society and information search is an essential part of it. These skills need constant training and maintenance and thus, innovative and engaging approaches to teach and learn information literacy and searching are needed. In this paper, we present a serious game to enhance information literacy skills, focusing on skills in seeking information. The experimental research setting widely used in search engine development provides means to gamify information seeking.

Keywords: Information retrieval · Search engines · Information literacy

1 Introduction and Related Work

Information literacy refers to the skills to recognize the information need, locate the information, evaluate the information found, and finally to use the chosen information ethically and effectively [15]. These abilities are widely seen as civic skills that everyone needs in today's society. Information search is an important part of information literacy. It is the first step in the interaction with available information [13]. Without relevant search results, it is difficult to proceed further: into evaluating and using information. Earlier research indicates that users often have problems with query formulation and reformulation [19]. An ability to use the search engine is essential, and thus the terms *search (engine) literacy* and consequently, *algorithmic literacy* have been adopted in the academic discussions. These kinds of literacies mean the ability to make effective use of a wide array of search engines, including a familiarity with their full functionality as well as their limitations [10].

The pedagogical approach of utilizing games in education is called *game-based learning* (GBL) or *digital game-based learning* (DGBL). Definitions of GBL mostly emphasize that it is a type of game play with defined learning outcomes. [18] Games that are used in (D)GBL are mainly *serious games*. A common definition of serious games is "games that do not have entertainment, enjoyment, or fun as their primary purpose" [16]. Serious games have the goal to transfer knowledge, to teach skills or to stimulate behavioural change.

© The Author(s), under exclusive license to Springer Nature Switzerland AG 2022
K. Kiili et al. (Eds.): GALA 2022, LNCS 13647, pp. 323–328, 2022.
https://doi.org/10.1007/978-3-031-22124-8_33

DGBL has been found to enhance students' motivation, participation, confidence, perception, attitude and learning performance [7, 21]. Accordingly, several researchers have implemented educational games to help students develop information literacy. The studies have shown positive effects [14, 22]. Games are widely accepted by new generations of learners and encourage creativity in information literacy training [9].

Competition is classified as a characteristic of a serious game [4]. Competition may have potential to optimize GBL. Earlier research has reported several benefits that competition in games may bring. Competition is considered as a useful technique to increase motivation and enhance students' learning by improving students' engagement and persistence in learning activities [6, 7, 22]. Competition has been found to be beneficial also in information literacy education [4]. Nonetheless, also some negative consequences of competition have been reported. Competition may cause feelings of anxiety, discouragement, frustration, and pressure [5]. However, virtual competition has been proposed to address these disadvantages as there is no direct competition between each player in virtual competition, and players compete with computers instead of real persons [8].

There are gamified approaches to information retrieval or search [17] of which our approach has similarities to *Query Performance Analyzer* [20], which was built upon a standard test collection of Finnish newspaper articles, topics, and related relevance assessments. The system did not consider judging documents' relevance, but it did measure query performance using the laboratory model and metrics available at that time. In a more recent approach called *Query Aspect Game* [8], relevance judgements for a topic are constructed with different queries and used for classification.

2   Game Design

We have designed a game that trains information search skills using multilingual Wikipediae. For technical details, see the demonstration publication in Arvola and Alamettälä [1]. It has also been used in workshops (hackathon) e.g., in Arvola and Alamettälä [2] and in undergraduate level university education.

The aim is for the teachers (hosts) to facilitate competitions for students (players) to search information from Wikipediae on a certain topic and measure the outcome, enabling scores for individuals or groups and provide leaderboards. Our game mechanics has its theoretical foundation in so called *Information Retrieval Laboratory evaluation model* [11, p. 4–5] and evaluation of information interaction [13].

In general, the laboratory model aims to measure and quantify the quality of the search results delivered by a search engine based on query and matching method. The main components of the framework consist of (1) a (test) collection of documents to search, (2) test topics and corresponding queries, (3) relevance judgements, i.e., data on which documents in the collection are relevant for the given topic, and (4) evaluation metrics. Our game design is an application of the laboratory model where students are players, and a teacher works as a host who selects, modifies, or creates topics for the players to play. Instead of competing algorithms or search engines, the players' queries about a topic are measured with a given search engine. So, the query is the search method to be measured.

First, the host – such as a teacher – develops a topic according to his or her preferences. The host can use topics that have been made earlier by someone else or create an own. For example, the host creates a topic named "Vaccination in preventing diseases to spread"[1]. In addition to the topic name, the host adds a topic description for the players (the students) to grasp what kind of documents they should search for. The language of the game is set here as well. As Wikipediae are considered here as document collections, virtually any language is viable, and the relevance judgements translated to other languages [1]. After setting the topic, the teacher judges the result documents relevant or not relevant according to his/her expertise using the assessment tool (Similar to Fig. 5). It is worth noting that the relevance judgments are usable ever after.

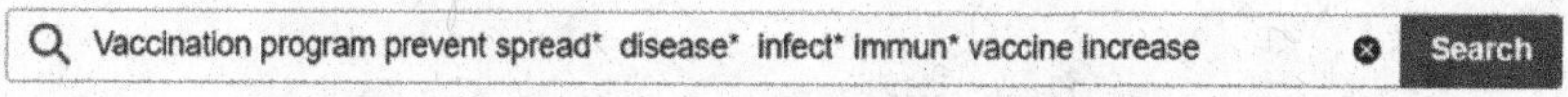

Fig. 1. Standard search box. Best performing query for the vaccine topic in the English Wikipedia edition

The user input is by default a standard search box (Fig. 1). This allows the player to freely insert any query they see fit following the *query language* provided by the search engine specifications[2]. Another alternative is to restrict the possibilities by offering a fixed set of query words and let the player choose the best possible combination of them (Fig. 2).

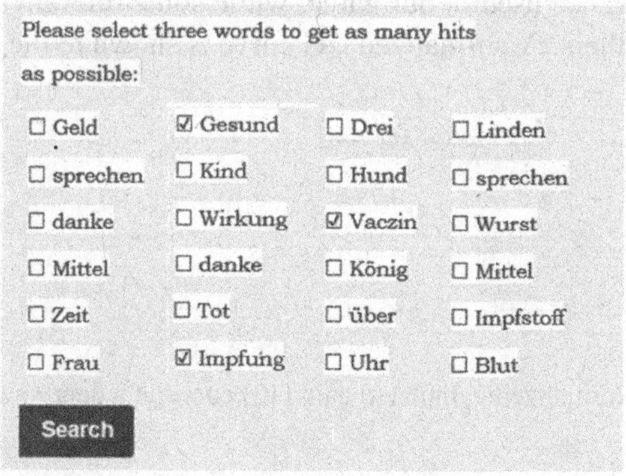

Fig. 2. An alternative form of game. Instead a query box, the player is given a restricted set of possible query expressions. Here for the German edition of the vaccine topic the user is required to select three words for the query. (Note a misspelled word).

The game delivers feedback based on the player's query performance in relation to the gold standard (relevance judgements). The feedback is immediate and comes in the form of precision-recall measures as well as corresponding diagrams, such as Euler diagrams (Fig. 3) and precision-recall curves.

---

[1] Topic translated from Finnish matriculation exam.

[2] https://www.elastic.co/elasticsearch/

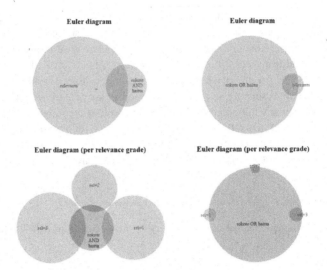

Fig. 3. Euler diagrams[3] as feedback for the player on how two different result sets overlap with the relevant document sets (binary and graded) using the queries "rokote AND haitta" and "rokote OR haitta".

Obviously, there are many other metrics available [3], of which the widely used Cumulated Gain (CG) [12] metrics for ranked lists is used in this study. This metrics supports graded relevance used in our game, while some relevant documents are more relevant than some others. A normalized CG curve is shown to the player (Fig. 4).

Fig. 4. Normalized cumulated gain [12] curve of a query evaluation.

Players themselves may judge the documents as well (Fig. 5). When players contribute to the relevance judgements in a gamified and *collaborative* effort, it results in more complete recall bases.

---

[3] https://github.com/benfred/venn.js

Rank

Link to document and snipett

Graded relevance score (0,1,2,3 or ?)

Relevance judgement for collaboration

Fig. 5. Result list presented to the player after executing a query. The host can use the same view for judging the relevance.

3 Discussion and Conclusions

The laboratory research setting is widely used in search engine development, spam filtering, (text) classification, and recommender systems, and many others. To provide a realistic, familiar and inspiring environment, we have adopted the online Wikipediae as the test collections and a freedom for the host to create or use virtually any topic - or language - for the players to play with. In our game design query or seeking success is measured explicitly, which enables competitive elements with leaderboards, see [4].

Consequently, the game presented in this paper is a challenge, where the players control the game with queries and exploit the explicit and measurable feedback. This results preferably in growing competence after seeing and comparing the different search strategies.

Acknowledgements. This work was partially funded by the European Union Erasmus+ programme with grant number 2021-1-FI01-KA220-SCH000029713.

References

1. Arvola, P., Alamettälä, T.: IRVILAB: Gamified searching on multilingual wikipedia. In: Proceedings of ACM SIGIR'22 Conference, pp. 3329–3333. ACM, New York (2022). https://doi.org/10.1145/3477495.3531662
2. Arvola, P., Alamettälä, T.: Information retrieval workshop. In: 30th BOBCATSSS Symposium - Book of Abstracts, p. 43 (2022). https://doi.org/10.5281/zenodo.6484810
3. Buttcher, S., Clarke, C.L., Cormack, G.V.: Information Retrieval: Implementing and Evaluating Search Engines. MIT Press, Cambridge (2016)
4. Cagiltay, N.E., Ozcelik, E., Ozcelik, N.S.: The effect of competition on learning in games. Comput. Educ. **87**, 35–41 (2015). https://doi.org/10.1016/j.compedu.2015.04.001
5. Chen, C.H., Liu, J.H., Shou, W.C.: How competition in a game-based science learning environment influences students' learning achievement, flow experience, and learning behavioral patterns. J. Educ. Technol. Soc. **21**(2), 164–176 (2018)
6. Chen, C.-H., Shih, C.-C., Law, V.: The effects of competition in digital game-based learning (DGBL): a meta-analysis. Educ. Tech. Res. Dev. **68**(4), 1855–1873 (2020). https://doi.org/10.1007/s11423-020-09794-1
7. Chen, S.Y., Chang, Y.M.: The impacts of real competition and virtual competition in digital game-based learning. Comput. Hum. Behav. **104**, 106171 (2020). https://doi.org/10.1016/j.chb.2019.106171

8. Di Nunzio, G.M., Maistro, M., Zilio, D.: Gamification for IR: the query aspects game. In: CLiC-it/EVALITA (2016)

9. Encheva, M., Tammaro, A.M., Kumanova, A.: Games to improve students information literacy skills. Int. Inf. Library Rev. **52**(2), 130–138 (2020). https://doi.org/10.1080/10572317.2020. 1746024

10. Hockly, N., Dudeney, G., Pegrum, M.: Digital Literacies. Routledge, London (2014)

11. Ingwersen, P., Järvelin, K.: The Turn - Integration of Information Seeking and Retrieval in Context. The Kluwer International Series on Information Retrieval (2005)

12. Järvelin, K., Kekäläinen, J.: Cumulated gain-based evaluation of IR techniques. ACM Trans. Inf. Syst. **20**(4), 422–446 (2002). https://doi.org/10.1145/582415.582418

13. Järvelin, K., et al.: Task-based information interaction evaluation: the viewpoint of program theory. ACM Trans. Inf. Syst. **33**(1), 1–30 (2015). https://doi.org/10.1145/2699660

14. Li, Z., Zou, D., Xie, H., Wang, F.L., Chang, M.: Enhancing information literacy in Hong Kong higher education through game-based learning. In: Jong, M., et al. (eds.) The 22nd Global Chinese Conference on Computers in Education: Conference proceedings, pp. 595–598. South China Normal University, Guangzhou (2018)

15. Library and Information Association. What is information literacy? (2018). https://www.cilip. org.uk/page/informationliteracy

16. Michael, D.R., Chen, S.L.: Serious Games: Games That Educate, Train, and Inform. Thomson Course Technology, Boston (2005)

17. Muntean, C.I., Nardini, F.M.: Gamification in information retrieval: state of the art, challenges and opportunities. In: Proceedings of the 6th Italian Information Retrieval Workshop (IIR'2015) (2015)

18. Plass, J.L., Homer, B.D., Kinzer, C.K.: Foundations of game-based learning. Educ. Psychol. **50**(4), 258–283 (2015)

19. Rieh, S.Y., Xie, H.: Analysis of multiple query reformulations on the web: the interactive information retrieval context. Inf. Process. Manag. **42**(3), 751–768 (2006). https://doi.org/10. 1016/j.ipm.2005.05.005

20. Sormunen, E., Hokkanen, S., Kangaslampi, P., Pyy, P., Sepponen, B.: Query performance analyser- a web-based tool for IR research and instruction. In: Proceedings of the 25th Annual International ACM SIGIR Conference on Research and Development in Information Retrieval, p. 450 (2002)

21. Subhash, S., Cudney, E.A.: Gamified learning in higher education: a systematic review of the literature. Comput. Hum. Behav. **87**, 192–206 (2018). https://doi.org/10.1016/j.chb.2018. 05.028

22. Zou, D., Zhang, R., Xie, H., Wang, F.L.: Digital game-based learning of information literacy: effects of gameplay modes on university students' learning performance, motivation, self-efficacy and flow experiences. Australas. J. Educ. Technol. **37**(2), 152–170 (2021)

BIG GAME: Balancing Player Preferences and Design Considerations in a Serious Game About Environmental Issues

Mikhail Fiadotau[1]([✉]) [iD], Michela Tramonti[2] [iD], Heli Brander[3], and Peadar Callaghan[1]

[1] Tallinn University, Narva mnt. 29, 10120 Tallinn, Estonia
fiadotau@tlu.ee
[2] EU-Track, Viale Europa 95, 04019 Terracina, Italy
[3] University of Turku, Joukahaisenkatu 3, 20520 Turku, Finland

Abstract. The article reflects on the benefits, challenges, and limitations of accommodating player preferences in serious game design. Based on a case study from an ongoing game development project (an environmentally themed multiplayer game for middle-schoolers), it discusses how player preferences need to be balanced against design considerations such as practicality and educational value.

Keywords: Player preferences · Case study · Serious games

1 Introduction

BIG GAME: Immersive and Multidisciplinary STEM Learning through a Cooperative Story-Driven Game (https://big-game.eu-track.eu/) is an Erasmus+ project coordinated by the University of Turku and involving research institutions and middle schools from Finland, Italy, Estonia, and Romania. The focus is on creating a serious game that connects STEM education to environmental themes, challenging participating middle-schoolers (ages 11–16) to use their problem-solving skills and knowledge from across STEM disciplines to tackle climate change, pollution, loss of biodiversity, and other issues.

The project started in late 2021 and, as of the time of writing, is at an early stage whereby the team is creating a pilot of the game to be tested with the participating schools in early 2023. Recognizing the value of player-centered and participatory approaches in serious game design [3,8], the team decided to involve teachers and students in the design process. A key, if often overlooked [1], aspect of player-centered design is to investigate player preferences [2,6]. As

This research was supported by the European Commission through the Erasmus+ KA2 program (Cooperation Partnerships in School Education). Grant agreement no. 2021-1-FI01-KA220-SCH-000024098.

K. Kiili et al. (Eds.): GALA 2022, LNCS 13647, pp. 329–334, 2022.
https://doi.org/10.1007/978-3-031-22124-8_34

such, one of the early steps in the pre-production process involved a conducting a survey of player preferences from the participating schools.

However, upon collecting player preference data, the team struggled to agree on how the data should be used. Is it background information helping designers understand their audiences better? Or should the goal be to accommodate player preferences in the game itself as much as possible? This short article thus reflects on a question that is more practical and exploratory than theoretical: how can serious game designers use player preferences and to what extent should they?

2   Survey Results and Discussion

The 20-question, English-language student questionnaire focused on students' experience and preferences with regard to games, as well as their priorities and concerns relating to the environment. The online questionnaire was sent out to teachers in the partner schools, who then distributed it to their students.

The survey yielded 251 unique responses. 175 (69.7%) came from the two Romanian schools (which was expected given they have more students than their Finnish and Estonian counterparts.) 78 of the respondents (31.1%) were in the 11–12 age bracket, 60 (23.9%) were 13–14 years old, and 113 (45%) were 15 or 16. No gender data was collected. Tables with detailed response statistics, broken down into age brackets, can be found at http://www.tlu.ee/~fiadotau/big_game.pdf. The key results are discussed below.

2.1   Game Preferences

A key question was "What kind of games do you play most often? (choose up to 2)", with the options being: action and shooter; adventure and puzzle; role-playing and massively multiplayer online games; strategy and multiplayer battle arena games; simulation and sports; party games; board and pen-and-paper games.

While almost half of the respondents in every age group (46.7% on average) reported action games among their favorite genres, accommodating this preference would be difficult both from an educational (creating meaningful challenges) and technical perspective. Action games are also among the most alienating genres for those with limited videogame experience, and the preference for them tends to be gendered, which makes them a risky choice for classroom use [4].

Elements from the other popular genres, such as simulation (22.5%), roleplay (21.9%), and adventure (26.6%), can be integrated into the game more easily. For example, having open-ended scenarios in which players' actions can affect the ecosystem is consistent with the simulation genre, while roleplaying elements can include things like experience points and attributes, as well as framing the scenarios as a series of quests.

Notably, 9.6% of the students reported not playing games at all, while a further 12.8% favor board and pen-and-paper games (although the preference decreases with age, presumably as children are permitted more access to digital technology). This means that the game must be approachable to non-gamers and presuppose no familiarity with gaming conventions from any genre.

A related technical question was "What devices do you usually play on? (Check all that apply)". The results, excluding those who do not play digital games at all, show that players' preference for personal computers and gaming consoles (64.7%) is about the same as for smartphones and tablets (63.7%), although mobile devices are somewhat more popular with the youngest students (68.7% compared to 59.7% for PC/console). This served as a reminder that it is desirable for the game to be available in both a desktop and mobile version.

In response to the question "How do you prefer playing games? (Choose one option)", online social play was preferred across the age groups at 53.2%. Children's preference for playing with others in the same physical space decreased with age (from 33.8% in the 11–12 bracket to 22.6% in the 15–16 bracket), while the preference for solo play increased from 12.7% in the 11–12 group to 38% in the 15–16 group. The fact that a majority of players preferred online social play suggests that the pilot game could, too, emphasize social interaction and provide an online environment for students to engage in it.

We also asked players what they enjoyed about playing games in the first place (they could check multiple options). Options included: Overcoming challenges and getting good at the game; Competing against other players; Experimenting and discovering new things; Creating and developing a character; Immersing yourself in the story. Results indicate that mastery and competition are both seen as key factors by over 50% of the respondents, suggesting that it is desirable to have elements of competition and progression in the game. At the same time, competition must be approached carefully, as overemphasizing it can be demotivating for less competitive or skillful players [7]. This can be mitigated by combining inter-team competition with intra-team collaboration, thus reducing individual performance anxiety.

Roleplay and exploration were also moderately important "fun aspects" at some 40% each, highlighting the need for incorporating these elements into the game. By contrast, narrative was viewed as essential by only a quarter of the respondents. Yet, implementing it in the present project appeared inevitable due to the need to provide context for the quests, as well as to create persistence and continuity between them.

Another question in the questionnaire was "Where do you prefer for games to take place? (check up to 3)". The results suggest that real-world settings, in particular in the present day, are the most popular at 57.9% (although the preference for them diminishes with age). This preference, however, was not compatible with the basic premise of this specific project: "solving" major environmental issues in the game would create discontinuity with the real world, where they remain unsolved. At the same time, opting for a setting too remote from the real world (e.g., a space colony or a sword-and-sorcery fantasy realm) would make it more challenging to transfer knowledge from the fiction of the game into real life. As such, near-future Earth appears to be a good compromise, offering enough artistic license to develop a variety of scenarios, but also sufficient similarity to the real world for students to learn from the experience.

2.2 Environmental Concerns and Awareness

We asked participants to evaluate how concerned they are about a selection of environmental issues (chosen from a list brainstormed with teachers) using Likert items from 0 ("Not at all") to 4 ("Extremely"). For each environmental issue, respondents could also check "I don't know what this is".

Overall, the results suggest that students are moderately concerned about environmental issues (total median value of 2 out of 4). Climate change, air pollution, and deforestation are the three most concerning issues. Students also demonstrated good awareness of the issues: over 95% are familiar with pollution issues (air, water, and land) and climate change. Loss of biodiversity, light pollution, and deforestation were somewhat less known. (Upon reflection, "loss of biodiversity" could be replaced with a less technical term such as "extinction.of species").

This part of the survey was intended as more of a barometer than an indication of which issues to prioritize in the game. For example, just because students appear to be less concerned about water pollution than about air pollution, does not mean that the latter issue that requires less attention in the game. Rather, it may be a sign that students need to be further educated about the severity and implications of water pollution. Similarly, students' lower awareness of biodiversity loss is perhaps a sign that the game needs to introduce the concept of biodiversity rather than avoid mentioning it. As such, the concern here is less with what students would like to learn about (even though it can to some extent be accommodated), but with how to build on their existing knowledge and perceptions in order to maximize the learning outcomes.

Informed by the above considerations (and instructional design considerations that are beyond the scope of this article), our vision for the pilot of the game is briefly discussed below.

3   Gameplay Description

BIG GAME is a problem-based, seminar-style [5] simulation game where teams of students roleplay as elite squads of experts tasked with tackling urgent environmental issues. These are presented as missions taking place in a shared fictional world: near-future Earth. The game time matches real-world time: a week in the world of the game elapses in seven real-world days. A new mission is released every two weeks and made available via the game's web portal.

Following the release of a new mission, students in each team formulate and submit their proposed solution to it using the web portal. In order to do so, the teams conduct independent research, brainstorm for solutions, choose and develop one, and present it according to the specified format.

Submissions then go through a double-blind peer evaluation using the website and based on a set of criteria (clarity, feasibility, effectiveness, practicality). Then, the best ranking submissions are analyzed by the game development team, who choose one submission (or multiple similar ones) and integrate it into the fictional world of the game. This is reflected in a narrative update, made available shortly before the next mission is released. The "winning" team is rewarded with a custom badge visible in the web interface.

In addition to the core mechanic outlined above, the game also incorporates basic roleplaying elements for additional engagement. Each team has a set of attributes, which start at one but whose value can increase over time: Persuasion, Pragmatism, Problem-Solving, Resource Management, and Innovation. These are based on the peer evaluation criteria outlined above: if a team scores among the top 25% in a category, its corresponding attribute increases by one. This acts as a form of aggregated feedback to the teams, highlighting their strengths and areas requiring more attention.

4   Discussion

4.1   Takeaways

The case study above demonstrates that balancing player preferences against design considerations (both educational and practical) can be a delicate and challenging task. In light of this, we would like to put forward the following twofold argument.

First, accommodating player preferences in serious game design is not always practical or indeed desirable, and thus should not be viewed as an inherent virtue or an end goal. Second, understanding player preferences and expectations is nonetheless vital to creating a serious game that is meaningful and accessible to its intended audience. Which player preferences to accommodate and to what extent should be a conscious choice on the designer's part aimed at finding a balance between engaging the player and accomplishing the game's serious goal.

Three further considerations strike us as being relevant here. First, there is value to distinguishing between target users' learning preferences and their preferences in entertainment. The former may include things that support more personalized or self-regulated learning (e.g., issues that the target users are particularly passionate about, or their learning style). The latter arguably matter less, as accommodating them may not improve learning outcomes as such. This connects to the second point: just because a game does not accommodate a player's reported preference for a specific genre or visual style, does not automatically mean it will not be engaging for them (nor does accommodating the preference guarantee that it will be). People can enjoy things that lie outside of their usual media consumption habits and tastes.

The third consideration is that accommodating players' entertainment (including gaming) preferences in serious games is impossible due to how diverse the player body is. Whereas entertainment games target players based on their shared tastes in gaming, the intended audiences for serious games typically have little in common beyond studying in the same program or sharing the same workplace. In the case study above, very few preferences were shared by an outright majority, meaning that even the most popular option may not align with the personal preferences of a sizeable number of players.

Designing and implementing a serious game is thus a three-way negotiation process between the game's serious goals, its players' preferences and expectations, and the practical constraints faced by the creators.

4.2 Limitations

This paper only reports on preliminary observations from a work in progress, often while glossing over potentially interesting tangents (such as age group differences) owing to a lack of space. Overall, the survey design could be significantly improved: for example, asking players to name their favorite games could be more reliable than asking about their preferred types and aspects of games.

Crucially, student preferences are highly contingent, and the results presented above may not be true of, and thus should not be extrapolated to, other contexts. (For example, while our respondents expressed a preference for present-day real-world settings, undergraduate pharmacology students in a 2015 study by Chang et al. preferred "post-apocalyptic fantasy" [2]).

References

1. Aubert, A.H., Bauer, R., Lienert, J.: A review of water-related serious games to specify use in environmental multi-criteria decision analysis. Environ. Modell. Softw. **105**, 64–78 (2018). https://doi.org/10.1016/j.envsoft.2018.03.023
2. Chang, H.Y., Poh, D.Y.H., Wong, L.L., Yap, J.Y.G., Yap, K.Y.L.: Student preferences on gaming aspects for a serious game in pharmacy practice education: a cross-sectional study. JMIR Med. Educ. **1**(1), e3754 (2015)
3. Khaled, R., Vanden Abeele, V., Van Mechelen, M., Vasalou, A.: Participatory design for serious game design: truth and lies. In: Proceedings of the First ACM SIGCHI Annual Symposium on Computer-Human Interaction in Play, pp. 457–460. ACM, New York (2014). https://doi.org/10.1145/2658537.2659018
4. Khan, A., Ahmad, F.H., Malik, M.M.: Use of digital game based learning and gamification in secondary school science: the effect on student engagement, learning and gender difference. Educ. Inf. Technol. **22**(6), 2767–2804 (2017). https://doi.org/10.1007/s10639-017-9622-1
5. Perla, P.P.: What wargaming is and is not. Naval War Coll. Rev. **38**(5), 70–78 (1985)
6. Procci, K., Bohnsack, J., Bowers, C.: Patterns of gaming preferences and serious game effectiveness. In: Shumaker, R. (ed.) VMR 2011. LNCS, vol. 6774, pp. 37–43. Springer, Heidelberg (2011). https://doi.org/10.1007/978-3-642-22024-1_5
7. Ravyse, W.S., Seugnet Blignaut, A., Leendertz, V., Woolner, A.: Success factors for serious games to enhance learning: a systematic review. Virtual Reality **21**(1), 31–58 (2016). https://doi.org/10.1007/s10055-016-0298-4
8. Sajjadi, P., Vlieghe, J., De Troyer, O.: Evidence-based mapping between the theory of multiple intelligences and game mechanics for the purpose of player-centered serious game design. In: 2016 8th International Conference on Games and Virtual Worlds for Serious Applications (VS-GAMES), pp. 1–8. IEEE, New York (2016)

An Ontological Model to Design the Specifications of Effective Educational Games

Ilenius Ildephonce[1]([✉])[ID] and Claudine Allen[2][ID]

[1] The University of the West Indies - Five Islands, St. John's, Antigua and Barbuda
ilenius.ildephonce@uwi.edu
[2] The University of the West Indies - Mona, Kingston, Jamaica
claudine.allen@uwimona.edu.jm

Abstract. Educational games' effectiveness is dependent on the harmony between pedagogy and entertainment. However, finding the balance between abstract concepts such as fun with concrete ones such as learning gains is difficult. This difficult task lacks prescriptive methodologies to guide conceptualizing and communicating the specifications of a standard educational game. This research sought to develop an ontological structural model applied to produce the specifications of educational games. The model is beneficial to educational game designers by facilitating them to make informed design decisions through careful mapping of learning and game elements, improving the produced games' quality.

Keywords: Educational games specifications · Ontological model · Design methodology

1 Introduction

The research on educational games (EGs) has produced few methodologies and theories that sufficiently show how to design effective EGs. However, some are solely focused on one game genre, such as the UAdventure platform [13]; while others lack practicality such as the Four-Dimensional framework (4DF) [5]. So far there is no existing standard for how an EG is to be designed and implemented [1]. Similarly, a method utilized to build a successful EG cannot guarantee similar results if applied to create another game [1]. Crafting EG is done in an ad-hoc manner. This approach presents limitations on the meaningfulness and pedagogy of EGs [7]. EGs as a didactic medium need standards to define their effectiveness and prescriptive methods for designing and sharing a standard EG or its resource. This study focused on developing an ontological model to produce design specifications for effective EGs. The model facilitates identifying suitable game elements for particular learning design constraints.

Supplementary Information The online version contains supplementary material available at https://doi.org/10.1007/978-3-031-22124-8_35.

2   Literature Review

There has not been well-established theoretical and practical evidence of a standard scientific method to develop an EG [9]. Many EGs design models have been proposed to tackle the need to integrate pedagogy into the mechanical elements of the gameplay [2,6]. Among the models is the Learning Mechanics-Game Mechanics (LM-GM) model, which supports serious games (SG) analysis and design by reflecting on the various pedagogical and game elements in an SG [2]. This model was the first successful in matching learning elements to game elements as it has been applied to design various EGs [3]. Similarly, a model for serious games analysis and design called Activity Theory-based model for Serious Games (ATMSG) was proposed [4]. This model aimed to fill the gap of lack of concrete association between high-level EG requirements to low-level game mechanics. Moreover, [11] demonstrated a simplified process to map pedagogy to game elements within mathematics-based games. Limitations such as the lack of knowledge structures of the associations of the elements and the complexity of the models create demands for an ontological or domain-based model.

3   Methods

A questionnaire focusing on how various learning elements influence the design of various game elements was developed and sent to experts in the fields of educational games development. A total of 17 participants from 9 countries responded to the questionnaire. 8 of the participants had more than 10 years of experience, 5 had between 6–10 years, and 4 participants had 1–5 years of experience.

The results from this survey revealed evidence-based associations among various elements. For example, it showed that various instructional or learning elements are constraints when designing the mechanics of an Effective EG. The survey revealed other interesting ideas such as learning styles are not used when designing Effective EGs. Moreover, EG design is highly creative and the separation between procedural and creative activities is blurry. Observation from this research informed the design of the model, specifically the valid associations or mappings between various learning elements and game elements.

4   Proposed Model

This study proposes an Ontology-based Model to design the Specification of effective EGs (OMSEGs) as in the Fig. 1. OMSEGs covers learning and game elements associations as well as the translation of the selected elements pairs into game mechanics.

The learning elements represents the constraints relevant to defining the educational context and needs of the game. The learning elements included in the model are as follows:

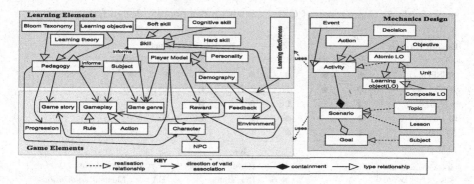

Fig. 1. The ontological model to design specifications of effective educational games (OMSEGs)

- *Player modelling* refers to abstracting of the target player based on characteristics which influence their learning experience. Examples in this study are personality, their demographic data, their cultural differences and game preferences. Player personality focuses on players' intelligence and personality types such as the Keirsey's personality & Bartle's gamer classifications.
- *Pedagogy* refers to the choice of instructional strategies, tools, skill articulation, content and other elements relevant to plan, structure and deliver content. Examples in this study are learning theory, bloom's taxonomy of learning outcomes, skills and learning content. Content covers elements such as learning games types, subject context, and scaffolding. Learning objectives include the description of instructional goals. Learning effectiveness focus on elements resulting to improved learning experience such as player experience, immersion, engagement, and assessment.

Game elements represent the decomposition of game systems into classes of elements which have been a research subject, specifically how they are associated with learning elements to achieve optimum learning in EGs. Examples include gameplay, rewards, feedback, environment, character, game genre, and game story were studied. Gameplay represent how mechanics are unfolded during play including elements such as drill and practice, cut scenes, and time pressure. Game environment covers elements such as game assets and aesthetics such as decorations, animations, and sound effects. Progression is for elements such as dialogue tree and goal setting. Feedback represent the design of elements such as hints.

4.1 Game Mechanics Design

This study adopted a template-based approach to understanding and proposing the structure of game mechanics. The template-based approach provides consistent means to design mechanics. The adopted template was introduced in [10]. This is beneficial to facilitate the modularity of OMSEGs.

Table 1. Comparison of OMSEGs with other popular design frameworks

Design Models	Evaluation criteria						
	P	PM	R	M	A	EA	MED
OMSEGs	●	●	●	●	●	◐	●
4DF	●	●	○	○	◐	◐	○
SG-ISD	●	○	◐	●	●	○	○
LM-GM	●	○	●	◐	◐	●	●
ATMSG	●	○	●	◐	○	◐	◐

Key

●= Covered, ◐= partially	PM = Player Modelling	A = Assessment
& ○= Not covered	R = Reusability	EA = Element associations
P = Pedagogy	M = Modularity	MED = Micro-design (Data level)

- *Activity:* In a game, an activity can be an event, an action or a decision. An activity, therefore, can be regarded as a tuple of the format described by the expression 1.

$$(P, S, O, R) \implies (PC, OS) \tag{1}$$

where: P - preconditions defining the current state; S - subject; O - object(s); R - set of rules (constraint for the action); PC - post conditions; OS - outcome (resulting state).

- *Scenario:* This is a set of related activities which are used to construct and convey meaning. In a game setting, a scenario can be understood as a mission or a quest. Scenarios are a meaningful set of activities built to create a complete unit of instruction that can be assessed.
- *Goal/Story:* A story does not mean describing events of the past but encapsulates the flow of elements or narratives. It encapsulates how scenarios snowball in the creation of a complete and meaningful gameplay experience. Effective storytelling incites an effective and meaningful EG [8,12].

Games, in general, are complex media with many creative aspects, from elements in the game, their representation to meaning conveyed through story structures [14]. Identification of fun elements, a good game theme/story, and Easter eggs are examples of creative activities. It is not easy to express such abstraction in a model. The dependency between mechanics design and learning elements accounts for abstractions in OMSEGs.

5 OMSEGs Evaluation

The quality of the proposed model was evaluated by comparing it with other existing models against predefined evaluation criteria. The evaluation criteria were developed based on the objectives and goals of this study. The comparison in Table 1 show the model contributions and its foundations by comparing OMSEGs to others from the state of the art.

Table 2. NetCom Quest learning elements and game elements design

Learning element	NetCom Quest element instance
Learning theory:	Experiential
Learning outcomes:	Bloom learning outcome taxonomy: remembering and understanding
Learning objectives:	TCP/IP devices, protocols
Player model Skills	Personality: Explorers (Bartle's gameplay personalities) and extroverts decision making, critical thinking and discovery
Visualisation of learning elements to game elements (link to OMSEGs)	

E:Asset name=Animation	**GR:Genre** name=Adventure	**gp5:Gameplay** name=Single player
En:Environment name=graphics		
FBK:Feedback name=Mini map	**SK:Skill** name=Decision making type=soft	**PL:Personality** name=Explorer type=Bartle gamer
FBK:Feedback name=Visual type=HUD	**L1:Learning theory** name=Experiential	**SK:Skill** name=Critical thinking type=soft	**PL:Personality** name=Extroverted	**En2:Environment** name=background music
FBK:Feedback name=Hints type=HUD	**OT:Learning Outcome** name=Remembering	**SK:Skill** name=Discovery type=soft	**gp4:Gameplay** name=time-pressure
Key	**OT:Learning Outcome** name=Understanding	**SB:Subject** name=Computer networks topic=Packet communications
Learning elements	**ag:Demographic** name=young adult type =age group age range=15-25	**OT:Learning objective**	**STR:Game Story**
Game elements		**C1:Character** name=Router Type=NPC	**GR:Genre** name=Simulation	**A:Asset** name=Billboard

Another evaluation was through applying the model to design an educational game known as NetCom Quest. Netcom Quest's foremost goal is to instruct players on TCP/IP packet communications. The objective covers the process involved in transmitting a packet from the source host to its destination on an IP network. The game covers network layout, network devices, packet information, and the TCP/IP concepts. The plot of the game is centred on the character playing the role of a mail deliverer. Details on other pedagogy design specifications for NetCom Quest are summarized in Table 2. NetCom Quest's mechanics design involved the template presented in the OMSEGs' mechanics design component in Fig. 1. Figure 2 presents Netcom Quest scenarios and activities as high-level

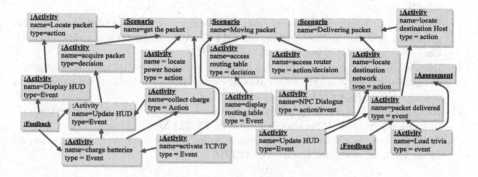

Fig. 2. NetCom Quest mechanics design instantiation

instantiating of the model. These instances demonstrate the feasibility of the OMSEGs when applied to design an educational game.

6   Conclusion and Future Work

This research's main contribution is the development of a design framework (OMSEGs) based on discovered knowledge structures on the association between learning elements and game elements. This is beneficial for educational game designers to decide which elements are best suited for their design problem. A limitation in this work was the absence of extensive user evaluation to test the model for a range of different kinds of games design scenarios. Future work is to automate processes involved in systematically mapping learning elements to game mechanics.

References

1. Arnab, S., Clarke, S.: Towards a trans-disciplinary methodology for a game-based intervention development process. Br. J. Edu. Technol. **48**(2), 279–312 (2017)
2. Arnab, S., et al.: Mapping learning and game mechanics for serious games analysis. Br. J. Edu. Technol. **46**(2), 391–411 (2015)
3. Callaghan, M., Savin-Baden, M., McShane, N., Eguíluz, A.G.: Mapping learning and game mechanics for serious games analysis in engineering education. IEEE Trans. Emerg. Top. Comput. **5**(1), 77–83 (2017)
4. Carvalho, M.B., et al.: An activity theory-based model for serious games analysis and conceptual design. Comput. Educ. **87**, 166–181 (2015)
5. De Freitas, S., Oliver, M.: A four-dimensional framework for the evaluation and assessment of educational games (2005)
6. De Troyer, O., Van Broeckhoven, F., Vlieghe, J.: Linking serious game narratives with pedagogical theories and pedagogical design strategies. J. Comput. High. Educ. **29**(3), 549–573 (2017)
7. Engström, H., Brusk, J., Erlandsson, P.: Prototyping tools for game writers. Comput. Games J. **7**(3), 153–172 (2018)
8. Ferguson, C., van den Broek, E.L., van Oostendorp, H.: On the role of interaction mode and story structure in virtual reality serious games. Comput. Educ. **143**, 103671 (2020)
9. Furuichi, M., Aibara, M., Yanagisawa, K.: Design and implementation of serious games for training and education. In: 2014 UKACC International Conference on Control (CONTROL), pp. 691–695. IEEE (2014)
10. Ildephonce, I., Mugisa, E., Allen, C.: Learning objects in instructional serious game design. In: 2018 IEEE 18th International Conference on Advanced Learning Technologies (ICALT), pp. 119–121. IEEE (2018)
11. Kalloo, V., Mohan, P., Kinshuk, K.: A technique for mapping mathematics content to game design. Int. J. Serious Games **2**(4), 73–92 (2015)
12. Naul, E., Liu, M.: Why story matters: a review of narrative in serious games. J. Educ. Comput. Res. **58**(3), 687–707 (2020)

13. Perez-Colado, I.J., Perez-Colado, V.M., Martínez-Ortiz, I., Freire-Moran, M., Fernández-Manjón, B.: UAdventure: the eAdventure reboot: combining the experience of commercial gaming tools and tailored educational tools. In: 2017 IEEE Global Engineering Education Conference (EDUCON), pp. 1755–1762. IEEE (2017)

14. Tavinor, G.: Tension and opportunity: creativity in the video gaming medium. In: Video Games and Creativity, pp. 263–284. Elsevier (2015)

Understanding the Advantages of a Hybrid Setting Over the Virtual Setting in Serious Game Application

Kevin Tan(✉) 📵, Sophie Mobbs, Håvard Vibeto, and Meisam Taheri

Game School, Inland Norway University of Applied Science, Hamar, Norway
{kevin.tan,sophie.mobbs,havard.vibeto,meisam.taheri}@inn.no

Abstract. The conventions of Virtual Reality (VR) controllers trace their lineage from decades of controllers used within the predominantly 2D computer world. Such controllers are not always precise or deft enough to adequately train people through Serious Games (SG) Applications. Virtual Reality environments open up huge opportunities for training "in the round" and while efforts are being made to refine controllers for use in this 3D VR medium, we propose that there is a case to be made now for a mixed medium approach, combining the freedom (and safety) of VR training with tactile, real-world equipment, integrated into the software. While not all VR training requires this level of specialism, it is an avenue worth exploring when trainees are learning skills that could save lives, or where full precision, at speed, could mean the difference between life and death. This paper presents a preliminary study within the context of our own case study of the creation and testing of a SG, VR based training application for the correct use of fire extinguishers, and how to use them to control a fire swiftly and safety.

Keywords: Virtual Reality · Serious games · Mixed medium approach · Extension embodiment · Tactile touch feedback

1 Introduction

The average yearly death count from fires in Norway is around 61 people, some of whom might have been spared had the correct training and education been provided [1]. VR can be an efficient replacement for real life fire safety training [2–4], allowing users to train in a cost effective manner, without fear of making mistakes, wasting valuable and expendable equipment or placing themselves or others in danger. There is proven research that a VR version of fire extinguisher training is more efficient in terms of memory retention, compared to solely watching training videos [5].

To test our hypothesis that memory retention can be improved by a mixed training approach that combines real-world tactile feedback inside a VR environment, we created a portable prototype of fire extinguisher training, comparing the use of conventional VR joystick controllers with a more realistic approach using real extinguishers. Not all training applications require this type of mixed training approach, but when training involves skills that could make life or death differences, we feel that a mixed method delivery has huge potential for practicing and retaining vital skills, and should, if possible, be explored as part of a toolbox for developing VR based training applications.

2 Advantages of VR in Fire Safety Training

Training with real loaded extinguishers and flames is messy, wasteful and can cost almost 10x more than a ready-built VR training application [6]. While a trained firefighter can take as little as 5 seconds to extinguish a small fire [7], a trainee might need to empty many extinguishers unsuccessfully, all while at risk from smoke inhalation, heat injury, and the fire spreading in an uncontrolled manner. VR solutions enable a trainee to make mistakes, and practice safely again and again at low cost, without the need to be supervised by professional firefighters for their own safety.

VR development has always been focused in visualization and simulation to enhance the feeling of how one might feel inside the virtual world [8], and researchers and developers use different techniques to achieve the best rendered display, (within the time and financial limitations available to them). However, when it comes to interaction, many VR-based SG still rely on using controllers [9] to hold, manipulate or mimic the effect of "pushing" a virtual object in the VR world. In other words, the feel of what is "seen" and "held" in the virtual world, does not really correspond to what is actually "touched" and "held" in the user's real hands. This disjunction of seeing and touching can make the whole experience awkward and uncomfortable [10].

Touch "as feel" is one of the five main senses that we use in the real world [11]. Moreover, touch improves retention of all that we experience, including the temperature, weight, and shape of an object [12]. The learning pace can be described as a power function that relates to an individual's responses and can become progressively faster [13]. This response indicates that initial learning is fast, but progress can slow over target repetitions [14]. It would seem that our brains appear to be hard-wired to quickly recognize and assimilate these elements. This may, in turn, aid in memory retention when trying to perform a learning task where one needs to hold the "actual" object itself, rather than a VR controller [15]. This can be especially valuable for training non-computer literate trainees, who might otherwise struggle with controllers that more computer savvy users might take for granted. One must "learn" which buttons to press in order to "visualize" how to perform the task itself. This is not necessarily a deal breaker for all training simulations, but in situations where accuracy of training can mean the difference between life and death, any steps that can be made to bring the controllers closer to a real-life tactile experience deserve to be explored.

3 A Custom-Made VR-Based Fire Training Application

In order to demonstrate the concept of tactile feeling for a training application, we took inspiration from Real-training [7] and hoped to reiterate from previous research in fire extinguisher evaluation applications [3]. Our project replicates a similar concept to build a VR training simulation, but with the aim to expand and explore upon the advantages that might be gained from a tangibly tactile effect.

Our mixed learning experience combines the heft and weight of a real extinguisher (filled with sand to make up the weight) with the timing and effects of simulated expulsion of matter onto simulated fire and smoke as shown in Fig. 1.

Fig. 1. Holding the "real" nozzle, and press the "real" handle to spray "virtual" foam to extinguish "virtual" fire

3.1 Method Discussion

A total of 10 participants, both experienced and novices in using VR and aged between 20–50 years old were required to test and compare between 2 extinguisher training applications, one purely VR based and the other using our mixed learning application. Our aims where to observe:

1. Would the threshold between the learner and the technology during the learning be lowered?
2. Would skills retention be improved?

The participants described their experience of the 2 methods of learning in focus groups and in response to a questionnaire. Examples of responses presented below.

Response to the VR only training application.

– "The trigger is confused, that spraying can be triggered un-intentionally".
– "Difficult to grab the nozzle, as it is imprecise with the controller and the virtual nozzle".
– "When grabbing the extinguisher with the controller it had a tendency to grab the pin instead, causing you to pull the pin out when you try to lift it. And the fire extinguisher controller often didn't properly register that the pin was removed".
– "The nozzle did not feel realistic since it was very loose and jiggly. Using the Oculus Controllers also did not feel like the real deal, since it gave no feel of location or weight or aim".

Response to the mixed (VR and real extinguisher) training application.

– "Having a physical object to interact with greatly increases the immersion and retention".

- "The weight was drastically different and as such, the experience of the feeling that real equipment is instant".
- "Training muscle memory would be more efficient with the actual tools in preference to VR controllers, just because you can feel actual pin when you pull it, the weight of the extinguisher and the force required on the handle for the correct amount of stream output, in addition to more accurate aiming practice".

4 Conclusions and Research Perspectives

It should be stressed that the number of participants was small and the testing and data gathering was preliminary and limited in scope. We present this as a prototype proof of concept designed to encourage further research and exploration of mixed learning approaches. There are existing examples that show benefits from this mixed delivery technique, such as performing surgical laparoscopic tasks [17], firearm training [18], and commercially available fire extinguisher training [6]. However, this type of mixed training approach has not generally been the specific focus point in SG applications, especially within VR environments.

However, even within this small study, certain interesting outcomes were observed. All the participants preferred the tactile feel and touch option, where one can "touch" to "feel" the virtual tank, pin and handle overlaid onto the real objects, to spray virtual foam while experiencing tangible heft and cumbersome weight of a real extinguisher. This seemed to indicate that the skills and concepts of putting out fires with an extinguisher where much easier to grasp (literally) with the help of the VR experience overlaid with a real extinguisher [3]. A standard 2-L fire extinguisher tank can weigh about 3.2 kg, and in a VR environment scenario, the weight that the user can feel is only the weight of the two VR controllers (approximately 150 g), on top of which, a virtual extinguisher in VR is entirely weightless. An inexperienced trainee might find lifting a real extinguisher something of a shock, after only experiencing a weightless virtual extinguisher.

With this mixed approach, a trainee can practice not just how to how to lift the extinguisher and direct the nozzle in a manner safe for extinguishing fires, but also practice manipulating it in a manner that places minimal strain on their back and body, to avoid strains or injuries.

While the preliminary study is about fire extinguisher training, it is the tactile feedback concept that should be considered for other similar SG training, where one might need to work with specific tools or equipment. In particular, where precise and memorable learning is needed to prepare a trainee for a potentially dangerous scenario, where inexperience could lead to panic or being over adrenalized [19, 20].

In this type of situation, it can be difficult to think clearly, but having experienced and felt the heft and spray sequence that might be expected from using an extinguisher in this training, a person will be better prepared to tackle a potentially life-threatening real-life scenario, swiftly and with confidence. We propose that this kind of mixed method approach should be considered for other SG training apps, in particular those where precision and clear learning retention could make all the difference for keeping the trainee and those around them safe from being hurt or placed in danger.

References

1. Direktoratet for samfunnssikkerhet og beredskap: Omkomne i brann. https://www.dsb.no/menyartikler/statistikk/omkomne-i-brann/
2. Sturm, L.P., Windsor, J.A., Cosman, P.H., Cregan, P., Hewett, P.J., Maddern, G.J.: A systematic review of skills transfer after surgical simulation training. Ann. Surg. **248**, 166–179 (2008)
3. Saghafian, M., Laumann, K., Akhtar, R.S., Skogstad, M.R.: The evaluation of virtual reality fire extinguisher training. Front. Psychol. **11**, 593466 (2020)
4. Tvenge, N., Ogorodnyk, O., Østbø, N.P., Martinsen, K.: Added value of a virtual approach to simulation-based learning in a manufacturing learning factory. Proc. CIRP **88**, 36–41 (2020)
5. Lovreglio, R., Duan, X., Rahouti, A., Phipps, R., Nilsson, D.: Comparing the effectiveness of fire extinguisher virtual reality and video training. Virtual Reality **25**(1), 133–145 (2020). https://doi.org/10.1007/s10055-020-00447-5
6. Real-Training. https://realtraining.no/
7. Arve Aasmundseth: VR branntrening for helsepersonell. Bærekraftig og kosteffektivt med høyt læringsutbytte
8. Gallace, A., Ngo, M.K., Sulaitis, J., Spence, C.: Multisensory presence in virtual reality: possibilities & limitations. In: Multiple Sensorial Media Advances and Applications: New Developments in MulSeMedia, pp. 1–38. IGI Global (2012)
9. Novacek, T., Jirina, M.: Overview of controllers of user interface for virtual reality. PRESENCE: Virtual Augment. Reality 1–100 (2022)
10. Davison, T., Samavati, F., Jacob, C.: LifeBrush: painting, simulating, and visualizing dense biomolecular environments. Comput. Graph. **82**, 232–242 (2019)
11. Shabgou, M., Daryani, S.M.: Towards the sensory marketing: stimulating the five senses (sight, hearing, smell, touch and taste) and its impact on consumer behavior. Indian J. Fundam. Appl. Life Sci. **4**, 573–581 (2014)
12. Gallace, A., Spence, C.: Tactile aesthetics: towards a definition of its characteristics and neural correlates. Soc. Semiot. **21**, 569–589 (2011)
13. Newell, A., Rosenbloom, P.: Mechanisms of skill acquisition. Cogn. Skills Acquisit. (1981)
14. Moll, K., De Luca, M., Landerl, K., Banfi, C., Zoccolotti, P.: Interpreting the comorbidity of learning disorders. Front. Hum. Neurosci. 767 (2021)
15. Gallace, A., Spence, C.: In Touch with the Future: The Sense of Touch from Cognitive Neuroscience to Virtual Reality. OUP, Oxford (2014)
16. Chan, J., Torah, R.: E-textile haptic feedback gloves for virtual and augmented reality applications. Eng. Proc. **15**, 1 (2022)
17. Giannotti, D., et al.: Play to become a surgeon: impact of Nintendo Wii training on laparoscopic skills. PLoS One **8**, e57372 (2013)
18. de Armas, C., Tori, R., Netto, A.V.: Use of virtual reality simulators for training programs in the areas of security and defense: a systematic review. Multimed. Tools Appl. **79**(5–6), 3495–3515 (2019). https://doi.org/10.1007/s11042-019-08141-8
19. Shusterman, R.: Muscle memory and the somaesthetic pathologies of everyday life. Hum. Move. **12**, 4–15 (2011)
20. Friedman, J.: Muscle memory: performing embodied knowledge. In: Text & Image, pp. 156–180. Routledge (2017)

Correction to: Comparison with Self vs Comparison with Others: The Influence of Learning Analytics Dashboard Design on Learner Dashboard Use

Timothy Gallagher⬤, Bert Slof⬤, Marieke van der Schaaf⬤,
Ryo Toyoda⬤, Yusra Tehreem⬤, Sofia Garcia Fracaro⬤,
and Liesbeth Kester⬤

Correction to:
Chapter "Comparison with Self vs Comparison with Others:
The Influence of Learning Analytics Dashboard Design
on Learner Dashboard Use" in: K. Kiili et al. (Eds.):
***Games and Learning Alliance*, LNCS 13647,**
https://doi.org/10.1007/978-3-031-22124-8_2

In an older version of this chapter, there was error in affiliation and values in Tables was incorrect. This has been corrected as per author request.

The updated original version of this chapter can be found at
https://doi.org/10.1007/978-3-031-22124-8_2

Author Index

Printed in the United States
by Baker & Taylor Publisher Services